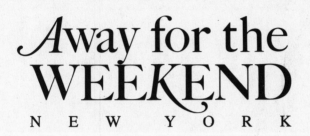

Away for the WEEKEND

NEW YORK

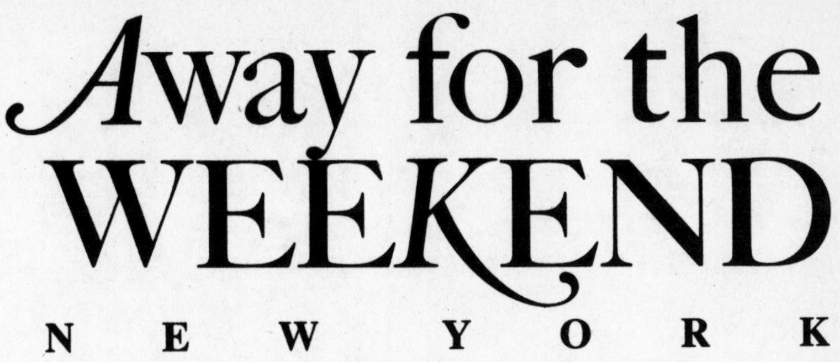

N E W Y O R K

Great Getaways
Less than 200 Miles from
New York City for
Every Season of the Year

ELEANOR BERMAN

Revised and Updated

CROWN
TRADE
PAPERBACKS

Published by Crown Trade Paperbacks, 201 East 50th Street, New York, New York 10022. Member of the Crown Publishing Group.

Random House, Inc. New York, Toronto, London, Sydney, Auckland

Manufactured in the United States of America

Library of Congress Cataloging-in-Publication Data

Berman, Eleanor.
Away for the weekend: New York : great getaways less than 200 miles from New York City for every season of the year / by Eleanor Berman—Rev. and updated.
Includes index.
1. Middle Atlantic States—Guidebooks. 2. New England—Guidebooks. 3. New York Region—Guidebooks. I. Title.
F106.B47 1994
917.404′43—dc20 94-4829
CIP

ISBN 0-517-88166-7

10 9 8 7 6 5 4 3 2 1

Fourth Revised Edition

Contents

FALL

WINTER

MAPS

Acknowledgments

I am grateful to all the state and local tourist offices as well as the innkeepers and local residents who supplied information and guidance during my travels for this fourth update and revision of *Away for the Weekend.* Thanks also to the innkeepers and readers who have taken time to write, helping me to follow who is in and out of business. Keeping up to date on the attractions, inns, and restaurants included in fifty-two trips in six states would be a daunting task without the help of these many friends.

A special word of appreciation also is due to my editor, Shirley Wohl, for her unfailing good humor and support, and to editorial assistant Leyla Morrissey for help far beyond the call of duty.

Before You Begin . . .

WEEKEND GETAWAYS—a change of scene, refreshment for mind and spirit—are what this book is all about. In the pages ahead you'll find suggestions for trips for every season of the year; jaunts with and without children; visits to country fairs and music festivals, Colonial towns and seaport villages, gardens and galleries . . . with parks, beaches, rivers, lakes, and mountains all along the way.

Some of these destinations may be familiar to you, but I hope that *Away for the Weekend* will prove to be for you, as it was for me in the writing, a source of discoveries and unexpected pleasures even in places you may have visited before.

Human nature being what it is, it is the faraway places that beckon most alluringly, often causing us to overlook attractions nearer at hand. We travel thousands of miles to look at scenery, monuments, mansions, and museums and ignore many equally fine places just a few hours from home. Nature's bounty, 300 years of history, and the many talented residents of our region, past and present, have combined to bless us in the New York area with an abundance of treasures to explore. I've tried to highlight some of the special places that are easy to miss, particularly the unusual once-private collections that are now unique and pleasurable small museums. Wherever possible, I've also provided just a bit of background on the colorful people who have amassed these treasures for us.

All of the trips outlined here are less than 200 miles from New York and its environs, most within three hours' driving time (minus traffic jams), so that they are easily manageable for a weekend sojourn. Their proximity offers still another bonus. Not only are these places easy to get to, but once having found them it's easy to go back!

There are a few things you should know before you start reading. This is, of necessity, a somewhat personal and selective guide to places I have visited and enjoyed. It does not include many large resorts or amusement parks for two reasons: I usually don't like them, and you usually don't need a book to find them.

Nor will you necessarily find every single sightseeing attraction or lodging available in the areas covered. I've tried to stick to places I've either been to myself or have had personally recommended by frequent visitors to the destination or local sources—people whose judgment I consider reliable.

This is a guide to destinations, not to country inns. Sometimes motels are the only accommodations available in a particular area. When inns are mentioned, it is because they are the best lodgings in the vicinity, not the pick of all possible inns as you find in books devoted to this subject. Keep that in mind if, occasionally, you find some place listed here a little disappointing compared to the ''dream'' inns you've visited elsewhere. However, when one offers something special, I've tried to say so.

BASIC INFORMATION

As for the basic format of the trips, they are laid out assuming you are spending a normal two-day weekend, arriving on Friday night and departing late on Sunday. There usually is a recommended itinerary, with added suggestions to accommodate varying tastes and time schedules. Sometimes there is more than enough to do for a long weekend, and a symbol at the start will indicate trips fitting that category.

If you want to spend more time in any area, check also for trips listed under other seasons for the territory near where you are going. Bucks County, for example, could fill several days if itineraries for both the lower and upper portions were combined. The same is true of the Hudson Valley, much of Connecticut, the Massachusetts Berkshires, and the Brandywine Valley.

The trips are arranged by season not only because activities change with the calendar, but to give you time to read about upcoming special events and reserve rooms before it is too late. Advance notice may also enable you to plan a whole weekend around a special show or open house, rather than see it as a last-minute day trip and miss all the sights and activities in the area nearby.

Since attractions do vary from season to season, you will find some areas mentioned more than once, or, as in the case of Philadelphia, recommended in different ways depending on whether children are along.

Don't, however, feel bound by the calendar. Many of these destinations are equally enjoyable and also less crowded when nothing special is going on, and are appealing both in and out of season. Think especially about the seashore in the fall, when you can enjoy the scenery and the best accommodations in the Hamptons or Cape May without the summer crowds—and sometimes at bargain rates.

Symbols will indicate which trips seem most appropriate with children, though you are the best judge of your own family's interests and may find others that sound right for you. There are also symbols for trips that are manageable without a car. Unfortunately, such trips are few. One possibility is to take public transportation to a central point and rent a car for a day for the sights you can't see without one.

The symbols to watch for indicating these varying categories are these:

 = recommended for children

 = can be done at least in part via public transportation

 = recommended for long weekends

As for prices, dollar signs indicate the range for a double room:
$ = under $70
$$ = $70 to $100
$$$ = $100 to $135
$$$$ = over $135
$$$$$ = over $200

and for restaurants:
$ = entrees mostly under $12
$$ = entrees averaging $12 to $20
$$$ = entrees averaging $20 to $25
$$$$ = expect to pay over $25 per person
$$$$$ = over $35 (usually means a prix fixe menu)

Some accommodations may also include some meals in their rates, and letter symbols following prices will indicate these. CP (Continental Plan) provides both bed and breakfast; MAP (Modified American Plan) includes breakfast and dinner; and AP (American Plan), all three meals.

Since there is always a lapse of several months between the writing and the publication of a book, I have used general price categories rather than specific figures, knowing that rates change rapidly in these inflationary times. Even so, it is likely that some the places listed will raise prices in the future, placing them into the next category. So use the book as a guide—I hope you will find it an accurate one on the whole—but *always* check for specific prices when you plan your trip.

Innkeepers and chefs also change, as do hours and fees for attractions, so do call ahead to check for current information.

If you find information that has become seriously inaccurate—if a place has closed or gone way downhill—I hope you will write me in care of the publisher so that it can be corrected in the future. If you discover places that I have missed, I hope you'll share them as well.

As for maps, there was just no way to provide maps detailed enough to take in every attraction or accommodation mentioned. There are basic area maps here to help you get your bearings and one map showing ways out of the city, but don't make the mistake of starting off without a really good road map of your destination. One way to get a detailed map free is by writing to the travel or tourism offices in the states included here. These offices offer not only maps but also informative brochures on their states. All have toll-free numbers for travelers seeking these materials.

In most cases, there is a source listed for further information at the end of each itinerary. Do write away, for the more you know about your destination ahead of time, the more pleasurable your trip will be.

Anyone who has ever tried to leave the city on a Friday knows that departing as well as returning at peak weekend traffic hours can be a frustrating experience, and can add an hour or more to your driving time. If you can't get away before 4 P.M. on Friday, particularly in the summer, consider having an early dinner in town and departing after 7 P.M., when the roads are more likely to be clear. If your destination is a particularly popular place, such as the Hamptons, you might find it more pleasant to take a train or bus, hop a local cab to your lodgings, and then pick up a car (or maybe a bike) the next day. Just remember to ask about the availability of local car rentals when you make your room reservation and be sure to reserve a car in advance.

Public transportation is subject to its own delays, of course, but sometimes it can be less aggravating to let someone else do the driving and fretting rather than begin or end a relaxing weekend stuck in a traffic jam.

Since the nicest lodgings tend to be expensive, this edition includes a list of bed-and-breakfast registries, handy whether you are on a budget or just seeking last-minute reservations. There can be confusion about what "bed-and-breakfast" means, since many inns label themselves this way. Here, it refers to rooms in private homes.

One last word: When it comes to inn reservations, plan ahead if you don't want to be disappointed. If you want to visit popular places at peak summer or fall seasons, three to four months ahead isn't too soon. Most places do offer refunds on deposits with reasonable notice, so remember that old adage and be safe rather than sorry.

With that out of the way, the only thing left to say is *Read on*—and have a wonderful time!

INFORMATION

Any of the state offices listed here will provide maps as well as information and literature on attractions throughout their states:

Tourism Division
Connecticut Department of
Economic Development
865 Brook Street
Rocky Hill, CT 06067
(203) 258-4355
Toll free: (800) CT-BOUND

Delaware Tourism Office
99 Kings Highway
Dover, DE 19901
(302) 739-4271
Toll free: (800) 441-8846

Division of Travel and Tourism
State of New Jersey
PO Box CN 826
Trenton, NJ 08625
(609) 292-2470
Toll free: (800) JERSEY-7

Division of Tourism
New York State Department of Economic Development
One Commerce Plaza
Albany, NY 12245
(518) 474-4116
Toll free: (800) CALL-NYS

Massachusetts Division of Tourism
100 Cambridge Street
Boston, MA 02202
(617) 727-3201
Toll free: (800) 447-MASS

Travel Marketing Bureau
Department of Commerce, State of Pennsylvania
453 Forum Building
Harrisburg, PA 17120
(717) 787-5453
Toll free: (800) VISIT-PA

Rhode Island Tourism Division
7 Jackson Walkway
Providence, RI 02903
(401) 277-2601
Toll free: (800) 556-2484

BED-AND-BREAKFAST REGISTRY SERVICES

Bed-and-breakfast registries are reservation services with a number of listings in their areas. Rates can range from $65 to $150, depending on the accommodations. Be specific about what you are looking for—extras such as private bath and private entrance, or economy. Most state tourist offices also keep listings for their own states; write for the latest update:

COVERING SEVERAL STATES

Covered Bridge Bed & Breakfast
(Berkshires, Hudson Valley, Rhode Island shore)
PO Box 447A
Norfolk, CT 06058
(203) 542-5944

The American Country Collection
(Northeast New York, western Massachusetts, Vermont)
4 Greenwood Lane
Delmar, NY 12054
(518) 439-7001

New England Hospitality Network
(Rhode Island, Connecticut, Massachusetts)
P.O. Box 3291
Newport, RI 02840
(401) 849-1298
Toll free: (800) 828-0000

CONNECTICUT

Nutmeg Bed and Breakfast
PO Box 1117
West Hartford, CT 06107
(203) 236-6698

Bed and Breakfast Ltd.
PO Box 216
New Haven, CT 06513
(203) 469-3260

Four Seasons International Bed & Breakfast
(Farmington Valley)
11 Bridlepath Road
West Simsbury, CT 06092
(203) 651-3045

DELAWARE

Bed and Breakfast in Delaware
Box 177
3650 Silverside Road
Wilmington, DE 19810
(302) 479-9500

MASSACHUSETTS

Berkshire Bed and Breakfast Homes
(Western Massachusetts, adjacent New England states)
PO Box 211
Main Street
Williamsburg, MA 01096
(413) 268-7244

NEW JERSEY

Bed and Breakfast Adventures
(Serves the entire state)
103 Godwin Avenue
Suite 132
Midland Park, NJ 07432
(201) 444-7409
Toll free: (800) 992-2632

NEW YORK

New York State Bed & Breakfast Association
(Covers the entire state; send $3 for listings)
PO Box 862
Canandaigua, NY 14424
(315) 474-4889

A Reasonable Alternative, Inc.
(Long Island)
117 Spring Street
Port Jefferson, NY 11777
(516) 928-4034

Bed and Breakfast USA Ltd.
(Hudson Valley, Rockland, Catskills, Albany–Saratoga)
PO Box 606
Croton-on-Hudson, NY 10520
(914) 271-6228

Ulster County Bed and Breakfast
(Listings for Woodstock, Kingston, New Paltz)
Ulster County
Public Information Office
PO Box 1800
Kingston, NY 12401
(914) 331-9300
Toll free: (800) DIAL-UCO

PENNSYLVANIA

Bed and Breakfast, Center City
(Philadelphia)
1804 Pine Street
Philadelphia, PA 19103
(215) 735-1137

Bed & Breakfast of Valley Forge
(Philadelphia, Brandywine and Valley Forge area)
PO Box 562
Valley Forge, PA 19481
(215) 783-7838
Toll free: (800) 344-0123

Bed and Breakfast Connections
(Philadelphia and suburbs)
PO Box 21
Devon, PA 19333
(215) 687-3565
Toll free (outside PA): (800) 448-3619

Bed and Breakfast of Chester County
(Brandywine Valley)
PO Box 825
Kennett Square, PA 19348
(215) 444-1367

Guesthouses
(Brandywine Valley and Philly Main Line)
PO Box 2137
West Chester, PA 19380
(215) 692-4575

Hershey Bed & Breakfast
PO Box 208
Hershey, PA 17033
(717) 533-2928

Pennsylvania Travel Council B & B Directory
902 N. Second Street, Dept. 931
Harrisburg, PA 17102
(Send self-addressed, legal size envelope with 52 cents postage for statewide directory)

RHODE ISLAND

Newport Bed and Breakfast
44 Everett Street
Newport, RI 02840
(401) 846-0362

Rhode Island Visitor's Guide
(Includes listings for entire state)
Rhode Island Tourism Division
7 Jackson Walkway
Providence, RI 02903
(401) 277-2601
Toll free: (800) 556-2484

Anna's Victorian Connection Rhode Island Bed and Breakfast Reservation Service
5 Fowler Avenue
Newport, RI 02840
(401) 849-2489

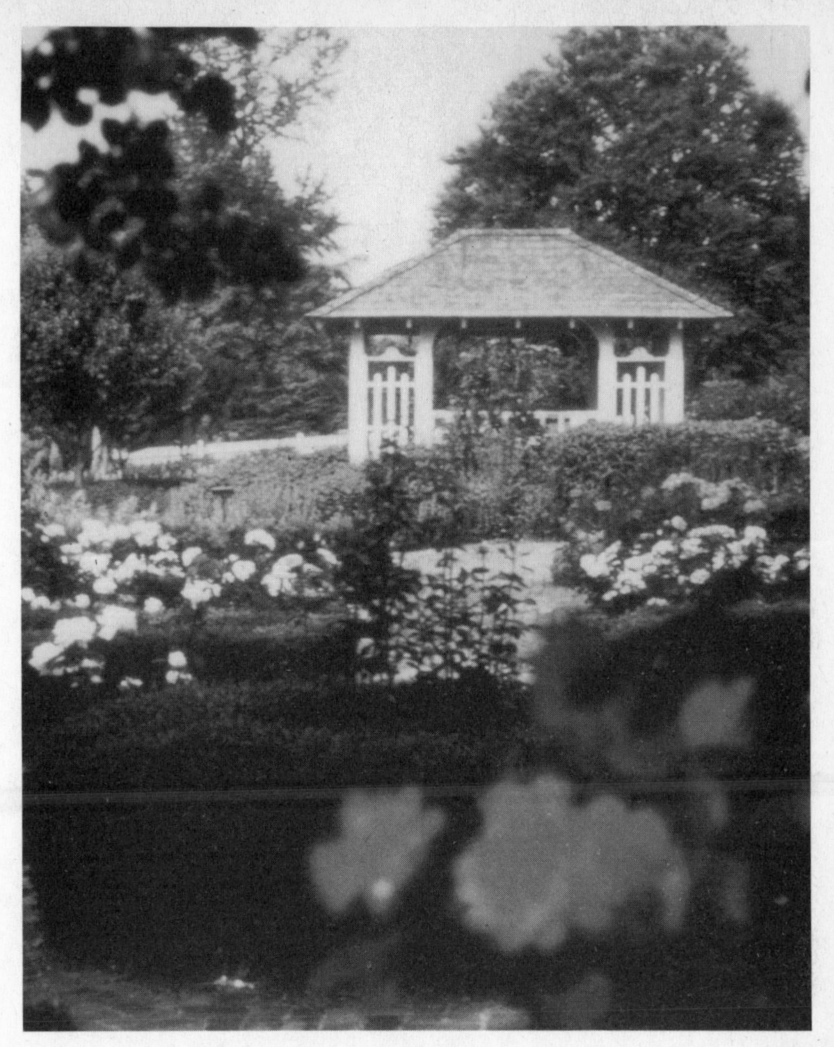

Spring

Gardens in bloom in Hershey, Pennsylvania
Photo courtesy of Hershey Entertainment and Resort Co.

Greeting Spring in Spring Lake

"You won't need that umbrella," the innkeeper assured us. "It never rains in Spring Lake."

Despite the clouds above, we were reluctant to doubt her, for it is obvious they don't permit many unwelcome intrusions here.

Some years back, Spring Lake was chosen by the producers of the movie *Ragtime* to represent the New Jersey shore as it was at the turn of the century—and with good reason. Pass the stone portals marking the village limits and you have returned to the past. Snack bars and arcades may mushroom in towns right next door, but nary a one has been allowed across the line to mar Spring Lake's pristine two-mile boardwalk.

Many of the grand hotels and gracious Victorian homes that marked one of the shore's most exclusive early enclaves remain intact. Swans still glide tranquilly on the picturesque spring-fed lake that gave the village its name. Rimmed by weeping willows and spanned by picturesque wooden footbridges, the lake and the park around it run for five blocks in the heart of town. The lake is a favorite landing pad for sea gulls shuttling back and forth between its serene waters and the ocean, just a shell's throw away.

When the first warm, sunny days of spring make you long to get away, there's no nicer place to greet the season than this oasis on the ocean, a town made to order for strolling.

The first to spot the unique attraction of a shore site with its own freshwater lake was a group of Philadelphia businessmen back in 1875. They formed the Spring Lake Beach Improvement Company, acquired the 285-acre property then known as Osborn Farm, and hired engineer Frederick Anspach to plan a whole new resort town. The centerpiece of the development was the ultra-elegant Monmouth House Hotel, completed in 1876, with 270 bedrooms, a dining room seating 1,000 guests, and large parlors overlooking the ocean.

A success from the start, it was quickly joined by more elaborate hotels and guest houses. Soon millionaires were building mammoth "summer cottages" in Spring Lake. A fire in 1900 slowed things temporarily, but the town rebuilt and remained a thriving part of the privileged people's shore.

Some of the hotels and many of the homes were transported here by wealthy businessmen directly from the 1876 Centennial Exposition in Philadelphia. Brochures from the town historical society point you to these and many other buildings remaining from the turn of the century.

The Monmouth House Hotel is gone, but you'll need no map to find many other sprawling wooden hotels of that earlier era. The huge Essex-Sussex, where *Ragtime* was filmed, retains its prized spot across from the beach, while the Hewitt Wellington looks out at the lake as it has for decades. You can still dance sedately after dinner at the Warren, or have a meal at the Breakers just as Victorian vacationers did.

Time, however, has brought a new generation of visitors, and with them have come changes to Spring Lake. You'll see modern homes here and there where Victorian beauties once stood. The Hewitt Wellington is now a condominium complex, with many of the newly elegant rooms available for weekend rentals. The Essex-Sussex has followed this trend. Hotels like the Warren have been refurbished, and the Breakers has added air-conditioning, TV, and other modern comforts.

Best of all, some of the old homes have become delightful bed-and-breakfast lodgings. Among the most pleasant are the Normandy Inn, La Maison, and Ashling Cottage.

Spring Lake acquired its nickname, the Irish Riviera, for the many Irish families who were among the earliest to establish summer mansions here. The head of one prominent family, philanthropist Martin Maloney, built the town's showplace, St. Catherine's Church, in 1901, as a memorial to his daughter, who died at the age of 17. The ornate Romanesque architecture, marble altar, and frescoed ceilings, modeled after a Vatican chapel, are proudly shown off to visitors by the natives.

One remaining sign of the Irish influence is the Irish Center—a boutique on Third Avenue, the town's main shopping street—where you will find fisherman sweaters, Donegal tweeds, Celtic jewelry, walking sticks, and a wide assortment of foods, all imported from the Emerald Isle.

The three-block "downtown" of Spring Lake is more preppy than touristy, but it does make for some interesting browsing for gifts and clothing.

If you want a light lunch, Jeffrey's or Who's On Third on Third Street will oblige, and the Sundae Times on Atlantic and First streets is guaranteed to satisfy your sweet tooth.

What to do on a warm spring day in Spring Lake? Take a jog or a stroll along the boardwalk to sniff the sea air. Then have a look at the cupolas and gingerbread ornamentation of the town's fine houses, either on foot or by bike. Most inns will either lend you a bike or help you rent one.

All of the blocks between Ocean and Third avenues have prize homes to be seen. Check out Coalbrook, Martin Maloney's 26-room carriage house at 105 Morris Avenue. On Monmouth Avenue, the Rolin House (circa 1888) at 207 and its neighbor at 214 are in the aptly named Spring Lake Beach Victorian style and are also worth a look (especially the latter, a gingerbread classic with Carpenter Gothic shingles, floor-to-ceiling windows, and stained glass). Two survivors from the Centennial Exhibition are the Missouri State Building at 411 Ocean Road and the Portuguese Government Pavilion at 205 Atlantic Avenue.

The beautifully planted lawn at Green Gables on Ocean Avenue between Washington and Madison streets contains two regulation-size croquet courts, which are used every Thursday in season by the local croquet club, nattily attired all in white. In September they are joined by players from all over for a prestigious annual invitational croquet tournament.

When your tour is done, you can get in a game of tennis in the park or some rounds of golf at nearby facilities. If you come back in summer, the local inns will provide passes for the residents-only beach.

For more sightseeing, drive north along the shore to Ocean Grove, a former religious colony by the sea with a fascinating collection of Victorian houses. Or head south to the Deserted Village, a restored ironworking town in Allaire State Park. The site of a historic iron and brass foundry, Allaire was once a self-sustaining community, and it retains some of the furnaces, forges, and casting houses that used to turn out pots, kettles, stoves, and screws used by residents. The old town bakery, a barn and carriage house, and a general store and post office also remain, giving an interesting and vivid picture of an industrial community of the past. The Pink Creek Railroad here offers steam train rides.

If you to go to Allaire, consider staying in the area for dinner, as the Farmingdale House in Farmingdale gets excellent reviews for its Northern Italian fare.

Evenings are quiet in Spring Lake; the most action you're likely to find is a production at the community theater. Things may be a bit livelier next door in Sea Girt, another particularly pleasant shore town.

Even in midsummer Spring Lake remains tranquil. Mainly, this is a town for an after-dinner amble by the lake or the sea and quiet talk in the Victorian parlor of your inn—pleasures of a less-hurried era in a town that remains a picture book from the past.

Spring Lake Area Code: 908

DRIVING DIRECTIONS Spring Lake is on the Jersey shore at exit 98 on the Garden State Parkway. Follow Route 34 south to the traffic circle, then Route 524 (Allaire Road) east into town. Total distance: about 60 miles.

PUBLIC TRANSPORTATION New Jersey Transit trains ([201] 762-5100) travel from Penn Station to Spring Lake Heights, on the edge of town. Take a cab to an inn or in the summer season, try using the town trolley. You can manage in town without a car.

ACCOMMODATIONS Among the houses-turned-inns are *Normandy Inn*, 21 Tuttle Avenue, 07762, 449-7172, nicest of all, $$$ CP • *Ashling Cottage*, 106 Sussex Avenue, 07762, 449-3553, charming ambience, $$$ CP • *La Maison*, 404 Jersey Avenue, 07762, 449-0969, beautifully decorated rooms, $$-$$$$ CP • *The Lodge at Spring Lake*, 15 Mercer Avenue, 07762, 449-6002, modest outside, stylish inside, pool, $$$$ CP • *Sea Crest by the Sea*, 19 Tuttle Avenue, 07762, 449-9031, nicely redone Victorian, $$-$$$$ CP • *Hollycroft*, 506 North Boulevard, 07762, 681-2254, change of mood, secluded lodge with knotty pine walls, log beams, opens late May, $$-$$$ CP. Modernized hotels include *Hewitt Wellington*, 200 Monmouth Avenue, 07762, 974-1212, best and priciest in town, $$$$ • *The Breakers*, 1507 Ocean Avenue, 07762, 449-7700, outdoor pool, $$$$ • *The Warren Hotel*, 901 Ocean Avenue, 07762, 449-8800 (open Memorial Day to mid-October), pool, tennis, putting green, $$$$. One pleasant motel deserves mention for its location on the park: *The Chateau*, 500 Warren Avenue, 07762, 974-2000, $$-$$$; cooking units, $$$$. All inns require 2- or 3-night minimum reservations in season; all rates are less off-season.

DINING *The Old Mill*, Route 71, Spring Lake Heights, 449-1800, delightful ambience, but no reservations taken, so expect waiting lines, $$$ • *The Breakers* (see above), Italian, $$$ • *The Sandpiper*, Ocean and Atlantic avenues, 449-9707, Continental menu, $$$ • *The Beach House*, Warren Hotel (see above), 449-9646, $$-$$$ • *Eggiman's Tavern*, 2031 Highway 71, Spring Lake Heights, 449-2626, $-$$ • *Yankee Clipper*, Chicago and Ocean avenues, Sea Girt, 449-7200, ocean view, $$-$$$ • *Rod's Olde Irish Tavern*, 507 Washington Boulevard, Sea Girt, 449-2020, informal, $-$$ • *Scarborough Fair*, 1414 Meeting House Road, Sea Girt, 223-6658, Continental menu, very popular, can be noisy, $$-$$$. Sea Girt's pubs, such as the *Parker House*, are where many younger vacationers go for nightlife. Other recommendations: *Evelyn's Fish Market*, 507 Main Street, Belmar, 681-0236, no frills, good fresh fish, $$ • *Farmingdale House*, 105 Academy Street, Farmingdale, 938-7951, excellent Italian, a top choice, $$-$$$.

SIGHTSEEING *Allaire Village*, Allaire State Park, off Garden State Parkway exit 98, Farmingdale, 938-5524. Hours: Park open daily

8 A.M. to dusk. Visitor Center, Memorial Day to Labor Day, Monday to Friday, 10 A.M. to 5 P.M., Saturday and Sunday to 4 P.M.; weekends only September and October. Buildings open Memorial Day to Labor Day, Wednesday to Sunday, 10 A.M. to 5 P.M., weekends only September and October. Parking fee, $5 weekends, $4 weekdays; train rides, $1.50. Building tours, $1.50.

FOR FURTHER INFORMATION Greater Spring Lake Chamber of Commerce, PO Box 694, Spring Lake, NJ 07762, 449-0577 • For complete list of lodgings, write to the Spring Lake Hotel and Guest House Association, PO Box 134, Spring Lake, NJ 07762.

Spring Spectacular: The Dogwoods of Fairfield

Isaac Bronson would hardly believe his eyes.

A retired Revolutionary War surgeon-turned-farmer, Bronson decided back in 1705 that his Fairfield, Connecticut, property could be enhanced if he transplanted some of the native wild dogwood trees blooming so prodigiously in the nearby woods.

Bronson propagated, and so did his trees. By 1895 the blooms nurtured by the family were so outstanding that the Greenfield Hill Village Improvement Society took on care of the dogwoods as an official project, adding many new plantings, including pink varieties that were not native to Connecticut. Today Greenfield Hill boasts 30,000 dogwood trees, and if you drive up early in May, you can enjoy a view of the steepled church, village green, and Colonial homes enveloped in clouds of pink and white blossoms. Bronson's original trees, carefully tagged, are still an integral part of the show.

Thousands turn out each year to revel in this spring spectacular and to attend the annual Dogwood Festival sponsored by the women of the Greenfield Hill Congregational Church. Usually held for several days overlapping Mother's Day in the second week in May, the festival offers daily guided walking tours, concerts, an art show, handmade gifts, and homemade food. Phone the church for this year's dates.

The town of Fairfield, named literally for the "fair fields" that attracted settlers from Hartford, was founded in 1639, just 19 years after the Pilgrims landed in this country. The 55 families who chose to settle in Greenfield Hill, two miles from the town center, made a lucky move, since it was the only part of town not burned by the British during the Revolutionary War. Now designated a historic district, it was a prime source of food for the American army, and the steeple of the original Congregational Church on the green served the army as a lookout for the British fleet.

Dogwood Festival concerts are presented in the church sanctuary, allowing visitors to see its handsome Early American interior, with just 23 pews in a room painted white, with red velvet cushions and carpet, and chandeliers of Colonial blue wood.

The interesting Heritage Walking Tour goes past many surviving Colonial homes as well as later Federal and Greek Revival houses. Down dogwood-festooned Bronson Road, the old windmill that once pumped water for Bronson's farm has been restored in his memory. Also on this road is Ogden House, a saltbox farm restored by the Fairfield Historical Society. Most of its authentic eighteenth-century furnishings have a history of local ownership. The lean-to kitchen and traditional English herb garden here make it well worth a visit, dogwoods or not.

The actual Historical Society headquarters, a red brick building, is near the town center in one of Fairfield's two other historic districts. For a small museum, it offers an unusually large collection of early Americana. Dolls, doll houses, and children's toys fill an entire top floor, and the lower level features an old country store and a country kitchen as well as every conceivable tool for every kind of Colonial craft, from candle-making to carriage-making. Many of the wooden tools on the wall are almost works of art in themselves.

The corner of the Historical Society block, Beach and Old Post roads, was the central point of the original "four squares" of the town laid out in 1639. You can while away a pleasant hour exploring these two roads on foot. Though only four of the original homes survived the British fires, there are many beautiful post-Revolutionary homes to see, as well as historic churches and the town hall, whose central section remains as it was when it was rebuilt in 1790. It was on the town hall green that residents refused to submit to a royal proclamation, an act that led to the town's burning.

Save some foot power for Southport, the picturesque harbor area, which has also been named a historic district. Boats laden with onions from the Greenfield Hill farms used to sail out of this harbor. Now it is the home of the Pequot Yacht Club and the Fairfield Country Club; the hilly surrounding residential area, with water views at every turn, is one of the most exclusive and attractive along the Connecticut shore.

Southport's tiny village is an antiques center. There are four shops within about two blocks on Pequot Avenue, as well as the Fairfield Women's Exchange, which combines antiques and gifts with many original articles.

For a lunchtime snack, try the Firehouse Deli on Reef Road, and for dessert, visit Timothy's Ice Cream just down the road. An even nicer lunch suggestion: Pack a picnic and eat on Greenfield Hill's green or by the shore on the sandy Fairfield beaches that stretch for seven miles on and off along the Long Island Sound.

Except for Dogwood Festival days, Fairfield's charms draw surprisingly few visitors, and it remains a peaceful and non-touristy place. The main shopping area on the "new" Post Road, U.S. 1, is typically small town, and the shopping centers on Black Rock Turnpike are fairly standard. There's an interesting little gallery of limited-edition art prints at the Greenwich Workshop just off the Post Road at 61 Unquowa Road, but for serious shopping, boutiques and the like, follow the Post Road a few miles west into more sophisticated Westport.

It's possible that the beautifully wooded residential sections of Westport boast more celebrity residents than any other single Connecticut town (Paul Newman and Joanne Woodward among the more prominent). The town itself is hardly a country village. There is a Main Street about two blocks long, with pleasant small shops and a bookstore that is something of a local landmark. The rest of the shopping area stretches along State Street, which is actually busy U.S. 1, and is divided into little modern shopping centers. There's plenty of browsing potential, but by car rather than on foot.

If you continue farther west on U.S. 1 into Norwalk and bear left to West Avenue, you'll come upon two Fairfield County shopping standbys. One is a branch of Loehmann's, well known to bargain-conscious, fashionably dressed women, and down the road a bit is Decker's, a haven for men. Gant shirts here sell for half their prices at New York stores, there are good buys on many other quality labels that vary from visit to visit, and the entire side wall is stacked with classic Shetland or cashmere sweaters at excellent prices. There are women's sweaters, too, and a few women's shirts, but this is primarily a man's world. On the same block as Decker's are outlet stores for silver and for sheets and towels.

While you are in Norwalk, visit SoNo, the revitalized section of South Norwalk that has blossomed into an arty center for interesting shops and restaurants. The local branch of the Brookfield Craft Center, off busy Washington Street, has a gallery and shop well worth a look.

The Maritime Center at the foot of Washington Street is a great stop for families, or for anyone interested in the sea. Part aquarium and part museum, it includes hands-on exhibits such as a wind tunnel, which demonstrates how sailors use the wind's force by giving visitors a chance to maneuver a sail. Wood hulls are carved before your eyes in the boat-building area, and the aquarium offers a touch tank where kids can stick their hands into saltwater and feel the slippery sea creatures who live there. If you reserve ahead, you can actually go out to sea by signing on for a ride aboard the *Oceanic*, the thirty-eight-passenger cutter that is the center's chief research vessel. There's also an IMAX theater here offering a variety of exciting films.

If you're more interested in the out-of-doors, back in Fairfield the Connecticut Audubon Society and its Larsen Sanctuary have more than six miles of trails along 168 wooded acres. The sanctuary is a managed wildlife area where you will find not only woods but meadows, streams, marshes, and ponds. The Birdcraft Museum of the society is a refuge for songbirds, the first of its kind in New England.

The closest lodgings to the dogwoods are motels, but there are more interesting places to stay a short drive away. The Inn at Longshore, a former estate on Long Island Sound, was acquired by the town of Westport as a recreational facility for its residents. The renovation included fourteen pleasant guest rooms, some with water views. The surroundings are super—golf course, beach, tennis, beautiful grounds.

Near the center of Westport are the intimate Cotswold Inn, exquisite, albeit expensive, and the recently renovated Inn at National Hall, in an 1873 building along the Saugatuck River.

On the more traditional New England side is Silvermine Tavern, a 200-year-old inn on a millpond, with ten simple Colonial rooms upstairs. The food here is average, but the low-ceilinged dining room filled with old tools and the deck overlooking ducks and geese on the pond are so pleasant that you won't mind, especially if you come for the generous Sunday brunch.

The Silvermine Guild of Artists is just across the way (though its official address is New Canaan). It's an art school housed in barns that has changing exhibits and a gift shop of paintings and handcrafts.

For dinner, Fairfield's best bet is the popular Tuscan-style Spazzi, featuring an oak-fired grill. Westport selections are far wider, though the offerings do seem to change with the seasons. Some old standbys that have stood the test of time are Le Chambord and Chez Pierre for French cuisine, and Allen's for seafood. Current favorites are listed below, but if they have vanished by the time you read this, don't say I didn't warn you.

Another good bet for interesting places to dine these days is Norwalk, especially in SoNo. And if you want to end your weekend with a Sunday dinner that makes the most of the Connecticut countryside, head home on the Merritt Parkway, detour at exit 42, and go about four miles north on Route 57 to Cobb's Mill Inn. It's the perfect country hideaway, full of antiques and with a view of trees, a waterfall, and a stream that is picture-perfect.

Fairfield Area Code: 203

DRIVING DIRECTIONS Via I-95 to exit 21 to Fairfield, go left on Mill Plain Road, left on Sturgess, then right on Bronson to the

Greenfield Hill Congregational Church and the Dogwood Festival. Via the Merritt Parkway, take exit 44, make immediate right on Congress Street to Hillside, then left on Hillside to Old Academy Road and the church.

Total distance: 52 miles.

ACCOMMODATIONS *The Inn at Longshore*, 260 Campo Road South, Westport, 06880, 226-3316, $$$ • *Cotswold Inn*, 76 Myrtle Avenue, Westport, 06880, 226-3766, $$$$-$$$$$ • *Inn at National Hall*, 2 Post Road West, Westport, 06880, 221-1351, $$$$-$$$$$ CP • *Silvermine Tavern*, Silvermine and Perry avenues, Norwalk, 06850, 847-4558, $$, CP • *Fairfield Motor Inn*, 417 Post Road, Fairfield, 06430, 255-0491, $$ • *Westport Motor Inn*, 1595 Post Road East, Westport, 06880, 259-5236, $$-$$$.

DINING *Spazzi*, 1229 Post Road, Fairfield, 256-1629, $$ • *Centro Ristorante*, 1435 Post Road, Fairfield, 255-1210, another popular and trendy Italian, $$ • *Sole E Luna*, 25 Powers Court, Westport, 222-2827, much lauded Northern Italian, $$ • *Restaurant Zanghi*, 2 Post Road West, Westport, 221-7572, attractive setting, eclectic and excellent menu, $$ • *Pompano Grill*, 1460 Post Road East, Westport, 259-1160, Continental, seafood, and grill specialties, $$-$$$ • *Meeting Street Grill*, 1563 Post Road East, Westport, 256-3309, American fare, $$ • *Da Pietro's*, 36 Riverside Avenue, Westport, 454-1213, Northern Italian and country French, $$$ • *Chez Pierre*, 146 Main Street, Westport, French cafe, 227-5295, $$$ • *Allen's Clam & Lobster House*, 191 Hills Point Road, Westport, 226-4411, $$-$$$ • *Le Chambord*, 1572 Post Road East, Westport, 255-2654, formal French, $$$-$$$$ • *Cobb's Mill Inn*, Weston Road, Weston, 227-7221, $$-$$$ • *Silvermine Tavern* (see above), $$-$$$ • *Pasta Nostra*, 116 Washington Street, South Norwalk, 854-9700, tiny and usually packed, excellent pasta, $$-$$$ • *La Provence*, 86 Washington Street, South Norwalk, 855-8958, charming French cafe, $$ • *Maria's Trattoria*, 172 Main Street, Norwalk 847-5166, popular Italian cafe, gets crowded, $-$$ • *Miche Mache*, 18 South Main Street, Norwalk, 838-8605, much lauded New American, $$.

SIGHTSEEING *The Dogwood Festival*, Greenfield Hill Congregational Church, 1045 Old Academy Road, Fairfield, 259-5596. Write or phone for information and brochure giving current dates and rates.

Silvermine Guild of Artists, 1073 Silvermine Road, New Canaan, 966-5617. Hours: Tuesday to Saturday 11 A.M. to 5 P.M., Sunday noon to 5 P.M. Donation • *Connecticut Audubon Society, Fairfield Nature Center*, 2325 Burr Street, Fairfield, 259-6305. Hours: Tuesday to Saturday 9 A.M. to 4:30 P.M. Free. Sanctuary open daily, dawn to dusk. Trail fee: adults, $2; children, $.50 • *Birdcraft Museum and Sanctuary*, 314 Unquowa Road, Fairfield, 259-0416. Hours: Saturday and Sunday, noon to 5 P.M. Donation • *Brookfield/SoNo Craft Center*, Brookfield Alley off 127 Washington Street, South Norwalk, 853-6155, Tuesday to Saturday 10 A.M. to 5 P.M.; Sunday noon to 5 P.M. Free • Maritime Center of Norwalk, North Water Street, 852-0700. Hours: daily 10 A.M. to 5 P.M. Admission for Maritime Hall and Aquarium: adults, $7.50, children, $6.50; IMAX theater, adults, $6, children, $4.50; combination ticket, adults, $11.75, children, $9.50. *Oceanic* cruises, phone for schedules, rates.

FOR FURTHER INFORMATION Fairfield Chamber of Commerce, 1597 Post Road, Fairfield, CT 06430, 255-1011; Greater Fairfield Tourism District, 297 West Avenue, Norwalk, CT 06850, 854-7825 or (800) 866-7925.

The Other Side of the Delaware: Discoveries in New Jersey

It was bound to happen. With all those tourists heading for Pennsylvania's Bucks County, it was only a matter of time until someone noticed that there were some appealing little towns right across the Delaware in New Jersey.

First it was a few antiques dealers who made the crossing. Priced out of New Hope, they began to open shops just a footbridge away across the river in Lambertville—and this sleepy side of the Delaware began to wake up. Lambertville's once-neglected Federal row houses and pointy-roofed Victorian homes began to be bought up and spiffed up. More shops followed. Next came several good restaurants to accommodate the shoppers, and then inns were opened so that diners could spend the night.

Now the New Jersey side of the Delaware is a delightful destination in its own right, still peaceful but with plenty to offer for a happy weekend of inning and antiquing. As a bonus, you are within easy striking distance of Flemington outlet stores, the many attractions of Princeton, and some lesser-known pleasures on the back roads where some of the state's historic past still lives on.

The area's choicest place to stay is Chimney Hill Farm, a beautifully restored and furnished 1820s stone and frame farmhouse, set high on a hill just outside Lambertville. In Lambertville itself are two small and rather elegant bed-and-breakfast inns, the York Street House and the Bridgestreet House, a cozy Victorian guest house that offers a garden and outdoor Jacuzzi. The Inn at Lambertville Station, adjacent to the town's restored train station, is really a small hotel. It isn't heavy on charm, but it does offer fireplaces in some of the suites.

Fireplaces can also be found at Colligan's Stockton Inn in Stockton, just a few miles upriver. The inn still has the wishing well that is said to have been the inspiration for the Rodgers and Hart song "There's a Small Hotel." Its long-established restaurant continues to thrive and now has a small gourmet addition, The Fox. Rooms are upstairs in the main building and in adjacent historic homes and buildings, including the old carriage house and wagon house. Oversized and luxurious, the rooms are done in high Federal style with canopy beds and decorator fabrics.

Another winning Stockton location is the Woolverton Inn, a very private, mellowed-stone country house tucked away high on a hill, surrounded by lawns and meadows populated with sheep. The sheep-fancying owners have a lineup of miniatures on the mantel in the main house, as well.

Lambertville now has a choice of fine dining, with Hamilton's Grill, Manon, and Anton's at the Swan Hotel among the current favorites.

The most elegant art showcase in town is the Genest Gallery and Sculpture Garden at 121 North Union Street. It features large works of fine and decorative arts. Coryell Gallery is another recommended stop. At either, you can pick up the New Hope–Lambertville Gallery Association guide for a full listing of the local scene.

You'll need no guide for shopping, since Lambertville's "downtown" totals about four square blocks. Antiques abound here. The Antique Center at The People's Store on North Union is a co-op offering wares from 20 dealers, Bridge Street Antiques holds some 14 shops in one location, and the Porkyard on Coryell, a onetime sausage factory, has been converted into a complex selling country furniture, art, and antiques. Other intriguing shops offer imported clothing and tapestries, arts and crafts by local artisans, Scandinavian country furniture and gifts, and hand-fashioned gold jewelry. The Lambertville Trading Company is the place for gourmet foods, including raspberry jam that is billed as "the best in the universe"; it's also a good place for a cappuccino break.

Stockton's main attraction is Country Tiles, featuring a wide selection of decorative tiles from Mexico, Brazil, Holland, France, and Italy.

You might want to have a look at the restoration of Prallsville Mills just north of Stockton, a National Historic Landmark restoration of an old mill complex that also hosts a variety of exhibits and special events. A biking and hiking path has been completed on the old railroad bed along the canal from the mill past Bull's Island, running about 15 miles north to Frenchtown.

There are more antiques shops waiting to be explored in Frenchtown, as well as across the river in Bucks County, but you may want to save some time for another kind of shopping—discount bargain hunting in Flemington.

This major outlet center includes lots of big names, such as Anne Klein, Adidas, Calvin Klein, Corning, Mikasa, and Dansk. You'll find Quoddy Moccasins, Health-Tex clothing for kids, Fieldcrest and Cannon towels and linens, and just about everything else you can think of—from luggage to furs to butcher-block tables. The shops are in several locations, clustered in two main complexes known as Liberty Village and Turntable Junction, along Main and Broad streets, at the Flemington Outlet Center, and along Route 202. One easy way to get to them is to park and take the Flemington Trolley, which makes a continuous loop connecting the major shopping. On your own, you can write ahead for a map or pick one up in most of the stores when you arrive.

Take time for a stroll on Main Street, for in spite of all the shops, the center of town has managed to retain a quaint look that reflects the town's 1712 origins. The 1828 Greek Revival courthouse, also in the center of town, was the scene of the famous Lindbergh kidnapping trial. The old Union Hotel makes an atmospheric stop for lunch.

You can also take a nostalgia break aboard the Black River & Western Railroad, which runs steam trains on hour-long trips to Ringoes from mid-April through December. The train also runs from Lambertville.

You'll need advance reservations for a different kind of perspective on the Delaware Valley landscape. Harrison Aire in Ringoes will show you the sights from a hot-air balloon, which usually takes off three hours before sunset, and sometimes at sunrise as well.

On Sunday, once again you can pick and choose your destinations. Stop off, if you like, at one of two area flea markets held every Saturday and Sunday from 8 A.M. to 5 P.M.; one is located on Route 179, 1½ miles north of Lambertville, and the other is on Route 29, about the same distance to the south. Farther south on Route 29 you might want to stop at Washington Crossing State Park, which commemorates the famous river crossing that was a turning point in the Revolutionary War. The park runs on both sides of the Delaware. On the New Jersey side you can visit the Ferry House, a restored Colonial inn where Washington and his men once spent the night, and the Flag Museum showing the evolution of the nation's flag.

Then it's back-roads time, taking Route 546 to Route 31, then off the main road to Pennington, which has many Federalist and Georgian buildings dating to Revolutionary times. From Pennington go west, then north on Route 579 to Harbourton, where the historic district is typical of a crossroads farm settlement of the eighteenth and nineteenth centuries.

Continue north to Route 518 and east past Hopewell, then detour south on Route 206 to Kingston, once an old stagecoach stop and a town where the Delaware and Raritan Canal (now a state park) was a vital transportation link. Near the canal you can still see the mill house used at various times during the last 200 years to produce lumber, flour, and woolen fabrics. Many other old buildings, which also still stand, aid the small shops and antique stores that dot the village.

Stay on Route 206 south to Princeton, which could fill a weekend on its own with its magnificent campus and historic homes. Sign up for the free one-hour campus walking tours offered by the Orange Key Guide Service in Maclean House to the right of the main campus gate at 1:30 P.M. and 3:30 P.M., or pick up literature in their office for a do-it-yourself tour. At Bainbridge House, the headquarters of the Princeton Historical Society on Nassau Street, you can buy a little map guide to other historic places and interesting architecture in town.

On campus visit Nassau Hall, which was the country's capital back in 1783; the beautiful Gothic University Chapel with its collection of stained glass by American artists; the University Art Museum; and the enormous outdoor sculpture collection that dots the entire idyllic campus with works by Calder, Epstein, Lachaise, Lipchitz, Moore, Nevelson, Noguchi, and many others.

Off campus there are historic sites like Rockingham, Washington's onetime headquarters; Morven, the former official residence of the governor of New Jersey; the Quaker Meeting House; the homes of Woodrow Wilson, Albert Einstein, and Aaron Burr, and hundreds of fine eighteenth- and nineteenth-century homes in either direction on Nassau Street and on the side streets around it. Alexander, Mercer, and Stockton are some of the many streets it is a pleasure to drive down or stroll on.

You could easily and happily spend the day in Princeton, and have dinner at the Nassau Inn on Palmer Square or one of the many other restaurants in town. If you decide to make your headquarters here or come back for a longer stay, Scanticon, a conference center/resort with special weekend rates, offers stylish modern accommodations, a variety of sports facilities, and fine dining. The Nassau Inn is the traditional spot to dine; and for cozier atmosphere, there's the Peacock Inn, formerly a pre-Revolutionary War home.

But there's yet another attraction that may cause you to cut this visit short: Duke Gardens on Route 206 in Somerville, right on the way home. It's a choice you'll have to make in advance, since reservations are needed to tour these 11 classic gardens under glass, and they are worth a visit anytime you are in the area since the blooms change according to the season.

If Somerville gets your vote, you'll also discover a selection of good restaurants in the neighborhood for Sunday brunch or dinner. What nicer way to wind up the weekend?

Princeton, Lambertville, and Stockton Area Code: 609

Flemington and Somerville Area Code: 908

DRIVING DIRECTIONS New Jersey Turnpike south to exit 10, then Route 287 north again to exit 10, and Route 22 west for 2½ miles. Exit at Flemington–Princeton, follow Route 202 south for about 25 miles, get off at Lambertville before the Delaware River Bridge, and follow Route 29 north to Lambertville and Stockton.

Total distance: roughly 75 miles.

PUBLIC TRANSPORTATION Bus service is available from New York to Flemington and Lambertville via Trans-Bridge Lines; the trip takes about two hours. Bus information: (800) 962-9135 or (215) 868-6001.

ACCOMMODATIONS *Stockton Inn*, Route 29, Stockton, 08559, 397-1250, $$-$$$$ CP • *Woolverton Inn*, RD 3, PO Box 233, Stockton, 08558, 397-0802, $$-$$$ CP • *Chimney Hill Farm*, Goat Hill Road, Lambertville, 08530, 397-1516, $$$-$$$$ CP • *York Street House*, 42 York Street, Lambertville, 08530, 397-3007, $$-$$$ CP • *The Bridgestreet House Guest Lodging*, 67 Bridge Street, Lambertville, 08530, 397-2503, $$-$$$ CP • *The Inn at Lambertville Station*, 11 Bridge Street, Lambertville, 08530, $$-$$$ CP • *Scanticon-Princeton*, Princeton Forrestal Center, 100 College Road East, Princeton, 08540, 452-7800, $$-$$$$$ CP (ask for weekend packages) • *Nassau Inn*, Palmer Square, Princeton, 08646, 921-7500, $$$-$$$$ • *Peacock Inn*, 20 Bayard Lane, Princeton, 08540, 924-1707, $$-$$$ CP.

* * *

DINING *Anton's at the Swan,* 43 South Main Street, Lambertville, 397-1960, period hotel setting, creative menu with a French accent, $$ • *Hamilton's Grill Room,* 8½ Coryell (adjoining the Boat Yard), Lambertville, 397-4343, a favorite in the area, $$ • *DeAnna's,* 18 South Main Street, Lambertville, 397-8957, Italian, homemade pastas, $-$$ • *Manon,* 19 North Union Street, 397-2596, tiny storefront, eclectic menu, French chef, $$ • *Lambertville Station,* 11 Bridge Street, Lambertville, 397-8300, standard fare, $$ • *Siam,* 61 North Main Street, Lambertville, 397-8128, plain decor, excellent Thai food, $-$$ • *The Ferry House,* 21 Ferry Street, Lambertville, 397-9222, a best bet for Sunday brunch, $$ • *Colligan's Stockton Inn and the Fox* (see above), $$-$$$ • *Palmer's,* Nassau Inn (see above), Colonial decor, $$-$$$ • *Black Swan,* Scanticon-Princeton (see above), Continental, elegant, $$$-$$$$ • *Tivoli Gardens,* Scanticon-Princeton (see above), Scandinavian specialties; buffet brunch, $$-$$$$ • *Le Plumet Royal,* Peacock Inn (see above), Continental, $$$-$$$$ • *Lahiere's, 5* Witherspoon Street, Princeton, 921-2798, formal French, $$$-$$$$ • *Alchemist and Barrister,* 28 Witherspoon Street, Princeton, 924-5555, Colonial ambience, pub in the rear, $$-$$$ • *Acacia,* 2637 Main Street (Route 206), Lawrenceville (south of Princeton), 895-9885, top reviews for this innovative New American in the old post office, $$-$$$ • *La Cucina,* 125 West Main Street, Somerville, 526-4907, popular Italian, $$ • *Filippo's,* 132 East Main Street, Somerville, 218-0110, tiny cafe, tasty southern Italian, $$ • *Max's,* 63 West Somerset Street, Raritan, 725-4553, creative Italian, $$-$$$.

SIGHTSEEING *Harrison Aire Balloon Rides,* Box 330 Wertsville Road, Ringoes, (609) 466-3389, phone for information and rates • *Black River & Western Steam Railroad,* Box 200, Ringoes, (908) 782-9600, steam train excursions from Lambertville, May through October; from Flemington, April through December. Phone for current rates and schedules • *Princeton University,* guided tours from Maclean House, 73 Nassau Street, 258-8603. Hours: Monday to Saturday 10 A.M., 11 A.M., 1:30 P.M., and 3:30 P.M.; Sunday 1:30 P.M., 3:30 P.M. Free • *Bainbridge House,* 158 Nassau Street, Princeton, 921-6748. Hours: Daily noon to 4 P.M. Guided walking tours Saturday morning and Sunday at 2 P.M., $3 • *Duke Gardens,* U.S. 206, Somerville, 722-3700. Hours: October 1 to June 1, daily noon to 4 P.M. Adults, $5; children 6–12, $2.50; children under 6 free. Reservations required by mail or phone. No high heels allowed.

* * *

FOR FURTHER INFORMATION Lambertville Area Chamber of Commerce, 4 South Union Street, Lambertville, NJ 08530, (609) 397-0055. For map of Flemington outlets, contact Flemington Chamber of Commerce, 76 Main Street, Flemington, NJ 08822, (908) 782-7456. Chamber of Commerce of the Princeton Area, Nassau Street, PO Box 431, Princeton, NJ 08542, (609) 921-7676.

"The Mercer Mile" and Other Bucks County Byways

We stepped inside the doorway, looked up six stories to the ceiling—and stopped in our tracks. Almost everyone who came behind us did the same.

Hanging above us, suspended at various levels from a vast central core, were Early American objects of every conceivable size and shape—chairs, barrels, cradles, whaleboats, baskets, bellows, sleds, cigar store Indians, a full-size buckboard, even a Conestoga wagon.

Next to the spiral stairs that circle the room are display cubbies, jammed and crammed with the hand tools that made these items and scores of others—tools used by butchers, dairymen, cooks, coopers, carpenters, weavers, leathermakers, and printers; tools for doctors, clockmakers, surveyors and seamstresses—130 crafts represented in all and a total of almost 50,000 objects.

It is an eye-boggling display that greets visitors to the Mercer Museum—the largest collection of early hand tools and their finished products ever assembled. But the museum, located in Doylestown, the county seat of scenic Bucks County, Pennsylvania, is only the first of three extravaganzas in an area that has come to be called the Mercer Mile.

And the Mercer Mile is just the start of the many attractions in this county along the Delaware River, a setting of rolling hills, covered bridges, and distinctive stone houses that served as country retreats for some of the nation's best-known authors and entertainers. Shopping and shunpiking are two major activities here, and though there's history galore, it comes in lively form—riding on a steam train, gliding downstream on a mule-drawn canal barge, watching an antique printing press or a water-powered gristmill in action, or seeing Mr. Mercer's dream houses, monuments to a man who was an authentic American genius—and eccentric.

Henry Chapman Mercer was one of the nation's leading archaeologists when his personal passion for collecting Early American tools led to a surprising midlife career change. Mercer became so intrigued with the tools used by the old Pennsylvania German pottery and tile makers that he became determined to perpetuate the dying craft. He apprenticed himself to an old German potter, rented a decrepit kiln, and by 1898 exhibited a talent that brought him a new kind of fame. Mercer tiles can be seen today from the casino at Monte Carlo to the Gardner Museum in Boston, from a high school in Havana to the King Ranch in Texas. His largest work is the tile floor in the Pennsylvania state capitol at Harrisburg.

Mercer called his enterprise the Moravian Pottery and Tile Works. The factory is now a living museum, part of the Mercer Mile, still turning out his original patterns according to his formulas and methods. You can pick up a few as souvenirs in the museum gift shop, which also has a fine selection of early Pennsylvania crafts—boxes of Pennsylvania Dutch designs, tinware, unusual weathervanes, and the like. If you are searching for books on Early American art or antiques, you'll find hundreds of titles here.

The most incredible display of tiles, however, awaits in Mercer's own home, Fonthill, a castlelike concrete fantasy that took 106 men more than two years to build. Mercer's mansion is a fantastic mélange of columns, balconies, beams, towers, arches, and winding stairs. Tiles are everywhere—on columns and beams, serving as headboards, tabletops, and ceilings, even lining the stairs. There is a copy of an English tapestry in tile, the story of the discovery of the New World told in tile, and in addition to Mercer's own creations, fine specimens of historic tiles he gathered from every part of the world.

Fonthill and the museum that Mercer built in 1913 to house his enormous collection of tools and artifacts established Mercer as an eccentric prophet of modern architecture. The October 1960 issue of *Progressive Architecture* says: "Though the effect is often weird and theatrical . . . [Fonthill] with its unique spatial plan and its frank and bold techniques . . . [is] one of the important forerunners of the modern movement."

The Mercer Mile can take a good half day, but there should be enough time left to enjoy some of the many other pleasures of Bucks County. Right across the street from the Mercer Museum on Pine Street is the James A. Michener Art Museum, housed in a handsome 1884 stone structure that was once the Bucks County Jail. The former prison yard is now a sculpture garden. A showcase for twentieth-century art, the museum was endowed by and named for the famous author, who was born in Doylestown and still maintains a residence here. A special exhibition honoring Michener's life and work includes furnishings from his early Doylestown office. An addition that doubled the display space in 1993 also added a pleasant tea room that opens onto a terrace in the sculpture garden.

A walking tour of Doylestown center is another enjoyable diversion. Main Street, State Street (Route 202), and Oakland Avenue are the main streets in town and are lined with interesting homes dating from early to late nineteenth century. Heading back east on 202 you'll come to Buckingham, a tiny village that maintains the early flavor of Bucks County and is also the site of the Buckingham Farmers' Market on 202 held on Saturdays from 9 A.M. until the farm produce is sold. (Bountiful Acres, a little farther east on Route 202, also has fresh-picked produce in season.)

Another famous Saturday event in Buckingham is Brown Brothers auction on Route 413 just south of Route 263. It begins at 9 A.M. with box lots and, as the day progresses, moves on to bigger and better things, including all kinds of antiques, furniture, and accessories that change by the week.

Lahaska, farther east on Route 202, is for shoppers. Peddler's Village, a nicely landscaped Colonial-style complex, has dozens of shops crammed with clothes, crafts, jewelry, and gifts. The newest addition here is a carousel museum that includes an operating 1926 Grand Dentzel Carousel boasting ornately carved animals and a melodious German band organ. The Golden Plough Inn is a convenient stop for lunch.

Afterward, cross the street to an antiquer's haven, the Lahaska Antique Courte, with a dozen shops featuring all kinds of collectibles.

All of Bucks County is an antiquer's paradise. A recent printed guide listed some 50 stores. There are three big annual shows in and around Doylestown, the last usually held in mid-October. Write to the Bucks County Tourist Commission for this year's dates and locations.

Finally, follow Route 202 north to where all roads in Bucks County lead eventually—New Hope, the picturesque artists' colony on the banks of the Delaware. Take a nostalgic ride here on the last operating mule-drawn canal barge in the country. Beginning in May, you can also hop a huffing, puffing steam train for an 8½-mile loop through the countryside that includes the famous trestle from the rescue scene in *Perils of Pauline.*

New Hope's labyrinth of paths and alleyways offers lovely old homes, almost 100 shops and art galleries, and lots and lots of shoppers, a good reason to avoid the busiest summer months.

Two favorite attractions in town are the Parry Mansion, which displays in ten rooms the furnishings and decor that might have been used by the one family who lived here for 182 years from the late eighteenth to the early twentieth century, and the Bucks County Playhouse, the famous old summer theater in a restored gristmill that now has a season almost year round.

Take time to mingle with that mass of shoppers in New Hope. Though there are lots of touristy offerings, some shops have interesting wares.

Save a good chunk of your Sunday for a back-roads tour to see the rural countryside and the stone farms and barns that are the special trademark of Bucks County. Part of the fascination is that no two of the houses are alike. Even the color and texture of the homes vary according to the native stones that were used for construction. You'll see mostly limestone and shale in central Bucks and craggy granite in the upper regions. Notice the double houses with twin doors, the big tri-level barns, and the "bride and groom" trees that flank many doorways. The trees were planted long ago for good luck by newlyweds who hoped their love would flourish along with the saplings.

The main roads are the River Road (Route 32), 611, and 413, and you can't go wrong making your own way back and forth. One possible route is to follow the River Road north. The thin strip of land running along the canal is officially called Delaware Canal State Park, but is generally just referred to as the tow path, named for its historical use as a path for the mules that pulled barges down the canal. Now you'll see hikers and bikers using it.

The drive takes you through the sleepy town of Lumberville and to Point Pleasant, where you may be tempted to spend an hour looking at the river from one of its nicest perspectives—from a canoe. Point Pleasant Canoe can provide all the necessary equipment, and even novices need not worry about this placid stretch of water. Rubber rafts and tubes are also for rent, or you can opt for a "pedal and paddle" tour allowing you to bike one way along the river and return via canoe.

In Ralph Stover State Park near Point Pleasant you can see the Big Red Bridge, and there are other covered bridges farther north in Erwinna and Uhlerstown. Stover Mill in Erwinna still has its old machinery intact and is a local historic site. There's also a restored Federal-style home in Tinicum Park on River Road, as well as picnic facilities if you want to take a break.

Two and half miles west of River Road in Upper Black Eddy is a strange geologic formation, 3½ acres of huge boulders, which are known as Ringing Rocks because many of the rocks, when struck, do actually ring.

From Upper Black Eddy continue west on 32 to the connection with 611 and proceed south once again through more charming towns such as Pipersville (near the Cabin Run and Loux covered bridges and another restored mill) and Plumsteadville. Not far away in Dublin is a home with a special kind of history. It is Green Hills Farm, where Pulitzer and Nobel prize–winning author Pearl Buck lived and worked for forty years. Mrs. Buck's 1835 stone house is filled with Oriental antiques in a rustic setting of Pennsylvania beams, wide-board oak floors, and big stone fireplaces.

There are winery tours at the Bucks County Vineyards near New Hope and the Buckingham Valley Vineyards in Buckingham. And there are more covered bridges (12 in all) and more historic sights all over the area. For a more comprehensive listing, write for the Bucks County guide before you make your trip.

The final bonus is the large number of historic houses that have been converted to atmospheric inns and restaurants. Three prize winners are in Doylestown.

Highland Farm was the home of song writer Oscar Hammerstein II, and the place where he wrote some of his most famous lyrics. The family lived in the Victorian farmhouse from 1941 to 1961, enjoying their tennis court and kidney-shaped pool. Henry Fonda was married in the grape arbor and Stephen Sondheim spent summers here with his boarding school roommate, the Hammersteins' son. Now the house is a bed-and-breakfast inn done in high-style Victoriana, with bedrooms named and decorated for musicals like *Carousel*, *Showboat*, and *The King and I*.

The Inn at Fordhook Farm is the estate of W. Atlee Burpee, who founded the famous seed company. Now an inn, the elegant eighteenth-century home is still owned by the Burpees, and the rooms are filled with family photos, antiques, and memorabilia. It sits on 60 acres of gardens, meadows, and woods.

While there is no celebrity owner, Pine Tree Farm in Doylestown is one of the most appealing of inns, an eighteenth-century home furnished in the best of taste.

Bucks County has a host of other lodgings to fit every mood: For country charm, try Barley Sheaf Farm; for Victoriana, it's Evermay, a period beauty with a fine dining room. The list of appealing choices is long—and you can hardly go wrong.

Bucks County Area Code: 215

DRIVING DIRECTIONS Take the New Jersey Turnpike south to exit 10, then go north on U.S. 287 15 miles to Route 22 (287 widens to five lanes just before the exit, so stay left). Drive west on Route 22 for about 3½ miles, then turn right at the sign marked Flemington–Princeton for Route 202 south to Doylestown.

Total distance: about 85 miles.

ACCOMMODATIONS *Highland Farm,* 70 East Road, Doylestown, 18901, 340-1354, $$$-$$$$$ CP • *The Inn at Fordhook Farm,* 105 New Britain Road, Doylestown, 18901, 345-1766, $$-$$$$ CP • *Pine Tree Farm,* 2155 Lower State Road, Doylestown, 18901, 348-0632, $$$-$$$$ CP • *Barley Sheaf Farm,* PO Box 10, Route 202, Holicong, 18928, 794-5104, $$$-$$$$ CP • *1740 House,* River Road (Route 32), Lumberville, 18933, 297-5661, $$-$$$ CP • *Evermay,*

River Road, Erwinna, 18920, 294-9100, $$-$$$$ CP • *Auldridge Mead,* 523 Geigel Road, Ottsville, 18942, 847-5842 1772 stone farmhouse, $$-$$$ CP • *Mill Creek Farm,* Quarry Road, Box 816, Buckingham, 18912, 794-0776, eighteenth-century home, horse farm on 100 acres, $$-$$$ CP • *Golden Pheasant,* River Road, Erwinna, 18920, 294-9595, rooms above the restaurant in French country decor, canal views, 862-9608, $$-$$$ CP • *Bucksville House,* Route 412 and Buck Drive, Kintnersville, 18930, 847-8948, $$-$$$ CP • *Ash Mill Farm,* Route 202, Holicong, 18928, 794-5373, eighteenth-century farmhouse, $$-$$$ CP • *Whitehall Inn,* Pinevile Road, New Hope 18938, 598-7945, pool, tennis, afternoon concerts, $$$-$$$$ CP • *Tattersall Inn,* Cafferty and River roads, Point Pleasant, 18950, 297-8233, gracious manor house, good value, $$ CP. Most inns have two-night minimums; these two do not: *Golden Plough,* Route 202, Peddler's Village, Lahaska, 18931, 794-4004, nicely furnished small hotel, $$-$$$$ CP • *Plumsteadville Inn,* Route 611 and Stump Road, Plumsteadville, 18949, 766-7500, well-furnished rooms above a popular restaurant, $$-$$$ CP.

DINING *Inn at Phillips Mill,* River Road, New Hope, 862-9919, romantic, French menu, $$$ • *Harrow Inne,* Routes 611 and 412, Ottsville, 847-2464, highly praised chef, Continental menu, $$$-$$$$ • *Cafe Arielle,* 100 South Main Street, Doylestown, 345-5930, French fare in a restored stable, $$-$$$ • *Conti Inn,* Routes 313 and 611, Doylestown, 348-9600, old-timer, dependable fare, Colonial ambience, $$-$$$ • *La Bonne Auberge,* Village II, New Hope, 862-2462, classic French, elegant, $$$$ • *Jean Pierre's,* 101 South State Street, Newtown, 968-6201, former Le Bec Fin chef, $$$-$$$$ • *Evermay* (see above), superb five-course prix fixe dinner served Friday through Sunday, $$$$$ • *Golden Pheasant Inn,* River Road, Erwinna, 294-9595, beautifully restored 1857 inn, excellent French chef, $$$-$$$$ • *Forager House,* 1600 River Road, New Hope, 862-9477, popular, mesquite grill and imaginative dishes, $$-$$$. The best are all expensive; for nongourmet, casual dining, New Hope has a variety of informal cafes such as *Mother's,* 105 South Main Street, 862-9897, $$; *Karla's Restaurant,* 5 West Mechanic Street, 862-2612, $$; and *Havana,* 105 South Main Street, 862-9897, $$. For a scenic brunch by a waterfall (but not recommended for dinner), try the *Cuttalossa Inn,* River Road (Route 32), Lumberville, 297-5082.

SIGHTSEEING *The Mercer Mile: Mercer Museum,* Pine Street, Doylestown, 345-0210. Hours: Monday to Saturday, 10 A.M. to 5 P.M.;

Sunday noon to 5 P.M. Adults, $5; children, $1.50 • *Fonthill,* East Court Street, Doylestown, 348-9461. Hours: open only for guided tours, by reservation, daily 10 A.M. to 5 P.M. Adults, $4.50; children, $1.50 • *Moravian Pottery and Tile Works,* Swamp Road (Route 313), Doylestown, 345-6722. Hours: daily 10 A.M. to 5 P.M. Adults, $2.50; children, $1 • James A. Michener Art Museum, 138 South Pine Street, Doylestown, 340-9800. Hours: Tuesday to Friday 10 A.M. to 4:30 P.M.; Saturday and Sunday 10 A.M. to 5 P.M. Adults, $4; students, $1.50 • *Green Hill Farm,* 520 Dublin Road, Perkasie, 249-0100. Hours: March to December, by guided tour only, Tuesday to Saturday 10:30 A.M., 1:30 P.M., and 2:30 P.M.; Sunday 1:30 P.M. and 2:30 P.M. Adults, $5; students, $4; family rate, $12 • *Parry Mansion,* 45 South Main Street, New Hope, 862-5652. Hours: May through October, Friday to Sunday 1 P.M. to 5 P.M. $4 • *Carousel World Museum,* Peddler's Village, Route 202, Lahaska, 794-4000. Hours: daily 10 A.M. to 9 P.M. Adults, $5; children, $4 (includes carousel ride) • *Mule-Drawn Barge Rides,* New Street at southern end of New Hope, 862-2842. Hours: April to mid-November, phone for current schedules. Adults, $6.50; children 2–11, $3.75 • *New Hope and Ivyland Railroad,* Bridge Street (Route 179) near the center of New Hope, 862-2332. Hours: daily April to November, weekends January to March, special Santa rides in December. Hours vary with the season; check for current hours and rates. • *Point Pleasant Canoe Rental and Sales,* Point Pleasant, 197-TUBE. Check for current canoe, raft, and tube rental rates.

FOR FURTHER INFORMATION Bucks County Tourist Commission, 152 Swamp Road, Doylestown, PA 18901, 345-4552.

Stony Brook and the North Shore: A Springtime Ramble

A set designer couldn't have done better. Old white Colonial homes, a peaceful harbor, an eighteenth-century grist mill, tiny tots toddling down the sloping green to feed the ducks on the pond. Even the shopping center of Stony Brook is built in Early American style so as not to spoil the picture.

This little North Shore town, so atypical of many people's visions of Long Island, is one of the island's most historic enclaves, but it owes its present look to a modern benefactor, Ward Melville, founder of the Thom McAnn shoe chain. In 1939, inspired by Colonial Williamsburg, Melville proposed that the town center be remodeled. He generously provided funds to pay for the project, and established the nonprofit Community Fund, which continues to work to preserve and maintain the village.

In keeping with Melville's vision, Main Street was re-routed and residences and businesses were moved or refurbished to open up vistas to the harbor and create a crescent-shaped village center just off the green, with a cluster of shops built in Colonial style. At the center of the crescent is a popular town landmark, the post office, adorned with a mechanical eagle that flaps its wings every hour on the hour.

Recently, two more shopping complexes have been added to the original Stony Brook Village Center, following its architecture. Shoppers now have a choice of over 40 stores, including a number of top name manufacturer's outlets behind the Colonial facades. The center shops sponsor many free events from jazz concerts on the green to story time for tots.

Across the green is the perfect inn to complete the picture. Three Village Inn, a handsome, white, 1751 structure, was until 1867 the home of Captain Jonas Smith, a New York City shipbuilder who became Long Island's first millionaire. Ward Melville's mother, Jennie, used the house as a meeting place for the women of the village. They began serving tea, and that custom eventually evolved into a restaurant, and then an inn.

Now there are seven rooms upstairs in the main inn, and another 25 in cottages tucked into pretty landscaping out back. The Early American–style furnishings are not distinguished but the ambience is very pleasant, especially in the cottages, where some rooms offer fireplaces and others a water view.

The dining room, decorated in fresh flowery prints, has a menu that includes Continental fare as well as such traditional dishes as chicken pot pie, roast beef with popovers, Yankee pot roast, and Long Island duckling. The big Sunday brunch is a local tradition. For a change of pace, you can try another historic dining spot, the Country House, circa 1710, or the cafes in the village center.

The newest attraction in town is the venerable Stony Brook Grist Mill, which was built around 1751 and was still grinding wheat and corn for local farmers as late as the 1950s. The mill was closed for several years for needed restoration. It reopened in 1993 as Long Island's most completely equipped working mill. Youngsters love watching the millstone turn, powered by the water from Mill Pond.

The Museums at Stony Brook are another major sightseeing stop.

The nine-acre site includes a History Museum, Carriage Museum and Art Museum, as well as four historic buildings. Among the major exhibits are decoys, miniature rooms, horse-drawn carriages, costumes, toys, and the paintings of William Sidney Mount, a well-known nineteenth-century Long Island artist.

There's more to be seen at the State University of New York at Stony Brook. The expansive modern campus north of the village, with 105 buildings on 1,100 acres, offers art galleries in the Melville Library and exhibits on local natural history at the Museum of Long Island Natural Sciences. The Statler Center for the Arts hosts a variety of events year round, including a Bach Aria Festival and an International Theater Festival in the summer.

Save time for exploring some of the historic neighborhoods in the area known as the Three Villages—Stony Brook, Setauket, and Old Field.

Follow Route 25A east to North Country Road and turn left to see the Thompson House, a fine example of early architecture, built in 1720. The timber-frame house is know for its unusually high ceilings, massive fireplaces, and wide floor boards. It contains a notable collection of early Long Island furniture. Guides will take you through the house, point out the decorative details on the exposed beams and the most interesting furnishings, and tell you all about the original inhabitants. An herb garden and the Thompson family cemetery are on the grounds of the house, as are an ice house, a barn, a corncrib, and the 1800s building that is the headquarters for the Society for the Preservation of Long Island Antiquities.

Drive a bit farther on North Country Road as it turns into Main Street and you'll come to the original settlement area around the Setauket Mill Pond. The village green here dates back over 300 years. The Setauket Presbyterian Church was built in 1812, but its graveyard goes back to the late 1600s. The Caroline Church, circa 1729, is the oldest Episcopal church building in New York State. The dam and mill on the pond are reconstructions, dedicated in memory of Frank Melville, Jr., in 1937.

The Three Village Historic Society has compiled a library of material on the early history of the area, housed in the century-old Emma S. Clark Library on the green. They offer occasional walking tours and a candlelight house tour in late November.

Come back to Route 25A and continue north to East Setauket, and the Dyer's Neck Historic District on Setauket harbor, once a thriving shipbuilding center. Located on Main Street (25A) is the Brewster House, a quaint saltbox that is the oldest home in the Three Village area, dating back to 1665. South of Route 25A are Coach Road and Old Post Road, two of the many byways where you can see shingled farmhouses that reflect the rural character of early Long Island.

If you continue east a few miles on 25A to Port Jefferson, you'll find a far different scene, the lively dock area where the ferry to Connecticut is berthed. There are shops galore to tempt you, and if there is no room at the inn in Stony Brook, Danford's Inn here is the closest alternative, pleasant though pricey.

On Sunday, you can spend an enjoyable day winding your way back home with a choice of attractions along the North Shore. Route 25A west will bring you to Northport and—just past the town—the Vanderbilt Museum, also known as Eagle's Nest for its lofty perch above Long Island Sound.

The estate, a 24-room Spanish-style mansion on 43 wooded acres, was given to Suffolk County by former owner William K. Vanderbilt II. The lavish mansion reveals clearly the life-style of the Gold Coast days when this stretch of the North Shore was the province of wealthy society. Besides the mansion itself, there are natural science exhibits created by Mr. Vanderbilt with collections from his family's travel to exotic places, which include dioramas of animals in their natural habitats.

Up the hill is a Marine Museum, built in 1922 and known as the Hall of Fishes, exhibiting the fruits of Vanderbilt's cruises of scientific exploration. Among the mounted specimens from the sea and the land are an anaconda, a python, a moose, a tortoise, and a devil ray. The second floor contains hundreds of marine vertebrates. A new building erected in 1971, funded by the Vanderbilt Foundation, houses a planetarium that is among a dozen of the largest and best equipped in the United States; it has the largest public-use telescope in the New York City region.

This is a rare and worthwhile stop, but even if you don't want to visit the museum, at least detour to enjoy the spectacular view from the semicircular overlook bordered by ancient Corinthian columns from the ruins of Carthage.

Continue along 25A until you come to Cold Spring Harbor, just south of Huntington, a perfectly delightful old whaling village that has been declared a National Historic District. There are several appealing shops here, as well as a small whaling museum that is one of the best of its kind, filled with harpoons, scrimshaw, paintings, ship models, and an old Long Island whaling boat.

A little farther on you'll come to Oyster Bay, with two major attractions that can easily occupy a full day—Sagamore Hill and the Planting Fields Arboretum.

Follow the signs off 25A to Theodore Roosevelt's ''bully'' home at Sagamore Hill, a three-story, 22-room Victorian affair with a big shaded porch where Teddy used to sit and rock and look at the sunset. It was here on this porch that he learned of his nominations for governor of New York and vice-president of the United States.

There's no mistaking whose home this is. Teddy's huge hunting trophies, buffalo heads, elephant tusks, bearskins, and the like are all over the place. There's a wastebasket made from an elephant's foot and an inkwell from a rhinoceros foot.

But the guided tour here recalls, too, the many other sides of this great man. He was a conservationist who was responsible for many of our national parks, a diplomat who received a Nobel Peace Prize for bringing about peace between Russia and Japan following the Russo-Japanese War, and the president who was responsible for the building of the Panama Canal. The great north room where the president entertained foreign dignitaries contains some of their gifts, including samurai swords, ivory, paintings, and photographs.

The rest of the house reflects a warm family life with six active children. Edith Roosevelt's touch is most evident in the pretty pale blue parlor, where she was allowed to decorate according to her own taste with patterned brocades and fancy lampshades.

Also on the grounds is the Old Orchard Museum, the former residence of Theodore Roosevelt, Jr. In the museum, a film about the former president is shown, and there are exhibits about his political and family life, and about his children's lives.

Since Sagamore Hill reopened in 1993 after extensive renovations, the guided tours have proven so popular that weekend afternoons are often sellouts, so morning tours are strongly recommended. To do this, you may want to consider spending a night near Oyster Bay or driving directly to Sagamore Hill from Stony Brook on Sunday morning.

You'll have no difficulty filling the rest of your day in Oyster Bay. Planting Fields Arboretum, recently named a State Historic Park, was originally another Gold Coast country estate, with a 65-room Tudor mansion built from 1918 to 1921 by William Robertson Coe. Coe's appreciation for rare and unusual plants led him to the famous landscape architects, the Olmsted brothers, who transformed the 409-acre estate into a horticultural showplace with 160 acres of gardens and rare plant collections.

Coe deeded his property to be enjoyed by the people of New York State. It includes sweeping lawns, a spectacular display of trees and shrubs, a rose garden, showy beds of spring bulbs, and over 600 species of rhododendrons and azaleas that are at their most dazzling in the month of May. Extensive greenhouses include seasonal displays and a camellia house that shows the nation's largest collection of camellias under glass, at their best in midwinter.

Free family walks are given on Sunday afternoons May through September, ending with a magic show or storytelling.

Planting Fields hosts outdoor concerts in a handsome tent on the grounds in late spring and summer, including the Long Island Mozart Festival, over Memorial Day weekend, the Long Island Jazz Festival, and a summer classical music festival. A recently added program of chamber music indoors in the Hay Barn will take place on selected

Sunday afternoons from September through April. It's hard to imagine a nicer setting for listening to music.

Oyster Bay offers casual cafes in town and fine dining at the Mill River Inn or Cafe Girasole in neighboring East Norwich. Or you can end the weekend on a nautical note with a seafood dinner at Steve's Pier I, on the water in nearby Bayville.

Long Island Area Code: 516

DRIVING DIRECTIONS Long Island Expressway (Route 495) to exit 62. Proceed north on Nicolls Road and turn left on Route 25A into Stony Brook. *Total distance:* about 58 miles.

PUBLIC TRANSPORTATION Long Island Railroad service is available from New York's Penn Station to Stony Brook. Take a cab or a ¼-mile walk from the station to the museums, then taxi or walk to the inn. From the inn, you can walk to the village sights.

ACCOMMODATIONS *Three Village lnn,* 150 Main Street, Stony Brook, 11790, 751-0555, $$$ • *Danford's Inn,* Bayles Dock, 25 East Broadway, Port Jefferson, 11777, 928-5200, $$$-$$$$$ • *Marriott Wind Watch Resort,* 171 Vanderbilt Motor Parkway (at exit 57 of the Long Island Expressway), Hauppauge, 11788, 232-9800, $$$$ • *East Norwich Inn,* Routes 25A and 106 (near Oyster Bay), 922-1500, $$$$ • *Radisson Plaza Hotel,* 1350 Old Walt Whitman Road, Melville, 11747, 423-1600, indoor pool, packages offered with Planting Fields concerts, $$-$$$.

DINING *Three Village Inn* (see above), dinner $$$-$$$$; brunch, $$ • *Country House,* Route 25A, Stony Brook, 751-3332; dinner, $$-$$$; lunch, $$ • *Pasta Viola*, Village Center, Stony Brook, 689-7755, Italian cafe, $$ • *Coffee Cafe*, Inner Court, Village Center, Stony Brook, 751-1232, refreshments by day, live music Thursday through Saturday nights, $ • *Mill River Inn,* 160 Mill River Road, Oyster Bay, 922-7788, contemporary American cuisine, $$-$$$, or prix fixe $$$$$ • *Canterbury Ales,* 26 Audrey Avenue, Oyster Bay, 922-3614, pub with seafood specialties, oysters, $$ • *Calamari Kitchen,* 628 South Street, Oyster Bay, 624-7781, casual, southern Italian menu, $-$$ • *Taby's Restaurant*, 28 Audrey Avenue, Oyster Bay, 624-7781, casual dinner menu, juicy hamburgers, good lunch choice, $ • *Cafe Girasole,* 1053 Oyster Bay Road, East Norwich, 624-8330, Italian $$-$$$ • *Steve's Pier I,* 33 Bayville Avenue, Bayville, 628-2431, seafood on the Sound, $$-$$$.

SIGHTSEEING *Museums of Stony Brook,* Route 25A, Stony Brook, 751-0666. Hours: Wednesday to Saturday 10 A.M. to 5 P.M., Sunday noon to 5 P.M. Adults, $6; students, $4; children 6–12, $3; family rate, $15 • *Stony Brook Grist Mill,* off Main Street, Stony Brook, 751-2244. Hours: Wednesday to Friday 11 A.M. to 4:30 P.M., Saturday and Sunday noon to 4:30 P.M. Free • *Statler Center for the Arts,* State University of New York at Stony Brook, phone 632-7235 for events schedule • *Thompson House,* North Country Road, Setauket, 941-9444. Hours: late May to mid-October, Friday to Sunday, 10 A.M. to 4 P.M. Adults, $2; children 7–14, $1 • *Vanderbilt Museum,* Little Neck Road, Centerport (watch for signs on 25A), 262-7880. Hours: Memorial Day to Labor Day, Tuesday to Saturday 10 A.M. to 4 P.M.; Sunday and holidays noon to 5 P.M. Rest of year, Tuesday to Sunday, noon to 4 P.M. Grounds: adults, $5; students, $3, under 12, $1; mansion and planetarium fees, each $3 extra; all-inclusive ticket, adults, $11; students, $9; under 12, $7. *Cold Spring Whaling Museum,* Main Street (Route 25A), Cold Spring Harbor, 367-3418. Hours: Memorial Day to Labor Day, daily 11 A.M. to 5 P.M; rest of year, closed Monday. Adults, $2; children over age 6, $1 • *Sagamore Hill,* Cove Neck Road, Oyster Bay, 922-4447. Hours: daily 9:30 A.M. to 5 P.M. Adults, $2; under 17 and over 62, free • *Planting Fields Arboretum State Historic Park,* Planting Fields Road, Oyster Bay, 922-9201. Hours: grounds open daily 9 A.M. to 5 P.M.; Camellia House, 10 A.M. to 4 P.M.; main greenhouse, 10 A.M. to 4:30 P.M. Parking, $3.

FOR FURTHER INFORMATION Stony Brook Village Center, Box 572, Stony Brook, NY 11790, 751-2244.

Down to the Sea at Mystic Seaport

Wait for the weather forecast. Make sure it's going to be the kind of perfect spring day when breezes billow the square sails, masts and rigging stand out against the blue sky, and the sun warms you while you listen to sea chanteys being sung on the green.

That's the kind of day to save for the Mystic Seaport Museum, not only a place for ships but a 17-acre total re-creation of a nineteenth-century maritime village. You can pick your weekend at the last minute only if you go to visit the Northeast's major maritime attraction before summer tourists fill the local motels. And you'll enjoy your visit even more without summer humidity and crowds.

Mystic's shipbuilding history dates back to the 1700s. When wooden shipbuilding was at its peak in the 1800s, Mystic's shipyards produced some of the fastest clippers on the seas; many were built at the George Greenman and Company Shipyard, the site of the present Seaport Museum. Three town residents formed a Marine Historical Association back in 1929 to preserve some of the objects from the town's maritime past, and sea-minded friends from all over soon became involved, helping the museum grow to include more than 60 historic buildings, 4 major vessels and more than 400 smaller boats, important collections of maritime artifacts and paintings, and a planetarium to teach the secrets of celestial navigation.

There is no question that for most visitors the most exciting part of Mystic is the ships, especially the big three: the *Charles W. Morgan,* America's last surviving wooden whaling ship; the full-rigged training ship *Joseph Conrad;* and the fishing schooner *L. A. Dunton.*

You can come right aboard, pace the decks, examine the intricate rigging and enormous masts, go below to see the crew's cramped quarters and the officers' cabins, even take an imaginary turn at the wheel. On the *Morgan,* the whaleboats, tryworks, sails, and rigging are all in place. Aboard the *Dunton,* crew members show another kind of fishing expertise in action—the cleaning, splitting, and salting of cod for drying. Fishermen's skills like trawling, weaving nets, and building lobster pots are also demonstrated.

Smaller boats once used for oystering, lobstering, salmon fishing, clamming, and other kinds of fishing are moored near the *Dunton,* and you can see the fishing gear used by three generations of one family at the Robie Ames Fishing Shack nearby.

Almost as interesting as seeing the boats is learning how they were built. Mystic's Henry B. du Pont preservation shipyard is a unique facility with the equipment and craftsmen to perform almost any task in the restoration and preservation of wooden boats. A visitors' gallery overlooks the carpenters' shops, rigging loft, and other areas where older vessels are maintained and new ones are built.

In the Small Boat Shop, boat builders are at work crafting small wooden sailboats or rowboats. Some are sold to finance the seaport's boat-building apprenticeship program, which keeps the old craft alive. Others are part of a fleet of nineteenth-century dories, wherries, canoes, split-sail boats, and catboats that are sailed and rowed on the river, enlivening the waterfront.

All of this goes on against the backdrop of a nineteenth-century seafaring village with more than 20 authentic structures—grocery store, printer's shop, school, chapel, ship chandlery, sail loft, shipsmith, cooperage, and buildings housing other necessary services. Some of these shops and houses are on their original sites; others were moved here from the town of Mystic or from other New England communities. All are furnished with authentic period items, and in many, craftsmen are on hand to explain and demonstrate their trades.

There are several galleries on the grounds displaying maritime art and artifacts, ship models, paintings, and scrimshaw. One exhibit traces the development of the maritime industry from the seventeenth to nineteenth centuries; another tells the story of fishing, America's oldest industry. One of the most delightful displays for adults is the collection of ships' figureheads and wood carvings in the Wendell Building. Children are invariably charmed by the Children's Museum, done up like the interior of the ship's quarters for a captain's family. Young visitors can climb into the bunks to peer out of portholes at a mock sea and play with reproductions of toys that might have been used to amuse children on a sea voyage long ago.

It's all educational, but they also keep things lively here with demonstrations—sail setting and furling, whaleboat rowing and sailing, and a breeches buoy rescue drill. And there are "sailors" all around the grounds ready to break into a sea chantey at the drop of a sea breeze. It's almost impossible to absorb it all in a single visit. You can opt for a two-day ticket that allows you to rest up and come back for more. At least take a long break for a clamburger at the Galley snack bar and a cruise down the river on the jaunty little steamboat *Sabino* to rest between bouts of seeing the sights.

And don't think the sights of Mystic are finished when you leave the seaport. The Mystic Marinelife Aquarium is almost as popular with youngsters as the museum itself for its dolphins and seals. The Penguin Pavilion is a real winner, starring a colony of showoffs who receive guests in formal black-and-white attire. The windows that reveal the penguins swimming underwater are special favorites here. And there's the Denison Pequotsepos Nature Center if you want to take a spring walk in the woods.

The town of Mystic is also appealing, with many fine old homes (ask for the walking tour at the information center in Olde Mistick Village). A nautical flavor remains downtown with the river running through; check out the riverside art gallery and the railroad station that was the model for millions of toy train sets for years.

There are shops galore in Olde Mistick Village, a pseudo-Colonial shopping mall, and in two sections of the growing Mystic Factory Outlets nearby. In town, Mystic River Antiques Market has 30 dealers, and there are all manner of shops, as well as art galleries. And don't overlook the Seaport Store, which serves as headquarters for nautical paraphernalia, books, paintings, and memorabilia, and has an old-time country store and bakeshop as well.

Just outside Mystic you can visit Whitehall, a 1770 country mansion that has been restored and authentically furnished by the Historical Society of neighboring Stonington.

As if all that isn't enough, there is Stonington village just four miles away. This is one of the most picturesque towns on the Connecticut shore, filled with eighteenth- and nineteenth-century homes that belonged to sea captains of another age, a Greek Revival town center, a village green with requisite white churches, and a lighthouse that dates from 1823. Should you be here in summer, don't miss the little museum in that lighthouse or the view of the sound from its tower.

If you are totally taken with Stonington (and many people are), while away some time getting a closer look at the town's charming homes. There are several excellent antiques shops for browsing on Main Street and a few good places to eat—informal Noah's or the Skipper's Dock, or the very elegant Harbour View. J. P. Daniels, back toward Mystic, is another good choice.

Dining in Mystic offers something for every taste and pocketbook. For an elegant evening, visit the Floodtide at the Inn at Mystic or the Mooring at the Hilton. Seamen's Inne at the Seaport is reliable and pleasant, and the Captain Daniel Packer Inne is a charming historic house on the Mystic River. There are many informal, reasonably priced cafes as well, many specializing in seafood. For a real change of pace, head for Randall's Ordinary in North Stonington, where cooks in Colonial garb make meals over the open hearth. This place is so unusual that the hosts made *People* magazine.

For lobster, Abbott's in nearby Noank, a no-frills establishment with outdoor picnic tables, has been famous for years; Noank has other fairly priced seafood restaurants on the water, as well.

If you want to try your luck at the big Foxwoods Casino, it is about a 15-minute drive from Mystic to Ledyard, and the food choices, while nothing to write home about, are ample.

Where to stay? The Red Brook Inn is the most charming of the inn choices, offering two 1700s houses filled with antiques and a warm and welcoming hostess who also likes to cook breakfast over an open hearth. The Applewood Farms Inn in Ledyard, an 1826 homestead on 33 acres, is filled with authentic country charm.

In town, the Whaler's Inn offers attractive rooms in a renovated period building, while the even nicer Steamboat Inn puts you in quarters directly overlooking the Mystic River.

Among the many motels, the Inn at Mystic is the pick, with attractive quarters and harbor views. Units in the new east wing come with fireplaces and canopy beds. And up the hill behind the motel units is a true inn, a former private estate with formal gardens, the place where legend says Humphrey Bogart and Lauren Bacall spent part of their honeymoon. The hilltop water views are unbeatable, and if you want to leave the kids at home and make Mystic a romantic nautical getaway for two, this is definitely the place.

Connecticut Area Code: 203

DRIVING DIRECTIONS Take I-95 to exit 90. Mystic Seaport is about one mile south of the exit on Route 27. *Total distance:* about 127 miles.

PUBLIC TRANSPORTATION Amtrak trains ([800]523-8720) and Greyhound buses ([800]531-5332) serve Mystic.

ACCOMMODATIONS *Steamboat Inn,* 73 Steamboat Wharf, Mystic, 06355, 536-8300, romantic quarters on the river, $$$-$$$$ CP • *Whaler's Inn,* 20 East Main Street, Mystic, 06355, 536-1506, convenient in-town location, $$-$$$ • *Red Brook Inn,* 10 Welles Road, Old Mystic, 06372, 572-0349, bed-and-breakfast in two historic houses, $$-$$$$ CP • *The Old Mystic Inn,* 58 Main Street, Old Mystic, 06372, 572-9422, nicely furnished B&B home, $$-$$$ CP • *Applewood Farms Inn,* 528 Colonel Ledyard Highway, Ledyard, 06339, 536-2022, country charmer 10 minutes from Mystic, $$$ CP • *The Inn at Mystic,* Route 1 at Route 27, Mystic, 06355, 536-9604, motel units and a traditional inn, $$-$$$$$ • *Howard Johnson,* Route 27 at I-95, Mystic, 06355, 536-2654, $$-$$$ • *Days Inn,* off I-95 at exit 90, 06355, 572-0574, $-$$$ • *The Mystic Hilton,* 20 Coogan Boulevard, Mystic, 06355, 572-0731, $$-$$$$$ • More possibilities a few miles up the coast: *Palmer Inn,* 25 Church Street, Noank, 06340, 572-9000, gracious, old, columned mansion near the water, $$$-$$$$ CP • *Shore Inne,* 54 East Shore Road, Groton Long Point, 06340, 536-1180, modest home with an incredible water view, closed in winter, $$-$$$ CP • *Lasbury's Guest House,* 24 Orchard Street, Stonington, 06378, 535-2681, modest bed-and-breakfast home, $$ CP.

DINING *Seamen's Inne,* Greenmanville Avenue, Mystic, 536-9649, seafood specialties, lunch, $; dinner, $$-$$$ • *Floodtide,* Inn at Mystic (see above), 536-8140, Continental, $$-$$$ • *The Mooring,* Mystic Hilton (see above), $$-$$$ • *J. P. Daniels,* Route 184, Old Mystic, 572-9564, $$ • *Captain Daniel Packer Inne,* 32 Water Street, Mystic 536-3555, $$ • *Giaco's Ship's Lantern,* 21 West Main Street, Mystic, 536-9112, seafood, good for family dining, $$ • *Anthony J's,* 6 Holmes Street, Mystic, 536-0448, Italian, $-$$ • *Drawbridge Inne,* 34 West Main Street, Mystic, 536-9654, casual, steaks and seafood, $$ •

Harbour View, 60 Water Street, Stonington, 535-2720, $$-$$$ • *Skipper's Dock,* 60 Water Street, Stonington (behind Harboor View), 535-2000, $$ • *Noah's,* 113 Water Street, Stonington, 535-3925, $-$$$ • *Abbott's Lobster in the Rough,* Route 215, Noank, 536-7719, open May to Columbus Day, $-$$$ • *The Fisherman,* Groton Long Point Road, Noank, 536-1717, $$-$$$ • *Randall's Ordinary,* Route 2, North Stonington, 599-4540, open-hearth cooking, prix fixe, $$$$$.

SIGHTSEEING *Mystic Seaport Museum,* Route 27, Mystic, 572-0711. Hours: April to mid-June, September and October, 9 A.M. to 5 P.M.; mid-June to September, 9 A.M. to 8 P.M.; November to March, 9 A.M. to 4 P.M. Adults, $15.00; children 6–12, $7.50; under 5, free. Steamboat *Sabino* rides; adults, $3; children, $2. (Many special weekends are scheduled: photography, sea music festival, and lobster festival, among others. Phone for specific dates.) • *Mystic Marinelife Aquarium,* Route 27, Mystic, 536-3323. Hours: daily 9 A.M. to 4:30 P.M., to 5:30 P.M. in summer; hourly dolphin, sea lion, and whale demonstrations from 10 A.M. Adults, $9; children, $5.50 • *Denison Pequotsepos Nature Center,* Pequotsepos Road, Mystic, 536-1216. Hours: April to October, Tuesday to Saturday 9 A.M. to 5 P.M.; Sunday 1 P.M. to 5 P.M.; rest of year, 9 A.M. to 4 P.M. Adults, $3; children, $1; under 6, free • *Whitehall,* Route 27, just north of I-95 Mystic Seaport exit, 535-1131. Hours: May 1 to October 31, Tuesday to Sunday 1 to 4 P.M. Adults, $2; children, $1 • *Old Lighthouse Museum,* 7 Water Street, Stonington, 535-1440. Hours: May to October, Tuesday to Sunday 11 A.M. to 4:30 P.M. Adults, $2; children, $1 • *Foxwoods High Stakes Bingo and Casino,* Route 2, Ledyard, 885-3000 or (800) PLAY BIG. Hours: open 24 hours daily.

FOR FURTHER INFORMATION Southeastern Connecticut Tourism District, PO Box 89, 27 Masonic Street, New London, CT 06320, 444-2206.

Winterthur and Other Delaware Delights

Who could have foreseen what lay ahead in 1923 when Henry Francis du Pont acquired his first American-made antique, a simple Pennsylvania chest dated 1737?

A man of extraordinary taste as well as wealth, du Pont recognized the distinctive work of Early American craftsmen before collecting native antiques had become fashionable. He saw the nation's early culture reflected in its decorative arts and was soon amassing not only the finest furniture from the period between 1640 and 1840, but also curtains, bed hangings, rugs, lighting fixtures, silver pieces, and ceramics.

Even that wasn't enough to satisfy him. It wasn't long before du Pont was combing the eastern seaboard for paneling, fireplace walls, doors, and ceilings from the finest homes of the period, dismantling and reinstalling them at Winterthur as proper background for his collections.

Eventually there were almost 200 room settings, and after living pleasurably with his antiques for almost 30 years, du Pont turned his home into a museum and educational facility in 1951 so that the rest of the world could appreciate it with him.

Winterthur is now one of the outstanding attractions in the Northeast, with a handsome museum building recently added to further enhance its riches. There is no better place to see the very best of America's early arts. Nor is there a more beautiful place to visit in spring, since the du Pont gardens are also a showplace, a 64-acre woodland wonderland of rare azaleas, rhododendrons, and other prize plants.

Come on the first Sunday in May and you can add to your agenda the color of the annual Winterthur Point-to-Point Race, a steeplechase event that also features a parade of antique carriages.

What stands out after touring Winterthur is the variety of the settings and the progression of styles. Among the memorable re-creations are a simple seventeenth-century dining room with tables and benches before an open hearth; the Readbourne Parlor with woodwork and appropriate accompanying furnishings from a 1733 Maryland home; a drawing room with New England Queen Anne furniture; and an equally elegant parlor from Port Royal, with yellow carved sofas and wing chairs, Chippendale side chairs and highboy, Oriental rugs, marble fireplace, and crystal chandeliers. Among the prize furnishings are a set of six silver tankards by Paul Revere and a 66-piece dinner service of Chinese export porcelain made for George Washington.

Complementing the room settings are the Galleries, a museum building that opened in 1992 with a permanent exhibit on the first floor that is an introduction to American decorative arts, and on the second floor, a furniture-exhibition gallery and space for changing displays. The "Touch-It Room" allows visitors to learn about the people of the past by examining the objects they used. It includes a child-sized period room setting, a small general store, and kitchen and lighting exhibit tables. The exhibits are geared to children, but are equally interesting to adults.

The gardens, like the original room settings, were created under du Pont's personal direction, with meticulous care to make them appear as natural growth among the native trees and shrubs that have been preserved around them.

Tanbark and turf paths wind through shaded woodland and over rolling hillsides, bringing spectacular vistas into view at every turn. The Azalea Woods for which the gardens are most noted reach their peak in the first half of May, a mist of white, pink, and salmon as far as the eye can see under a canopy of flowering dogwood and tall tulip trees. Be sure to see the quarry area as well, which is in full bloom in May with Asiatic primroses in deep jewel colors.

A visit to Winterthur is a wonderful way to welcome spring, and one pleasant way to do it is to arrive late morning, spend time in the house and galleries, have lunch in the cafeteria-style Garden Pavilion, and then wander the gardens in the afternoon. You can take a tram tour or make your own path or follow the arrows posted to give you the best route for seeing the peak of the blooms. The 2½ miles of paths can be covered in a leisurely hour and a half.

Although Wilmington isn't thought of as a tourist city, it is an interesting one. If you want to live like a du Pont, choose the recently renovated Hotel du Pont with its carved ceilings, marble stairs, and antiques. The Christina Room has a million dollars' worth of Wyeths on its walls. The Holiday Inn Downtown offers an indoor pool, and Guest Quarters is an all-suite hotel. Fairville Inn is an attractive country inn near Winterthur, just across the Pennsylvania border.

Take a walk from your hotel down to the Market Street Mall to see the Grand Opera House, a cast-iron, highly decorative neoclassical building recently restored to become Delaware's Center for the Performing Arts. Wilmingtown Square, the 500 block on the mall, is a historic complex of six eighteenth-century houses. The Old Town Hall, dating to 1798, has displays of decorative arts and a restored jail inside.

On Sunday there are many more diversions to choose from. The excellent Delaware Art Museum in Wilmington is dedicated to Howard Pyle. His Brandywine School turned out illustrators like N. C. Wyeth and Frank Schoonover, whose distinct works of art enlivened countless magazines and books early in this century. Pyle's own works are generously included in the exhibits. The museum's other speciality is Pre-Raphaelite art, a London school of the mid-1800s represented here by Dante Gabriel Rossetti, Sir John Everett Millais, and Ford Madox Brown, the gift of a Wilmington industrialist and art collector, Samuel Bancroft, Jr.

The evolution of industry in the Brandywine Valley and in the nation as a whole is shown at the Hagley Museum on Route 141 in Greenville. The history of the du Pont Company, which dominates the valley, is prominent. The buildings include the original du Pont "black powder" mills, consisting of an 1814 cotton spinning mill, an operating waterwheel, and a water turbine. The first office of the du Pont Company is also part of the exhibits, as is company founder E. I. du Pont's first home, Eleutherian Mills. Not the least of the attractions of the Hagley is its lush setting along the banks of the Brandywine River, which powered these and many other mills.

If you want to appreciate the fruits of the first Mr. du Pont's labors, pay a visit to Nemours, the Louis XVI chateau built by descendant Alfred I. du Pont in the early 1900s. The 77-room house and formal gardens do full credit to the French chateau country that inspired them.

A more down-to-earth way to pass the time is to take a ride on the old steam train at the Wilmington and Western Railroad in Greenbank—a huffing, puffing hour's excursion into the countryside.

An even more delightful visit to the past is the easy six-mile drive south along I-95 to New Castle, where you walk cobbled streets into Colonial times. Historic New Castle was Delaware's first capital and a meeting place for the Colonial assemblies. Later overshadowed by Wilmington and Philadelphia, it fell out of the mainstream of commerce, and its lack of prosperity kept architectural changes to a minimum. Today the old town, with its mellow red-brick town houses and public green, hardly seems changed by the passing of time. Many of the old homes are exquisitely furnished and open to the public, as is the Old Court House that once housed the state assembly. The handsome cupola atop the Court House is distinguished by being the center of the 12-mile circle surveyed by Mason and Dixon, part of which delineated Delaware's northern boundary with Pennsylvania. Several guest houses and the David Finney Inn in the Historic District are perfect hostelries for this town; there's even an appropriately atmospheric dining place, the New Castle Inn, in an old arsenal behind Delaware Street.

The third Saturday in May each year is designated as "A Day in Old New Castle," and many of the private homes and gardens in town are open to the public. If you can time your trip to coincide, set aside the day and save Sunday for Winterthur.

Also note that the first Saturday in May each year is Wilmington Garden Day, a once-a-year opportunity to visit some of the city's finest houses and gardens, and another reason to postpone Winterthur until the next day.

Either event, plus Winterthur in the spring, makes for a blooming combination.

Delaware Area Code: 302

DRIVING DIRECTIONS Take the New Jersey Turnpike to the end, cross the Delaware Memorial Bridge to Route 295, and turn north on I-95 into Wilmington. From Wilmington to Winterthur, take Route 52; the entrance is on the right about two miles past the railroad tracks at Greenville Shopping Center. To get from Wilmington to New Castle, follow I-95 south to Route 141 east.
Total distance: about 125 miles.

PUBLIC TRANSPORTATION Amtrak serves Wilmington. Bus No. 14 (Kennett Pike line) goes from the train station to Winterthur daily. Check for current schedule at station.

ACCOMMODATIONS *Hotel du Pont,* 11th and Market streets, Wilmington, 19899, 594-3100, $$$-$$$$; ask about special weekend package plans • *Holiday Inn-Downtown,* 700 King Street, Wilmington, 19801, 655-0400, $$-$$$; check for current packages • *Holiday Inn-North,* 4000 Concord Pike, Wilmington, 19803, 478-2222, $$ • *Guest Quarters Suites,* 707 King Street, Wilmington, 19801, 656-9300, all-suites, $$-$$$$ CP • *Sheraton Suites,* 422 Delaware Avenue, Wilmington 19806, another all-suite possibility, $$$ • *William Penn Guest House,* 206 Delaware Street, New Castle, 19720, 328-7736, $ (no private baths) • *Janvier-Black Bed & Breakfast,* 17 The Strand, New Castle, 19720, 328-1339, restored Federal home, 2 suites, $$$ CP • *Terry House Bed & Breakfast,* 130 Delaware Street, New Castle, 19720, 322-2505, nineteenth-century town house, $$ CP • *David Finney Inn,* 216 Delaware Street, New Castle, 19720, 322-6367, $$-$$$ CP • *Fairville Inn,* Route 52, Mendenhall, PA 19357, (215) 388-5900, convenient for Longwood Gardens, $$$-$$$$ CP.

DINING *Brandywine Room,* Hotel du Pont (see above), walnut paneling, a million dollars' worth of Wyeths on the walls, $$$-$$$$ • *Green Room,* Hotel du Pont (see above), old-world elegance, $$$-$$$$ • *Buckley's Tavern,* 5812 Kennett Pike, Centreville (outside Wilmington), 656-9776, charming, roof terrace open in spring, $$-$$$ • *Harry's Savoy Grill,* 2020 Naamans Road, 475-3000, handsome traditional decor, $$ • *Columbus Inn,* 2216 Pennsylvania Avenue, Wilmington, 571-1492, Colonial flavor in historic building, $$-$$$ • *Tiffin,* 1208 North Market Street, 571-1133, contemporary decor, a local favorite, $$-$$$ • *Griglia Toscana,* 1412 North Dupont Street,

Wilmington, 654-8001, northern Italian, $$ • *The Silk Purse,* 1307 North Street, Wilmington, 654-7666, fine dining, $$-$$$, also casual dining upstairs at The Sow's Ear, $-$$ • *Waterworks Cafe,* 16th and French streets, Wilmington, 652-6022, restored mill on the Brandywine, lunch, $-$$; dinner $$-$$$$ • *New Castle Inn,* behind the Court House, New Castle, 328-1798, historic arsenal buildings with specialty chicken and oyster pot pie, dinner $$-$$$; Sunday brunch, served 11 A.M. to 2 P.M., $ • *David Finney Inn* (see above), $$ • *Country Mouse Cafe*, Route 52, Greenville, 656-7626, ideal lunch spot, located between Winterthur and Hagley, $.

SIGHTSEEING *Winterthur Museum,* Winterthur, (800) 448-3883. Hours: Tuesday to Saturday 9 A.M. to 5 P.M., Sunday noon to 5 P.M. General admission: adults, $8; children 12–18, $5; under 12, $3. General admission includes a tour of the Galleries, a self-guided garden walk and year-round tram. The Introduction to Winterthur ticket, $5, adds a guided tour of a selection of period rooms. Reservations are suggested for tours • *Delaware Art Museum,* 2301 Kentmere Parkway, Wilmington, 571-9590. Hours: Tuesday to Saturday 10 A.M. to 5 P.M., Sunday noon to 5 P.M. Adults, $4; children, $2.50 • *Hagley Museum,* Route 141, Greenville, 658-2400. Hours: April to December, daily 9:30 A.M. to 4:30 P.M.; January to March, Monday to Friday one tour at 1:30 P.M.; Saturday and Sunday 9:30 A.M. to 4:30 P.M. Adults, $9.75; children 6–14, $3.50 • *Wilmington and Western Railroad,* Routes 2 and 41, Greenbank Station, 998-1930. Hours: one-hour steam train ride from Greenbank to Mt. Cuba Picnic Grove. Hours: May to November, Sunday afternoons; June to August, Saturday and Sunday afternoons; phone for time schedules. Adults, $6; children, $4 • *Wilmington Old Town Hall,* 512 Market Street Mall, Wilmington, 655-7161. Hours: Tuesday to Friday noon to 4 P.M.; Saturday 10 A.M. to 4 P.M. Donation • *Nemours Mansion,* Rockland Road, Wilmington, 651-6912. Tours from May to November by reservation. Hours: Tuesday to Saturday 9 A.M., 11 A.M., 1 P.M., and 3 P.M.; Sunday 11 A.M., 1 P.M., and 3 P.M. Over 16 only, $8 • *Amstel House Museum,* 2 East 4th at Delaware Street, New Castle, 322-2794. Hours: April to December, Tuesday to Saturday 11 A.M. to 4 P.M., Sunday 1 to 4 P.M. Adults, $2; children 5–12, $1; combination ticket with Old Dutch House, adults, $3.50; children, $1.50 • *Old Court House,* 2nd and Delaware, New Castle, 571-3059. Hours: Tuesday to Saturday 10 A.M. to 4:30 P.M., Sunday 1:30 to 4:30 P.M. Free • *Old Dutch House,* 32 East 3rd Street, New Castle, 322-9168. Oldest dwelling in state, early eighteenth-century furnishings. Hours: April to

December, Wednesday to Saturday 11 A.M. to 4 P.M., Sunday 1 P.M. to 4 P.M. Adults, $2; children 5–12, $1 • *George Read II House,* 42 The Strand, New Castle, 322-8411. Georgian home with period antiques, formal garden. Hours: March to December, Tuesday to Saturday 10 A.M. to 4 P.M., Sunday noon to 4 P.M.; January and February, Saturday 10 A.M. to 4 P.M., Sunday noon to 4 P.M. Adults, $4; ages 12–21, $3.50; children 10–12, $2.

FOR FURTHER INFORMATION Greater Wilmington Convention and Visitors Bureau, 1300 Market Street, Wilmington, DE 19801, 652-4088, or (800) 422-1181.

On the Back Roads in Connecticut's Laurel Country

All of Connecticut may be known as the Laurel State, but it is the northwest corner that seems to have cornered the most magnificent displays of the state flower—and a little-known spot near Torrington has the most spectacular show of all.

Known as Indian Lookout, it's actually the private property of the Paul Freedmans, who some 35 years ago began clearing their 6 acres of mountainside to allow the wild laurels to spread, then gradually landscaped the area to provide a balanced natural setting. The 6 acres grew to 100 and the pale pink clouds of laurel enveloping the mountain grew more beautiful with the seasons until, in 1958, the owners decided it was too beautiful to keep to themselves.

So visitors are now welcome to come to Indian Lookout for laurel season only, from mid to late June. Come dressed for the occasion—you'll have to climb the hill on foot unless you are one of the senior citizens who are allowed to drive through on weekdays from 5:30 to 6 P.M. But the view is worth every step of the climb.

Having literally scaled the heights when it comes to laurel watching, you're now all set for further excursions into the countryside, a rural ramble through little towns where the residents still patronize the general store, past historic homes and unexpected museums, in and out of antiques stores. You'll have plenty of opportunity to get back to nature, to hike, or possibly even to paddle your way down the Housatonic River.

All along the way, the laurels lend a pastel glow to the scenery. Just a few miles north of Torrington along Route 8 is Winsted, a tiny town that calls itself the Laurel City. Until the late 1960s, Winsted celebrated the appearance of its bountiful blossoms every year with a weekend festival. Recently town residents have revived the custom, staging a true bit of small-town Americana with bands and a homemade float parade, the crowning of a Laurel Queen, booths of homemade goodies set around the village green, and an old-fashioned square dance on Saturday night.

Festival or no, Winsted usually posts markers to send visitors on self-guided auto tours of the most scenic laurel views. While you're in town stop at the corner of Lake and Prospect streets to see the Solomon Rockwell House, an antebellum mansion that is a national historic landmark, furnished with Hitchcock chairs, Thomas and Whiting clocks, and memorabilia dating to the Revolutionary War.

Take Route 20 north from Winsted to Riverton for a closer look at Mr. Hitchcock's famous chairs in a museum building that was once an old church meetinghouse. The Hitchcock Museum has an extensive collection of the originals; the modern factory nearby makes reproductions, using some of the traditional handcraft procedures, and you can visit a showroom and a gift shop there.

There are a couple of antiques shops in Riverton, an herb shop, and a contemporary crafts gallery. For lunch, the Catnip Mouse Tearoom will serve your sandwich on homemade bread, and the Village Sweet Shoppe has tempting chocolates and ice cream for dessert.

From Riverton, plot your course according to your inclinations. If you want to get out and hike, there are two possibilities. The People's State Forest on Route 44 in Barkhamsted offers miles of well-marked trails. Or, since it's laurel season, you might want to go back toward Winsted and follow Route 44 northwest to Haystack Mountain State Park or Dennis Hill State Park, both in Norfolk. Each park has summit buildings with magnificent views, but Dennis Hill is a particularly good choice if you are looking for laurel vistas.

If you prefer to continue traveling the back roads by car there are two possible routes. Head south to the junction of Routes 44 and 219, then north to the Lake McDonough Recreation Area for a scenic ride and perhaps a pause for a picnic or a rowboat ride. At the junction of routes 219 and 318, drive west to the Saville Dam and Spillway for a picture-perfect scene of rolling hills and lakes, with rushing white water cascading down the spillway in spring. Don't forget the camera.

Or you might take Route 183 out of Winsted to Colebrook, where you'll find a genuine one-room schoolhouse and a general store that has been in operation since 1812. The town hall dates to 1816. You couldn't have found a more authentic, nontouristy New England village. And there's also a haven for book buffs, the Book Barn, with more than 5,000 selections, some rare, some just secondhand.

Catching up with the hikers in Norfolk, you'll find a drive through the local parks an enjoyable outing. Norfolk is also the site of the Yale Summer School of Music and some excellent summer concerts beginning in late June. It may be a bit early, but check locally to see if the season has begun. Music Mountain, not too far away in Falls Village, also begins its season in mid-June (running through early September), with mostly chamber groups, and a bit of Gilbert and Sullivan and jazz mixed in for spice.

For a look at some lovely spring blooms, stop at Hillside Gardens on Route 272. This is a nursery that specializes in unusual perennials, and their extensive display gardens include some 1500 varieties.

There's a happy choice of country-inn headquarters for this weekend. Norfolk offers three winners. Mountain View is homey Victorian, while Manor House is just what the name implies—a grand and spacious manor with handsome paneling, Tiffany windows, and oversize rooms. Greenwoods Gate is Colonial and decorated with high style and taste. The Old Riverton Inn in Riverton is a different type of Colonial charmer, a wayside inn that has been welcoming travelers since 1796.

On Sunday you can continue shunpiking west on Route 44 through Canaan to Salisbury, Lakeville, and Sharon, and you'll be passing through three of the loveliest northwest Connecticut towns. Salisbury's Sweethaven Herb Farm will charm you with its Peter Rabbit garden, populated with whimsical little creatures. In Sharon the Northeast Audubon Center on Route 4 offers self-guided nature trails over 684 acres of sanctuary.

If your timing is right and a race is scheduled, you may also decide to take in the speeding autos at Lime Rock Park, just a few miles east of Lakeville.

In your own car, don't be afraid to venture off onto the side roads. One of the real pleasures of this kind of weekend is discovering your own memories—a white steepled church, a picture-book Colonial farmhouse, or a babbling brook.

But to really make the most of the Connecticut springtime, there's nothing to compare with the country scenery and quiet on a cruise down the Housatonic River by canoe. Follow Route 7 south out of Canaan to Falls Village, and a place called Riverrunning Expeditions will provide everything you need. Don't be frightened by the name—the portion of the river from Falls Village to West Cornwall is almost all placid flat water, and if you remember your strokes from those long-gone days at summer camp, you'll have no trouble at all. They'll give you a quick refresher or a whole day of instruction if you really want to prepare for running a river—even the whitewater. And if you don't trust yourself at all, you can splurge and hire a guide who'll lead you safely down the river, filling you in on the history and the wildlife and vegetation of the area as you float by.

If you debark at Cornwall Bridge, you're in just the right place for a last bit of picturesque scenery—the covered bridge that gives the town its name. Proceed across the bridge into town to Freshfields, and you can have a drink or a meal with a waterfall view, the perfect end to a country ramble whether by land or by canoe.

Connecticut Area Code: 203

DRIVING DIRECTIONS Hutchinson River Parkway to Merritt Parkway. Follow the Merritt past Bridgeport, then take Route 8 north to Torrington. Follow Route 4 through Torrington and past town to Mountain Road and Indian Lookout. *Total distance:* about 109 miles to Torrington.

ACCOMMODATIONS *Mountain View Inn,* Route 272, Norfolk, 06058, 542-5595, $$-$$$ CP • *Manor House,* PO Box 447, Maple Avenue, Norfolk, 06058, 542-5690, $$-$$$$$ CP • *Greenwoods Gate,* Greenwoods Road East, Norfolk, 06058, 542-5439, $$$-$$$$ CP • *Old Riverton Inn,* Route 20, Riverton, 06065, 379-8678, $$ CP • *Cobble Hill Farm,* Steele Road (off Route 44), New Hartford, 06057, 379-0057, $-$$ CP. Also see Salisbury, page 245.

DINING *Mountain View Inn* (see above), $$-$$$ • *Old Riverton Inn* (see above), $$-$$$ • *Yankee Pedlar Inn,* 93 Main Street, Torrington, 489-9226, $-$$ (rooms also available, $-$$) • *Freshfields,* Route 128, West Cornwall, 672-6601, $$-$$$ • *The Tributary,* 19 Rowley Street, Winsted, 379-7679, pleasant and unpretentious, $-$$ • *The Pub & Restaurant,* Station Place, Norfolk, 542-5716, English pub flavor in a historic building near the green, $-$$ • *The Cannery Cafe,* Route 44, Canaan, 824-7333, creative menus, $$.

SIGHTSEEING *Indian Lookout,* Mountain Road, Torrington. Hours: weekdays, 1:30 to 6 P.M., weekends, 11 A.M. to 6 P.M. Free, but donations accepted • *Solomon Rockwell House,* Lake and Prospect streets, Winsted, 379-8433. Hours: June 15 to September 15, Thursday to Sunday 2 to 4 P.M. (Hours are extended for the Laurel Festival weekend.) Adults, $1; children, $.50 • *Hitchcock Museum,* Route 20, Riverton, 738-4950. Hours: April to December, Thursday to Sunday noon to 4 P.M. Donation • *Sharon Audubon Center,* Route 4, Sharon, 364-0520. Hours: Monday to Saturday 9 A.M. to 5 P.M., Sunday 1 to 5 P.M. Adults, $3; children, $1.50 • *Riverrunning Expeditions Ltd.,* Main Street, Falls Village, CT 06031, 824-5579. Write or call for brochure and current rates. Canoe rentals are also available at *Clarke Outdoors,*

Route 7, West Cornwall, 672-6365 • *Norfolk Music Festival,* Route 44, Norfolk, box office (during season), 542-5537, information (off-season), 432-1966 • *Music Mountain Chamber Series,* off Route 7, Falls Village, 496-2596 • *Lime Rock Park Auto Races,* Box 111, Lakeville, 435-0896.

FOR FURTHER INFORMATION Litchfield Hills Travel Council, PO Box 968, Litchfield, CT 06759, 567-4506.

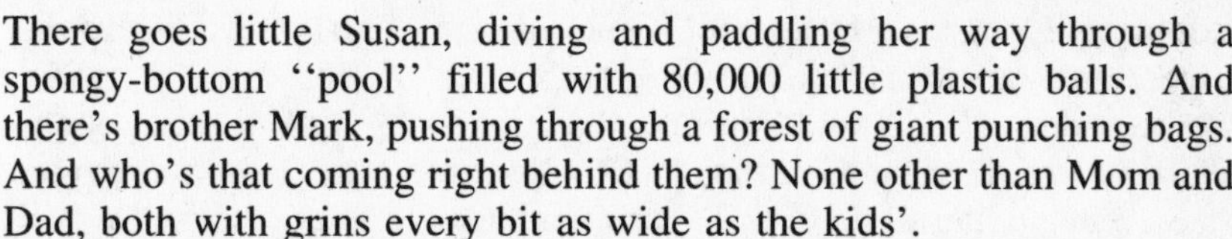

Big Bird to Ben Franklin: Family Fun Near Philadelphia

There goes little Susan, diving and paddling her way through a spongy-bottom "pool" filled with 80,000 little plastic balls. And there's brother Mark, pushing through a forest of giant punching bags. And who's that coming right behind them? None other than Mom and Dad, both with grins every bit as wide as the kids'.

Sesame Place, a "family play park" in Langhorne, Pennsylvania, just south of Trenton and north of Philadelphia, is a place where 3- to 13-year-olds can exercise mind and muscle cavorting on one of the nation's most innovative playgrounds, trying do-it-yourself science experiments, splashing through a water park and making their way through bigger-than-life Twiddlebug Land, where there is a giant vegetable garden maze and a wave pool with a seven-foot-tall water nozzle.

This is a totally "kid-powered" park, run on the energy of the eager youngsters who come to play. Indeed, there's enough energy flying around to light a small city. The kids gliding, tumbling, climbing, sliding, and bouncing about never stop to miss the passive roller coasters and rides that have no place in this park.

Do-it-yourself science exhibits challenge young minds. At the Sesame Neighborhood, a replica of the storefronts and building facades of the TV set, children can mingle with some of their favorite TV characters, watch street entertainers, dress up as a firefighter and sit behind the wheel of a real fire engine, or play mechanic at Oscar the Grouch's Garage. A musical revue in the Big Bird Theater gives another chance to see favorite Sesame Street Muppet characters come alive.

Bring bathing suits because there's a lot of water play. Big Bird's Rambling River is an adventure for all the family, who board single or double inner tubes for a 1,000-foot river float, with swirling waters and bubbling geysers along the way. The Big Slipper is a flume ride winding down to a splash-pool finale.

Sesame Place gets crowded, so it is a good idea to make it your first destination in the morning, enjoying a few hours of fun and then lunching in the restaurant where the see-through kitchen makes even food preparation a learning experience.

When you can convince the family to leave, you're ready to proceed to Philadelphia. Families love Philly because it offers not only the perennial historic pleasures but also a host of innovative attractions for kids.

Everyone seems to get a special kick from seeing the real Liberty Bell, crack and all. The bell is just one of the sights in a complex called Independence National Historical Park, which is billed rightly as America's most historic square mile. Start at the visitors' center at 3rd and Chestnut streets to see a 30-minute film to put it all in perspective, then take the walking tour map and see the sights. These include Independence Hall, where the Declaration of Independence was adopted; Congress Hall, the home of the legislature in the late eighteenth century; Franklin Court, the site of Benjamin Franklin's home and of a lively underground museum; Old City Hall; Carpenter's Hall, where the first Continental Congress met; the First and Second U.S. Banks (literally); City Tavern; and any number of other historic homes, churches, and businesses. It's all free, and you can take in as much or as little as your family can absorb, a neat little American history lesson to close out the day.

Get a good night's rest because Sunday offers a delightful choice of directions. The Treehouse at the Philadelphia Zoo, for example, was specially designed for 4- to 11-year-olds. It is unique, letting youngsters experience for themselves what it might feel like to climb through a 35-foot-high honeycomb for a bee's-eye view of the world, or to hatch out of a giant egg in the Everglades Swamp. The recently enlarged zoo is also the only place in the U.S. where you can see white tigers and has a terrific new exhibit known as the "Carnivore Kingdom." It is easily reached from downtown on the Fairmount Park trolley.

Even the youngest won't get restless at the "Please Touch" Museum, the first in the nation to be designed especially for children under 7. They are enthralled here, dressing up as fire-fighters or ballerinas, ringing up sales in their own grocery store, or running a doctor's office. This is also one of the few museums offering an attended "Tot Spot" for children under 3. Big brothers and sisters will find computer games and other things to keep them busy, as well.

"Discovering Dinosaurs," the $2.5 million exhibition at the Academy of Natural Sciences, is an eye-opener for all ages, changing old perceptions about these fascinating prehistoric giants. The dozen or so specimens on display are not lumbering slowpokes, but graceful, quick-footed animals, fitting the latest picture that scientific research has revealed. The interactive exhibits allow kids to dig for fossils, step into a dinosaur's footprints, play archaeologist at the "build-a-dino" station, work a dinosaur jaw, or call up pictures, facts, and figures on a sophisticated video disk system. A favorite corner is the one where film clips give a hilarious review of how dinosaurs have been treated in the movies.

One of the best of Philadelphia's many museums is the imaginative Franklin Institute, a place where visitors find out about science by climbing aboard a 350-ton steam locomotive, observing the solar system in action, or taking a walk through the chambers of a giant walk-through heart. Even physics is far from boring here, when you discover that by finding the right distance, you can use a rope and pulley to lift a giant weight by yourself.

The museum recently added the nation's first Futures Center, the ultimate do-it-yourself trip to tomorrow. Here you can advance to the frontiers of medicine, standing inside a human cell a million times larger than life, or manipulate a robot on the surface of the moon. Even the youngest will enjoy touring a space station and imagining themselves as astronauts. The museum offers a leaflet suggesting other exhibits that can be enjoyed by children under age six.

Other popular attractions here include the Fels Planetarium and the Omniverse Theater, where a giant screen puts the audience in the midst of the action.

A different kind of fun awaits at Penn's Landing on the Delaware River waterfront, where there are ships and a submarine for boarding, and exhibits at the Philadelphia Maritime Museum.

At the "Workshop on the Water," a barge operated by the museum, a boat-building shop is in operation in warm weather.

You can take a pedal boat out into the marina, hop the Penn's Landing Trolley for a round trip around the waterfront area, or board the Riverbus Ferry for a ride across the Delaware to Camden's New Jersey State Aquarium, which is sure to please all, with its cascading waterfalls and birds skipping along the barrier beach.

During the summer season, there is entertainment every weekend at Penn's Landing, including special programs for the kids every Sunday from 2 to 4 P.M.

Even eating can be a new adventure in the City of Brotherly Love. Kids invariably love soft pretzels from the ever-present street vendors, and cheese steaks like those at Jim's at 4th and South streets. Or you can head for the colorful food stalls and the reasonably priced Italian restaurants in South Philly, or have lunch amid the bustling action at Reading Terminal Market, where generations of Philadelphians have shopped for fresh produce and meat. Knowing locals descend here at lunch for freshly carved turkey sandwiches—or Peking duck, gyros, or enchiladas.

However you slice it, Philly is a feast of fun for families.

Philadelphia Area Code: 215

DRIVING DIRECTIONS From New York to Sesame Place, take the New Jersey Turnpike south to exit 9, bear right after toll booth to Route 18 north. Follow signs to U.S. Route 1 South through Trenton into Pennsylvania to the Oxford Valley exit. Turn left onto Oxford Valley Road, go to third traffic light and turn right.

ACCOMMODATIONS Most of these hotels have no additional charge for children under 18 in parents' rooms. Ask at all about weekend packages. Closest accommodations to Sesame Place are: *Sheraton Bucks County Hotel,* 400 Oxford Valley Road, Langhorne, 19047, 547-4100, just across the road, $$-$$$$$, • *Red Roof Inn,* Langhorne, 19047, 750-6200 or (800) THE-ROOF, ½ mile away, $ • Most reasonable Center City Philadelphia lodgings include: *Comfort Inn at Penn's Landing,* Delaware Avenue and Race Street, 19106, 627-7900, $$-$$$ • *Ramada Inn–Center City,* 501 North 22nd Street, 19130, 568-8300, $$ • *Quality Inn Historic Downtown Suites,* 1010 Race Street, 19107, 922-1730, $$-$$$. For more Philadelphia lodgings, see pages 239–40.

DINING See Philadelphia Dining, pages 240–41.

SIGHTSEEING *Sesame Place,* Oxford Valley Mall off U.S. 1 bypass, Langhorne, 752-7070. Hours: July through Labor Day, 9 A.M. to 8 P.M. Shorter hours in spring and fall, generally 10 A.M. to 5 P.M., but they vary, so it's best to call and check. Admission $20.95; under 2 free. There is also a charge for parking. Best value is the twilight rate of $13.95, available three hours before closing • *Independence National Historical Park,* 3rd and Chestnut streets, Philadelphia, 597-8974. Hours: daily 9 A.M. to 5 P.M. Free • *Penn's Landing,* Delaware and Spruce streets, Philadelphia, 923-8181. USS *Olympia* and USS *Becuna,* 922-1898. Hours: daily 10 A.M. to 4:30 P.M., summer to 6 P.M. Adults, $5; children under 12, $3 • *Philadelphia Maritime Museum,* 321 Chestnut Street, 925-4539. Hours: Tuesday to Saturday 10 A.M. to 5 P.M., Sunday 1 to 5 P.M. Adults, $2.50; children, $1 • *Franklin Institute,* 20th Street and Benjamin Franklin Parkway, 564-3375. Hours: Science Center, daily 9:30 A.M. to 5 P.M.; Futures Center,

Thursday to Sunday until 9 P.M. Science Center and Futures Center: adults, $9.50; ages 4–11, $8.50; Omniverse Theater: adults, $6; 4–11, $5; Fels Planetarium: adults, $5; 4–11, $4. Combination tickets, any two attractions: adults, $12; 4–11, $10.50; all three attractions: Adults, $14.50; 4–11, $12.50 • *Philadelphia Zoological Garden,* 34th Street and Girard Avenue, Fairmount Park, 243-1100. Hours: daily 9:30 A.M. to 5 P.M. Adults, $7; children, $5.50 • *Please Touch Museum for Children,* 210 North 21st Street, 963-0666. Hours: daily 10 A.M. to 4:30 P.M. Admission: $6 • *Academy of Natural Sciences Museum,* 19th and Benjamin Franklin Parkway, 299-1020. Hours: Monday to Friday 10 A.M. to 4:30 P.M.; Saturday and Sunday 10 A.M. to 5 P.M. Adults, $5.50; children 3–12, $4.50 • *New Jersey State Aquarium,* 1 Riverside Drive, Camden (609) 365-3300. Hours: daily 9:30 A.M. to 5:30 P.M. Adults, $9; children, $6 • *Riverbus*, Penn's Landing, (800) 634-4027, Delaware River Ferry to and from the Aquarium. Hours: mid-September to mid-May, Monday to Friday 7 A.M. to 6:45 P.M., Saturday 9 A.M. to 8:45 P.M., Sunday 9 A.M. to 5:45 P.M.; later evening hours rest of year; departures from Philly every half hour, on the quarter hour. Adults, $2 each way; children, $1.50.

FOR FURTHER INFORMATION Contact Philadelphia Convention and Visitors' Bureau, 16th Street and JFK Boulevard, Philadelphia, PA 19102, 636-1666. For free information packet, including weekend package information, phone toll free (800) 537-7676.

Mansion Hopping Along the Hudson

Though the Hudson River is lovely seen from either side, it is the east bank that has long captivated artists *and* millionaires. The spectacular river views capped with the Catskill and Shawangunk Mountains beyond inspired the first cohesive group of American artists, aptly known as the Hudson River School, and also attracted people like the Vanderbilts, Roosevelts, and Livingstons, who built their mansions on sites overlooking the majestic river.

Today, many of those magnificent estates are open to the public, offering both a living lesson in American history and a firsthand look at the life-style of a more opulent era. A weekend of mansion hopping provides an ample helping of river scenery, with special towns, antiques, and unexpected pleasures to be found along the way.

Ideal headquarters for a Hudson River ramble is the pretty town of Rhinebeck, home of the hotel that proudly calls itself the oldest in America. The Beekman Arms, a stagecoach stop dating to 1700, has fascinated modern visitors with its venerable guest books. Washington, Lafayette, and Aaron Burr stayed here, along with later notables like Horace Greeley, William Jennings Bryan, and many of our presidents. Franklin Roosevelt, who lived nearby at Hyde Park, wound up every campaign with an informal talk on the inn's front porch.

The inn also manages the 1844 Delamater House and other vintage village houses, along with new look-alike structures around a court, which form a little complex that is even nicer to stay in than the main building. Many of the rooms have working fireplaces. And there are pleasant bed-and-breakfast inns in the area, as well.

As soon as you make your inn reservations, call to reserve for lunch or dinner at the Culinary Institute of America in Hyde Park, the most unusual dining place in the Hudson Valley.

The beautiful campus of the nation's top school for chefs is a pleasure to visit, but weekend reservations can be hard to get unless you call far ahead. Glass walls along the corridors let you look in on the classrooms of America's soon-to-be-great chefs, and display cabinets show off some of their homework in menu and restaurant design. White-jacketed students in their final semester of the school's 21-month program cook and serve for the dining rooms on campus, and their fare bodes well for the future of America's culinary arts.

Most formal is the handsome Escoffier Room, where classic French fare is served. The equally attractive American Bounty Room shows off American cookery, while regional Italian is the theme for the Caterina de Medici Room, the first formal restaurant experience for students. The delicious, price-fixed meals here are a real value.

The informal St. Andrews Cafe gives young chefs the chance to practice delicious meals that are also healthful. Guests here can get a computerized nutritional analysis of their meal. Note that Caterina de Medici and St. Andrews are open only Monday to Friday, so plan accordingly.

The CIA has also raised the level of food in the area, thanks to some of its alumni, including Larry Forgione, owner of New York's "An American Place," who took over the dining room at the Beekman Arms a couple of years back.

A good weekend plan is a first day of touring to the north and a second day of making mansion stops downriver on the way home. There are too many places to fit into one weekend, so you'll have to pick and choose. You'll also want to save time for sightseeing, and for the area's choice antiquing. Rhinebeck has many shops, including the excellent Antiques Market, a converted barn behind the Beekman Arms housing 30 dealers.

A unique attraction here is the Old Rhinebeck Aerodrome, a

one-of-a-kind place with antique airplanes both on display and in the air for shows held every weekend. Everything's in the spirit of the old glory days, including the pilots who wear uniforms dating from World War I.

Rhinebeck is also the site of an excellent crafts fair in late June and the old-fashioned Dutchess County Fair in August, both held at the fairgrounds.

Another diversion you might want to include is a boat ride on the river, one more fine way to appreciate its beauty.

You can begin your mansion tour just outside Rhinebeck at Wilderstein, the most recently opened of the great houses on the Hudson. Built in 1852 as an Italianate villa by Thomas Suckley, a wealthy importer, the house was remodeled by his son, Robert, in 1888 in the then-popular Queen Anne style, adding verandas, gables, and a handsome five-story round tower affording fine views of the grounds and the river. The parklike lawns and walkways were planned by Calvert Vaux of Central Park fame and Joseph Burr Tiffany (a cousin of the more famous Louis Comfort Tiffany) was commissioned to create the interiors, including numerous stained-glass windows. The last Suckley descendant lived in the house until 1991. It is open weekends while a nonprofit corporation undertakes restoration, providing a rare chance to see a home before and after.

Three grander mansions await to the north, along scenic Route 9G. Two are associated with the Livingstons, one of the Hudson Valley's most prominent early families. Montgomery Place in Annandale, maintained by Historic Hudson Valley, is an opulent 23-room home built in 1805 by Janet Livingston Montgomery, widow of Revolutionary War hero General Richard Montgomery. It was remodeled in 1860 by Alexander Jackson Davis, who is considered America's leading nineteenth-century architect. Seven generations of Livingstons and Delafields, an offshoot of the family, lived here. The house is filled with their possessions. The estate offers almost 400 acres of beautiful grounds, and gardens with outstanding river and mountain views. The extensive orchards on the estate are in full bloom in spring. From mid-June on, you can pick your own fruit here, from strawberries and raspberries to peaches and apples.

Next stop is Clermont, the ancestral home of Robert R. Livingston, who lived from 1746 to 1813 and was a chancellor of New York State. It is now a museum and state park. The beautiful grounds overlooking the river are open free for picnicking or just enjoying the view.

About four miles below Hudson you'll come to Olana, the Persian castle built by painter Frederic Edwin Church, well-known member of the Hudson River School. Whether your interest is art, gardens, decorating, or architecture, you'll find something special in the domain of the well-traveled Mr. Church. The unusual structure and decor of the house and the meticulously planned grounds are strong personal expressions of his taste, and outside the windows there is a virtually flawless Hudson River School painting, with sweeping views of the river and the mountains beyond.

More estates await when you turn south. The first is the Mills Mansion in Staatsburg, yet another Livingston property, an 1895 neoclassical 65-room affair that was the home of Ruth and Ogden Livingston Mills. The lavish house was designed by Stanford White and furnished in fancy Louis XV and Louis XVI styles.

Next is the even more opulent palace owned by Frederick Vanderbilt, grandson of ''The Commodore,'' in Hyde Park. Built by the famous firm of McKim, Mead and White in the late 1890s, the enormous beaux-arts structure was large enough to entertain hundreds. The landscaped grounds and Hudson views are magnificent.

Justifiably the most famous of all Hudson River estates is the home and library of Franklin Roosevelt in Hyde Park. Springwood, the main house, is not so much a showplace as a warm testament to an exceptional family who left the home stamped with their own personalities. Franklin Roosevelt was born and grew up here, and he and his wife, Eleanor, and their children returned here each summer to visit his mother, Sara. Both Franklin and Eleanor are buried in the rose garden beside the house.

This is a home filled with warmth, family photos, and mementos. In Roosevelt's room, the leash and blanket of his dog, Fala, are on the Scottie's own chair. Scattered about are the books and magazines that were here at the time of Roosevelt's last visit in March 1945, as though he had just stepped out the door.

In the library is more memorabilia, from FDR's boyhood pony cart to papers that shaped world history. The collection is arranged chronologically, and seeing it is a wonderful way to learn or remember what happened here and abroad between the years 1932 and 1945. There are also records of Eleanor's humanitarian activities extending to 1962. In 1984, Eleanor's own modest home, Val-Kill, was opened to the public. Situated just two miles from the big house, it was her private retreat while her husband was alive, and the place where she chose to spend her last years.

Hyde Park antiquing includes the Village Antique Center with 20 dealers and the Hyde Park Antiques Center with 54 dealers. Both are right on Route 9.

Art lovers may want to detour into Poughkeepsie for a look at Vassar's fine, new Frances Lehman Loeb Art Center, a $15 million soaring showplace designed by Cesar Pelli to display the school's collection of over 12,500 works of art, including a fine group of Hudson River School paintings. A sculpture garden is part of the complex.

If time and energy remain, there is still another worthwhile mansion tour downriver at Boscobel in Garrison. This stately nineteenth-century home with its columns and porticoes is an out-standing example of New York Federal architecture. It was built by States Morris Dyckman, another prominent New Yorker, in 1804, and rescued from the wrecker's ball and moved piece by piece to its present lovely site in 1961. Candlelight mansion tours and many outdoor concerts and special events are scheduled through the year.

Just one mile above Garrison is Cold Spring, a tiny town whose main street is another antiquer's delight. Cold Spring's bandstand, jutting out on the river at the very end of Main Street, faces one of the most dramatic mountain perspectives anywhere along the Hudson. It is a fine place to watch a sunset—and to make a vow to return to see what you have missed in the extraordinary Hudson River Valley.

Rhinebeck Area Code: 914

DRIVING DIRECTIONS New York Thruway to exit 19, across the Rhinecliff Bridge to Route 9G south, then make a right turn onto Route 9 south. Or take the Saw Mill River Parkway onto the Taconic Parkway and get off at Route 199, following 308 left to Route 9 in Rhinebeck. *Total distance:* about 100 miles.

PUBLIC TRANSPORTATION Amtrak service (800) USA-RAIL to Rhinecliff, three miles from Rhinebeck (the Beekman Arms will meet guests). Also bus service via Short Line from Manhattan to Rhinebeck; for information call (212) 736-4700.

ACCOMMODATIONS *Beekman Arms,* Route 9, Rhinebeck, 12572, 876-7077. Main House, $$; Delamater House, $$ CP; Carriage House, $$-$$$ CP; Delamater Courtyard, $$$ CP • *Village Victorian Inn,* 31 Center Street, Rhinebeck, 12572, 876-8345, Victorian frills in an 1860 home, $$$$$ CP • *Whistle Wood,* 11 Pells Road, Rhinebeck, 12572, 876-6838, rustic horse farm outside town, $$-$$$$ CP • *Mansakenning Carriage House,* 29 Ackert Hook Road, Rhinebeck, 12572, 876-3500, rooms in stylishly furnished house and converted stable, $$$$-$$$$$CP • *Fala House,* 46 East Market Street, Hyde Park, 12538, 229-5937, small pleasant B&B, $$ CP • *Inn at the Falls,* 50 Red Oaks Mill Road, Poughkeepsie, 12603, 462-5770, attractively furnished small hotel-inn, $$$-$$$$ CP • *Fox Run,* 936 Country Route 6, Germantown, 12526, 537-6945, 1810 Colonial near Clermont, $-$$ CP • *Le Chambord,* Route 52, Hopewell Junction, 12533, 221-1941, a bit of a drive, but pleasant rooms in a new wing and good food, $$$ CP.

DINING *Culinary Institute of America,* Route 9, Hyde Park, 471-6608, reservations necessary at all restaurants for lunch or dinner, phone between 8:30 A.M. and 5 P.M.; jackets required. *Escoffier Room,* classic French, open Tuesday to Saturday, lunch, $$, dinner, $$-$$$; *American Bounty,* regional U.S. specialties, open Tuesday to Saturday, lunch, $$, dinner $$-$$$; *Caterina de Medici,* Italian, lunch $$, prix fixe $$$; *St. Andrews Cafe,* light, healthy fare, open Monday to Friday, lunch, $, dinner, $-$$ • *Beekman 1776 Tavern,* Beekman Arms (see above), excellent New American cuisine, $$-$$$ • *La Parmigiana,* 37 Montgomery Street, Rhinebeck, 876-3226, Italian in an old church, wood-fired pizza ovens, $ • *Chez Marcel,* U.S. 9, Rhinebeck, 876-8189, pleasing French cafe, $$ • *Green & Bresler, Ltd.*, 29 West Market Street, Red Hook (north of Rhinebeck), 758-5992, rave reviews make this worth the drive, $$ • *Chambord* (see above), $$$.

SIGHTSEEING *Old Rhinebeck Aerodrome,* Stone Church Road, off Route 9, Rhinebeck, 758-8610. Display hours: mid-May to October, Monday to Friday 10 A.M. to 5 P.M. Adults, $4; children 6–10, $2. Admission and air shows, mid-June to mid-October, Saturday and Sunday afternoons 2:30 to 4 P.M. Adults, $10; children, $5 • *Wilderstein,* Morton Road, Rhinebeck, 876-4818. Hours: June to September, Saturday and Sunday noon to 4 P.M., $4 including afternoon tea • *Clermont State Historic Park,* Route 6 (off Route 9G), Germantown, 537-4240. Hours: mid-April to October, Wednesday to Sunday (and Monday holidays) 10 A.M. to 5 P.M. Grounds open all year. Free • *Olana State Historic Site,* Route 9G, Hudson, 828-0135. Hours: mid-April to October, Wednesday to Sunday (and Monday holidays) 10 A.M. to 4 P.M. Adults, $3; children, $1. Grounds open daily. Free • *Montgomery Place,* Route 9G, Annandale-on-Hudson, 758-5264. Hours: April to October, daily except Tuesday 10 A.M. to 5 P.M.; November, December, and March, weekends only. Adults, $6; ages 6–17, $3 • *Mills Mansion and State Park,* U.S. 9, Staatsburg, 889-8851. Hours: May 1 to Labor Day, Wednesday to Sunday (and Monday holidays) noon to 5 P.M.; September and October, Wednesday to Sunday noon to 5 P.M. Free • *Franklin D. Roosevelt National Historic Site,* U.S. 9, Hyde Park, 229-9115. Hours: April to October, daily 9 A.M. to 5 P.M.; rest of year closed Tuesday and Wednesday. Adults, $4; under 16, free • *Eleanor Roosevelt National Historic Site,* 229-9115. May to October, daily 9 A.M. to 5 P.M.; November, December, April, weekends only. Free • *Vanderbilt Mansion National Historic Site,* Route 9, Hyde Park, 229-7821. Hours: April to October, daily 9 A.M. to 5 P.M.; rest of year closed Tuesday and Wednesday. Adults, $2; under 16, free • *Frances Lehman Loeb Art Center,* Vassar

College, Poughkeepsie, 437-5235. Hours: Wednesday to Saturday 10 A.M. to 5 P.M., Sunday 1 to 5 P.M. Free. • Boscobel, Route 9D, Garrison, 265-3638. Hours: April to October, daily except Tuesday 9:30 A.M. to 5 P.M.; March, November, and December, to 4 P.M. Adults, $6, age 6–14, $3 • *Shearwater Cruises,* RD #2, Box 329, Rhinebeck, 876-7350, Hudson River cruises, phone for schedules and rates • *Riverboat Tours,* 310 Mill Street, Poughkeepsie, 473-5211, Hudson cruises from Poughkeepsie, phone for details.

FOR FURTHER INFORMATION Hudson River Heritage, PO Box 287, Rhinebeck, NY 12572, 876-2802; Dutchess County Tourism, 3 Neptune Road, Poughkeepsie, NY 12601, 463-4000.

Horsing Around in New Jersey

"We raise 'em, we ride 'em, we race 'em."

Way out west in New Jersey, the subject was horses and a gentleman was explaining to us that in this state, which is better known for turnpike traffic than green pastures, there probably are more cowboys to be found than anywhere else east of Texas. The reason is that raising horses is one of the state's principal industries, particularly in Monmouth County, not far from the Jersey shore.

The horse farms are in full view along the roads, concentrated in a triangle between Holmdel, Freehold, and Colts Neck—a particularly pretty sight in spring when the colts are in the fields grazing beside their mothers. The trotters run at Freehold and the thoroughbreds at Monmouth Park. And you can see where the winningest trotters are trained, and take in a variety of horse shows. With all of that within easy reach of interesting historic sights and just a breeze from the shore, what better plan for a late May to early June weekend than a sampling of horse country? If you like, you can even saddle up and take a ride.

An excellent base is Red Bank, where you can choose between the Molly Pitcher Inn, an imposing red Colonial structure with a beautiful view of the Navesink River out the dining room windows, or the modern Oyster Point Hotel, just around the bend and with its own river views. Some alternatives are hotel/motels in Freehold or Tinton Falls, closer to the horse country.

Since you are only heading about 45 miles out of the city if you choose Red Bank, it should be easy to make it for Friday night dinner. A highly recommended restaurant for fine French food is the Fromagerie in nearby Rumson. The tiny Little Silver Spoon in neighboring Little Silver also gets high marks from reviewers for its creative New American fare. In Red Bank itself, the current star is Cucina Di Roma, an elegant northern Italian restaurant. Other good choices include the Little Kraut for German and the very informal little Everybody's Cafe, with an interesting, eclectic menu.

If you want to see future trotter champions in training, save Saturday morning for a visit to Showplace Farms on Route 33 in Englishtown, known as one of the top horse training and therapy centers in the country. There are usually some 450 horses in residence and 200 employees looking after them. The horses start their training as two-year-olds, jogging clockwise around the track in morning workouts. One day a week there are time trials heading counter-clockwise. It looks like there could be trouble, what with sulkies going in both directions, but the clockwise joggers are careful to keep to the outside lanes.

Inside the central building on Monday through Friday, you can see the horses clip-clopping down a ramp into the pool for therapy sessions. Many of these "patients" have had leg injuries or recent surgery. Treatments are all over before 11 A.M., so don't tarry if you want to watch.

If you follow Route 33 east into Freehold, you're ready for a horse farm tour. Follow Route 537 out of town to Colts Neck, then turn north on Route 34 to Route 520 and Holmdel, and you've hit the main corners of the triangle. Feel free to turn off onto smaller lanes. You're not likely to get lost, and even if you do for a bit, you'll have fine scenery as compensation. Route 537 between Colts Neck and Red Bank offers several pick-your-own orchards and you'll pass the home of Laird's Applejack whiskey, an institution since 1780.

Save time for a look around Red Bank. Masted schooners once plied the river here, carrying shellfish, farm produce, and other goods from the area to the world markets in New York. Later on, romantic paddlewheel steamers brought vacationers from the city to this quaint Victorian town perched on the red soil banks for which it was named. Carriages in Red Bank would take them to the races or the shore or out into the gentle countryside, and it is the same kinds of diversions that attract visitors today. Red Bank grew as a shopping hub as well as a racing and boating center, but it never completely lost its Victorian feel. The shops along Front, Broad, Monmouth, and Maple have kept their old facades, making for a pleasant stroll on a spring morning. Red Bank's 1878 railroad station is on the National Register of Historic Places.

At 99 Monmouth Street, you'll find the Monmouth Arts Center and its Count Basie Theater. Once a movie palace and vaudeville stage, the theater now showcases a variety of entertainment. It is named after the late pianist and bandleader who was born in Red Bank. The house where Basie grew up still stands at 229 Mechanic Street. Marine Park at the foot of Wharf Avenue is the most popular recreation spot in town.

For antiquers, the biggest attraction in Red Bank is its Antiques Center, a complex along West Front Street and Shrewsbury Avenue that just keeps growing. There are some 100 dealers congregated here, spread over several buildings, and there isn't much in the way of antiques that is not for sale.

On the way east into Shrewsbury on Route 35, the Outlet Center has some interesting tenants, including Anne Klein.

There are some interesting bits of history to be found along Route 35. The Allen House in Shrewsbury is furnished to simulate the tavern it was in Colonial days, and has changing exhibits upstairs. An interesting stop in Middletown is Marlpit House, an old Dutch cottage circa 1685, enlarged in the English style in 1740 and furnished with fine period pieces.

If you're going to the races, you can schedule Monmouth for Saturday or Sunday afternoon, but Freehold runs on Saturday only. Freehold is in action through May at 1 P.M., resuming again later in August. Monmouth opens in late May and continues through early September with races starting at 1:05 P.M.

On Sunday, you can pick your destination. There are a couple of interesting stops in Freehold, site of the Revolutionary War Battle of Monmouth, where Molly Hays took over for her wounded husband and brought water to the parched troops, earning her place in the history books as Molly Pitcher. Monmouth Battlefield State Park commemorates the site with an audio-visual display and an electric relief map tracing the battle. Craig House is a restored 1710 home that the British used as a hospital; Owl Haven is a nature center with live animals. The Monmouth County Historical Museum has many exhibits of Revolutionary to Civil War memorabilia, and rooms furnished in period furniture from the seventeenth to early nineteenth centuries. The kids love the attic, filled with toys, dolls, and dollhouses played with by children of another age.

Holmdel, one of the oldest communities in Monmouth County, offers tours of the Holmes-Hendrickson House, built in 1754, and the chance to step back to the 1890s at Longstreet Farm, a living historic farm where costumed guides explain life as it was lived here a century ago. This is also the home of the Garden State Arts Center, an amphitheater offering musical performances and ethnic festivals in May through October. You might want to check the current schedule.

One of the biggest flea markets around—five buildings with everything from antiques to live chickens—takes place every weekend to the west in Englishtown.

If a horseback ride is on the agenda, horses for trail rides are available to the south at New Horses Around, Inc., in Farmingdale, where trails wind through more than 400 acres of woodland behind Allaire airport, or at Circle A Riding Stables in Howell. Both offer guided rides through Allaire State Park.

Or you can watch other riders go through their paces at the Horse Park of New Jersey in Upper Freehold Township. Horse shows are held here regularly, open free to the public.

Another pleasant option on a fine spring day is a scenic drive along the Navesink River Road, Route 12A, out of Red Bank toward panoramic views at Atlantic Highlands. Follow the road as it bends north into Route 8A, then turn east again on Navesink Avenue, Route 8B, to the Mt. Mitchell Scenic Overlook for a fabulous view of Sandy Hook Bay and the Gateway National Recreation Area. Ocean Boulevard continues into town past a line-up of fine homes.

It's only a few minutes drive from here to Highlands and Doris and Ed's, considered by many to be the best seafood restaurant on the shore. No reservations are taken, so be prepared for a line. When your dinner arrives, you won't regret the wait.

Red Bank Area Code: 908

DRIVING DIRECTIONS Garden State Parkway southbound to Route 109, Red Bank. Route 34 runs into Rumson. Take Route 109 west and Route 50 south to Route 537 east to Freehold. *Total distance:* about 50 miles.

ACCOMMODATIONS *Molly Pitcher Inn,* 88 Riverside Avenue (State Highway 35), Red Bank, 07701, 747-2500, $-$$ • *Oyster Point Hotel,* 146 Bodman Place, Red Bank, 07701, 530-8200, $-$$ • *Courtyard by Marriott,* 600 Hope Road, Tinton Falls, 07724, 389-2100, $$ • *Days Inn,* 11 Center Plaza, Tinton Falls, 07724, 389-4646, $ • *Holiday Inn,* Hope Road at Garden State exit 105, Tinton Falls, 07724, 544-9300, $$ • *Freehold Gardens,* Route 537 and Gibson Place, Freehold, 07728, 780-3870, $$.

DINING *Fromagerie,* 26 Ridge Road, Rumson, 842-8088, $$$-$$$$ • *Cucina Di Roma,* 6 Linden Place, Red Bank, 747-5121, $$ • *Little Kraut,* 115 Oakland Street, Red Bank, 842-4380, $-$$$ • *Everybody's Café,* 79A Monmouth Street, Red Bank, 842-4755, $ • *Left Bank Café,* 8 Linden Place, Red Bank, 530-5930, $-$$ • *Colts Neck Inn,* Routes 34 and 537, Colts Neck, 462-0383, $$-$$$ • *Little Silver Spoon,* 496 Prospect Street, Little Silver, 747-4044, $$ • *Farm House,* 438 Branch Avenue, Little Silver, 842-5017, American food in 150-year-old farmhouse, $$-$$$ • *Shadowbrook,* off Route 35, Shrewsbury, 747-0200, Georgian mansion with gardens, $$$-$$$$ •

Doris and Ed's, 348 Shore Drive, Highlands, 872-1565, tops for seafood, $$-$$$.

SIGHTSEEING *Freehold Raceway,* Park Avenue at U.S. 9 and Route 33, Freehold, 462-3800. Hours: year-round except June and July, Tuesday through Saturday, 1 P.M. $2 parking • *Monmouth Park,* Oceanport Avenue (Garden State exit 105), 222-5100. Hours: late May to early September, Tuesday, Wednesday, Saturday, and Sunday 1:05 P.M., Friday 3 P.M. Grandstand, $1.50; clubhouse, $4. • *Monmouth Battlefield State Park,* Route 33, Freehold, 462-9616, Visitor Center hours: Memorial Day to Labor Day 10 A.M. to 6 P.M., rest of year, to 4 P.M. Free • *Monmouth County Historical Museum,* 70 Court Street, Freehold, 462-1466. Hours: Tuesday to Saturday 10 A.M. to 4 P.M.; Sunday 1 to 4 P.M. Adults, $2; ages 6–18, $1 • Other Historical Society properties, all using the same telephone number and with the same hours and admission fees, include: *Allen House,* Route 35 at Sycamore Avenue, Shrewsbury; *Marlpit Hall,* 137 Kings Highway (Route 35), Middletown; *Holmes-Hendrickson House,* Longstreet and Roberts roads, Holmdel • *Englishtown Auction Sales,* 90 Wilson Avenue (Route 527), Englishtown, 446-9644. Hours: Saturday 7 A.M. to 5 P.M., Sunday, 9 A.M. to 5 P.M. • *Longstreet Farm,* Holmdel Park, Longstreet Road, Holmdel, 946-3758. Hours: daily, Labor Day to Memorial Day, 10 A.M. to 4 P.M.; summer hours 9 A.M. to 5 P.M. Free • *Garden State Arts Center,* Telegraph Hill Park, Holmdel, 442-9200. Phone for current offerings • Horseback riding: *New Horses Around, Inc.,* Belmar Boulevard, Farmingdale, 938-4480. *Circle A Riding Stables,* 667 Herbertsville Road, Howell, 938-2004 • Horse shows: *The Horse Park of New Jersey,* off Route 524, PO Box 118, Allentown, (609) 259-0170.

FOR FURTHER INFORMATION Monmouth County Public Information and Tourism, 27 East Main Street, Freehold, NJ 07728, toll free (800) 523-2587.

Chocolate and Roses in Hershey, Pennsylvania

The streetlights are Hershey kisses, the signs are chocolate colored with candy-bar lettering, the main intersection of town is at Chocolate and Cocoa streets, and they hand you a Hershey bar when you check into a hotel.

There's no mistaking the main attraction in Hershey, Pennsylvania, where even the grand hotel is placed to include the chocolate factory in its hilltop view. And there are few better places for a family weekend than this ''company town,'' where chocolate really is only the beginning of the fun.

Magnificent gardens, a major theme park, a zoo, a museum of American life, and sports facilities that include five golf courses are all waiting after the chocolate tour is over.

It's all a bit ironic since Milton Hershey, who made a fortune satisfying America's sweet tooth, probably never expected further profits from tourists. When the former farmboy came back to his hometown of Derry Township to build a chocolate factory in 1904, his main aim was to make the town a pleasant place for his workers to live. The first park, gardens, museum, and zoo were strictly for their benefit.

But from the very start people wanted to see how this new confection called milk chocolate was made, and the factory began offering tours to meet the demand. Savoring the sweet smells, the free samples, and the pleasant atmosphere of this unusual small town, visitors told their friends to come. In 1928 the count was 10,000; by 1970 it was pushing a million and the factory could no longer accommodate the crowds. The Chocolate World Visitors' Center was built to take the place of the old tour, and it is now almost everyone's first stop in Hershey.

The free 12-minute trip in a Disney-like automated car whisks you off to the cacao plantations of Ghana. You watch the story of chocolate unfold from bean to candy bar, from picking and shipping the beans, grinding and blending them with milk in a simulated factory, to the wrapping of the bars. You exit from the tour into a tropical garden containing some 99 varieties of trees, including cacao, and hundreds of flowering plants and shrubs. You're also facing stands stacked high with Hershey bars and dozens of other souvenirs, chocolate and otherwise. And there's a refreshment pavilion specializing in you-know-what. There's no more chocolate smell or free samples—but over a million people take the tour each year anyway.

Opposite Chocolate World is Hersheypark, once a place where factory employees came to picnic, play ball, go boating, and be entertained at the pavilion. Mr. Hershey kept improving the facilities, adding a swimming pool and a convention hall that doubled as an ice-skating rink. Hershey Zoo was actually Hershey's own private animal collection, one of the country's largest, housed at the park for all to see. And for the kids he bought a carousel and, as a twentieth birthday present to the town, a roller coaster.

As the crowds grew the notion of an actual amusement park seemed a natural one, and in 1971 redevelopment began. Unless you have a total aversion to theme parks, it's hard not to like this clean and pretty one, where you stroll through a mock English town called Tudor

Square and an eighteenth-century German village named Rhine Land. All come complete with appropriate costumes, music, shops, and restaurants. It's undeniably commercial, but the happy crowds don't seem to care.

The antique 1919 carousel at the park now has a lot of company, including three roller coasters. The scariest is the Sidewinder, which turns you upside down and backwards to boot. Water rides include Canyon River Rapids, simulating a raging whitewater rafting trip; Frontier Chute-Out, a quadruple-flume waterslide ride; the Coal Cracker, featuring a 35-mile-per-hour splashdown; and Tidal Force, billed as the tallest, wettest boat ride in the world. There are some 50 rides in all, from "scream machines" to gentle rides for tots. You can get a view of the whole 87-acre park from the kiss-shaped windows of the 330-foot Kissing Tower or take the Monorail for a scenic ride with an audio accompaniment.

Town tours are also offered by Hershey Trolley Works, aboard old-fashioned trolley reproductions manned by "conductors" and "motormen" dressed in period uniforms.

There is also continuous live entertainment at four theaters scattered through the park. The adjoining arena continues after the park closes for the season, hosting not only the Ice Capades and hockey games but also name entertainers such as Kenny Rogers, Billy Joel, and Diana Ross.

Almost everyone's favorite souvenir of the park is a photo taken with the life-size candy-bar characters that greet visitors. In summer, the characters also take part in a daily event billed as "The Sweetest Parade on Earth," at Chocolate World and Hersheypark. Don't forget your camera.

The zoo, too, has come a long way. It now represents the major natural regions of North America—waters, desert, woodlands, plains, and forest, with native plants and animals of each zone in their native habitat. You'll see alligators in the swamps; pumas, bison, and eagles in Big Sky Country; black bear and timber wolves in the forest; wild turkeys, bobcats, otters, and raccoons at home in the woodlands.

There's more than enough to fill a Saturday here—but more still to fill your Sunday. All ages can appreciate the beauty of the Hershey Gardens, which have grown in 40 years from an old-fashioned rose garden into 23 acres featuring 700 varieties of roses, as well as six classic gardens—English, Oriental, Colonial, and Italian, a rock garden, and a fountain garden.

Even the Hershey Museum proves to be more than you might expect. It's less overwhelming than a lot of museums and for that very reason makes its points unusually well. The main exhibit tells the story of the town's founder, Milton Hershey, which includes a history of the town. Other displays include Milton Hershey's two exceptional collections of Native American and Pennsylvania Dutch artifacts. The Pennsylvania objects illustrate the settlement and growth of this region. Visitors can work with a computer to find out about small-town life in Pennsylvania in the 1850s, or work on the nineteenth-century style two-harness loom.

Try to time your museum visit to coincide with the performance of the Apostolic Clock, 15 minutes before each hour, with moving carved figurines that depict the Last Supper.

One other unique sight in Hershey has nothing to do with tourists. The Milton Hershey School was founded in 1909 by childless Milton and Catherine Hershey to provide a free home as well as an education for orphan boys. Now co-ed, the school tries to re-create the feel of family living for its residents with 92 campus homes spread across 10,000 acres of campus. Each house shelters 12 to 16 children with house parents. The schooling, which extends through high school, is unusual in many ways. It includes time working on community farms and the opportunity to learn a trade or prepare for college, according to each student's talents and inclinations.

Founders Hall, a striking domed marble building that is a tribute to the Hersheys, is awesome architecturally, yet it serves well as church, theater, and concert hall for 1,300 very energetic orphaned children. Some of the profits from Hershey's current commercial ventures are used to supplement the endowment Milton Hershey left for his school. Founders Hall is well worth a visit—if you can only find the time, with everything else there is to do.

Where to stay in Hershey? The natural choices are the excellent Hershey-run accommodations, not cheap but not as expensive as you might think when you figure all the admissions included in weekend packages. Hotel Hershey does seem a bit steep and elegant for a family jaunt, but it is a grand hotel in every sense. Mediterranean in style, the lobby is reminiscent of a small Spanish town, with a tiled fountain and arcaded stucco walls. The circular dining room has windows all around that look out at gardens and grounds, and the food is a match for the setting. There are pools indoors and out, four tennis courts, and a golf course. You could happily spend a weekend here without ever venturing off the grounds.

The Lodge is motel-style and obviously more family-oriented, as you can tell when you drive up and spot the children feeding the ducks on the pond out front. There are pools here, too, a playground, tennis and paddle tennis, a golf course and a par-3 pitch-and-putt, a game room for the kids, and movies at night.

June is the perfect time for Hershey, when the roses are in evidence but the summer crowds are not. The only problem may be how to see it all in one weekend. You may decide to take it in parts. That way you can see the gardens with tulips or mums as well as roses in bloom.

Hershey Area Code: 717

DRIVING DIRECTIONS Take I-80 or 78 to the I-81 west exit at Route 743 (exit 28) and follow signs to Hershey. *Total distance:* about 183 miles.

PUBLIC TRANSPORTATION Amtrak service to Harrisburg. Hotel Hershey and Hershey Lodge limousine service for guests; free shuttle service to all attractions from late May to Labor Day. Bus service to Hershey via Capitol Trailways.

ACCOMMODATIONS *Hershey Resorts,* Hershey, 17033, toll free (800) 533-3131. *Hotel Hershey,* $$$$-$$$$$ MAP; *Hershey Lodge,* $$-$$$ (children under 18 free in same room as parents). Both hotels offer many summer package plans including meals, lodging, and admissions and much lower off-season rates; call for information and brochure • For less expensive lodgings, try *Best Western Inn,* 533-5665, $$$, including movies in room and Continental breakfast, $$$ • *Days Inn,* 350 Chocolate Avenue, Hershey 17033, 534-2162, $$ • *White Rose Motel,* 1060 East Chocolate Avenue, Hershey, 17033, 533-6923, $-$$ • *Milton Motel,* 1733 Chocolate East Avenue, Hershey, 17033, 533-0369, $-$$ • *Spinner's Motor Inn,* 845 East Chocolate Avenue, Hershey, 17033, 533-9157, $$ CP • *Comfort Inn,* 1200 Mae Street, Hummelstown, 17036 (one mile from Hershey), 566-2050, indoor pool, $$-$$$ • *Union Canal House,* 107 South Hanover Street, Union Deposit, 17033, 566-0054, B&B in a historic building, $$ CP.

DINING First choices, once again, are the Hershey properties: *Hershey Lodge,* three choices: the *Tack Room,* $$; the *Hearth,* $$, and the *Copper Kettle* for family dining, $. *Hershey Hotel,* elegant dining room, jackets requested, $$$ • Other recommendations: *Harvey's on Chocolate,* 814 East Chocolate Avenue, 533-7450, owner-chef gets good reports, $$ • *Spinner's Restaurant,* 845 East Chocolate Avenue, 533-9050, wide variety, $$-$$$ • *Union Canal House* (see above), Colonial decor, basic menu, steaks and seafood, $$ • *Dimitri's,* 1311 East Chocolate Avenue, 533-3403, Greek and Continental, $-$$ • *The Dream Family Restaurant,* 1500 Allegheny Street, 696-3384, Italian and American, $.

SIGHTSEEING For all Hershey attractions, phone toll free (800) HERSHEY. *Hersheypark.* Hours: mid-May to Labor Day, selected September weekends. Opening time 10:30 A.M., closing varies with season, usually 10 P.M. or 11 P.M. in summer, 6 P.M. to 8 P.M. spring and fall. Best to phone for current operating hours. Age 9 to adults, $23.95; ages 3–8, $14.95 • *Hershey Museum of American Life.* Hours: daily 10 A.M. to 5 P.M., Memorial Day to Labor Day, to 6 P.M. Adults, $4; children 3–15, $1.75 • *ZOOAMERICA.* Hours: daily 10 A.M. to 5 P.M., to 8 P.M. mid-June through August. Adults, $4.50; children 3–12, $3.25 • *Hershey Gardens.* Hours: April through October, daily 9 A.M. to 5 P.M. Adults, $4; children 3–15, $1.75 • *Hershey Chocolate World.* Hours: daily 9 A.M. to 4:45 P.M., open later in summer season. January through March, Sunday hours are noon to 4:45 P.M. Free. Check for current package rates for savings.

FOR FURTHER INFORMATION *HERSHEY,* 300 Park Boulevard, Hershey, PA 17033, toll free (800) HERSHEY.

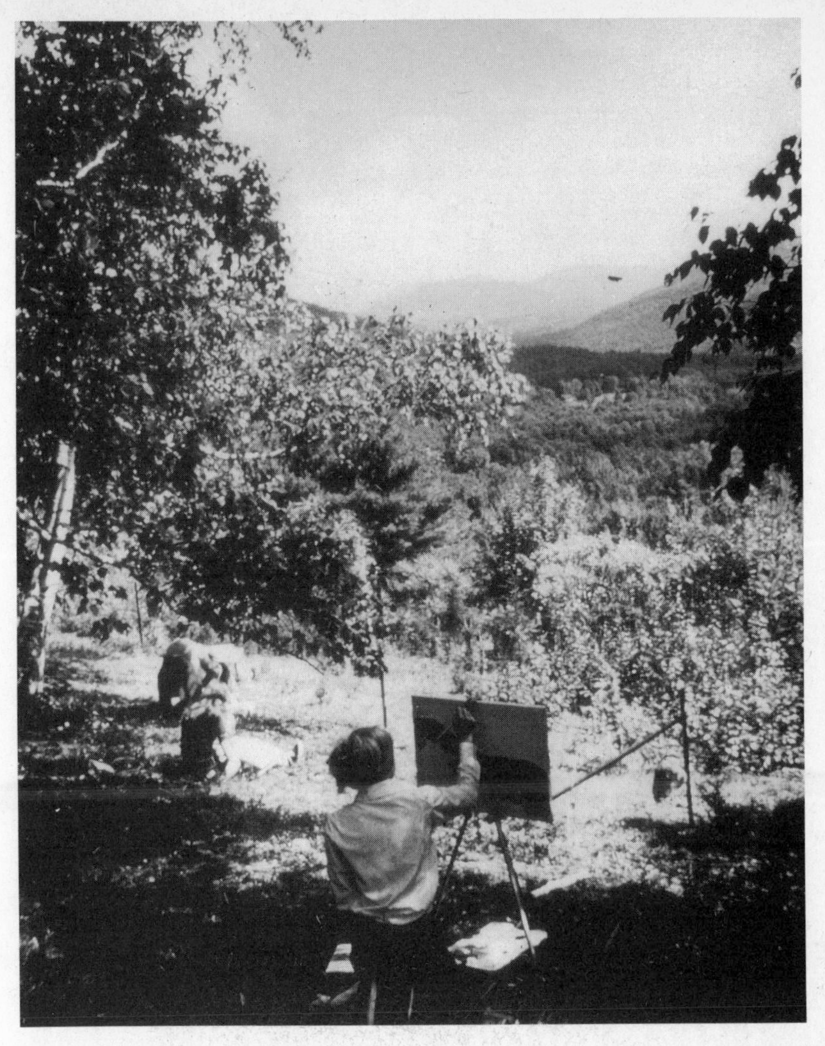

Summer

Capturing New York's Catskills on canvas
Photo courtesy of New York State Commerce Department

Summering with the Arts in Saratoga Springs

Should it be the racetrack or the golf course? Sightseeing or the health spa? The ballet or a jazz concert under the stars?

The only problem planning a visit to Saratoga Springs, New York, is choosing among what may well be the Northeast's most bountiful helping of summer entertainment.

Saratoga's original attractions are legendary. As far back as George Washington's day, people flocked to this little town north of Albany for the mineral springs said to cure everything from gout to sinus. In the nineteenth century it was the racetrack and gambling casinos that drew the rich and famous and flamboyant, people like J. P. Morgan, Diamond Jim Brady, and Lillian Russell.

Things went downhill when gambling was outlawed in the 1950s, but the Whitneys and Vanderbilts and the rest of the horsey set never stopped coming for the gala racing season. Then the state stepped in to preserve the precious waters and to add new incentives for a visit.

The revival started with the opening of Saratoga State Park, a 2,200-acre playground with two golf courses, four swimming pools, tennis courts, a dozen picnic areas, bike and walking paths, and a nature trail. The Roosevelt and Lincoln Bathhouses remain, now owned and under renovation by the state so that guests can still enjoy the fizzy mineral baths and massages that once put Saratoga on the map. Reserve well in advance at (518) 584-2011.

The Crystal Spa is a new arrival in town, for those who want their mineral soaks in glitzier surroundings.

The Saratoga Performing Arts Center (SPAC) in the park has something outstanding happening almost every night all summer long. The New York City Ballet takes a turn on stage in July, the Philadelphia Orchestra takes up residence in August, the New York City Opera makes an annual appearance, and many big-name popular performers are also on the agenda. The jazz greats take over in late June, playing from noon until night. Seats are in the 5,100-seat open amphitheater, or on its outdoor ''mezzanine'' of sloping grounds that can accommodate as many as 30,000.

Theater and modern dance are also on Saratoga's agenda, presented in the park's Little Theater, a 500-seat indoor arena. Write to SPAC for a full schedule.

For many, Saratoga's foremost attraction remains America's oldest and one of its most beautiful racetracks. The top thoroughbreds run here in August, with the Travers Stakes, a main event on the national racing circuit, the highlight of the season. It is the occasion for a week of festivities in town, including antique and art shows, a parade, and matches at the Saratoga Polo Grounds, where many top polo players compete throughout the month of August. Rates double in August at local lodgings, but racing fans are willing to pay the price.

If you come during racing season, save a morning for one of its nicest traditions, breakfast at the track, watching the thoroughbreds go through their practice paces, then enjoying a free, behind-the-scenes tour of the paddocks. You can have a sit-down breakfast on the clubhouse porch or settle for a cup of coffee and a muffin from a stand. The morning is special either way.

There's another reason to get up early. Unless you line up at 8 A.M. to snag one of the 1,000 general admission grandstand seats, you'll watch the races standing up. The seats, both clubhouse and grandstand, are mostly sold out by mail the previous fall. Note that you can bring folding chairs to set up on the rail, on the ground floor of the grandstand, or under a shade tree.

Even if you aren't a fan, you'll enjoy a visit to the National Museum of Racing, fresh from a $6 million refurbishing. The colorful silks, equestrian paintings, and magnificent silver trophies here are beautifully displayed, and some excellent and imaginative exhibits will teach you a great deal about what makes a top thoroughbred and re-create the excitement of being at the track.

Another unique attraction is the National Museum of Dance, which is housed in a restored bathhouse. It includes a Hall of Fame honoring the greats of American dance—Isadora Duncan, Agnes de Mille, Fred Astaire, and George Balanchine, to name a few.

All the summer activity has inspired a rejuvenation of Saratoga's downtown, now abloom with boutiques and sidewalk cafes. This is also prime antiquing country. The Regent Street Antique Center, with many dealers under one roof, is also a mini-museum displaying stoneware, canes, and other collectibles.

A sense of history remains throughout town. A stop at the Urban Cultural Park Visitor's Center in Drink Hall, a former trolley station right at the center of town on Broadway, will supply you with free maps and guides to help you explore some of the city's elegant past. Walking tours are also available.

On your own, a good place to start is right across the street from the Information Center at Congress Park and The Casino, whose grand halls attest to its role as a flourishing gambling establishment during the town's grand old days.

Upstairs, the Hall of History traces Saratoga's development from frontier village to flamboyant resort. On the third floor, the Walworth Museum presents a sampling of rooms from the home of Reuben Hyde Walworth, whose wealthy and prominent family lived in Saratoga for 125 years.

Move on to North Broadway, Circular Street, and Union Avenue to see the architecture of the mansions that have survived from Saratoga's opulent past, and to Franklin Square to examine the Doric columns and pediments of the 1830s Greek Revival homes under restoration there.

Wherever you go, you'll see natural springs bubbling up with the mineral water that first made Saratoga famous—in Congress Park, in front of City Hall, and even at the racetrack. Many of them offer samples of the healthy though none-too-tasty water.

Outside Saratoga proper you can visit the campus of Skidmore College and the grounds and garden at Yaddo, the gray stone mansion that has been an inspirational refuge for writers and musicians such as Aaron Copland, Carson McCullers, and Saul Bellow.

On U.S. 4 in Schuylerville, Saratoga National Historic Park marks the Battle of Saratoga, one of the critical encounters of the Revolutionary War. The Visitor Center offers a 20-minute film and the route for a nine-mile self-guided driving tour of the battlefield.

For further evening amusement, a festival of baroque music goes on in town, and there is harness racing every summer night except Sunday, regardless of whether the thoroughbreds are running.

Book early if you want to stay at the only hotel remaining from Saratoga's grand Victorian days, the Adelphi. Broadway is lined with motels and lodgings, and the Gideon Putnam remains a stately standby in the park, but the best news for visitors is the appearance of many new bed-and-breakfast inns in some of the Victorian homes in and around town, some of them right on Union Avenue, the handsome boulevard leading to the track.

Saratoga has many good restaurants, but tops for many years is Eartha's Kitchen. Be sure to make reservations early. You'll find that fine cuisine is just one more of the arts that make Saratoga Springs a special summer destination.

Saratoga Area Code: 518

DRIVING DIRECTIONS New York State Thruway to exit 24 at Albany-Northway (Route 87) to exit 13N, Saratoga. *Total distance:* 175 miles.

PUBLIC TRANSPORTATION Amtrak or Greyhound to Saratoga. It's easy to get around town via minibus (schedules at visitors' center).

ACCOMMODATIONS Expect minimum stays in season; all rates are *doubled* in August, but ask about racing and weekend packages. *Adelphi Hotel,* 365 Broadway, 12866, 587-4688, $$-$$$$ • *Gideon Putnam Hotel,* Saratoga Springs State Park, 12866, 584-3000, $$$-$$$$ • *The Inn at Saratoga,* 231 Broadway, 12866, 583-1890,

$$$ • *Sheraton Saratoga Springs,* 534 Broadway, 12866, 584-4000, $$$-$$$$ • *Holiday Inn,* Broadway and Circular Street, 12866, 584-4550, $$-$$$ • *Eddy House,* Nelson and Crescent Avenue, 12866, secluded beautiful grounds, handsome decor, shared baths, $$ CP • *Union Gables,* 55 Union Avenue, 12866, 584-1558, grand Queen Anne Victorian, $$ CP • *Westchester House,* 102 Lincoln Avenue, 12866, pleasant Victorian, 587-7613, $$-$$$ CP • *Willow Walk Inn,* 120 High Rock Avenue, 12866, 584-4549, small, nicely decorated, $-$$ CP • *Six Sisters,* 149 Union Avenue, 12866, 583-1173, cozy small Victorian, $$ CP • *Lombardi Farm,* 41 Locust Grove Road, 12866, homey 1850s farmhouse, animals, hot tub, $$$ CP • *Wayside Inn,* 104 Wilton Road, Greenfield, 12833, 893-7249, farmhouse just outside Saratoga with adjacent crafts workshop, $-$$$ CP • *The Mansion,* Route 29, PO Box 77, Rock City Falls, 12863, 885-1607, elegant Victorian decor, $$ CP.

DINING *Eartha's Kitchen,* 60 Court Street, 583-0602, grill specialties, $$-$$$ • *Olde Bryan Inn,* 123 Maple Avenue, 5872990, varied menu, atmospheric oldest building in town, $-$$ • *Sperry's,* 30½ Caroline Street, 584-9618, good bistro fare, art deco decor, $$ • *Old Firehouse Restaurant,* 543 Broadway, 587-0047, basic American menu, $-$$ • *Gideon Putnam* (see above), try the lavish brunch, $-$$$ • *Hattie's Chicken Shack,* 45 Phila Street, 584-4790, traditional Southern fried chicken and ribs (new owners, so ask your innkeeper if it has changed), $ • *Ash Grove Inn,* Church Street, Route 9N, 587-1278, Italian, country views from the picture windows, $-$$$ • *The Wheat Fields,* 440 Broadway, 587-0534, casual, gourmet pasta, $-$$ • *Bruno's,* 237 Union Avenue, 583-3333, pizza from a wood-fired oven, across from the racetrack, $ • *The Wishing Well,* Route 9, Gansevoort, 3 miles north of town, 584-7640, 1823 farmhouse, $$-$$$ • *Chez Pierre,* U.S. 9, Wilton, 793-3350, French fare, $$.

SIGHTSEEING *Saratoga Performing Arts Center,* Saratoga Springs, 587-3330. Phone or write for schedule of performances. Prices vary with attractions. Tickets are also available at Ticketmaster. • *Saratoga Spa State Park Recreation Center,* South Broadway (Route 9), 584-2535. Pool, tennis, golf, par-3 golf course. Call for fees and hours. • *Saratoga Spa Mineral Bathhouses,* Saratoga Spa State Park, *Roosevelt Baths*, open year round, 584-2011; Lincoln Baths, July and August, 583-2880. Phone for hours and mineral-bath reservations. Bath with massage: $30–$32 • *National Museum of Racing,* Union Avenue and Ludlow Street, 584-0400. Hours: Racing season, daily 9

A.M. to 5 P.M.; rest of year, Monday to Saturday 10 A.M. to 4:30 P.M., Sunday, noon to 4:30 P.M. Adults, $3; children, $2 • *The Casino, Walworth Museum, and Historical Society of Saratoga Springs,* Congress Park, 584-6920. Hours: June to October, Monday, Tuesday, Thursday, Friday, and Saturday 10 A.M. to 4 P.M., Wednesday and Sunday 1 to 4 P.M.; November to May, Wednesday and Sunday only, 1 to 4 P.M. Adults, $2; students, $1.50; children under 7, free • *Saratoga Racetrack,* Union Avenue, 584-6200, August; daily except Tuesday, 1:30 P.M. Call for this season's exact dates. Grandstand seats, $4; general admission, $2; clubhouse admission, $5; parking, $3. Free admission for breakfast workouts, 7 to 9:30 A.M. Advance ticket orders by mail from Saratoga Reserved Seats, PO Box 257, Elmont, NY 11003, (718) 641-4700, ext. 4306 • *National Museum of Dance,* South Broadway, 584-2225. Hours: mid-June to Labor Day, Tuesday to Sunday 10 A.M. to 6 P.M.; early June, weekends only. Adults, $3; students, $2; under 12, $1 • *Saratoga Raceway* (harness track), off Route 9, 584-2110. Hours: Races February through November, Monday to Saturday 7:45 P.M. Call for off-season schedules. Grandstand, $1.75; clubhouse, $3; parking, $1 • *Urban Cultural Park Visitor's Center,* 297 Broadway, 587-3241. June to Labor Day, daily 9 A.M. to 4 P.M.; spring and fall closed Tuesday and Wednesday; phone for winter schedules. Walking tours daily in summer, 10:30 A.M. Adults, $2; under 12, free • *Saratoga Polo,* Seward Street, 584-3255. August only. Matches usually held Tuesday 3 P.M., Friday and Saturday 6 P.M. Best to phone to check current schedule. • *Saratoga National Historic Park,* U.S. 4, 664-9821. Hours: daily, 9 A.M. to 5 P.M.; July and August, to 5:30 P.M. Free.

FOR FURTHER INFORMATION Contact Chamber of Commerce, 494 Broadway, Saratoga, NY 12866, 584-3255.

Litchfield and Lake Waramaug: A Connecticut Double Feature

Lake what? Even in Connecticut, lots of people haven't heard of this placid blue oasis just north of New Milford in the Litchfield Hills. Just over eight miles around, ringed by wooded hills and as smooth as a looking glass, Lake Waramaug has a small public beach at one end and at the other, a state park, with boating and swimming facilities as well as walking trails—and not a commercial facility in sight. All you'll find around the lake are summer homes and some fine small country inns.

Each of the inns is different and has something special to offer. The largest, the Inn at Lake Waramaug, is a mini-resort with its own beach and dock, sailboats and canoes, a little paddlewheel showboat to cruise you around the lake, tennis, and an indoor pool. There are a few rooms in the inn building, a 1795 Colonial house, but most are in motel-type lodges on the grounds. Hopkins Inn across the way is a pretty yellow house with a porch looking out at the lake, with 10 modest Colonial bedrooms upstairs, and a highly regarded dining room.

The Boulders Inn, literally built with boulders in its fieldstone walls, is the most appealing of all. The antique-filled living room has fine lake views from a big picture window, as does the dining room and a pleasant outdoor dining deck. Boulders accommodates 45 people, a dozen in the pretty inn rooms and the rest in cottages on the grounds.

A pleasant inn, good food, and plenty of outdoor activity could fill a weekend on their own, especially if you add the cache of interesting crafts and antique shops in New Preston, the little town closest to the lake. But an added attraction at Lake Waramaug is its proximity to some of Connecticut's loveliest Colonial towns. Prime among them is Litchfield, invariably on every list of the most beautiful Main Streets in America and considered by many experts to be the finest unrestored, unspoiled Colonial town in America.

One of the nicest things about visiting Litchfield is that its three dozen or so choicest homes—those forming the central Historic District around the village green—are easily strollable, concentrated on two long blocks, North and South streets, just off the green.

You may recognize the steepled Congregational Church on that green; it shows up in countless photographs of typical New England scenes. Next door is the 1787 parsonage where Harriet Beecher Stowe's family lived when she was born here in the 1800s.

Across the way on South Street are two homes that help to explain why Litchfield has remained unique and unchanged. The Moses Seymour House was completed in 1817 for Jane Seymour, who married Dr. Josiah G. Beckwith. The Beckwith family remained in the house well into this century. The Seymour House next door, one of the best examples of Federal architecture of this period, was built by Moses for his son Ozias; it was later occupied by Origen Seymour, chief justice of Connecticut, and remained in the Seymour family until 1950. Litchfield's families didn't move on to greener pastures; they stayed to tend to their green.

Tapping Reeve opened the nation's first law school in his superb 1773 home with his brother-in-law, Aaron Burr, as his first pupil. Eventually, the pupils outgrew the house and a school building was erected in 1784. Among its alumni were 3 Supreme Court justices, 2 vice-presidents, 14 governors, 28 senators, more than 100 congressmen, and 16 chief justices of Connecticut.

John C. Calhoun was a student here, lodging in the rectory next door and planting some of the elms that remain along the street. Farther down the street is the 1736 home where Ethan Allen, Revolutionary War leader of the fabled Green Mountain Boys, is believed to have been born.

Beautiful white Colonials of the 1700s seem to go on and on, including the home of Oliver Wolcott, Jr., now the town library, and the obligatory structure boasting ''George Washington slept here,'' in this case the Elisha Sheldon Tavern. With the exception of the law school and the town Historical Society Museum, almost all of these homes are private residences. Like so many towns, Litchfield has one day set aside for its annual open house of historic homes. It is usually the second Saturday in July (check with the Travel Council to be sure), and it is well worth timing your visit to coincide.

The Litchfield Historical Society Museum recently renovated its fine quarters on the corner of South Street, and a stop will tell you a lot about Litchfield's development. You'll learn, for example, that this was also home to the Sarah Pierce Academy, the nation's first academy for women, conveniently located for socializing with Mr. Reeve's law students.

Litchfield has a growing number of art galleries in town, including the gallery of Frank Federico, who has won many awards. For dining, the West Street Grill, a stylish bistro on the green, gets critics' raves for its innovative menu.

Outside of town are two expert glass artists, Tony Carretta and Larry LiVolsi, who invite visitors into their studios to watch them create beautiful sculptures of glass.

If the day is fine, you may prefer to forget the shops and head for the White Memorial Foundation Conservation Center, just west on Route 202. It is the state's largest nature center, with 4,000 acres and many appealing hiking trails in the hills and valleys. Bantam Lake is also part of the center, offering swimming at Sandy Beach and boats for renting at the landing at Folly Point.

Another magnificent strolling place is Topsmead State Forest, a former estate whose grounds and gardens are now open to the public for hiking and picnicking with fabulous views of the Litchfield Hills.

For anyone interested in flowers, particularly unusual perennials, White Flower Farm is a must. This is no ordinary nursery. Garden lovers make pilgrimages here to see the eight-acre formal display garden and to browse among the 1,200 varieties of unusual plants over 20 acres of growing fields. Delphiniums are a specialty, as are tuberous begonias.

It would be easy to spend a week, rather than a weekend, enjoying the out-of-doors and the other Colonial towns near Lake Waramaug—

Washington, Kent, and Woodbury, to name just a few. At least mark it down for a return visit in the fall, when flaming foliage rings the lake in a blaze of color.

Connecticut Area Code: 203

DRIVING DIRECTIONS Henry Hudson Parkway to Saw Mill River Parkway to Route 684 north to Brewster, Route 84 east to Danbury, exit 7 to Route 7 north to New Milford, then Route 202 east to New Preston and Route 45 to Lake Waramaug. *Total distance:* 85 miles.

ACCOMMODATIONS *The Inn on Lake Waramaug,* 107 North Shore Road, New Preston, 06777, 868-0563 or (212) 724-8775, $$$$ MAP (three-day minimum in summer) • *Boulders Inn,* Route 45, New Preston, 06777, 868-7918, $$$$ MAP • *Hopkins Inn,* 22 Hopkins Road, New Preston, 06777, 868-7295, $ (closed January and February) • *Tollgate Hill,* Route 202, Litchfield, 06759 482-6116, attractive decor in 1700s Colonial, $$$-$$$$ • *Mayflower Inn,* Route 47, Washington, 868-9466, fabulous gardens, ultimate luxury in a beautifully restored country-house hotel, one of the best in the state, $$$$$.

DINING *Inn on Lake Waramaug* (see above), $$-$$$ • *Hopkins Inn* (see above), $$ • *Boulders Inn* (see above), $$ • *Le Bon Coin,* Route 202, New Preston, classic French in a country house, $$$ • *West Street Grill,* 43 West Street, Litchfield, 567-3885, $$-$$$ • *Tollgate Hill* (see above), Colonial ambience, traditional menu, $$-$$$ • *The Cafe,* Route 45, New Preston, 868-1787, $$-$$$ • *Mayflower Inn* (see above), fine dining, $$-$$$.

SIGHTSEEING *Litchfield Historical Society Museum,* South Street on the Green, 567-4501. Hours: April to mid-November, Tuesday to Saturday 11 A.M. to 5 P.M., Sunday 1 to 5 P.M. Adults, $2; under 16, free; includes admission to *Tapping Reeve House and Law School,* South Street, Litchfield, 567-4501. Hours: mid-May to mid-October, Tuesday to Saturday 11 A.M. to 4 P.M., Sunday 1 to 5 P.M. Adults, $2; children, free • *White Flower Farm,* Route 63 South, Litchfield, 567-8789. Hours: April to October, weekdays 10 A.M. to 5 P.M., weekends 9 A.M. to 5:30 P.M. Free • *White Memorial Foundation Center,* Route 202, Litchfield, 567-0857. Hours: grounds open daily, museum open year-round Tuesday to Saturday 9 A.M. to 5 P.M., Sunday 11 A.M. to 5 P.M. Adults, $1.50; children, $.75. Grounds: free. • *Topsmead State*

Park, Buell Road off East Litchfield Road (Route 118), Litchfield, 845-0226. Daylight hours. Free • *Glass artists*: (best to phone before stopping by: *Tony Carretta*, 513 Maple Street, The Milton Barn, Litchfield, 567-4851; *Larry LiVolsi*, Lorenz Studio and Gallery, Route 109, Lakeside, 567-4280.

FOR FURTHER INFORMATION Litchfield Hills Travel Council, PO Box 968, Litchfield, CT 06759, 582-5176.

A Midsummer Escape to Shelter Island

Some say the name came from the Quakers who found refuge on the island from religious persecution. Others believe it comes from the Indian term, *Manhansack-aha-quashawamock,* ''an island sheltered by islands.''

Whatever the origin of the name, here's a place for anyone saying ''gimme shelter'' from the usual commercial summer resorts.

Shelter Island's 12 square miles are tucked between the north and south forks of Long Island's east end, reachable only by ferryboat from Greenport to the north and Sag Harbor to the south. Though the population of 2,000 swells to about 8,000 in the summer, the effects of the influx are limited since most of the summer visitors own or rent homes—also limited in number, thanks to strict zoning. About a third of the island, 2,200 acres known as Mashomack Preserve, remains unpopulated.

The current visitors' guide lists about a dozen small hotels and/or restaurants, a small selection of bed-and-breakfast inns, a couple of gift and/or antiques shops, two art galleries, an ice cream parlor, and a few places where the locals buy clothing, food, and other necessities. Besides building and selling houses, the only local industry is fishing. The big summer events are the annual country fair, an arts and crafts fair, Fourth of July fireworks, and the Fireman's Barbecue in August. That's it.

So, what do you do on Shelter Island? You bike. Or hike. Sunbathe on crescent beaches. Rent a sailboat or go fishing. Play a little tennis or golf. Drive around to see the varied topography and homes. Mainly, you just plain relax and adjust to the calm pace of island life.

Despite its lack of commerciality today and its onetime reputation as a refuge for pirates (Captain Kidd is reputed to have hidden treasure here), Shelter Island was founded by four merchants. They were in the business of supplying sugar from Barbados and found that the many white oak trees on the island could be used for making barrels. One of them, Nathanial Sylvester, built the first home here in 1652. The present manor house, the residence of a descendant, was constructed in 1773. Sylvester Manor became a haven for Quakers who had been driven out of Boston, and Friends groups still conduct services here regularly. They also gather each fall at the Quaker Cemetery on the outer boundary of the manor to remember those who brought their faith to Long Island. The 1852 windmill nearby was restored in 1952 as a memorial to Sylvester.

The Shelter Island Historical Society maintains a small museum of local history in Manhaset Chapel and has furnished the 1743 Havens House, where the Havens family lived for seven generations, as a House Museum. It is located on Route 114 about a mile from the South Ferry.

This is an interesting island to explore because the contours change so rapidly, from steep hills to flat valley to beach. If you arrive via the North Ferry from Greenport, you are within walking distance of the Victorian homes in an area called The Heights. This is pretty much the center of activity, the site of the Chequit Inn, with its veranda for gazing out at the sailboats that often race in Dering Harbor. A walk down the hill brings you to Bridge Street and the town, such as it is, where you'll find day-trippers over from the Hamptons.

If you keep to the right instead of going down Bridge Street from the Chequit, you pass a nine-hole public golf course and descend a steep hill to Crescent Beach, a major gathering spot for the island's resident tourists, with a motel and a couple of hotels in the vicinity. Back across town is the modern Dering Harbor Resort Complex overlooking the harbor. It is on Winthrop Road, which leads to the village of Dering Harbor, the smallest but perhaps the richest per capita municipality in the state—200 acres and 30 homes. Adjoining it is an area called Hay Beach, a subdivision of new homes, and the Gardiners Bay Country Club.

Two causeways lead to the more rugged terrain of Big and Little Ram Islands with Gardiners Bay on one side and calm Coecles Harbor on the other. Mashomack Preserve is to the south across the harbor. Once private, it is now a public preserve maintained by the Nature Conservancy. It abounds with saltwater marshes, forests, beaches, and wildlife. Guided tours are offered on some weekends; check the current schedule. Among the intriguing sights are the huge nests of osprey, the eagles of the sea, which can be spotted atop the poles in the preserve and on the Ram Island Causeway.

On the other side of Route 114 are two other residential areas: Shorewood, populated mostly by summer renters, and Silver Beach, a residential area along the waterfront.

Though the number of hotels is not large, there is a choice of atmosphere. Chequit Inn is a gingerbread Victorian circa 1870 and puts you in the middle of what action there is in town. Dering Harbor Inn is built motel-style with private terraces, a pool and tennis courts, and a busy harbor where many guests arrive by boat. The Pridwin is an old-time resort with a big porch, white wicker chairs in the lobby, and cabins for guests who prefer them. Senior citizens' groups like to come here in the off-season. There is a private beach plus pool, water skiing and sailing, and three tennis courts for guests, as well as such diversions as croquet, shuffleboard, and Ping-Pong. Then there is the delightful Ram's Head Inn, the prototype country inn, with 16 rooms. It is located way off by itself on one of the most scenic areas of the island, and has tennis, a private beach, and sailing.

Some very pleasant bed-and-breakfast homes have appeared in recent years. First choice is Beach House, which has water views and its own private beach. Stearns Point House is a spacious home set apart but within just a short walk from the beach, and the House on Chase Creek, a small nineteenth-century Dutch Colonial, lets you walk to the ferry and the action in town, such as it is.

By night, the Chequit has a piano bar, the Ram's Head Inn or the Pridwin may have music on weekends, and there is entertainment in a converted barn called Inn Between on North Ferry Road. So much for Shelter Island nightlife.

Most vacationers on the island don't come expecting nighttime action and are perfectly happy being active during the day and turning in early. The one peril is bad weather. But if the clouds do roll in, all you need do is board a ferry boat in either direction to find diversion. The north fork of Long Island is coming into its own as a destination, and Greenport gains more interesting antiques and crafts shops every year. There are also vineyards to be visited in this direction. Palmer and Pindar, both west of Greenport on Route 25, are among the choicest.

In the other direction lies Sag Harbor. The old whaling center is nicer when you can really walk around, but it is a pleasant port in all except a real storm.

Wear a slicker if need be, and take the short walking tour beginning on Main Street that leads you past the town's exceptional architecture that ranges from early Colonial saltbox to Greek Revival mansions that once belonged to wealthy sea captains. Go into one of the mansions, the home of the Suffolk County Whaling Museum, to see the big scrimshaw collection and many other relics of the town's early industry. Then visit the Old Custom House and the Whaler's Church with its hand-carved whaling motifs.

There are plenty of shops to browse through in town, and the American Hotel is the perfect old-fashioned spot for a drink and fancy dinner. A stop at the information center off Main will provide a map and all the guidance you need to plot your way through the little village.

If this is the tail end of the weekend, you can drive directly home from Sag Harbor. Otherwise, you can take the four-minute ferry ride back to Shelter Island and leave the rest of the world behind.

Shelter Island Area Code: 516

DRIVING DIRECTIONS Midtown Tunnel to I-495, Long Island Expressway, to exit 73, Riverhead. Turn right and take Route 58, Old Country Road, east for about two miles to the traffic circle. Continue east past Central Suffolk Hospital for about two more miles on 58 until it turns into Route 25. Continue to Greenport and watch for a large sign, SHELTER IS FY, west of the shopping area to guide you off Front Street (Route 25) onto Fifth Street going south. Turn left at Wiggins Street (Route 114) to the ferry landing. North Ferry Service runs from 5:40 A.M. to midnight; in July and August boats run every 15 minutes. Information, 749-0139. Continual shuttle service to North Haven and Sag Harbor via South Ferry runs from the southern end of Route 114, 6 A.M. to 1:45 A.M. in peak season. Information, 749-1200. *Total distance:* 102 miles

PUBLIC TRANSPORTATION Sunrise Express Bus Service from New York City to Shelter Island, 6 A.M. to 11:50 P.M., information (516) 477-1200, or Long Island Railroad to Greenport, information (718) 454-LIRR. No need for a car on Shelter Island if you stay near the North Ferry Station or ride a bike.

ACCOMMODATIONS Expect minimum stays in peak season. *Chequit Inn,* Shelter Island Heights, 11964, 749-0018, $$$; rooms in adjacent cottage, $$-$$$ • *Pridwin Hotel and Cottages,* Crescent Beach, Shelter Island, 11964, 749-0476, $$$-$$$$ • *Ram's Head Inn,* 108 Ram Island Drive, Shelter Island Heights, 11964, 749-0811, $$-$$$ CP (more expensive rooms have private baths) • *Dering Harbor Inn,* PO Box AD, Shelter Island Heights, 11964, 749-0900, $$$$-$$$$$ • *Beach House,* 90 Peconic Avenue, Silver Beach, 11964, $$-$$$ CP • *Stearns Point House,* Stearns Point Road, Shelter Island, 11964, 749-4379, $$$ CP • *House on Chase Creek,* 3 Locust Avenue, Shelter Island, 749-4379, $$-$$$ CP.

DINING *Chequit Inn* (see above), dinner entrées $$-$$$; delightful terrace dining $-$$ • *Ram's Head Inn* (see above), dinner entrées,

$$-$$$ • *The Dory,* Bridge Road, 749-8871, $$ • *The Harbor Room,* Dering Harbor Inn (see above), $$-$$$ • *The Cook,* 15 Grand Avenue, Shelter Island Heights, 749-2005, Caribbean decor and specialties, outdoor dining, $-$$$ • *Cogan's Country Restaurant,* Route 114, 749-0018, $$-$$$ • *Bob's Fish Market,* Route 114, 749-0830, no frills, fresh fish, $-$$ • *American Hotel,* Main Street, Sag Harbor, 725-3535, 1846 inn, fine food, local gathering place, $$-$$$.

SIGHTSEEING *Shelter Island Historical Society, Manhaset Chapel Museum, and Havens House,* Route 114. Hours: July and August, Saturday and Sunday noon to 4 P.M. Contribution • *Mashomack Preserve,* 749-1001. Nature walks and talks held on weekends; phone for current schedule • *Sag Harbor Whaling Museum,* Main Street, Sag Harbor, 725-0770. Hours: mid-May to September, Monday to Saturday 10 A.M. to 5 P.M., Sunday 1 to 5 P.M. Adults, $3; children $1 • *The Custom House,* Main and Garden streets, Sag Harbor, 941-9444. Hours: July and August, daily 10 A.M. to 5 P.M.; May, September to mid-October, weekends only. Adults, $1.50; children, $1.

FOR FURTHER INFORMATION Shelter Island Chamber of Commerce, Box 598, Shelter Island, NY 11964, 749-0399.

Concerts and Colonial Greens: Bedford and Caramoor

Bedford Village is a bit of New England transplanted to the New York suburbs—village green, white-steepled church, Colonial homes, and all.

Caramoor is a bit of the Mediterranean, a house-museum filled with treasures from European palaces set on 100 sylvan acres, with a Venetian theater that is the site of the most elegant kind of outdoor summer music festival.

Put them together and you have a gracious summer getaway not much more than an hour from home.

Those who liken Bedford to a New England village are not far wrong, for it was actually part of Connecticut when settled in 1680. A royal decree settled a border dispute by placing Bedford in Westchester County, where it prospered and became the county seat.

In the mid-1800s, when the railroad made the town more accessible to New York, Bedford's scenic beauty attracted wealthy families who built their country estates on the hilltops nearby and acquired the nickname of "hilltoppers." A local historian of the period noted kindly that the newcomers—many of them world-famous—were generally "unobjectionable." The estates still make for pleasant sightseeing along the country roads near town.

The buildings surrounding the village green were built after the Revolution, since most of the town was burned by the British in 1779. Bedford's early residents set out to replace each building on its original site. Most of the structures still stand, thanks to the unusually active Historical Society.

In 1916 when the Methodists stopped holding services in their aging church on the green, the church was bought at auction by someone who planned to convert it into apartments. An indignant band of citizens raised the money to buy the building back, repair it, and turn it into a community house. That was the beginning.

The 1787 Court House, the oldest public building in Westchester County, was restored to appear just as it did early in the last century when William Jay, son of the first chief justice, presided on the bench. On the second floor the Bedford Museum was built to trace 300 years of the town from its earliest Indian origins. One ticket covers a visit to this building and the restored one-room schoolhouse across the green.

Posted in front of the Court House is a printed walking tour of the village, a stroll that takes you past the Old Burying Ground (1681), the general store (1838), the post office (1838), the library (1807), and beautiful homes from the early 1800s.

One of the white-pillared structures once housed an A&P, which was an unusual link in the chain because the storefront was not painted red. The tradition-conscious owner made it a condition of the contract that the facade not be altered.

That building is now Bedford Green, a shop offering fine antiques. More small shops line Bedford's main street, and if you turn off to Court Road, and you'll find another small shopping enclave in charming Colonial homes.

Even trees are considered worth saving in preservation-minded Bedford. Take a drive just north of town on Route 22 to see a towering white oak estimated to be 500 years old. Somehow that tree became a symbol of the town's attachment to the past. The owner, Harold Whitman, deeded its ground to the town of Bedford in memory of his wife back in 1947, making it the Bedford Oak in truth as well as sentiment.

Of all our founding fathers, few filled so many high offices as John Jay. He served as president of the First Continental Congress, first chief justice, governor and chief justice of New York State, minister to Spain, and author of the Jay Treaty. The Jay Homestead, located a few miles farther north on Route 22, has been designated a state historic site. An enlarged 1787 farmhouse, it is part clapboard, part shingle, and part stone, a blend of both Hudson Valley and New England building traditions. It was still occupied by the family as late as 1954. Their presence is tangible.

The house has been restored to the Federal era when widower John, son William with his wife and young family, and two of William's older sisters were in residence. Interpreters take you through, telling the story of the home and its occupants. The family treasures and living history presentation give a unique dimension to the tours. Afterward visitors are welcome to explore the 64-acre grounds or to relax in the period gardens surrounding the house. Special events take place on the grounds all summer long, from a vintage auto show to puppetry for the kids.

Follow Route 22 south again and turn left onto Route 137 to reach Caramoor, a totally different kind of homestead. Best known for its Venetian theater, Caramoor was the country home of Walter Tower Rosen, a lawyer and investment banker. Mr. and Mrs. Rosen built their pink stucco Mediterranean villa amid acres of woodland and formal gardens, then filled it with treasures from European palaces and villas. In fact, they installed whole rooms, complete down to wall panelings, molded ceilings, and priceless wall coverings. Down the narrow vaulted hallway, behind heavy, carved wooden doorways, are rooms representing styles from fifteenth-century Gothic to sixteenth-century Renaissance to eighteenth-century neoclassical. Some are hung with silk and wallpaper painted in China in the eighteenth century.

You visit an intimate library from a chateau in southern France, a small room from a palace in Turin, an English pine-paneled chamber from a home in Dorsetshire, a French Regency sitting room, or a Jacobean bedroom. You'll come upon Pope Urban VIII's bed and a chair owned by Spain's Ferdinand and Isabella, along with the most extensive collection of needlepoint upholstery in the Western Hemisphere. The needlework, both French and Italian, is displayed in almost overwhelming profusion in an 80-foot music room, the ceiling of which was carved for a palace in Italy 400 years ago.

To enter the theater area, you pass through great black and gold wrought-iron gates acquired by Mr. Rosen in Switzerland. The stage of the Venetian theater is built around a set of pink marble columns that once stood in a fifteenth-century garden near Venice. On a moonlit night this is a magical setting for music.

Caramoor offers picnic tables in an apple grove near a grape arbor, or bring a blanket for an elegant picnic before the concert. Seating is on folding chairs, both in the main theater and in the Spanish courtyard where Sunday afternoon concerts are held. The music of these concerts varies from opera to symphony to chamber music; the season runs from late June through late August.

If you don't want to hear music on Sunday, you can take a drive to North Salem to one of Westchester County's most unexpected attractions, the Oriental Stroll Gardens at the Hammond Museum. There's no more serene setting for a summer stroll than these 15 formal Oriental landscapes where weathered tree trunks, weeping willows, dwarf fruit trees, flowering shrubs, artfully placed stones, moss and pebbles, reflecting pools, and a mirror-still lake blend to form a setting of rare tranquillity.

The Hammond's other special claim to fame is an elegant three-course luncheon service in a shaded flagstone courtyard centered by a fountain and dotted with cheerful red geraniums. It has been aptly compared to lunching in the French countryside.

The museum building itself is attractive, with a soaring beamed great hall. It calls itself a museum of the humanities, and exhibits range widely, from religious artifacts to modern art to places of entertainment to Mexican tapestries.

Another excellent place to see art is the Katonah Gallery, recently ensconced in its own new building. It holds six major exhibitions a year.

One final nearby attraction to note is Ward's Pound Ridge Reservation, a 4,600-acre park with some excellent hiking trails through the woods.

Lodgings in the area are strictly motel variety, unless you cross the line to nearby Ridgefield, Connecticut. Dining possibilities, however, will please the most finicky gourmet. Local favorites include the Inn at Pound Ridge, a restored farmhouse near the Bedford town line, and a host of highly rated French choices, including the Box Tree, a charming 1770 home in Purdy's; Le Château, a hilltop mansion, and L'Europe, with a highly regarded chef, both in South Salem; Thierry's Relais, a romanic hideaway in Bedford Hills; Bistrot Maxime in Chappaqua; and Maxime's in Granite Springs. The formal fare at Maxime's, Auberge Maxime in North Salem, The Arch in North Brewster, and La Crémaillère in Banksville are Manhattan class—with Manhattan prices. More moderate choices in Mt. Kisco include La Camelia, a Spanish restaurant with tasty tapas; Tuscan Oven for wood-fired brick oven pizza and other Italian specialties; and Kit 'N Caboodle, with old-fashioned decor, generous portions, and a menu that ranges from hamburgers to roast beef. Crabtree's Kittle House Restaurant, in a renovated Colonial home in Chappaqua, has been a favorite for years and offers nice golf-course views as well as excellent food. If you want to picnic at Caramoor, give a call to The Homemade Touch in Bedford Hills, and they'll whip up something elegant for you.

Westchester Area Code: 914

DRIVING DIRECTIONS Take the Hutchinson River Parkway north to the intersection of I-684, then north on 684 to Route 35, Katonah. Turn right and follow Route 22 south into Bedford Village; Caramoor is at the intersection of Route 137, about half a mile east of 22. *Total distance:* roughly 50 miles.

PUBLIC TRANSPORTATION Metro North often offers ''Caramoor Specials'' from New York on concert Saturdays. For information phone (212) 532-4900.

ACCOMMODATIONS *Ramada Inn,* Route 22, Armonk (south of Bedford), 10504, 273-9090, $$$ • *Holiday Inn,* Holiday Drive, Mount Kisco, 10549, 241-2600, $$ • Crabtree's Kittle House, 11 Kittle Road, Chappaqua, 666-8044, $$ CP • Also see Ridgefield, CT (page 146), about 20 minutes away.

DINING *The Inn at Pound Ridge,* Route 137, Pound Ridge, 764-5779, $$-$$$ • *Bistro 22,* Route 22, Bedford, 234-7333, $$-$$$ • *Thiery's Relais,* 352 North Bedford Road, Route 121, Bedford Hills, 666-9504, $$-$$$ • *La Camelia,* 234 North Bedford Road, Mount Kisco, 666-2466, $$-$$$ • *Kit 'N Caboodle,* 443 Lexington Avenue, Mount Kisco, 241-2440, $-$$ • *Crabree's Kittle House,* see above, $$-SSS • *The Arch,* Route 22, North Brewster, 279-5011, $$-$$$$ • *Tuscan Oven,* 360 North Bedford Road, Mt. Kisco Square Shopping Center, Mt. Kisco, 666-7711, $-$$ • *La Crémaillère,* four miles on right side from exit 31, Merritt Parkway, Banksville, 234-9647, $$$$ • *Box Tree,* Routes 22 and 116, Purdy's, 277-3677, $$$, or prix fixe, $$$$$ • *Le Château,* Route 35, South Salem, 533-6631, $$$-$$$$ • *L'Europe,* Route 123, South Salem, 533-2570, $$$ • *Auberge Maxime,* Ridgefield Road, Route 116, North Salem, 669-5450, $$-$$$ or prix fixe $$$$$ • *Maxime's,* Old Tomahawk Street, Granite Springs, 248-7200, prix fixe $$$$$ • For picnic dinners: *The Homemade Touch,* 25 Depot Plaza, Bedford Hills, 666-8222. (See also Ridgefield, CT, page 146.)

SIGHTSEEING *Bedford Museum,* Bedford Village, 234-9328. Hours: Wednesday to Sunday 2 to 5 P.M. Adults, $.75; children, $.25 • *John Jay Homestead State Historic Site,* Route 22, Bedford Village, 232-5651. Guided tours. Hours: mid-April to Labor Day, Wednesday to Saturday 10 A.M. to 4 P.M.; Sunday noon to 4 P.M., September and October, Wednesday to Sunday, noon to 4 P.M. Adults, $4; children, $2

• *Caramoor,* Route 137, PO Box R, Katonah, 232-5035. One-hour guided tours April to November. Hours: Thursday and Saturday 11 A.M. to 4 P.M.; Sunday 1 to 4 P.M. Adults, $5; children, $3; children under 10 not admitted. Write or call for summer music festival schedule and prices. • *Katonah Museum of Art,* Route 22 and Jay Street, Katonah, 232-9555. Hours: Tuesday to Friday and Sunday, 1 to 5 P.M., Saturday 10 A.M. to 5 P.M. Guided tours Tuesday, Thursday, and Sunday at 2:30 P.M. Free • *Ward Pound Ridge Reservation,* Route 121 at Route 35, Cross River, 763-3493. Hours: 9 A.M. to sunset. Parking: nonresidents, $2; residents, $1 • *Hammond Museum,* Deveau Road off Route 124, North Salem, 669-5135. Hours: April to December, Wednesday to Sunday 10 A.M. to 4 P.M.; rest of year, weekends only. Adults, $4; children, $3. Stroll Gardens open May to late October. Luncheon served May through September.

Crafts (Small and Otherwise) on the Connecticut Shore

Farm animals used to graze on the wide village green in Guilford, Connecticut. Colonial neighbors discussed the day's news under the shade of the trees, the local militia drilled here, and for a time the green even doubled as the local cemetery until someone decided such a central location really ought to be reserved for the livelier residents of the town.

The green remains the hub of Guilford centuries later, surrounded these days by shops instead of sheep. And come the middle of July each year, it is livelier than ever as it plays host to top craftsmen from all over New England: potters, weavers, glassblowers, smiths, carvers, and others who show their wares at the Guilford Handicrafts Exposition. Many are members of Guilford's excellent Handcraft Center.

Except for the annual big show held in Springfield, Massachusetts, this three-day affair is probably the area's biggest crafts exhibit. It is a perfect time to get acquainted with the quaint and historic towns that line the Connecticut shore from Guilford to Old Lyme.

Towns like Guilford, Madison, and Old Lyme owe their flavor more to their Colonial heritage than to their proximity to the Long Island Sound. They have long histories, many fine homes, some excellent small museums, and almost as an afterthought, proximity to the beach.

Most of the summer visitors here are people who own or rent the shingled cottages near the shore, so there is wonderfully little commercialism, yet there are some very appealing lodgings in the area. The Madison Beach Hotel has simple rooms and the grandest of views, right smack on the water. Water's Edge in Westbrook is a handsome hotel that also has water views, indoor and outdoor pools, tennis, a spa, and its own stretch of beach, and the elegant Saybrook Point Inn offers a scenic spot on the harbor and pools indoors and out. For inn lovers, Talcott House in Westbrook has the breezy, informal feel of a summer house and an unbeatable water view, while the nearby Captain Stannard House is cozily done up in Victorian decor.

And there are two real winners in Old Lyme. Whether you select the Bee and Thistle, an informal yellow Colonial house, or the Old Lyme Inn, an 1850s mansion with an elegant French menu in the dining room, you have a perfect base for exploring a very special little town. In fact, wherever you decide to stay, you may well want to begin your sightseeing in Old Lyme and work your way back to Guilford, saving the crafts for Sunday.

Old Lyme's entire wide, shaded main street lined with Colonial homes has been declared a historic district. One residence housed one of the nation's first art colonies. The columned Georgian mansion is known as Florence Griswold House for "Miss Florence," who put up and fed a group of painters, including Henry W. Ranger, Willard Metcalf, and Clark Voorhees. They eventually developed the "Ideal Lyme landscapes" that brought national attention to the area. The house is now headquarters for the Lyme Historical Society and contains paintings and panels left by the artists, an extensive china collection, and completely furnished period rooms such as the front parlor, circa 1830s, and the lady's bedroom from the early 1900s.

Next door the Old Lyme Art Association was founded in 1914 as a showcase for local artists and remains a prestigious gallery with changing exhibits of prominent current work.

Heading back down the coast, take time out for the picturesque harbor and excellent seafood restaurants in Old Saybrook. If you opt for an informal take-out lunch, you can sit outside on the docks and watch the boats go by.

Should you choose to spend Saturday afternoon at the beach, you can try two small beaches near Old Lyme off Route 156 (beach stickers required, available from the town hall on Lyme Street), or you can drive to Hammonasset, between Clinton and Madison (one mile south of I-95 exit 62), the largest Connecticut shoreline park. You'll still have to put up with the pebbles that are an unavoidable nuisance on Sound beaches, but the sand here stretches for two wide miles and the vistas of endless small boats offshore are a bonus.

Of course, if you choose a beachside lodging, all you have to do is come home for the afternoon.

If you want to see Madison's Allis-Bushnell House and Museum, you'll have to squeeze it in on Saturday between 1 and 4 P.M. It's a bit unusual for its corner fireplaces and its reproduction of a doctor's office from the early 1900s. There are also children's toys and costumes from the late 1700s to 1900s.

Even older is the Deacon John Grave House, circa 1685, where the hours are a bit more generous.

House tours or no, do take a drive down Madison's main and side streets and admire the handsome homes that are still private residences. This is also an ideal town for a shoreline drive to see those big rambling summer cottages.

Evenings are on the quiet side here—a long dinner, maybe a movie, or a local concert here and there. Ask at your inn what's happening currently.

On Sunday, take a slow drive back to Guilford on U.S. 1, detouring for some of the antiques stores along the way. When you get to the crafts exposition, pick and choose carefully among the dozens and dozens of exhibitors. Buying hastily can be a mistake because you never know what's waiting in the next tent. When you've bought your ceramic pitcher, goblets, carvings, or whatever, take time to see the three historic sites of Guilford.

This town boasts one of the oldest stone houses in the country, constructed around 1639 by the Reverend Henry Whitfield, founder of Guilford. It was built like a manor house in the English midlands that its owner used to call home, with a steeply pitched roof, small windows, and a great hall 33 feet long with a huge fireplace at either end. A partition in the middle hinged to a second-floor joist either turns the room into two or swings up to the ceiling out of the way. It's an unusually interesting house-museum and offers some exhibits of early crafts such as weaving and metalworking.

The Hyland House is also an early home, a 1600 saltbox with a "new" lean-to added about 1660. It is completely furnished as though a family could be living in it still, and has beautiful paneling and original hardware. Thomas Griswold House, circa 1735, is pretty enough to have once adorned a commemorative stamp, and is a repository for many of the historic artifacts of the town's long history.

If you like outlet bargains, you may want to continue beyond Guilford to Branford, where a new outlet center on Route 1 has shops for Chaus, Manhattan, Van Heusen, and American Tourister, among others. On the way you'll pass the Branford Craft Village at Bittersweet Farm on Route 1, where crafts are always on the agenda. Bishops Farm, south of Guilford, is a good spot to pick up fresh produce of the season, as is Hilltop Orchards in Branford.

One last possibility in Branford finally does take you out to sea. Legend has it that Captain Kidd visited the Thimble Islands offshore west of Guilford, and deposited his booty somewhere in the area when he fled the British in 1699. No one has found gold here yet, but a short cruise around the little-known islands does make for a rewarding and scenic tour. Take exit 56 off I-95 and follow signs to Stony Creek boats at Branford's Stony Creek dock make the trip regularly during the summer.

The most scenic way to navigate to Stony Creek from Guilford or Branford is via Route 146, which travels part way along the water. This a beautiful drive past lovely old homes, a worthwhile detour even if you haven't got time for the islands, and in Branford it will present you with some nice choices for a final seafood dinner at the marina section known as Indian Head.

Connecticut Area Code: 203

DRIVING DIRECTIONS Take I-95 to exit 70, Old Lyme; Guilford is at exits 57 to 59. *Total distance:* about 104 miles.

ACCOMMODATIONS *Bee and Thistle Inn,* 100 Lyme Street, Old Lyme, 06371, 434-1667, $$-$$$ • *Old Lyme Inn,* 85 Lyme Street, Old Lyme, 06371, 434-2600, $$$-$$$$ CP • *Madison Beach Hotel,* 94 West Wharf Road, Madison, 06443, 245-1404, $$-$$$ CP • *Water's Edge Inn and Resort,* 1525 Boston Post Road, Westbrook, 06498, 399-5901, out of state toll-free (800) 222-5901, $$$-$$$$ • *Captain Stannard House,* 138 South Main Street, Westbrook, 06498, 399-4634, $$ CP • *Talcott House,* 161 Seaside Avenue, Westbrook, 06498, 399-5020, $$ CP • *Saybrook Point Inn,* 2 Bridge Street, Old Saybrook, 06475, 395-2000 or toll free (800) 243-0212, $$$-$$$$ (check for special weekend packages).

DINING *Bee and Thistle Inn* (see above), $$-$$$ • *Old Lyme Inn* (see above), $$$ • *Dock and Dine,* Saybrook Point, Old Saybrook, 388-4665, good seafood with a harbor view, clam bar, $-$$$ • *Saybrook Fish House, 99* Essex Road, 388-4836, fish nets, wrapping paper for tablecloths, and the freshest seafood, $-$$ • *Saybrook Point Inn* (see above), elegant dining, $$-$$$ • *The Wharf,* Madison Beach Hotel (see above), fresh flowers, sea view, and mixed menu, $$-$$$ • *Friends & Company,* 11 Boston Post Road, Madison (on the Guilford line), 245-0462, informal, snacks or full meals, $-$$ • *Cafe Lafayette,* 725 Boston Post Road, Guilford 245-2380, Continental fare in a converted church, $$-$$$$ • *Bistro on the Green,* 25 Whitfield Street, Guilford, eclectic menu, $-$$ • *The Stone House,* Lower Whitfield Street, Guilford, 453-2566, restaurant and seafood market near the water, $$-$$$ • *Sachem Country House,* Goose Lane, Guilford, 453-5261, an eighteenth-century house, $$ • *Guilford Tavern,* 2455

Boston Post Road, Guilford, 453-2216, informal, $-$$ • *Lenny's Indian Head Inn,* 205 S. Montowese Street, Branford, 488-1500, seafood in a scenic part of town, $$ • U.S.S. Chowder Pot, 560 East Main Street, Branford, 481-2356, local landmark for seafood, $-$$.

SIGHTSEEING *Guilford Handicrafts Exposition.* For dates and this year's admission prices, contact the Guilford Handcraft Center, 411 Church Street, Guilford, CT 06437, 453-5947. Handcraft Center shop and gallery hours: Monday to Saturday 10 A.M. to 5 P.M., Sunday noon to 4 P.M. Free • *Henry Whitfield Museum,* Whitfield Street, Guilford, 453-2457. Hours: April through October, Wednesday to Sunday 10 A.M. to 5 P.M., rest of year to 4 P.M. Adults, $3; children 6–17, $1.50 • *Hyland House,* 84 Boston Street, Guilford, 453-9477. Hours: June to early September, open Tuesday to Sunday 10 A.M. to 4:30 P.M.; September to mid-October, Saturday and Sunday only. Adults, $2; children, $1.50 • *Thomas Griswold House*, 171 Boston Street, Guilford, 453-3176. Hours: mid-June to mid-September, Tuesday to Sunday, 11 A.M. to 4 P.M. Adults, $1; children, $.50; under 12, free • *Florence Griswold Museum,* 96 Lyme Street, Old Lyme, 434-5542. Hours: June to October, Tuesday to Saturday 10 A.M. to 5 P.M., Sunday 1 to 5 P.M.; rest of year, Wednesday to Sunday 1 to 5 P.M. Adults, $3; children under 12, free • *Lyme Art Association,* 90 Lyme Street, Old Lyme, 434-7802. Hours: May to mid-October, Tuesday to Friday noon to 5 P.M., Sunday from 1 P.M. Donation • *Lyme Academy of Fine Arts,* 84 Lyme Street, Old Lyme, 434-5232. Hours: Monday to Friday 9 A.M. to 4:30 P.M., weekends by appointment. Free • *Allis-Bushnell House,* 853 Boston Post Road, Madison, 245-4567. Hours: Thursday to Saturday, 1 to 4 P.M. Donation • *Deacon John Grave House,* 581 Boston Post Road, Madison, 245-4798. Hours: summer months, Wednesday to Friday, noon to 3 P.M., Saturday 10 A.M. to 4:30 P.M., Sunday noon to 4:30 P.M. $2 • *Thimble Island Cruises: Sea Mist II,* 64 Thimble Islands Road, Stony Creek Dock, Branford, 481-4841, or *Volsunga III,* PO Box 3284, Stony Creek Dock, Branford, 481-3345 • *Connecticut Sea Ventures,* PO Box 3302, Stony Creek Dock, Branford, 397-3921.

FOR FURTHER INFORMATION Connecticut River Valley and Shoreline Visitors Council, 393 Main Street, Middletown, CT 06457, 347-0028 or toll free (800) 486-3346.

Harmonious History in New Jersey

The Colonial dame, wearing a mobcap and a long homespun dress, was sweeping her front step. She smiled and nodded as we passed, as though this group in jeans and sneakers could have been just the Colonial family next door.

The village around her, too, seemed perfectly natural in its surroundings, a clearing next to the Morris Canal. Despite the visitors strolling its paths, it might have still been the settlement known as Andover Forge during the Revolutionary War.

Today it is called Waterloo Village and is a restoration consisting of more than 20 buildings along the canal in Stanhope, New Jersey. It isn't the biggest or most elaborate restoration you'll ever see, but there's something extraordinary about the place—a sense of entering a time warp and walking into the past. There is a church, a stagecoach inn, several houses and barns, a working gristmill, a smithy's shop, an apothecary shop, and a general store, all seemingly occupied by people going about their daily affairs. A potter works at his wheel, the smithy's hammer clangs, herbs are hung on the racks in the drying room at the apothecary.

You watch them at work, maybe chat as they dip the candles, weave the cloth, or grind the grain, and there you are, back in the past. There are no guides to break the illusion. It's a self-guided tour at your own pace, with plenty of time to pause under a tree or have a snack at a shady table outside or beneath the low beams of the tavern.

Stepping even further back in time, you can visit the newest part of the complex, Winakung, an authentic Lenape Indian village circa 1625, reconstructed on an island within the Waterloo Village complex.

This is a pleasant experience anytime, but come from May to October, there is double incentive to make the trip because Waterloo's annual Festival of the Arts fills the area with activity. On weekends, a whole range of special events are on the agenda, from crafts and antiques shows to a Civil War encampment and an annual Oktoberfest.

In the summer, the village concert tent and concert field host a wide range of musical events, from the Festival Symphony Orchestra to the Metropolitan Opera, John Denver to Ringo Starr. In spring 1994, ground was broken for a new performing arts center that will showcase a variety of programs.

Some very charming inns are in the Waterloo area. Right in Stanhope is the Whistling Swan, a gracious Victorian with a warm ambience that reflects the spirit of its friendly owners. Crossed Keys in

Andover is a nicely restored 1790 Colonial with working fireplaces and its original wide-board flooring.

The Inn at Millrace Pond in Hope is especially convenient if you want to spend some time enjoying the scenery and the great outdoors at the Delaware Water Gap National Recreation Area. The delightful, authentically furnished Colonial inn is part of a complex of historic buildings that includes a gristmill now transformed into a restaurant. Hope, a tiny town packed with history, merits a little walking tour on its own.

Another possibility is to head south and plan on Sunday in the Morristown area, where the Governor Morris Inn is an attractive hotel that offers an outdoor pool, lawn games, and bikes for guests. Morristown has many sightseeing attractions and good restaurants. The Bernards Inn in Bernardsville is known for its restaurant as well as its comfortable rooms.

Whatever your decision, reserve some time for driving around one of the wealthiest areas in New Jersey—or anywhere else, for that matter—the hunt country of Somerset and Morris counties. They rank themselves among the top 20 counties in wealth in the country, and you won't doubt it if you travel from Stanhope down Route 206 to Chester and on through towns like Far Hills, Peapack, Gladstone, Mendham, Liberty Corners, and Basking Ridge. The very heart of the area is south of Route 24 and north of I-78 and the very best addresses are south of Mendham.

Don't stick to the main roads. Try 525 or those wiggly lines on the map with no numbers to see the best estates of the horsey set. In the towns along the way you can explore the eclectic stores that occupy appropriately atmospheric Victorian houses. Antiques shops are legion, all along the way.

A few back roads, some sightseeing and shopping stops, and Waterloo Village make for a Saturday well spent, leaving you with a pleasant decision between history in Morristown and the great outdoors at the Delaware Water Gap on Sunday.

Morristown was actually the nation's military capital for a while, the site of Washington's headquarters and the main encampment of the Continental Army during the winter of 1779–80, when the general was fighting to rally and rejuvenate his starving, freezing, and sometimes mutinous forces. Morristown National Historical Park has three parts, each representing a different element of that crucial year.

The first, off Morris Avenue, is the museum, where you can see a color film about the area and exhibits of weapons and other pertinent artifacts. In front of the museum building is the Ford Mansion, the finest home in town in the 1770s, which was offered as headquarters to Washington and his wife by Mrs. Jacob Ford, a widow who obligingly moved with her four children into two rooms to create space for them. The house still has many of the original Ford furnishings.

Fort Nonsense, not far from the Morristown Green, got its name because no one could remember why soldiers had been obliged to work so hard to dig its trenches and embankments.

The actual Jockey Hollow encampment area is a few miles south of Morristown off Route 202. It contains typical log huts where the troops might have been quartered, as many as twelve to a shelter, plus the officers' huts, the parade ground where troops were drilled, and Wick Farm, a prosperous farm of the day used as headquarters for General Arthur St. Clair. It, too, retains some of its original furnishings. The area also includes a wildlife sanctuary with wooded hills, streams and flowers, and hiking trails.

There's more history to be tracked down in Morristown. Fosterfields Historical Farm is a turn-of-the-century ''living history farm'' with demonstrations of old-fashioned farming and a nineteenth-century Gothic revival home, The Willows, furnished to represent the period from 1880 to 1910. Acorn Hall, circa 1853, and headquarters of the Morris County Historical Society, also will delight lovers of both Victorian homes and gardens.

Historic Speedwell, a complex of nine buildings, has a unique background. It was the home and factory of Stephen Vail, who manufactured the engine for the first steamship that crossed the Atlantic. It was also the home of Vail's son, Alfred, who perfected the telegraph with Samuel Morse, demonstrating it publicly for the first time right here. The house has period furniture and there are various exhibits on engines and the history of the telegraph.

But how much can a person absorb on one summer afternoon? Perhaps you'd rather head for the Patriot's Path, a network of hiking and biking trails being developed along the banks of the Whippany River and across western Morris County. More than 20 miles are already in place between Speedwell Village, Jockey Hollow, and various other points.

Or you could take a stroll at the Frelinghuysen Arboretum, a 127-acre estate with rolling lawns, gardens, and stately trees in a traditional English park design. There are also nature trails here and the unusual fern configurations of a swamp area.

Best of all, head for the nature trails, waterfalls, and canoeing at the Delaware Water Gap, 70,000 acres of pristine woodland preserved by the National Park Service to provide a much-welcome wilderness respite for city dwellers. The area also has several interesting sites of its own, including a restored country village and a crafts village.

At the end of the day, you may want to look for just one more historic setting—a place to enjoy a fine dinner before you head home. A word to the wise: If you're in the mood for a splurge, dinner at Le Delice is worth a detour off Route 80 to Whippany.

New Jersey Area Code: 201

DRIVING DIRECTIONS To Waterloo Village, take I-80 to Route 206 (exit 25), drive north 2½ miles to Waterloo Road, then left another 2 miles to Waterloo Village. Watch for signs. Follow Route 206 south to Chester and Bernardville, Route 202 or 287 to Morristown, I-80 west to Delaware Water Gap. *Total distance:* 50 miles.

ACCOMMODATIONS *Whistling Swan Inn,* Box 791, 110 Main Street, Stanhope, 07874, 347-6369, $-$$ CP • *The Inn at Millrace Pond,* PO Box 359, Hope, 07844, (908) 459-4884, $$-$$$ CP • *Governor Morris Inn,* 2 Whippany Road, Morristown, 07960, 539-7300, $$$-$$$$ • *The Bernards Inn,* 27 Mine Brook Road, Bernardsville, (908) 766-0002, $$$-$$$$.

DINING *Black Forest Inn,* Route 206, Stanhope, 347-3344, fine German food in a turn-of-the-century stone house, $$ • *The Old Morris Canal,* 2 Walton Place, Stanhope, 347-9434, northern Italian, $-$$ • *The Chequers,* Route 183, Stanhope, 347-3777, pub fare, $-$$ • *Silver Springs Farm,* Drakestown Road, Flanders (south of Stanhope), 584-6660, country French, very popular, reserve ahead, $$$ • *Ron's Landmark,* 85 Main Street, Netcong, 347-9853, informal Italian, family-run, $ • *Inn at Millrace Pond* (see above), American, Continental, $$-$$$ • *Grand Cafe,* 42 Washington Street, Morristown, 540-9444, chic French, $$$ • *Khiva,* 11 South Street, Morristown, 267-4427, off-beat, Mongolian barbecue and American specialties, interesting sauces, popular locally, $$-$$$ • *Pierre's,* 26 Washington Street, Morristown, 539-7171, French bistro, $$ • *Settebello,* 2 Cattano Avenue, Morristown, 267-3355, popular Italian, $-$$ • *Calaloo Café,* 190 South Street, Morristown, 993-1100, informal, American menu, burgers to Cajun, $-$$ • *Llewellyn Farms,* Routes 10 and 302, Morris Plains, 538-4323, American, $$-$$$$ • *The Bernards Inn* (see above) • *Girafe,* 95 Morristown Road (Route 202), Basking Ridge, (908) 221-0017, Continental, $$$-$$$$ • *Le Delice,* 302 Whippany Road, Whippany, 884-2727, fine French, $$$$-$$$$$ • *Dennis Foy's Townsquare*, 6 Roosevelt Avenue, Townsquare Mall, Chatham, 701-0303, noted Manhattan chef gets highest marks, $$$.

SIGHTSEEING *Waterloo Village,* Waterloo Road off Route 206, Stanhope, 347-0900. Hours: mid-April to October, Tuesday to Sunday 10 A.M. to 6 P.M., November to December, 10 A.M. to 5 P.M. Weekend admission: adults, $8; children, $4. Weekdays: adults, $6.50; children,

$4. Concerts vary in price; phone for current schedule and prices • *Morristown National Historical Park,* Morris Avenue, Morristown, 539-2085. Hours: daily 9 A.M. to 5 P.M. Adults, $2 (paid at Historical Museum for all sights); under 16, free • *Speedwell,* 333 Speedwell Avenue, Morristown, 540-0211. Hours: April to October, Thursday and Friday noon to 4 P.M., Saturday and Sunday 1 to 5 P.M. Adults, $3; children 6–16, $1 • *Frelinghuysen Arboretum,* Whippany Road (entrance from East Hanover Avenue), Morristown, 326-7600. Hours: grounds open daily dawn to dusk. Free • *Acorn Hall,* 68 Morris Avenue, Morristown, 267-3465. Hours: March to December, Thursday 11 A.M. to 3 P.M., Sunday 1:30 to 4 P.M. Adults, $2, children, $.50. Gardens open daily until dusk. Free • *Fosterfields Farm,* Route 24 and Kahdena Road, Morris Township, 326-7645. Hours: April to October, grounds open Wednesday to Saturday 10 A.M. to 5 P.M., Sunday 1 to 5 P.M.; house open Thursday to Sunday, 1 to 4:30 P.M. Grounds free weekdays; Saturday and Sunday, adults $3, children $2. Additional fee for house tours. • *Delaware Water Gap National Recreation Area,* I-80 at New Jersey–Pennsylvania border, (717) 588-2435. Free. The information station at Kittatinny Point exit, New Jersey, is open April to October daily, the rest of year Friday to Sunday only. For a complete schedule of park activities, write to Superintendent, Delaware Water Gap, Bushkill, PA 18324.

Stone-House Hunting in Ulster County

It may seem an unlikely place to look for the past. First there are the fast-food signs, then the funky shops filled with students from the local college. But drive on to the end of Main Street (just before the bridge) and make a right turn—and the clock turns back 300 years.

A national historic landmark that celebrated its tercentennial in 1978, Huguenot Street is the oldest street in America with its original homes intact. The sturdy, steep-roofed stone houses on the block, their Old World architecture unique to New Paltz and its Ulster County environs, still evoke the feel of a rural European village as they did for the homesick French Huguenot families who built them so long ago.

The houses are an unusual start to a weekend of beautiful back roads Ulster County scenery and a visit to one of America's unique hotels, Mohonk Mountain House.

The settlers of New Paltz were a small band of Huguenot families from Flanders villages. Fleeing from the religious persecution of Louis XIV, they first moved to the Rheinland Pfalz, or Palatinate, in Germany. Eventually they emigrated to America and the Dutch settlements of Kingston (then known as Wiltwyck) and Hurley in the Hudson River Valley. In 1677 a dozen of these families banded together to buy from the Indians their own tract of land beside the Wallkill River. They named it New Paltz for the Rheinland Pfalz.

Happy to have found a safe haven at last, the Huguenots moved onto their land in the spring of 1678 and there they put down firm roots. Although their homes were enlarged as new generations grew and prospered, five of the first six houses on the street remained virtually unchanged for 250 years and were occupied by descendants of the original builders.

Even today many names of those original settlers—Deyo, Bevier, Elting, DuBois, and Hasbrouck—remain prominent in New Paltz life. In the 1950s these families were largely responsible for forming the Huguenot Historical Society to begin buying and restoring the earliest homes. Each house museum is supported by a family association of descendants.

A tour of the homes begins at Deyo Hall on Broadhead Avenue, half a block off Huguenot Street. Here, displays give visitors some insight into the history of the area. An excellent introduction is the Jean Hasbrouck Memorial House, whose steep, shingled roof, great chimney, and jambless fireplace have earned it a citation as the most outstanding example of medieval Flemish stone architecture in America. The gigantic internal chimney is one of the only originals of its kind in existence. Many of the furnishings, including the tavern table, Hudson Valley rush-bottom chairs, Dutch *kaas* (chests), and a cradle, belonged to the Hasbrouck family prior to 1700.

In the Abraham Hasbrouck House, unusual family heirlooms include an English four-panel chest that commemorated a 1609 marriage. There's also a rare seventeenth-century Dutch writing table with mother-of-pearl inlay and a cozy Dutch bed hidden behind paneled doors. The pride of this house is the mammoth medieval fireplace in the central "room of seven doors." As in most of the homes, you can still see much of the original woodwork, huge beams, and wide floorboards.

The two Hasbrouck houses, along with the equally interesting Hugo Freer and Bevier-Elting houses, represent living styles from the town's earliest days. The LeFevre House, built in 1799 with three stone walls and a front of brick, marks a transition to the Federal period on the street. Deyo House, dating from 1692, was remodeled in the 1890s into an elegant Edwardian residence.

Also on the street are two churches. A careful reconstruction of the

1717 French Church has been placed next to the original Huguenot Burying Ground. The 1839 red brick Dutch Reformed Church is a sign of the growing influence of Dutch neighbors on the Huguenots.

If you want still more Huguenot history, head four miles south on Route 32 to Locust Lawn, the other Huguenot Society property in the area. Built by Josiah Hasbrouck in 1814, this Federal-style house reflects the owner's travels to Washington and Virginia, and its furnishings are a textbook example of period decoration, from Queen Anne to early Victorian. Also nearby is the Terwilliger Home, where the Hasbroucks lived until Locust Lawn was completed. Many consider this appealing home their favorite of all the stone houses.

Just west of Locust Lawn, 20 acres of woodland, thicket, and pond have been set aside as a wildlife sanctuary. Nature trails through the area may be reached from the entrance on Jenkinstown Road.

There's more spectacular nature awaiting, however, six miles west of New Paltz at Mohonk Mountain House. This absolutely huge old-fashioned Victorian fantasy of towers and turrets is wrapped around one end of a natural marvel, a mountain lake atop the Shawangunk Mountains. The dark blue, 60-foot-deep, springfed lake lies in a small fault running across the main line of the mountain, surrounded by cliffs—a truly spectacular sight.

It was the natural beauty of this place, 1,200 feet high, that captivated the Smiley twins, Alfred and Albert, in 1869. Albert bought up 300 acres and a rundown tavern for $28,000, mortgaging his future in the process, while Alfred stayed at his teaching job to bring in some much needed cash. To add more to their income, the Smileys opened a ten-room hotel on their property in 1870—with drinking, smoking, dancing, and cards outlawed by its Quaker owners.

More than 100 years later, Mohonk still belongs to the Smiley family. It has grown to 305 rooms; the grounds now total 7,500 acres (5,000 of them in protected undeveloped land known as the Mohonk Trust); and there are award-winning gardens, a clifftop lookout tower to make the most of the view, artificial lakes, 30 miles of bridle trails, an 18-hole golf course and putting green, miles of gorgeous hiking trails, and tennis. There is still no bar and no smoking in the dining room, though drinks are allowed now at dinner or in your room. People come regardless of restrictions, for this remains a magnificent natural retreat, with special programs from hiking to choral singing to swing dancing all through the year.

You can happily spend a weekend or more at Mohonk, or you can stay in a nearby bed-and-breakfast and come as a day guest, paying admission to enjoy hiking in the woods, strolling the gardens, or taking out one of the horses for hire at the stable. If you have a meal in the dining room, there is no admission charge to the grounds.

Continue driving to the end of the Mohonk Road and you'll reach High Falls, a tiny town with one of the Hudson Valley's classic restaurants, the Dupuy Canal House, a historic stone structure that was once a lively tavern back in 1797. The old Delaware and Hudson Canal passed through High Falls. In a tiny and charming museum in an old church you can see replicas of the canal boats, panoramas of the canal and the adjoining towpath, and fascinating miniature dioramas of early life in High Falls.

There are a couple of unique shops in High Falls, such as the Bird Watcher's Country Store, stocking everyting for the bird lover including an art gallery. This is choice antiquing territory, as well. The Tow Path House by the D & H Canal should be able to supply a free current guide to all nearby shops published by the Antiques Dealers Association of Ulster County.

It's also choice back-roads country, the kind of area to just get lost on the side roads admiring the quaint stone houses and farms and the unspoiled Ulster County scenery.

One pleasant drive west on Route 213 brings you to Stone Ridge and more antiques shops, including The Thumb Print, in a picturesque old barn, and Elm Rock, a 1780 showplace with a large selection of furniture and collectibles.

Continue north on Route 209 to Hurley, site of the first Huguenot settlements in the county, and you'll see stone houses still occupied, transformed into attractive homes for today.

If you have more time, continue to Kingston, New York's first capital, with historical sites and museums, Hudson River cruises from the Rondout area, and its own store of stone houses. Or head up Route 28 and 375 to Woodstock, the artists' colony that is chockablock with intriguing shops.

Note that the Ulster County Fairgrounds in New Paltz hosts an annual Woodstock–New Paltz Crafts Fair on Memorial Day and Labor Day weekends, and a county fair each year in August.

Antiquers may want to head south from New Paltz along Route 208, driving past all farms that invite you to stop and pick your own produce, and into Gardiner. On Route 44-55 in the center of the village is the Country Store Antique Center, a collective that is filled with all manner of antiques and collectibles.

On the same road about two miles west of Gardiner is Widmark Honey Farms, with tours of the apiaries, animals that can be petted, honey tasting, and a store where you can stock up on honey. Last but far from least, there are performing black bears.

Finally, if you save your appetite and reserve in advance, you can enjoy an old-fashioned Italian luncheon feast at the Magnanini Winery, farther south and east in Wallkill. The dining room overlooking the vineyards comes complete with accordian music. Guaranteed, it's the closest you'll come to Italy in New York State.

Ulster County Area Code: 914

DRIVING DIRECTIONS George Washington Bridge to Palisades Parkway to exit 9N, New York Thruway to exit 18, New Paltz. Turn left onto Route 299, which becomes Main Street, then right onto Huguenot Street just before the river. *Total distance:* 85 miles.

ACCOMMODATIONS *Mohonk Mountain House,* Mohonk Road, New Paltz, 12561, 255-1000 or (800) 772-6646, $$$$$ AP (Inquire about many special weekends for nature lovers, photographers, tennis players, music fans—even fans of mystery novels.) There are many delightful bed-and-breakfast inns in this area. (For a complete list write to Ulster County Public Information Office, address below.) Here are some of the best: *Captain Schoonmaker's,* Route 213, Box 37, High Falls, 12440, 687-7946, 1760 stone house, canopy beds, some working fireplaces, waterfall on the grounds, charming, $$ CP • Baker's B&B, RD 2, Box 80, Stone Ridge, 12484, 687-9795, 1780 stone farmhouse on 16 acres, $$ CP • *Hasbrouck House Inn,* PO Box 76, Stone Ridge, 12484, 687-0736, 1757 estate manor house, pool, $$ CP • *Jingle Bell Farm,* 1 Forest Glen Road, New Paltz, 12561, 255-6588, delightful 1766 farmhouse, $$ CP • *Nieuw Country Loft,* 41 Allhusen Road, New Paltz, 12561, 255-6533, authentically restored 1740 Dutch stone house, country decor, $$ CP.

DINING *Dupuy Canal House,* Route 213, High Falls, 687-7700, great atmosphere, prix fixe $$$; cabaret entertainment on many weekends, small admission charge • *Northern Spy Cafe,* Route 213, High Falls, 687-7298, small pleasant cafe in an old house, American menu, $-$$ • *Egg's Nest,* Route 213, High Falls, 687-7255, local hangout for informal dining, $ • *The Locust Tree Inn,* 215 Huguenot Street, New Paltz, 255-7888, an old stone house in convenient location, Continental menu, lunch $, dinner $-$$$ • *Loup Garou,* 46 Main Street, New Paltz, 255-2536, interesting, eclectic menu, $$ • *Magnanini Vineyard and Restaurant,* 501 Straw Ridge Road, Wallkill, 895-2767, six-course Italian feast by reservation only, Saturday at 7 P.M., Sunday at 1 P.M. six courses prix fixe, $$$$. Open April through December.

SIGHTSEEING *Huguenot Street,* New Paltz, 255-1600. Hours: June through September, Wednesday to Sunday 9:30 A.M. to 4 P.M. 2¼-hour guided tours at 9:30 A.M. and 1:30 P.M. Adults: $6; children, $3; 1¼ hour tours, $3.50 per person, individual houses, $2.50 •

Delaware and Hudson Canal Museum, Mohonk Road, High Falls, 687-9311. Hours: Late May through Labor Day, Thursday to Monday 11 A.M. to 5 P.M., Sunday 1 to 5 P.M.; May, September, and October, weekends only. Donation • *Widmark Honey Farms,* Route 44-55, Gardiner, 255-6400. Hours: daily 10 A.M. to 6 P.M. Admission charged April to October, $2 weekdays, $3 weekends, with the money deducted from your purchase. • *Ulster County Fair,* held annually in August at New Paltz fairgrounds. Dates available from Ulster County Information Office • *Woodstock–New Paltz Arts and Crafts Fair,* held annually both Memorial Day and Labor Day weekends at fairgrounds, information from Quail Hollow Events, PO Box 825, Woodstock, 12498, 679-8087. For Woodstock sightseeing, see pages 152–153.

FOR FURTHER INFORMATION Ulster County Public Information Office, 244 Fair Street, PO Box 1800, Kingston, NY 12401, 331-9300, or New Paltz Chamber of Commerce, 257½ Main Street, New Paltz, NY 12561, 255-0243.

Weekending with the Boston Symphony

Is there anybody out there who doesn't know about Tanglewood?

The summer home of the Boston Symphony has been one of the most popular destinations in the Northeast ever since the concerts began in 1936. The 6,000 seats in the open-air shed are often sold out, and as many as 10,000 more people may be found on the lawn, spreading wicker baskets and wine bottles on blankets and settling back to enjoy a symphony concert under the stars.

Some people like the lawn even better on Sunday afternoon, when you can really appreciate strolling the 210 acres of William Aspinwall Tappan's former estate, viewing the formal gardens and the re-creation of the red house where Nathaniel Hawthorne worked, no doubt inspired by the beauty around him. The view of lake and mountains from the main house (now the administration building) is magnificent.

Does Tanglewood even need mentioning here, especially since the Berkshires come up again for other reasons in fall and winter? The answer is *yes,* since the fare of music as well as dance and theater is so rich in the summer that plans for a weekend seem in order, if only to inspire those who haven't gotten around to making the trip.

For first-timers, then, a word is in order about tickets and accommodations. As for tickets, lawn seats are always available, but write ahead to Tanglewood or watch for the very first ad that appears in the Sunday *New York Times* to order tickets if you want to be sure of reserved seating for the concert of your choice. For accommodations, the list is long and there are many terrific choices, everything from an Italian villa to simple country inns, with dozens of motels in between. You must make reservations several months ahead for the choicest of the inns, and even the motels may require you to stay a minimum of three nights. There are few bargains here with so much demand.

On warm summer days, it helps to have a pool nearby, so my first pick of inns provides this nice extra. At the delightful Apple Tree Inn, a 22-acre antiques-filled hilltop retreat, the pool as well as the many-windowed gazebo dining room come with soaring mountain views. This inn is also conveniently set near a gate to Tanglewood.

Weathervane Inn in South Egremont and Williamsville Inn in West Stockbridge are both country hostelries with antiques, warmth, and that all-important pool. The Applegate in Lee has the feel of a Southern mansion transplanted to New England, Brook Farm Inn in Lenox offers Colonial charm, poetry readings and concerts, and the Roeder House, a restored 1856 Federal farmhouse, is unbeatable for fine furnishings and good taste. If money is no object, you can live like a king at Blantyre, a veritable hilltop castle, or Wheatleigh, which shows you the good life as enjoyed by the contessa who once owned this villa.

In addition to these, a number of old mansions turned inn in Lenox offer spacious and gracious quarters, and there are other possibilities in Lee and Stockbridge, including the Red Lion, the granddaddy of all the inns, where everyone who is anyone shows up sooner or later.

Now that you have the basics, here's a quick rundown on some of the attractions you have to choose among, in addition to planning a night and/or afternoon at the symphony. In Becket, the Jacob's Pillow Dance Festival, the oldest such event in America, takes place in a rustic 100-acre setting in a barn named for its founder, Ted Shawn. The whole gamut of modern dance is performed here over the summer. Come early for free previews of works in progress, a guided tour of the grounds, or a picnic in a wooded glen. Dining is also available in a cafe under the tent.

The Berkshire Theater Festival in Stockbridge, housed in a building designed in 1886 by Stanford White, was only the second summer theater in the nation when it began performances in 1928. Now there's top-grade summer stock here in the Mainstage, and avant-garde new American plays at The Unicorn, where there are special events and children's matinees in the courtyard.

If drama is a special interest, don't overlook the excellent Williamstown Theater Festival, which has done some experimental productions that attracted much critical acclaim.

The Bard is the thing at Shakespeare & Company; the productions are staged in a natural amphitheater on the grounds of The Mount, Edith Wharton's former estate high above Laurel Lake. There are many plays alternating, and you can picnic on the lovely grounds. The house itself is open for daytime tours. Adaptations of Wharton novels and short stories are performed in the salon.

Aston Magna presents baroque concerts during July at St. James Church in Great Barrington, the Berkshire Opera offers weekend performances at the Cranwell Estate in Lenox, and the Berkshire Choral Festival brings choral masterpieces to the concert shed on the campus of the Berkshire School in Sheffield.

You won't have a lot of time to worry about sightseeing, especially if you have sunshine during the day and a pool or a pond at your disposal. A couple of possibilities for lake swimming are Pontcosuc Lake in Pittsfield, York Lake in New Marlboro, and Beartown State Forest near Great Barrington.

Save a little time for a drive around and a walk through both Lenox and Stockbridge—the former a town that was the summer mountain retreat for millionaires in its heyday, the latter a picture-book New England town immortalized by resident Norman Rockwell in his paintings. The impressive Norman Rockwell Museum on estate lands just outside town will give you new appreciation for Rockwell's skills as an artist and chronicler of the changing life-styles of America. The grounds offer soaring views of the Berkshires.

The museum is a haven if the clouds roll in. You might also consider Saturday and Sunday matinees at the various theaters in the area, or go shopping in West Stockbridge, or antiquing in Sheffield, or visit the marvelous Clark Art Institute in Williamstown. If you need further suggestions, check the attractions mentioned in the fall and winter Berkshire itineraries on pages 147 and 230.

You'll probably make plans to come back, because if a Berkshires weekend proves anything, it's that you really can't get too much of a good thing.

Berkshire Area Code: 413

DRIVING DIRECTIONS Saw Mill River Parkway north to the Taconic Parkway to the New York State Thruway Berkshire Spur (Route 90), then east to exit 2. Follow Route 102 to U.S. 20 into Lenox. Tanglewood is on West Street, Route 183 in Lenox. *Total distance:* 153 miles.

PUBLIC TRANSPORTATION Amtrak serves Pittsfield, toll free (800) USA-RAIL; Bonanza Bus Lines services much of the Berkshire area, (800) 556-3815. You might be able to stay close enough to walk to Tanglewood, but it is difficult to get around to other places without a car.

ACCOMMODATIONS Rates given are for weekends in July and August concert season and foliage season. All rates are less on weekdays and during September, and much less after October. All inns have minimum stays in season. *Apple Tree Inn,* 224 West Street, Lenox, 01240, 637-1477, $$-$$$$ CP (less expensive rooms are in a modern lodge on the grounds) • *Brook Farm Inn,* 15 Hawthorne Street, Lenox, 01240, 637-3013, $$-$$$$ CP • *Birchwood Inn,* 7 Hubbard Street, Lenox, 01240, (800) 524-1646 spacious historic house with canopy beds, handsome garden, $$-$$$$ CP • *Cliffwood Inn,* 25 Cliffwood Street, Lenox, 01240, 637-3330, Belle Epoque showplace, breakfast on the veranda overlooking the grounds, $$$-$$$$ CP • *Walker House,* 74 Walker Inn, Lenox, 01240, 637-1271, art-filled, off-beat, and interesting, $$-$$$$ CP • *Garden Gables Inn,* 141 Main Street, Lenox, 01240, 637-0193, cozy, Colonial decor, big pool, $$-$$$$ CP • *Merrell Tavern,* Route 102, Main Street South Lee, 01260, 243-1794, authentically restored 1800 stagecoach inn, $$-$$$$ CP • *Chambery Inn,* Main and Elm streets, Route 20, Lee, 01238, 243-2221, restored schoolhouse in the village, big rooms, $$-$$$$ CP • *Applegate Bed and Breakfast,* 279 West Park Street, Lee, 01238, 243-4451, $$$-$$$$ CP • *Williamsville Inn,* Route 41, West Stockbridge, 01266, 274-6118, $$-$$$ CP • *The Roeder House,* Route 183, Stockbridge, 01262, 298-4015, $$$-$$$$ CP • *Weathervane Inn,* Route 23, South Egremont, 01258, 528-9580, $$$$$ MAP • *The Red Lion Inn,* Main Street, Stockbridge 10262, 298-5545, $$$-$$$$ • *Staveleigh House,* Route 7, Sheffield, 229-2129, ideal for antiquers, good value for all, $$ CP. The top of the line: *Blantyre,* Route 20, Lenox, 01240, 298-3806, impressive 1902 manor, pool, tennis, $$$$$ • *Wheatleigh,* West Hawthorne Road, Lenox, 01240, 637-0610, elegant villa, nicely refurbished, $$$$$.

DINING *Wheatleigh* (see above), Continental, prix fixe, $$$$$ • *Blantyre* (see above), prix fixe, $$$$$ • *Williamsville Inn* (see above), Continental, lovely dining room, excellent, $$-$$$ • *The Old Mill,* Route 23, South Egremont, 528-1421, restored gristmill, long a local favorite, $$-$$$ • *Federal House,* Route 102, South Lee, 243-1824, Continental, $$-$$$ • *Gateways Inn,* 71 Walker Street, Lenox, 637-2532, Continental, $$$-$$$$ • *Church Street Café,* 69 Church Street, Lenox, 637-2745, excellent bistro, $$ • *Café Lucia, 90* Church

Street, Lenox, 637-2640, Italian, $$-$$$ • *The Dakota,* Route 7, Lenox/Pittsfield line, 499-7900, informal, fun, popular, $-$$ • *Apple Tree Inn* (see above), Continental with an Italian accent, $$-$$$ • *Lenox 218,* 218 Main Street (Route 7A), Lenox, 637-4218, Continental, $$-$$$ • *La Bruschetta,* 1 Harris Street, West Stockbridge, 232-7141, Italian, $$-$$$ • *The Old Inn on the Green,* Route 57, New Marlborough, 229-3131, worth the drive for five-course dinners in an eighteenth-century dining room, by reservation only, prix fixe $$$$$ • *The Red Lion Inn* (see above), New England fare, $$-$$$ • *The Painted Lady,* 285 South Main Street, Great Barrington, 528-1662, Northern Italian, $$-$$$ • *Elm Court Inn,* Route 71, North Egremont, 528-0325, good reviews, $$-$$$. For lunch, in Stockbridge try *The Café* in the Mews around the corner from The Red Lion; and in West Stockbridge, *Shaker Mill Tavern,* which also has light supper fare and entertainment. For Tanglewood picnics, call *Cheesecake Charlie's,* 637-3411.

SIGHTSEEING Check all for current schedules, ticket prices, and starting times. *Tanglewood,* West Street (Route 183), Lenox, 637-1940; before June, (617) 266-1492. Tickets also available from Ticketmaster, (212) 307-7171; Concerts: July and August • *Jacob's Pillow Dance Festival,* off Route 20 on George Carter Road, Becket, 243-0745, late June to August • *Shakespeare & Company,* The Mount, Route 7, Lenox, 637-3353, season late May through mid-December • *Berkshire Choral Festival,* Berkshire School, Sheffield, 229-3522, July and August • *Berkshire Theater Festival,* Main Street, Stockbridge, 298-5576, late June to early September • *Williamstown Theater Festival,* Park and Main (intersection of Routes 7 and 2), Williamstown, 597-3400, July and August • *Aston Magna Foundation,* PO Box 1035, Great Barrington, 528-3595, July to early August • *Berkshire Opera Company,* 17 Main Street, Lee, 243-1343 • *Berkshire Public Theater,* 30 Union Street, Pittsfield, 445-4634, performances year round.

FOR FURTHER INFORMATION Lenox Chamber of Commerce, Lenox Academy Building, 75 Main Street, Lenox, MA 01240, 637-3646, for general local information and lodging referral service; Berkshire Visitors Bureau, The Common, Pittsfield, MA 02101, 443-9186 or toll free (800) 237-5747 (BERKSHIR) outside MA, for information and free guide to the entire area.

Rhode Island's Unsung Shoreline

It was Sunday noon on a mid-July weekend, and all was right with the world at Weekapaug Beach—hot sun, ocean breeze, cloudless sky, and beach blankets spaced in a discreet checkerboard to allow everyone a patch of privacy to enjoy it all.

It is a scene repeated many times along 25 miles of sandy shoreline edging the area officially labeled Washington County but affectionately known to everyone in Rhode Island only as "South County." The county's five state parks, spaced between Westerly and Point Judith, draw their full share of sun worshipers, but the town beaches in between have plenty of room for all (by New York standards, at least). And so does this relatively unheralded vacation area.

South County doesn't ape the chicness of the Hamptons or the quaintness of Cape Cod. It's a down-to-earth, wide-open area with a couple of nice inns, a scattering of adequate motels, a smattering of small towns, lots of nature preserves and fishing grounds, and just enough shops to fill the bill on a rainy day. There's little traffic, less serious hassle—and few better places for a truly relaxing weekend.

Westerly, population 14,497, is the hub of the western end of the county, and within the bounds of Westerly township is a variety of accommodations that should suit almost anyone. One of the best choices is Shelter Harbor Inn, about four miles out of town, an informal restored country farmhouse and barn that offers seclusion, a pleasant sun deck, a tennis court, big full breakfast included in the rates, and guest passes to that delightful residents-only beach at Weekapaug.

Weekapaug Inn is quite another matter; it is a handsome, weathered, shingled summer place that has been run by the same family for three generations and has had some of its guests for almost as long. Here you'll find rockers on the porch, beautiful grounds with a water view, bowling on the lawn, tennis, sailing, golf privileges, and a private beach. It's expensive and has the atmosphere of a private club.

West of Weekapaug are two beaches that are poles apart. Misquamicut is a state beach, crowded with roller rink, water slide, seafood stands, tavern, discos, and all the other amusements of a slightly tacky beach area. Nevertheless, on one end is the nicest beachfront accommodation on the shore, a motel called the Pleasant View Inn.

Farther on, on a spit with Little Narragansett Bay on one side and the ocean on the other, is Watch Hill, an enclave of big Victorian homes and old wealth. But you can't exactly categorize Watch Hill. The shops here include expensive antiques and exclusive stores, but there are also souvenir places, a wonderful old used bookstore called the Book and Tackle Shop, and a very plain restaurant that is a local institution called the Olympia Tea Room.

The street runs directly across from the harbor so one of the major events of the day here is watching the sun go down over the masts of the sailboats. Park benches are thoughtfully provided. The oldest carousel in the country is at the end of the block, with horses hung on chains, and it fills the street at night with music to serenade strollers out for a homemade ice cream cone or fresh buttered popcorn.

Mansions notwithstanding, there's nothing forbidding about Watch Hill—it's a delightful place despite the fact that the lodgings are not the greatest. The huge old wooden Ocean House, the last remaining grand hotel, has seen better days. Hartley's Guest House also seems a bit down at the heels, but it has a great location between Main Street and the ocean beach. (The latter is free, reached by a craggy, hidden path; the bay beach charges admission.) The best bet is Watch Hill Inn, also an easy walk to the ocean beach, with simply furnished rooms and a front deck on the harbor that is the best spot in town for cocktails and sunset watching.

Among the bed-and-breakfast homes found along the shore, the nicest by far is Woody Hill, a charming antique-filled home with a very private pool out back.

Narragansett, whose famous old casino was lost in a hurricane some years ago, was quiet until recently when a mini building boom began. Now it boasts the biggest lodging along the shore, the Village Inn, a modern hotel complex overlooking Narragansett Bay and the busy town beach. It wouldn't be my first choice as a place to stay, but at this end of the shoreline, you'll find more space for sunbathing at Scarborough Beach, and you'll be near the picturesque fishing village of Galilee and the Block Island Ferry, as well as closer to Newport if you choose to drive over for a day.

If the weather is with you, you'll be more than content with just a place to stay and a few restaurant recommendations on the Rhode Island shore. But if the clouds roll in or you're beginning to burn, all is far from lost. Visit some of the lovely conservation areas along the shore, and take advantage of nature walks and field trips scheduled at the Kimball Wildlife Refuge and the Ninigret Conservation Area. If you are here the first Sunday in August, don't miss the annual all-day Charlestown seafood festival at Ninigret—a feast of good eating. And remember that this is fisherman's paradise—write ahead to the state tourist office for a free guide telling you where to cast for what.

Or go to Westerly and its library—not to read a book but to admire the wood paneling, fireplaces, stained glass, marble mosaic floors, and leaded-glass hanging lamps in this surprisingly lovely building. Look out back for another surprise. Wilcox Park is one of the prettiest to be found anywhere in a city this size. The park is used for free summer concerts, so check in the library for a schedule.

Also in Westerly, though open only on Sunday afternoons, is the 1732 Babcock-Smith House, one of Rhode Island's architectural landmarks, restored and elegantly furnished by the local historical society.

A growing sightseeing complex is the South County Museum on 175 acres of Canonchet Farm in Narragansett, where old-time crafts and farming techniques are demonstrated. Exhibit areas include a carpenter's shop, cobbler's shop, tack shop, and general store. Kids enjoy the collections of old toys, desks, and slates, and are impressed by the kitchen equipped with pre-electricity tools like rug beaters, cheese presses, irons, and washing machines, all powered by human energy.

If the weather sends you in search of indoor amusements, take a drive north on Route 1 to North Kingston, where Wickford Village, a settlement incorporated in 1674, has quaint shops as well as historic homes and churches. The Wickford Antiques Center includes several dealers and a variety of wares. Wakefield's Olde Towne Shoppe is another group shop, and the Dove and Distaff on Main Street specializes in Early American furniture and accessories. The tiny vilage of Peace Dale also has lures for antiquers. While you are in Wakefield, have a meal at the Larchwood Inn, a gracious antique-filled home in town. There are many more antique shops around; ask for the free printed guide to antiques dealers on the South Shore; most stores have them.

Fayerweather Craft Center on Route 138 in Kingston Village is not only a place to shop for crafts but one where you can see demonstrations of crafts in the making. An off-beat shopping stop on Route 1A is Charlestown's Fantastic Umbrella Factory, a crazy mishmash of pottery, china, posters, clothes, gifts, and what-have-you in ramshackle old farm buildings with a few goats and chickens still wandering in the barnyard.

For dining, Shelter Harbor is a good choice (the place to sample Rhode Island jonnycakes). The Watch Hill Inn serves Italian food and at the Olympia Tea Room you'll find fresh seafood and homemade bread as well as tea. George's in Galilee is the special spot for seafood, and Narragansett has turned into the shore's dining center, with several good new restaurants. Evening diversion is the Theater-by-the-Sea in Matunuck, which specializes in summer-stock musicals. Families should note that there are special children's performances on Fridays.

By all means, stop at some of the roadside stands near the beach (especially those near Weekapaug) where lobster goes for $6 or $7, a dozen clam cakes cost $3, and you take your meal and your chowder outside to the picnic tables in the back. The food, like the area, doesn't come in fancy wrappings, but it can't be beat.

<u>*Rhode Island Area Code: 401*</u>

DRIVING DIRECTIONS Take I-95 to Route 2 (exit 92), Westerly exit. Follow Route 2 into Route 78 (Westerly bypass) to U.S. 1 and bear north for Shelter Harbor Inn, Charlestown, or Narragansett (watch for town signs to guide you). Route 1A south leads to Watch Hill, Misquamicut, and Weekapaug. *Total distance:* 145 miles.

ACCOMMODATIONS *Shelter Harbor Inn,* Route 1, Westerly, 02891, 322-8882, $$-$$$ CP • *Weekapaug Inn,* Weekapaug, 02891, 322-0301, $$$$$ AP • *Pleasant View Inn,* 65 Atlantic Avenue, Misquamicut, 02891, 348-8200, $$$-$$$$$ • *Hartley's Guest House,* Larkin Road, Watch Hill, 02891, 348-8253, $-$$ • *Watch Hill Inn,* Bay Street, Watch Hill, 02891, 348-8912, $$-$$$$$ CP • *The Village Inn,* 1 Beach Street, Narragansett, 02882, 783-6767, $$$-$$$$ • *Winnapaug Inn,* 169 Shore Road, Westerly, 02891, 348-8350, motel on a golf course and convenient to the beach, pool, $$-$$$ • Some small bed-and-breakfast choices: *Woody Hill,* 300 Woody Hill Road, Westerly, 02891, 322-0452, charming home with Colonial decor, pool, $-$$ CP • *Grandview,* 212 Shore Road, Westerly, 02891, 596-6384, rambling turn-of-the-century home near the ocean, very reasonable, $-$$ CP • *The Villa,* 190 Shore Road, Westerly, 02891, 596-1054, small complex around a pool, $$-$$$$ CP • *Fairfield by the Sea,* 527 Green Hill Beach Road, Green Hill, 02879, 789-4717, $-$$ CP • *Larchwood Inn,* 176 Main Street, Wakefield, 783-5454, $. Narragansett has many small bed-and-breakfast properties; write for a full list. The Rhode Island Tourism Division Visitors Guide also includes bed-and-breakfast listings in every town. See address on page xiii.

DINING *Shelter Harbor Inn* (see above), $$ • *Mary's Italian Restaurant,* Route 1, Westerly, 322-0444, the name says it, $-$$ • *George's,* near the fishing dock, Galilee, 783-2306, $-$$ • *Wilcox Tavern,* Route 1, Charlestown, 322-1829, 1730 home, varied menu, $-$$ • *Charlestown Lobster Pot,* Route 1, Charlestown, 322-7686, good seafood $-$$$ • *Olympia Tea Room,* Watch Hill, 348-8211, $-$$ • *Watch Hill Inn* (see above). *The Deck,* informal, snacks, $; *Positano,* Italian, $$ • *Spain,* The Village Inn (see above), Narragansett, Spanish fare, $-$$ • *Coast Guard House,* 16 Ocean Road, Narragansett, 789-0700, seafood with a sea view, waterfront deck, $$ • *Basil's,* 22 Kingstown Road, Narragansett, 789-3743, unpretentious French, $$-$$$ • *Terminesi's,* 85 Boon Street, Narragansett, 783-7939, no-frills, good Italian, $-$$ • *Larchwood Inn* (see above), $-$$ •

Villa Trombino, Route 3, Ashaway Road, Westerly, 596-3444, Italian, salad bar, dependable, $-$$. Just FYI: Almost everyone in Narragansett has breakfast at *Dad's Place*, 142 Boon Street, 783-6420.

SIGHTSEEING *Westerly Public Library,* Westerly, 596-2877. Hours: Monday, Tuesday, Wednesday 8 A.M. to 9 P.M.; Thursday and Friday 8 A.M. to 5 P.M.; Saturday 8 A.M. to 3 P.M. Closed Saturdays in July and August. Free. Ask at library for schedule of free concerts in Wilcox Park • *Ninigret Conservation Area,* Route 1A (off Route 1), Charlestown, 364-7718, open daily sunrise to sunset. Free • *Kimball Wildlife Refuge,* Route 1, take Windswept Farms exit, 231-6444. Hours: daily, sunrise to sunset. Free. Ask at either refuge for current free nature programs • *Babcock-Smith House,* 124 Granite Street, Westerly, 596-4424. Hours: May to October, Sunday 2 to 5 P.M., July and August, also open Wednesday. Adults, $2; children under 12, $.50 • *South County Museum,* Route 1A across from the Beach Pavilion, Narragansett, 783-5400. Hours: May to October, Wednesday to Sunday 11 A.M. to 4 P.M. Adults, $2.50; children, $1.50; families, $8.

FOR FURTHER INFORMATION Greater Westerly Area Chamber of Commerce, 55 Beach Street, Westerly, RI 02891, 596-7761. Narragansett Chamber of Commerce, "The Towers," Ocean Road, Narragansett, RI 02882, 783-7121. South County Tourism Council, Inc., Oliver Stedman Government Center, 4808 Tower Hill Road, Wakefield, RI 02879, 789-4422 or toll free (800) 548-4662 outside RI.

A Taste of Victoriana at Nyack-on-Hudson

There was a lively argument the other day on a street corner in Nyack, New York. A young man, gesturing upward toward the round towers of an ornate Victorian home, kept insisting that this was the house to buy. His wife continued to shake her head and point across the street to an old house with a wraparound porch perched above the Hudson.

Neither house was for sale that day, but Nyack is a town that inspires first-time visitors to wishful house-hunting. An antiques and handicrafts shopping center, Nyack is also an old-fashioned village filled with delightful gingerbread Victorian homes. It is a town that proudly declares itself one of the last remnants of "Small Town, USA."

The town's scenic location on the west bank of the Hudson once made it a busy river landing and later allowed it to decline gracefully into a peaceful resort community. Grover Cleveland spent summers here, Ben Hecht and Carson McCullers found the atmosphere conducive to writing, and actress Helen Hayes bought a gracious white house on North Broadway. The old Tappan Zee Playhouse has been named for the late actress and was being renovated at press time into a performing arts center where live theatrical productions will be held. If it is complete when you visit, check to see what is playing.

Nyack's best-known native son, Edward Hopper, memorialized his town's homes in his paintings. His home at 82 North Broadway is now an art gallery.

Nyack had come on hard times, however, and its charm seemed threatened by the specter of housing developments and shopping centers. Instead, the combination of low rents and artistic atmosphere inspired the town's renaissance as a shopping and strolling mecca. On a pleasant weekend, the sidewalks are filled with visitors, especially when street fairs are in swing in May, July, and October.

A good plan would be to arrive Saturday morning, take in a few of the scores of shops on Broadway and Main Street, then buy a picnic lunch (there's a deli on Broadway) and go two miles north to Hook Mountain State Park. Picnic tables are right at the river's edge; the view is hard to beat. Thus refreshed, you'll be ready to explore the town at length.

Nyack's homes remain its pride. Most are not mansions but well-kept examples of comfortable Victoriana in its turn-of-the-century heyday, displaying the gables and porches, balconies and bay windows, cupolas, and whimsical carving that give this style its special appeal.

To appreciate the houses, you must get out and walk, preferably accompanied by the *Village Guide and Walking Tour,* a booklet available in most shops. It will give you a fast lesson in spotting Victorian architecture, and then point out the most interesting houses on the five different loops along the tree-lined village streets and the waterfront. If you're on your own, an easy route to follow is south on Broadway to Washington Avenue, then one block left to Piermont at the water's edge.

All roads eventually lead to Broadway and the shops. On one block alone (South Broadway between Hudson and Cedar Hill avenues), there are at least two dozen stores offering everything from baskets to beads, furniture to works of art. Stroll the side closest to the river and you can prowl among places like Thieves Market (chocolate molds, signs, and tins), Christopher's (lots of handsome oak furniture and a greenhouse), and Hand of the Craftsman (original crafts), which has grown to fill two shops. The second store located farther north at number 5 South Broadway houses their nationally known collection of artist-made kaleidoscopes. Stage Door Antiques and Gifts is filled with memorabilia that should interest music, theater, and film buffs.

There are more stores on Main Street, and if you continue on Route 9W into Upper Nyack you'll find another cache of shops, including a group gallery that calls itself the Upper Nyack Antiques Center.

When hunger pangs strike, if you choose not to picnic, there are lots of possibilities. For lunch, Eat Your Heart Out has sandwiches and salads, and Temptations, one of the local ice cream parlors, also serves light lunches. For something heartier, Old Fashion is a chop house with seafood, hot sandwiches, and tavern atmosphere; Slattery's is an Irish pub, complete with Irish music; and the Bully Boy is an English pub not far away in Congers. For more serious dining, Hudson House is highly rated for its American and Continental menu, and Piermont, a few minutes to the south, has developed into the culinary hub of Rockland County. Xaviar is expensive, but gets almost unanimous praise as one of the best restaurants in the region, and the less formal Free Lance Cafe next door also rates high marks. All of the restaurants along Piermont Avenue serve up a view of the Hudson as dessert.

Make it an early dinner, and you can then drive across the Tappan Zee Bridge for music under the stars at Lyndhurst. Concerts are held every Saturday night from July through mid-August on the 67-acre grounds of this Gothic revival mansion overlooking the Hudson River. It is located on Route 9, half a mile south of the bridge, and you can picnic there, too.

Spend the night at the Tarrytown Hilton or the Marriott and you can spend Sunday sunning or swimming or hitting a few tennis balls. A more historic choice is the Tarrytown House, the lavish former Biddle and King estates overlooking the Hudson River. They have been combined and converted to an executive conference center during the week, but on weekends the accommodations, pools, tennis courts, jogging paths, and other recreation are open to all. Rooms in the newer lodges are attractively furnished, but the prize spaces are the rooms in the King Mansion, especially the front rooms with river views.

You'll also be perfectly situated to explore the outstanding properties of Historic Hudson Valley that trace life along the river over the centuries. Starting with the destination farthest from Tarrytown, Van Cortlandt Manor at Croton-on-Hudson, you can visit a Revolutionary War estate where Benjamin Franklin was once a guest. The gracious 1680 stone house with its railed porch, double stairway, and pitched roof is surrounded by eighteenth-century gardens, peach, pear, and apple trees, and a brick-paved Long Walk lined with lush flowerbeds. Costumed hostesses take you through the house, pointing out the prized furnishings and telling of life during the home's heyday.

Sunnyside in Tarrytown was the home of Washington Irving, who immortalized the area with his stories about Rip Van Winkle and Ichabod Crane, the legends of Sleepy Hollow. Irving once described his Victorian home as "a little old-fashioned stone mansion, all made up of gable ends, and as full of angles and corners as an old cocked hat.'' The house stands on the east bank of the Hudson surrounded by orchards, gardens, and wooded paths planned by Irving himself. Much of his original furniture and personal possessions also remain, including his massive desk in the library.

Philipsburg Manor in North Tarrytown was also the preserve of a prominent family, one that once owned about a third of what is now Westchester County. The trilevel home bears witness to New York's Dutch-English origins. One of its most appealing rooms is the big, beamed kitchen, where the hostesses show you how food was prepared in Colonial times. At the gristmill and barn on the grounds, you'll learn about some of the daily activities on an early Colonial farm.

From here, a shuttle bus will take you to the newest property managed by Historic Hudson Valley. It is Kykuit, the 87-acre Rockefeller estate in Pocantico Hills. Built between 1907 and 1913, the 40-room mansion called Kykuit (Dutch for lookout and pronounced KYE-cut), was the home of John D. Rockefeller, his son John D. Rockefeller, Jr., and his grandson Nelson Rockefeller, who bequeathed the house to the National Trust for Historic Preservation before his death in 1979. The rooms are much as they were when used by Nelson and Happy Rockefeller and their children from 1963 to 1979. Furnishings include eighteenth- and nineteenth-century antiques from John D. Rockefeller, Jr.'s, collections, as well as Nelson's early Chinese ceramics and twentieth-century art, including works by Picasso and Warhol. The gardens contain over 70 pieces of modern sculpture by artists such as Henry Moore and Alexander Calder, and the coach house holds a collection of historic carriages and cars. The Hudson River views from the property are unsurpassed.

Historic Hudson Valley also oversees the church where the Rockefellers worshiped, the Union Church of Pocantico Hills, a modest stone sanctuary with exquisite stained-glass windows by Matisse and Chagall, a sight that should not be missed.

Their final property is Montgomery Place, another architectural landmark at Annandale, quite a bit farther up the river north of Rhinebeck. See page 51.

The Rockefellers have also ceded 800 acres of their properties in North Tarrytown to New York state as the Rockefeller State Park Preserve, an excellent spot for a picnic or a hike on a fine day. A new visitor center should be open on the property by the time you read this.

Though it may require another weekend to find the time, you may also want to return at some point to Lyndhurst for a house tour, stepping back into a gilded age when Jay Gould lived here very much like a king. The house is maintained by the National Trust for Historic Preservation.

More outstanding modern sculpture can be seen if you choose to make your weekend headquarters at Arrowwood, another attractive resort property with a pool, tennis, and golf, located a few minutes east of Tarrytown at Rye Brook. This is a corporate center during the week, and they often have attractive rates to draw people on the weekend. An indoor pool and golf center guarantee fun no matter what the weather.

Just down the road from Arrowwood in Purchase is the headquarters of PepsiCo and the Donald M. Kendall Sculpture Gardens, 112 acres of formally landscaped grounds that form an outdoor gallery for 40 works by a virtual *Who's Who* of important twentieth-century artists—Calder, Dubuffet, Rodin, Miró, and Moore among them. The grounds are open to the public daily free of charge, and you won't find a lovelier setting for a picnic or a stroll to appreciate the exceptional art.

Nyack and Tarrytown Area Code: 914

DRIVING DIRECTIONS Take the George Washington Bridge to New Jersey, then the Palisades Interstate Parkway north to exit 4. Continue north on 9W until you come to Broadway, then bear right into the center of Nyack. The Palisades Parkway also leads back to the Garden State Parkway and the connection to the Tappan Zee Bridge, which leads directly across the river into Tarrytown. *Total distance:* about 25 miles.

PUBLIC TRANSPORTATION For Nyack only: Take the IND A train to the George Washington Bridge Bus Terminal at 177th and Broadway in Manhattan, then board one of the Red & Tan buses that leave for Nyack every hour weekdays and weekends. Metro North serves Tarrytown.

ACCOMMODATIONS Ask at all for weekend packages. *Tarrytown House*, East Sunnyside Lane, Tarrytown, 10591, 591-8200, $$$-$$$$. • *Best Western-Nyack,* Route 59 and NYS Thruway, Nyack, 10960, 358-8100, $-$$ • *Tarrytown Hilton Inn,* 455 South Broadway, Tarrytown, 10591, 631-5700, $$$-$$$$ • *Marriott Westchester,* 670 White Plains Road (Route 119), Tarrytown, 10591, 631-2200, $$$$ • *Courtyard by Marriott,* 475 White Plains Road, Tarrytown, 10591, 631-1122, indoor pool, $$$ • *Arrowwood,* Anderson Hill Road, Rye Brook, 10573, 939-5500, $$$-$$$$ • *Alexander Hamilton House,* 49 Van Wyck Street, Croton-on-Hudson, 10520, 271-6737, pleasant alternative for bed-and-breakfast fans, $-$$$ CP, bridal suite with skylights, fireplace, and Jacuzzi, $$$$$ CP.

DINING *Old Fashion,* 83 South Broadway, Nyack, 358-8114, $-$$ • *Slattery's,* 9 North Broadway, Nyack, 358-9766, $-$$ • *Hudson*

House, 131 Main Street, Nyack, 353-1355, $$-$$$ • *Bully Boy Chop House,* 117 Route 303, Congers, 268-6555, $$-$$$$ • *Xaviar,* 506 Piermont Avenue, Piermont, 359-7007, lunch, $-$$, dinner prix fixe $$$$$ • *Freelance Cafe and Wine Garden,* 506 Piermont Avenue, Piermont, 365-3250, Xaviar's little brother, Nouvelle American, casual, $$-$$$ • *Turning Point,* 468 Piermont Avenue, Piermont, 359-1089, casual, Continental menu, blues club downstairs, $$ • *Piermont on Hudson,* 701 Piermont Avenue, Piermont, 365-1360, Continental, $$-$$$ • *Caravela,* 532 North Broadway (Route 9), Tarrytown, 631-1863, seafood, Portuguese specialties and decor, $$-$$$ • *Lago di Como,* 27 Main Street, Tarrytown, 631-7227, Northern Italian, $$-$$$ • For lunch or light fare in Tarrytown, try *Horsefeathers,* 94 North Broadway (Route 9), 631-6606, or *Dockside at the Tarrytown Boat Club,* 634 West Main Street, 631-2888, a nautical bar and grill with a river view.

SIGHTSEEING *Historic Hudson Valley,* 150 White Plains Road, Tarrytown, NY 10591, 631-8200. Five properties reached via Route 9 near Tarrytown, NY Hours: daily except Tuesday, 10 A.M. to 5 P.M., last tours at 4 P.M. Each house: adults, $6; children $3 • *Kykuit,* admission by tour from Philipsburg Manor. Hours: April to October, daily except Tuesday, 10 A.M. to 4 P.M., last tour 3 P.M. Adults, $18; students, $16 • *Union Church of Pocantico Hills,* Route 448, North Tarrytown, tours April to December, Wednesday to Friday 1 P.M. to 4 P.M., Sunday 2 to 5 P.M. $3 donation • *Lyndhurst,* Route 9, 635 South Broadway, Tarrytown, 631-0046. Hours: May to October, Tuesday to Sunday 10 A.M. to 4:15 P.M. Adults, $6; children 6–16, $3 • *Donald M. Kendall Sculpture Gardens,* PepsiCo, Inc., Anderson Hill Road, Purchase, 253-2000. Hours: sunrise to sunset daily. Free.

FOR FURTHER INFORMATION Free map, street fair calendar, and shopping guide booklet are available by mail from the Art, Craft, and Antiques Dealers Associations of the Nyacks, PO Box 223G, Nyack, NY, 10960, 358-8443.

Long Island Beaches for Beginners Part 1: The Fabled Hamptons

Yes, that was definitely Billy Joel at the next table in the restaurant. And yes, that was unmistakably George Plimpton coming down the aisle of the John Drew Theater. And just maybe that really was Peter Jennings stopped next to you at the last red light.

Celebrities are commonplace in the Hamptons. Socialites spend their summers in Southampton, artists and writers and publishing executives in East Hampton—and prominent faces from the worlds of arts and entertainment are easy to spot in either town or in any of the villages in between. But their presence is possibly the least of the reasons for planning a weekend on Long Island's eastern end.

The main attraction remains the thing that brought the beautiful people here in the first place—the beach. There are miles and miles of it, broad stretches of soft sand lined with sheltering dunes, some of it still amazingly unpopulated. You'll search hard to find better beaches anywhere, and if you are an ocean lover and a sun worshiper, you may never notice or care who else is around sharing nature's bounty with you.

There are other reasons for making the trip, of course. Lots of people enjoy the browsing possibilities in an area filled with chic shops and art galleries. Others are attracted by resort towns where picturesque windmills still stand and where a Colonial heritage remains dominant in spite of the influx of summer visitors. There are many fine restaurants to choose from. And let's face it—it's fun to peek at the mansions behind the hedges.

All in all, the popularity of the area is well deserved, and though you'll encounter annoying traffic not only driving out from the city but also clogging the streets of the shopping centers after you arrive, this remains a prime summer destination.

The Hamptons officially begin with Westhampton, which is considerably closer to the city than the rest, but that proximity seems its only advantage. It is by far the most built up of the towns, with houses and condominiums lining the beach road, and those houses, along with the beach, have suffered badly from storms in recent years.

Adjoining Westhampton Beach, however, is Quogue, a quiet village that is almost all gracious private homes, one of them an inn worth noting. The Inn at Quogue is an airy, comfortable summer place. With the acquisition of adjacent buildings, it has enlarged to 70 guest rooms and added things like TV in the rooms, which may change the ambience from the old summer-house feel. Still, this is a special spot less than a mile from the very private town beach. There is also a pool on the premises and guests have tennis privileges at the Quogue Racquet Club and can work out at the Hampton Athletic Club.

Southampton was discovered long before the beautiful people arrived—even earlier than you might have guessed. The marker at Conscience Point off North Sea Road bears a plaque reading: NEAR THIS SPOT IN JUNE 1640 LANDED THE COLONISTS FROM LYNN, MASS., WHO FOUNDED SOUTHAMPTON, THE FIRST ENGLISH SETTLEMENT IN THE STATE OF NEW YORK.

Visit the Old Halsey House here and you'll be entering the oldest frame house in the state. The Southampton Historical Museum offers relics even older, all the way back to Indian days—not to mention a whaling captain's living room, a Colonial bedroom, a one-room schoolhouse, a country store, a carpenter's shop, and exhibits of early farm equipment. The restored Silversmith Shop on Main first opened about 1750.

Many tourists overlook all the history, preferring instead to head for Main Street and Job's Lane to look at the galleries and antique shops and the fashions—both staid and strictly kicky—in boutiques along the way. The antiques shops on Job's Lane don't deal in junk-tique; if you don't believe it, just check the price tags.

While you're on Job's Lane, don't get so carried away with window shopping that you miss the Parrish Art Museum. The changing exhibits are well worth a look.

Southampton has long been a favorite watering hole for society, and its mansions are legendary. The best roads for seeing them are parallel to the ocean on Meadow Lane (also the site of the handsome town beach) and Gin Lane, and on intersecting streets such as Halsey Neck, Cooper's Neck, and First Neck lanes. Wait until you see the size of these shingled "cottages"—and the cars in their driveways.

If you want to stay in Southampton and share that inviting public beach, one of the pleasantest lodgings is the Old Post House, a 1684 house on the National Register of Historic Places that has been done up simply and cheerfully with quilts and country prints. The Southampton Inn, located just a block from Job's Lane shops, offers swimming, tennis, a pool, and a health club. Room decor is motelish, but does provide some wicker pieces to remind you that you are at the beach. Next door is the Village Latch Inn, also with its own pool and tennis court. Rooms are in a gracious main building and various houses on the property. They vary greatly in size and decor; ask questions when you book, and take a look at all the possibilities before you accept your room.

Driving farther east on Route 27 you'll pass through appealing small villages such as Water Mill (named for its windmill) and Bridgehampton—both have many shops for later exploring—and into East Hampton, where you could well be driving into another era. The approach as you turn left onto Main Street is pure Colonial, with handsome white houses facing a green and a narrow pond that was a cattle watering hole for early settlers and is a gathering spot for ducks today. The first stretch of Main Street is labeled Woods Lane, probably because it once ran through a forest.

East Hampton is another settlement founded more than three centuries ago, and in this case many descendants of the original families remain. Most of the older homes have been declared historic landmarks, and this town would make interesting strolling even if it were landlocked.

Almost every old home has a story to tell. On the west side of the pond, the second house from the V where Woods Lane turns into Main Street is The Studio, the home of noted watercolorist Thomas Moran. At 217 two doors down is the home that was the summer White House for President John Tyler. Across the green is the South End Burying Ground, and on James Lane, a short street bordering the eastern edge of the cemetery, are some of the oldest homes in town. Among them are Winthrop Gardiner's saltbox, Mill Cottage, and Home Sweet Home, a 1750 home named in honor of its owner, John Howard Payne, who wrote the song of the same title. It is open to visitors. Mulford Farmhouse next door, built in the 1650s, is the oldest of all the homes and was a working farm until the late 1940s.

Back on Main Street is Guild Hall, which is both art museum and home of the John Drew summer theater. It is the cultural center of East Hampton. Across the way is the town library and next door Clinton Academy, the first chartered secondary school in New York State. It is currently home to the East Hampton Historical Society, which regularly holds exhibits and lectures. Next is Towne House, a tiny 1730 structure that has been both schoolhouse and town hall and is currently being restored.

Hook Mill at the end of town in very much a landmark, and tours of the wind-powered grinding mill, which is still in working order, are a favorite with children. Hook Mill Burying Ground is even older than the South End cemetery, and it is not unusual to see people taking rubbings of the stones, which date from 1650.

The East Hampton Chamber of Commerce at the corner of Main Street and Newtown Lane has free walking guides to the village and lots of other printed information. Shops in town begin on Main and continue down Newtown. They grow more numerous and more interesting every year.

The beach in East Hampton is at the end of Ocean Avenue, a right turn south at a traffic light as you approach town. Lily Pond Lane, which runs west off Ocean Avenue, is this town's mansion row.

For your own weekend home there are some lovely inns here. One of the choicest is the exclusive Centennial House, an intimate 1876 charmer with just three guest rooms. Every room upstairs and down has been decorated with exquisite taste, from fabrics to prints on the walls. The house breakfast special is buttermilk pancakes—and they are special, indeed. There's also a very private pool in back, delightful if you want a quiet break from the beach.

There are other fine choices on Main Street. The Maidstone Arms, across from the green, has been beautifully renovated into a tasteful retreat in inviting English-country style. The 1770 House lives up to its name with Colonial decor, wide-planked floors, antiques, and canopy beds. Across the street, the Huntting Inn, which dates to 1751, is also Colonial in room decor. On the first floor is a classy outpost of New York's well-known restaurant The Palm. The Hedges Inn, another attractive old home turned inn, is under the management of the Huntting Inn, and has its own pleasant (and less pricey) restaurant, the James Lane Cafe. The Mill House is a more modest lodging with a country feel, with rates that are reasonable by East Hampton standards.

The House on Newtown, a short walk to town restaurants and shops and the jitney, is a choice that may save some the cost of a car rental. Courtside Bed and Breakfast, tucked away in a residential area, gives you access to the hosts' tennis court and pool.

Farther east is the town of Amagansett, which is really a Hampton in all but name. Boutiques and discount shopping complexes have altered what used to be a small unspoiled town with Colonial flavor, that was diluted only by the modernistic beach houses near the shore. But the shops haven't overrun the street yet; there are still enough saltbox homes, Colonial shutters, and geranium boxes to make Amagansett wonderfully appealing, and if the famous once-authentic farmers' market has gone upscale, it is still a great place for gourmet shopping and for lunch.

All the new shops do make for interesting browsing, and Balasses House, an old standby on Main Street, has beautiful English country antiques. If you need other diversions there is a little marine museum on Bluff Road, as well as a historical museum known as Miss Amelia's Cottage, with excellent period furniture, particularly clocks and other pieces made by the Dominy family, well-known Colonial craftsmen of East Hampton.

Amagansett has several town beaches. One of them, Atlantic Avenue Beach, is a popular singles territory, sometimes called "Asparagus Beach" for all the bodies standing around.

One of the most appealing places to stay in the whole area is in Amagansett. Just off Main, the Mill Garth is a 100-year-old main house with another half-dozen or so studios and apartments winding around a complex of lawns and gardens, all antique-filled and offering charm as well as privacy. It is only half a mile to the beach, but if you are feeling lazy, they will lend you a bike or provide parking passes. Gansett Green is a more modest but similar complex that was under renovation at press time and promises to be another excellent choice.

Amagansett also has two noteworthy bed-and-breakfast homes. Bluff Cottage is one of those beautiful homes you look at longingly when you drive around the area, a gracious Dutch Colonial within walking distance of the beach. The more modest Amagansett House, a 200-year-old farmhouse on Main Street, will interest New Yorkers without cars, since it is in the midst of the shops and eating places in town and an easy bike ride to the beach.

Hamptons weekends can't be run by schedules. Both East Hampton and Southampton can easily take half a day just for sightseeing, but if the weather is right, the beach and the ocean may be the only sights you care to see.

Not only is Amagansett pleasant to visit, but Water Mill and Bridgehampton also have many interesting specialty shops worth a stop. All of Route 27, in fact, offers galleries and shops that will tempt you to pull off the road for a bit.

If you want tennis, golf, or fishing, all are available; just ask at your lodging for the most convenient spot. And you can take a trip to Montauk, Sag Harbor, or Shelter Island.

There's enough to keep you busy here for many a day—and many a weekend. Why do you think all those people spend the summer here?

Hamptons Area Code: 516

DRIVING DIRECTIONS Long Island Expressway to exit 70, right for three miles to Sunrise Highway (Route 27) eastbound. Follow 27 to Southampton; it continues to be the only main route to Montauk and the end of the island. *Total distance to Southampton:* 96 miles.

PUBLIC TRANSPORTATION Long Island Railroad has regular service to the Hamptons, (718) 217-LIRR or (516) 822-LIRR. Hampton Express, (212) 861-6800 or (516) 653-6300, and Hampton Jitney, (212) 936-0440 or (516) 283-4600, provide bus service from New York. There are also small commuter airlines; check chambers of commerce for current schedules. Note that in summer Hampton Jitney runs local service from Southampton to Montauk.

ACCOMMODATIONS Many places have three-day minimums in summer, and most are much less expensive off-season and on weekdays. *The Inn at Quogue,* Quogue, 11959, 653-6560, $$$$$ (CP weekends only) • *The Village Latch Inn,* 101 Hill Street, Southampton, 11968, 283-2160, $$$$-$$$$$ CP • *The Old Post House,* 136 Main Street, Southampton, 11968, 283-1717, $$$-$$$$ CP • *Southampton Inn,* Hill Street at First Neck Lane, Southampton, 11968,

$$$$ • *The Maidstone Arms,* 207 Main Street, East Hampton, 11937, 324-5006, $$$$ CP • *1770 House,* 143 Main Street, East Hampton, 11937, 324-1770, $$$-$$$$ CP • *Huntting Inn,* 94 Main Street, East Hampton, 11937, 324-0410, $$$-$$$$ • *Centennial House,* 13 Woods Lane (Route 27), East Hampton, 11937, 324-9414, $$$-$$$$$ CP • *Hedges Inn House,* 74 James Lane, East Hampton, 11937, 324-7100, $$$-$$$$ CP • *The Mill House,* 33 North Main Street, East Hampton, 11937, 324-9766, $$-$$$$ • *The House on Newtown,* 172 Newtown Lane, East Hampton, 11937, 324-1858, $$$-$$$$ CP • *Courtside Bed and Breakfast,* PO Box 496, East Hampton, NY 11937, 324-0453, $$$-$$$$ CP • *The Mill Garth,* Windmill Lane, Amagansett, 11930, 267-3757, studios, $$$-$$$$; suites and cottages, $$$$-$$$$$ • *Gansett Green,* Main Street, PO Box 799, Amagansett, 11930, 267-3133, studios, $$; one- and two-bedroom apartments and cottages, $$$$ • *Bluff Cottage,* 266 Bluff Road, Amagansett, 11930, very special, $$$$ CP • *Amagansett House,* 1439 Main Street, Amagansett, 11930, 267-3808, $$-$$$$ CP.

DINING *The Inn At Quogue* (see above), fresh-caught seafood, fresh-grown vegetables, $$$ • *John Duck Jr.,* North Main Street, Southampton, 283-0311, no atmosphere, just home-style roast duckling and lots of it, $$ • *The Old Post House* (see above), pleasant outside dining, $$-$$$ • *Basilico,* 10 Windmill Lane, Southampton, 283-7987, Northern Italian, the place to be seen, offspring of East Hampton's Sapore di Mare, $$-$$$$ • *1770 House* (see above), prix fixe dinner, $$$$ • *Saint Ambroeus,* 30 Main Street, Southampton, 283-1233, for homesick New Yorkers, the same great pastries, excellent lunches, basic Northern Italian dinners, $$-$$$ • *Della Femina,* 99 North Main Street, East Hampton, 329-6666, the New York ad man turned very successful restaurateur, a power scene, $$$ • *East Hampton Point,* 295 Three Mile Harbor Road, East Hampton, 329-2800, Della Femina's second smash hit, harbor views, $$-$$$ • *Bostwicks Seafood Grill,* 313 Three Mile Harbor Road, East Hampton, 324-1111, seafood with Italian touches, ask for the deck on the water, $$-$$$ • *Maidstone Arms* (see above), excellent food in elegant surroundings, $$$ • *Sapore di Mare,* Route 27, East Hampton, 537-2764, superb Northern Italian food, reserve well ahead, $$$ • *Nick & Toni's Restaurant,* 136 North Main Street, East Hampton, 324-3550, Mediterranean, $$-$$$ • *James Lane Cafe,* Hedges Inn (see above), 324-7100, pricey but attractive and very popular bistro, $$-$$$ • *The Palm at Huntting Inn* (see above), $$-$$$$$ • *The Laundry,* 31 Race Lane, East Hampton, 324-3199, brick walls, skylights, mixed menu, popular, $$-$$$ • *Estia/Amagansett Fresh Pasta*, 177 Main Street, Amagansett, 267-6320, little ambience but good, affordable fresh pasta $-$$ • *Amagansett Fish Company,* Montauk Highway, Amagansett, 267-7592, again no decor to speak of, but very fresh seafood, $$-$$$ • *Honest Diner,* 74 Montauk Highway, Amagansett, 267-3535, 1950s diner decor, basic food, $-$$ • *The Station Bistro,* Water Mill, 726-3016, bistro menu, very popular, $$ • *Bobby Van's,* Main Street, Bridgehampton, 537-0590, entertainment on weekends, $$-$$$.

SIGHTSEEING *Southampton Historical Museum,* 17 Meeting House Lane off Main Street, 283-2494. Hours: June to September, daily except Monday 11 A.M. to 5 P.M. Adults, $2; children, $.50 • *Parrish Art Museum,* 25 Job's Lane, Southampton, 283-2118. Hours: mid-June to mid-September, Monday, Tuesday, and Thursday to Saturday 11 A.M. to 5 P.M., Sunday 1 to 5 P.M.; rest of year closed Tuesday as well as Wednesday. Admission $2 • *Old Halsey Homestead,* South Main Street, Southampton, 283-3527. Hours: June to September, daily except Monday 11 A.M. to 4:30 P.M. Adults, $2; children, $.50 • *Olde Mill,* Route 27, Water Mill, 726-4594. Hours: mid-June to September, Monday, Wednesday, and Saturday 10 A.M. to 4 P.M., Sunday 1 to 4 P.M. Donation • *Home Sweet Home House and Windmill,* 14 James Lane, East Hampton, 324-0713. Hours: May to November, Monday to Saturday 10 A.M. to 4 P.M.; Sunday 2 to 4 P.M. Adults, $2; children, $1 • *East Hampton Historical Society,* 101 Main Street, 324-6850, and all its properties: *Osborne Jackson House,* 101 Main Street; *Historic Mulford House,* James Lane; *Clinton Academy,* 151 Main Street. All open July to September, daily 10 A.M. to 5 P.M.; June and October, weekends only. Each property: adults, $2; children, $1 • *Hook Mill,* 36 North Main Street, East Hampton, 324-0173. Hours: late June to Labor Day, daily 10 A.M. to 4 P.M. Adults, $1.50; children, $1 • *Guild Hall Museum and John Drew Theater,* 158 Main Street, East Hampton, 324-0806. Hours: June to Labor Day, daily 10 A.M. to 5 P.M.; rest of year, Wednesday to Saturday 11 A.M. to 5 P.M., Sunday noon to 5 P.M.; closed January. $2 donation. Check for current summer theater schedule at John Drew Theater, 324-4050 • *Miss Amelia's Cottage,* Main Street, Amagansett, 267-3020. Hours: Friday to Sunday 1 to 4 P.M. • *East Hampton Town Marine Museum,* Bluff Road, Amagansett, 267-6544. Hours: July to September, daily 10 A.M. to 5 P.M.; June and October, weekends only. Adults, $2; children, $1. Note that hours and admissions for smaller properties are subject to frequent change; best to phone for current information.

FOR FURTHER INFORMATION Contact the Southampton Chamber of Commerce, 76 Main Street, Southampton, NY 11968,

283-0402. East Hampton Chamber of Commerce, 4 Main Street, East Hampton, NY 11937, 324-0362.

Long Island Beaches for Beginners Part 2: Unaffected Montauk

Boutiques and babies don't always mix. Small children and country inns aren't always comfortable with each other. And people who love wide open seascapes and shell searching often hate tourist-clogged sidewalks and busy town beaches.

That's why many people prefer to keep right on going when they get to the Hamptons. Instead of heading for the action, they want to get away from it on the easternmost end of Long Island.

The scene changes dramatically on Route 27 as soon as you pass the outer limits of Amagansett. No more shops. After a while, no more clumps of beach houses. At Napeague there is a lineup of condominium resort complexes along the shore. Many owners rent out their units, and these are choice lodgings with tennis, pools, and long stretches of very private beach. Sea Crest and Driftwood are among the oldest and best of these.

Finally, when the condos end, there is nothing ahead except beach grass and dunes and the unmistakable scent of the sea growing stronger all the time.

Bear right onto Old Montauk Highway and you'll see the sea, Hither Hills State Park with campgrounds and its famous ''walking dunes,'' and a few exceptional places for beach lovers. Gurney's Inn is the oldest and best known. Panoramic View, terraced up a steep hillside, offers dramatic sea views, private beach and pool, simpler accommodations, and a smaller tab. Wave Crest, now a condo, is another nearby spot for wave watching. All of these provide comfort and extraordinary private powdery beaches. Leave the small groups clustered in front of each hotel, and in either direction there's open space for walking, jogging, or shelling as far as the eye can see and the feet can carry you.

Children are in the definite minority here—very young ones, at least. They're more likely to be found farther on in Montauk, where about a dozen motels are grouped near the ocean; few of them offer much in the way of charm but all providing something equally hard to come by—direct access to the beach. There couldn't be a better place for young families. It's easy for one parent to take a little walk back to put the baby in for a nap while the other stays on the beach with the rest of the family. Many of these motels offer refrigerators and/or cooking facilities, which help to save on restaurant bills. And if there are children too old to want to sit around with parents in the evening but too young to drive, Montauk offers a special bonus. The beach (and the beach motels) are only a block off the Main Street of town, meaning that it's an easy walk to the local movie or minigolf course or pinball parlor.

Almost all of the oceanfront motels recently have become condominiums, which is both bad and good, depending on your budget. Many have been fixed up quite a bit, but their prices have risen as well. You have to look hard these days if you want to pay less than $100 a night for a motel room. Check the chamber of commerce and the bed-and-breakfast listing in the front of this book for less pricey accommodations.

If you want to enjoy Montauk's easy atmosphere and still live in style, the posh local spot is the Montauk Yacht Club, ideal whether you need a place to park yourself or your yacht.

But don't be misled by luxury accommodations. At heart this is still a fisherman's town. Until recently, the best place in town to find anything, including clothes, was White's Drug Store. The town center is filled with modest eating places serving breakfast, lunch, and dinner, a pizza place, and a handful of modest shops. The Carriage House has a variety of gifts, and new stores are opening, but there is nothing remotely like the shopping a few miles to the west.

So what do you do in Montauk when you're not on the beach? Get back to nature. Go hiking or biking on dirt roads beside the ocean, sound, lake, and fresh ponds. Watch for birds—you're in the crossroads of a major migratory pattern. Take a guided walk with the Nature Conservancy. Play tennis or golf at the Montauk Downs State Park; the Robert Trent Jones golf course was listed by *Golf Digest* as one of the 50 best public courses in America. Go berry picking for shadberries, blackberries, or blueberries—or in September, for beach plums and wild grapes. Watch the sunset at Hither Hills, Fort Pond Bay, or Montauk Harbor. Go horseback riding on the beach or sign up for lessons in wind surfing or sailing.

There are many ways to go out to sea in Montauk. You can sign on for the deep-sea fishing trips that go out of the harbor daily, or rent a sailboat, or take a day-long whale-watching expedition aboard the *Finback II,* a working scientific research boat. Or you can take the ferry to Connecticut or Block Island, just a 1½-hour cruise away.

Whether you get on a boat or not, you'll surely want to watch them returning to the docks with the day's fresh catch of fish. One prize spot for viewing is Gosman's Dock, where fresh fish is available in the fish store as well as in the restaurant, one of the most popular places on all Long Island.

Gosman's lobsters are legendary; there is often at least an hour's wait for a table on weekend evenings. There are no reservations; you'll just have to wait your turn, keeping occupied with a drink from the bar and the activity of the boats around you. If you don't want to wait, there is a clam bar and a takeout where you get "lobster in the rough" to eat at picnic tables nearby. If not as pleasant as the restaurant, it is, at least, cheaper. (The crowds at Gosman's, incidentally, have inspired the opening of the only shops in town that might qualify as touristy—all right at the dock.)

The other "don't miss" attraction in Montauk is its lighthouse, which has stood on the very eastern tip of Long Island since 1795. It is the oldest lighthouse in New York State, and stands some 110 feet tall, with a light that rotates every five seconds and can be seen for 19 nautical miles. Inside you can see the keeper's quarters, interesting old photographs, and a close-up view of some sizable lenses, including the Fresnel Bivalve Lense that served from 1903 to 1987. Climb the 86-step spiral staircase to the watch deck and you can view the new optic in the lantern room. On Lighthouse Weekend in August, there are Revolutionary War encampments, displays of Coast Guard and dory rescue equipment, and demonstrations of rescues at sea. Check for this year's dates.

If you find yourself stuck indoors with kids in the rain, there are just enough diversions within driving distance to save the day. Two standbys are the whaling museum in Sag Harbor and East Hampton's windmill. There's a small Indian artifacts museum in the County Park east of the Village, and if the children are old enough to appreciate a bit of history, you can also visit the museums in Montauk and in the various Hamptons towns. Hither Hills State Park offers family activities, many outdoors but still worth checking into, including square dancing, castle contests, and a puppet theater for kids.

Are the motels in Montauk tacky? Does the town lack class? Some Hamptons lovers might say so, but you couldn't prove it by the many people who swear by the place and can't wait to get back.

Long Island Area Code: 516

DRIVING DIRECTIONS Follow directions to Southampton (page 117); continue east on Route 27 to Montauk. *Total distance:* 120 miles.

PUBLIC TRANSPORTATION Same as Hamptons, page 117.

ACCOMMODATIONS Expect minimum-stay requirements in season. All rates down after Labor Day. *Gurney's Inn,* Old Montauk Highway, Montauk, 11954, 668-2345, $$$$$ MAP • *Panoramic*

View, Old Montauk Highway, 668-3000, with kitchenettes and terraces, $$$-$$$$ • *Wave Crest,* Old Montauk Highway, Box 952, 668-2141, $$$-$$$$ • *Royal Atlantic Motel,* South Edgemere Street, 668-5103, pool, some kitchenettes, $$$$ • *Crow's Nest Inn,* Route 27, 1½ miles east of town, 668-3700, nicely furnished motel units with water views, Jacuzzis, refrigerators, and coffeemakers, quiet location, $$$$ • *Ocean Surf,* South Emerson Avenue, 668-3332, some efficiencies, $$$-$$$$ • *Sea Crest,* Montauk Highway, Napeague, 267-3159, efficiencies, pool, tennis, $$$$-$$$$$ • *Driftwood,* Montauk Highway, Napeague, 668-5744, pool, tennis, efficiencies, $$$$$ • *Sun Haven Motel,* Montauk Highway, Route 27, Napeague, 267-3448, efficiencies, pool, tennis, $$$ • *Born Free,* PO Box 675, Montauk, 11954, 668-2896, two-room suites, $$$-$$$$ • *Surf Club,* South Essex and Surfside Avenue, 668-3800, beachside condos, pool, tennis, $$$$-$$$$$. Some lower-priced Montauk choices within easy walking distance to the beach: *Oceanside Beach Resort,* South Eton Street and Montauk Highway, Montauk, 11954, 668-9825, $$$ • *Sands,* Emerson Avenue and Emery Street, Montauk, 11954, 668-5100, $$-$$$ • *Malibu Motel,* Elmwood Avenue, PO Box 353, Montauk, 11954, 668-5233, $$ • *Sunrise Guest House,* RFD 1 Box 3, Old Montauk Highway, Montauk 11954, 668-7286, modest bed-and-breakfast home across the highway from the ocean, good for budget watchers, $ CP • Top of the line in Montauk: *Montauk Yacht Club & Inn,* Star Island, PO Box 5048, Montauk, 11954, 668-3100, $$$$$.

DINING *Dave's Grill,* Flamingo Road at Montauk Harbor, 668-9190, casual favorite for good fresh seafood by the water, $$ • *Gosman's Dock,* West Lake Drive, Montauk Harbor, 668-2549, join the line for lobster and the harbor view, a Montauk tradition, $$-$$$ • *The Waterfront,* West Lake Drive, 668-1300, lovely water views, $$ • *The Crow's Nest Inn* (see above), 668-4483, wonderful water views, early-bird lobster specials, good chowder, $$-$$$ • *Villa Testarossa,* Main Street, 668-4505, change-of-pace Italian, $-$$ • *Blue Marlin,* Edgemere and Flamingo streets, 668-9880, steaks and seafood, nice outdoor deck, $$ • *Napeague Restaurant,* Route 27, 267-3332, American menu, $$, children's plates, $ • *Ziegfield's,* Montauk Yacht Club (see above), 668-3100, perfect setting overlooking the marina, open for all three meals, dinner $$-$$$ • *Shagwong Restaurant,* Main Street, 668-3050, a fixture for 25 years for dependable, reasonable food, dinner prix fixe $$. For lunch: *The Lobster Roll,* Route 27, Napeague, $ • *Mimosa Beach Café,* right on the beach in Montauk, $.

SIGHTSEEING AND ACTIVITIES *Montauk Point State Park,* end of Route 27, 668-3245. Parking, $3 • *Montauk Point Lighthouse Museum,* in the park, 668-2544. Hours: daily Memorial Day to Labor Day 10:30 A.M. to 6 P.M. weekends only during off-season; closed January to mid-March. Adults, $2.50; children, $1 • *Montauk Downs State Park,* South Fairview Avenue, 668-5000, tennis, golf, pool. Phone 669-0570 for golf fees and reservations • *Hither Hills State Park,* Old Montauk Highway, 668-2554. Hiking trails, picnic areas, children's programs. Parking fee, $4 • Bicycle rentals, *Pfunds Hardware Store,* Main Street, 668-2456 • Wind-surfing and sailing lessons and rentals: *Wind and Surf Shoppe,* Montauk Yacht Club, Star Island, off West Lake Drive, 668-2300 • Sailboat rentals, mini golf: *Puff n Putt Family Fun Center,* Montauk Village, 668-4473 • Waterskiing instruction and boat rentals: *Uihleins,* Montauk Harbor, West Lake Drive Ext., 668-2545 • Horseback riding: *Deep Hollow Ranch,* Montauk Highway, 668-2744; *Rita's Stable,* Montauk Highway, 668-5453 • Fishing trips (including family trips with lesson), ferry to Block Island and Connecticut, whale watching, sunset sightseeing cruises: *The Viking Fleet,* Montauk Harbor, 668-5709. Phone for current rates; *Okeanos Whale-Watching Cruises,* PO Box 776, Hampton Bays, 728-4522. Daily cruises from Montauk Marine Basin at 10 A.M., returning approximately at 4 P.M. Adults, $28; children under 12, $15. Reservations required.

FOR FURTHER INFORMATION Contact the Montauk Chamber of Commerce, Box CC, Montauk, NY 11954, 668-2428.

Shipping Out in Connecticut

The call of the sea is strong on the Connecticut shore.

Once brave whalers shipped out from New London's piers, making the town wealthy and world renowned. Today it is the home of the Coast Guard Academy, the proud seagoing service whose mission since 1790 has been to rescue lives and property at sea.

In fact, New London and its neighbors, Groton, Mystic, and Stonington, cover the historic waterfront, from fishing skiffs and whaleboats to nuclear submarines. As an added summer bonus, New London offers a sandy shoreline on Long Island Sound. It's an ideal setting for a salty summer weekend.

The Coast Guard Academy is a good place to start. Though it is not visited as frequently as the army or navy academies, this is a fine campus, a cluster of handsome, traditional red-brick buildings on 100 acres high above the Thames River. There are inviting grounds, a museum, and a multimedia center at river's edge, where you can learn about the service's glory days from the era of George Washington to the present. The academy itself was founded in 1876 as a seagoing school aboard a schooner in New Bedford, Massachusetts. After outgrowing three other sites, the academy moved to its present location in 1932.

Colorful cadet dress parades are held on the Washington parade field in spring and fall, usually at 4 P.M. on Fridays, and there are many free concerts by the Coast Guard Band. Check for current schedules.

There's a special bonus when the *Eagle* is in port. Even in a nuclear age, the romance of the great sailing ships still captures the imagination, and this 295-foot bark that led America's Bicentennial Tall Ships Parade remains an object of fascination for all ages. Each summer, the *Eagle* becomes a floating classroom for cadets who test their mettle handling the great sails, learning the ways of wind and water. When it is not at sea, it is usually at home in New London, available for free tours of the deck and the quarters of officers and crew.

Near the academy on Mohegan Avenue is the campus of Connecticut College and the Lyman Allyn Art Museum, named in memory of a famous sea captain. It contains art, antiques, and a wonderful collection of dollhouses, dolls, and toys. Also on the campus is the Connecticut Arboretum, a particularly fine nature preserve, which offers 445 acres with hiking trails.

New London itself has lost the glory of its early days, and is, in fact, a bit down at the heels. But there are some interesting sights to be seen here. A walking tour might well start at the beautifully restored nineteenth-century train station, which stands at the busy dock where ferries leave regularly for Block Island and Orient Point. The dock is the site of a gala Sail Festival the weekend following the Fourth of July, ending with spectacular fireworks over the river.

Near the waterfront is a statue of the town's best-known resident, playwright Eugene O'Neill, shown here as a young boy. You can see the Dutch Tavern, the bar where the grown-up O'Neill was a regular, on Green Street, just off the main street, State Street. From the old-fashioned looks of the place, O'Neill would still feel right at home.

Also near the station is the restored Nathan Hale Schoolhouse, where the American hero taught prior to enlisting in George Washington's army. It was moved to this site to be more accessible to visitors.

Other interesting sites in town include the 1833 Customs House, whose front door was once part of the frigate *Constitution,* and the four imposing, columned whaling merchant's mansions now known as

Whale Oil Row. Another historic home, the Shaw Mansion, is now the headquarters and museum of the New London Historical Society.

As you proceed south from Whale Oil Row, you'll find several fine old homes on Hempstead Street. One of Connecticut's oldest, Hempsted House, is a 1678 homestead that was maintained by the family of the original owners until 1937. The only house remaining that escaped burning by British troops in New London in 1781, it is open to the public for a look into the past.

Head back to town via Starr Street, where the old homes have been restored to form a charming contemporary neighborhood.

Drive out toward Ocean Beach Park to 325 Pequot Avenue and you'll find Monte Cristo Cottage, the boyhood home of Eugene O'Neill. The Victorian home has been restored, and tours are available weekdays or by appointment. The Eugene O'Neill National Theater Institute in nearby Waterford holds an annual summer series of readings by promising new playwrights. Check to see what is scheduled while you are in town.

Next door to the institute is Harkness Memorial Park, a 234-acre waterfront estate that hosts Summer Music, a wonderful program of classical and popular music with big name performers. You can order tickets in the sheltered tent or sit on the lawn and enjoy a picnic under the stars. A picnic buffet is served on the grounds, but must be ordered in advance.

New Yorkers may find a familiar look to New London's Ocean Beach, since it was done by the designer of Jones Beach. There's a mile-long boardwalk, a water slide, miniature golf, and other family fun.

Across the Thames at Groton, the U.S. Navy Submarine Base, the largest in the world, provides still another perspective on America's maritime traditions. The submarine has a longer history in the New London area than most visitors realize. The first submarine, *The Turtle,* invented by David Bushnell of nearby Saybrook, was launched in 1776. It can be seen at the Connecticut River Museum in Essex. Although an attempt to sink a British flagship failed, the 7½-foot vessel paved the way for today's underwater fleet.

At the USS *Nautilus* Memorial at the base, you can trace the progress of submarines from those days to the nuclear age, and board the world's finest nuclear-powered sub. Working periscopes, an authentic submarine control room, and minitheaters are part of the exhibit.

Groton has its own share of nautical history. Up the hill from town is Fort Griswold State Park, where Colonial troops were massacred by Benedict Arnold's British forces in 1781. An obelisk standing 127 feet high marks the spot, and the fort still offers the same commanding view of the river that made it ideal as a lookout for British ships. Monument House nearby holds the D.A.R. collection of both Revolutionary and Civil War memorabilia.

All of this sightseeing is hardly going to leave enough time to do justice to Mystic Seaport, one of America's prime maritime attractions. There are the majestic sailing vessels to board; a whole nineteenth-century village with working shops to explore; buildings filled with rare boats, ship's models, figureheads, scrimshaw, and art; the chance to watch boats being built; and continuing demonstrations of arts such as sail setting, ropework, oystering, or fireplace cooking. It might be well to save Mystic for a weekend of its own or to tack an extra day onto your present tour.

Even if you postpone Mystic, don't overlook the little towns beyond it. Noank, jutting out into the west side of the Mystic River, offers spectacular views of Fishers Island Sound. The fine homes bespeak a time when this was a center for shipbuilding and lobstering. Later, it was an art colony, and galleries still display the work of local artists. Noank is a fine place for a walking tour and a seafood dinner. Abbott's Lobster in the Rough here is a longtime summer favorite on the shore.

Stonington, the village just beyond Mystic, is even more picturesque; it is also filled with fine sea captains' homes from the eighteenth and nineteenth centuries. Stonington is the home harbor of the last working fishing fleet in Connecticut. The blessing of the fleet, usually in late June or early July, featuring a parade of flower-festooned boats, is well worth a special visit. Call for this year's dates.

If you want to add a winery tour to your weekend agenda, Stonington Vineyards will oblige. If children are along, they'll enjoy the Thames Science Center, with its touch tank, salt marsh diorama, and other exhibits on nature and the sea. The imaginative Children's Museum of Southeastern Connecticut in Niantic, below New London, is another pleaser, filled with hands-on exhibits—learning and fun for everyone from toddlers to preteens.

Should you be feeling lucky, you can head inland for a change of pace at the Foxwoods High Stakes Bingo and Casino. You'll be amazed at the lavish facilities tucked away in the countryside in Ledyard on the Mashantucket Pequot reservation. There's even a Las Vegas–style theater where big name entertainers appear.

Each of the shore towns offers a variety of places to stay, from New London's elegant Lighthouse Inn, a Victorian mansion, to modest bed-and-breakfast homes to scores of motels. To be sure you don't miss a minute at the slots or the tables, you can even stay at hotels on the reservation, adjoining the gambling casino.

Note that each of these sea-centered communities also offers ample opportunity to actually get out on the water. New London's ferries ply back and forth to Fishers Island, Block Island, Montauk, and Orient Point. Whale watching and deep-sea fishing excursions go out of Waterford, and educational oceanographic cruises are available in Groton. The *Voyager,* a replica of a nineteenth-century schooner, sails out of Mystic harbor, and the jaunty little coal-powered steamboat, *Sabino*, runs the river at Mystic Seaport.

And if all that nautical atmosphere moves you to want to go farther out to sea, you can ship out on one of the windjammers, replicas of the two-masted nineteenth-century schooners that sail out of Mystic regularly for one-, two-, or five-day cruises.

Connecticut Area Code: 203

DRIVING INSTRUCTIONS I-95 to exit 83 for New London, exit 85 for Groton. *Total distance:* about 125 miles.

PUBLIC TRANSPORTATION Amtrak (800) 523-8720 has trains to New London from Grand Central, but it's hard to get beyond the center of town without a car.

ACCOMMODATIONS *Lighthouse Inn,* 6 Guthrie Place (off Pequot at Lower Boulevard, one-half mile east of Ocean Beach Park) New London, 06320, 443-8411, $$-$$$ CP • *Radisson Hotel,* 35 Governor Winthrop Boulevard and Union Street, New London, 06320, 443-7000, indoor pool, $$-$$$ • *Queen Anne Inn,* 265 Williams Street, New London, 06320, 447-2600, Victorian B&B, $$-$$$ CP (with afternoon tea) • *Gold Star Inn,* 156 Kings Highway, Groton, 06340, 446-0660, pleasant motel, indoor pool, $$. For Mystic and beyond, see page 33.

DINING *Lighthouse Inn* (see above), elegant, with water views, $$-$$$ • *Thames Landing Oyster House,* 2 Captain's Walk, 442-3158, popular for seafood, near station and dock, $-$$$ • *Ye Olde Tavern,* 345 Bank Street, 442-0353, New London, maritime decor, steak and seafood, $$-$$$ • *The Gondolier,* 92 Huntington Street, New London, 447-1781, Italian, $$ • *Two Sisters Deli,* 300 Bank Street, New London, 444-0504, favorite spot for lunch in New London, $ • *Diana,* 970 Fashion Plaza, Poquonnock Road, Groton, 449-8468, change of pace, Lebanese decor and menu, $$. See also Mystic, pages 33–34.

SIGHTSEEING *U.S. Coast Guard Academy,* Mohegan Avenue, New London, 444-8270. Hours: May to October, daily 9 A.M. to 5 P.M. Visitors' Pavilion open May to October. Museum open May to October, weekdays 8 A.M. to 4 P.M. weekends and holidays, 8 A.M. to 5 P.M. • *Eagle* ship tours, Friday, Saturday, and Sunday 1 to 4 P.M. whenever the ship is in port. Free. Check for schedules of *Eagle,* cadet dress parades, and Coast Guard Band concerts • *Shaw Mansion,* 11 Blinman Street, New London, 443-1209. Hours: Wednesday to Friday 1 to 4 P.M., Saturday 10 A.M. to 4 P.M. Adults, $2; children, $.50 • *Nathan Hale Schoolhouse,* Union Plaza, New London, 443-8331. By appointment. Free • *Hempsted House,* 11 Hempstead Street, New London, 247-8996. Hours: Tuesday to Sunday 1 to 5 P.M. Adults, $3; children under 18, $2 • *Ocean Beach Park,* Ocean Avenue, New London, 447-3031. Hours: Memorial Day to Labor Day, daily 9 A.M. to 6 P.M. Parking: weekdays, $7; weekends $9. Walk-in fees: non-resident adults and children, $2 • *Harkness Memorial State Park,* Route 213, Waterford, 443-5725. Hours: mansion open daily, Memorial Day to Labor Day, 10 A.M. to 5 P.M.; grounds open all year. Parking, summer weekdays $3–$4, weekends $4–6; rest of year free. Summer Music Concert information: 442-9199 • *Connecticut College Arboretum,* Connecticut College Campus, Williams Street, New London, 447-1911. Hours: daily during daylight hours. Free • *Lyman Allyn Art Museum,* 625 Williams Street (near college), New London, 443-2545. Hours: Tuesday, Thursday, Friday, and Sunday 1 to 5 P.M.; Wednesday 12:30 to 9 P.M.; Saturday 11 A.M. to 5 P.M. Donation • *Monte Cristo Cottage,* 325 Pequot Avenue, New London, 443-0051. Hours: early April to mid-December, Monday to Friday 1 to 4 P.M. and by appointment. Adults, $3; children $1 • *USS Nautilus Memorial and Submarine Force Library and Museum,* U.S. Naval Submarine Base, Route 12, PO Box 571, Groton, 449-3174. Hours: April 15 to October 14, Wednesday to Monday 9 A.M. to 5 P.M., Tuesday 1 to 5 P.M; rest of year, to 4 P.M. and closed Tuesday. Free • *Fort Griswold State Park,* Monument Street and Park Avenue, Groton, 445-1729. Park open daily dawn to dusk • *Groton Monument and Monument House*, Memorial Day to Labor Day, daily 10 A.M. to 5 P.M., Labor Day to mid-October, weekends only. Free • *Thames Science Center,* Gallows Lane off Williams Street, New London, 442-0391. Hours: Monday to Saturday 9 A.M. to 5 P.M., Sunday 1 to 5 P.M. Adults, $2; children, $.50 • *Children's Museum of Southeastern Connecticut,* 409 Main Street, Niantic, 691-1255. Hours: Monday and Wednesday to Saturday 9:30 A.M. to 4:30 P.M., Sunday 12:30 to 4:30 P.M. Admission: $2.50 • *Mystic Seaport,* Route 27, Mystic, 572-0711. Hours: daily 9 A.M. to 5 P.M., late June to Labor Day, to 8 P.M. Adults, $14; children 6–12, $7.75 • *Stonington Vineyards,* Taugwonk Road, Stonington, 535-1222. Hours: Tuesday to Sunday 11 A.M. to 5 P.M. Tours and tastings. Free • Boat trips: Check all for current schedules and rates. *Captain John's Sportfishing Center,* 15 First Street, Waterford, 443-7259, deep-sea fishing and whale watching. *Project Oceanology,* Avery Point, Groton,

445-9007, educational cruises aboard the Enviro-Lab. *Voyager Cruises,* Steamboat Wharf, Mystic, 536-0416, sailing excursions. *Steamboat Sabino,* Mystic Seaport, 572-0711. *Mystic Whaler and Mystic Clipper,* 7 Holmes Street, Mystic, 536-4218, one- to five-day windjammer cruises.

FOR MORE INFORMATION Southeastern Connecticut Tourism District, PO Box 89, 27 Masonic Street, New London, CT 06320, 444-2206.

Gingerbread by the Sea in Cape May

With more than 600 prize gingerbread Victorian houses within 2.2 square miles, how do you ever decide which ones deserve special status? In historic Cape May, New Jersey, they didn't even try. They simply declared the whole town a national landmark.

Hop aboard the sightseeing trolley or join one of the guided walking tours of the nation's oldest seashore resort and you'll soon know why. While erosion has diminished Cape May's once lavish beaches, fire has leveled the legendary nineteenth-century hotels that hosted presidents and royalty, and the usual quota of innocuous resort motels and eateries have sprung up around the beach, nothing has touched the tree-lined residential streets of old Cape May. They remain a serene world apart, a gracious enclave of pastel paint and lacy curlicues, mansard roofs and fish-scale shingles, ornate railings and columned porches, with widow's walks, cupolas, towers, and turrets looking out to sea.

Because of its unique heritage, the largest collection of Victorian homes in America, Cape May is a seaside retreat like no other—and possibly at its most appealing during the tail end of summer, after Labor Day. The water remains warm, there is more room for strolling on the beach promenade, and you have a better chance of getting reservations in the guest houses in the historic district where you will sample the best of Victorian living.

If you wait until early October, you can take in the Victorian Week festivities, a ten-day gala encompassing two weekends. There are special house tours, period fashion shows, and lectures on Victorian arts as well as an antiques show, entertainment, and other special activities.

On a Cape May tour, you'll learn that a destructive fire in 1878 accounts for the unusual concentration of 1880s homes. Before that date Cape May was the prime vacation spot on the East Coast. It had attracted Colonial luminaries from Philadelphia as early as the 1770s, and in the years following, local guest house and hotel registers included the names of seven U.S. presidents, including Andrew Jackson and Abraham Lincoln, as well as Henry Clay, Horace Greeley, actress Lillie Langtry, and composer John Philip Sousa. Huge old wooden hotels like the Mansion House, the Mount Vernon, and the United States had been vulnerable to fires all along, but the blaze of 1878 was so devastating that 30 acres of the town were laid bare by the flames.

Ironically, it was that disaster that prompted so many wealthy people, most from the Philadelphia area, to come in and build on the suddenly available tracts of land. They were further encouraged by the railroad, which offered a year's free transportation for anyone who would help recoup their tourist trade.

The homes that went up were smaller than Cape May's original structures, but were even showier, products of an era when having money meant flaunting it in the form of elaborate exterior home decoration. "The fancier the better" seems to have been the Victorians' motto.

Trolley tours of the town run regularly, but you'll get a much better look at the architecture on a walking tour sponsored by the Mid-Atlantic Center for the Arts. It takes you down streets like Ocean and Beach, Gurney and Stockton, Columbia and Howard, with an enthusiastic local resident to fill you in on who was who in the homes and hotels along the way. You'll learn how the Chalfonte Hotel on Howard Street, the only remaining survivor of the 1878 fire, once qualified for a local liquor license by counting linen closets and bathrooms as "accommodations"; about the wife of a sea captain living near Howard and Ocean who confessed in her diary that she was afraid when her husband went to sea, leaving her to deal with the Indians and pirates who roamed the Cape; and about the socialite from Baltimore who came to the Colonial Hotel in the summer of 1917 to plan her coming-out party. Her name was Wallis Warfield, later known as the Duchess of Windsor.

Most of the homes are private residences, but you can get a feel for their interiors by taking a Victorian Sampler tour or by visiting some of the guest houses in the historic district. The acknowledged show-place in town is the Mainstay Inn, also known as the Victorian Mansion, once an elegant gambling club, still with its original 14-foot ceilings, tall mirrors, ornate plaster moldings, elaborate chandeliers, and cupola with an ocean view. The current owners, Tom and Sue Carroll, have kept many of the original furnishings, and they offer tours and tea in the parlor (on the veranda, weather permitting) on Saturdays and Sundays at four.

The Abbey, just across the way, is another of the finer inns. These two are among many on Columbia, Hughes, Ocean, and Jackson streets that are an easy stroll to the center of town or to the beach. Among the nicer choices are Victorian Rose, the Queen Victoria, The Brass Bed, and Captain Mey's.

Farther from town are some other interesting possibilities. The Angel of the Sea, a large and elaborate 1881 "cottage" is the biggest of the town's inns. It offers ocean views from many of the rooms, as does Columns by the Sea, a 20-room mansion located directly across from the quietest end of the beach. The Wilbraham Mansion, another beautiful 1840 home just at the edge of West Cape May, has a unique feature for off-season guests, an indoor pool surrounded by stained glass.

No rooms at the inns? You'll have to settle for a hotel or motel and teatime tours. The Virginia Hotel has its own Victorian charm, as well as an excellent dining room.

Cape May's beaches are a lot slimmer than they used to be, but there is still enough room for sunning, and the promenade is perfect for walking or jogging with an ocean view. A 30-minute bike ride from town takes you to Cape May Point, where the Atlantic meets Delaware Bay and where you can sift through the sand for pieces of polished quartz known as "Cape May Diamonds." These have more sentimental than monetary value, but they are pretty and, when polished, can be set into jewelry souvenirs. Cape May Point State Park boasts one of the country's oldest lighthouses, dating to 1744. The Point's Sunset Beach is the favored local spot for sunset watching.

The point also is happy hunting grounds for bird-watchers. You'll be following in the footsteps of John James Audubon and Roger Tory Peterson if you head for the sanctuary in the park or the 180-acre Cape May Migratory Bird Refuge, owned by the Nature Conservancy. Both are sanctuaries for spotting birds of prey, such as hawks and falcons, as well as exotic and endangered species, like the least tern, black skinner, and piping plover, which stop for food and shelter before crossing the mouth of Delaware Bay.

Back in Cape May you can play tennis at the Cape May Tennis Club, next to the Physick Estate at 1048 Washington Street, and while you are in the neighborhood have a look at the elegant restoration of an 1881 home, finely furnished with Victorian pieces. The Cape May County Art League holds changing exhibits in the carriage house on the estate.

On Washington Mall you'll find three blocks of shops as well as sidewalk cafes, ice cream parlors, and a bookstore where you can pick up the Sunday papers. Just off the mall is the Pink House, an antiques shop that is the ultimate in Victorian frills. It's the house you see most of the time when you see a photo of Cape May.

You'll hardly need any further diversion if the weather is right, but for cloudy days or a very worthwhile detour on the way home, don't overlook Wheaton Village, about an hour away in Millville, New Jersey. This relatively unknown attraction is a re-created Victorian village on the site of a former glass factory. The 1888 factory has been restored and gives demonstrations of early glassblowing techniques daily. Those who want to learn how to shape molten glass can learn to make a paperweight (by advance reservation).

In addition to glassmaking, The Crafts and Trades Row demonstrates nineteenth-century arts such as woodcarving and pottery making, and you can watch a tinsmith at work in the Tin Shop. Also on the premises is a print shop displaying turn-of-the-century equipment, a restored 1876 schoolhouse and a Victorian-era pharmacy. Young visitors love the 3/4-mile train trip around the lake in an old-fashioned miniature train.

But the main attraction here is the Museum of Glass, one of the best collections of its kind anywhere, in an attractive building around a court that makes excellent use of its tall windows to highlight the glass displays. You'll view the first hand-blown bottles—used for drinks, strong and otherwise—goblets, pitchers, ornamental glass, medicine bottles, perfume and ink bottles, early lamps, pressed glass, cut-glass lead crystal, works of art by Tiffany, art nouveau glass, art deco glass—just about every kind of glassware ever made by hand or machine. You can buy glassware in the Village store and paperweights in a shop that has a most comprehensive collection of this art ranging in price from $3 to $3,000.

Wheaton Village is a surprise in this quiet, nontouristy farm area, and it is a fascinating look at another kind of 1880s—a perfect counterpoint to a weekend in Victorian Cape May.

Cape May Area Code: 609

DRIVING DIRECTIONS Garden State Parkway south to last exit. *Total distance:* 160 miles.

PUBLIC TRANSPORTATION Bus service via NJ Transit from the New York Port Authority; for schedules and rates, phone (201) 762-5100.

ACCOMMODATIONS (All zip codes 08204) *Mainstay Inn,* 635 Columbia Avenue, 884-8690, $$-$$$$ CP • *The Officers' Quarters of the Mainstay Inn,* same address and phone, adjacent cottage restored in 1994 as four suite lodgings, $$$$ CP, including afternoon tea at the Mainstay • *The Abbey,* Columbia Avenue and Gurney Street, 884-4506, $$-$$$$ CP • *The Brass Bed,* 719 Columbia

Avenue, 884-8075, $$-$$$$ CP • *Victorian Rose,* 715 Columbia Avenue, 884-2497, $$-$$$ CP • *The Queen Victoria,* 102 Ocean Street, 884-8702, $-$$$ CP • *Captain Mey's Inn,* 202 Ocean Avenue, 884-7793, $$-$$$$ CP • *The Angel of the Sea,* 5–7 Trenton Avenue, 884-3369, $$$-$$$$ CP • *Virginia Hotel,* 25 Jackson Street, 884-5700 or (800) 732-4236, $$$-$$$$ CP • *Colvmns by the Sea,* 1513 Beach Drive, 884-2228, $$$-$$$$ CP • *Wilbraham Mansion & Inn,* 133 Myrtle Avenue, 884-2046, $$-$$$ • *Inn at 22 Jackson,* 22 Jackson Street, 884-2226, all suites, $$-$$$$ • *The Manse,* 510 Hughes Street, 884-0116, $$-$$$ CP. Prices vary by seasons, are usually at the lower end in fall, winter, and early spring, highest in summer. Write to chamber of commerce for still more inns and a long list of motels.

DINING *410 Bank Street,* same address, 884-2127, Cajun, mesquite grill, $$$ • *Washington Inn,* 801 Washington Street, 884-5697, gracious 1856 home, $$-$$$ • *Ebbitt Room,* Virginia Hotel (see above), elegant and among the tops in town, $$$ • *Maureen,* 429 Beach Drive and Decatur Street, 884-3774, French, another "best," $$$ • *Mad Batter,* 19 Jackson Street, 884-5970, nouvelle cuisine in a gingerbread house, $$-$$$ • *Chalfonte Hotel,* 301 Howard, 884-8409, Southern specialties, $$ • *Louisa's,* 104 Jackson Street, 884-5882, many call this tiny place the best in town, no reservations, $$ • *Water's Edge,* Beach Drive and Pittsburgh Avenue, 884-1717, creative menus, $$-$$$ • *Frescos,* 412 Bank Street, 884-0366, excellent Northern Italian, $$-$$$ • *Freda's Cafe,* 210 Ocean Street, 884-7887, eclectic menu, ribs to filet, $$ • *Sugar Reef,* Beach Drive and Decatur Street, 884-8009, Caribbean, $$ • *Peaches on Sunset,* 1 Sunset Boulevard, West Cape May, 898-0100, interesting menu, Thai influence, $$-$$$ • *The Globe,* 110 North Broadway, West Cape May, 884-2429, international menu, good reviews, b.y.o.b., $$-$$$ • *The Lobster House,* Fisherman's Wharf, 884-8296, good seafood, long lines, come for lunch, $$-$$$$ • *A & J Blue Claw,* Ocean Drive, 884-5878, another fine seafood choice, $$-$$$ • Some moderately priced choices: *Peaches Cafe,* Carpenters Lane between Perry and Jackson, 884-0202, casual, interesting menu, $$ • *Pilot House,* 142 Decatur Street, 884-3449, tavern fare, open late, $-$$ • *Cactus Cantina,* Sunset Boulevard and Broadway, West Cape May, 898-0354, Tex-Mex, $-$$.

SIGHTSEEING For current schedules and rates of walking tours, trolley tours, and house tours, see the free pamphlet "This Week in

Cape May,'' available at all lodgings, or contact Mid-Atlantic Center for the Arts (MAC), 1048 Washington Street, PO Box 340, Cape May, NJ 08204, 884-5404. MAC can also provide a list and dates of special annual events such as antique and craft shows, Victorian Week, Christmas in Cape May, Tulip Week, and the spring Music Festival • *Wheaton Village,* Route 552, Millville (from Cape May take Route 47 north and west and watch for signs), 825-6800. Hours: April to December, daily 10 A.M. to 5 P.M., January to March, Wednesday to Sunday 10 A.M. to 5 P.M. Adults, $6; children 6–17, $3.50; family rate, $12.

FOR FURTHER INFORMATION Greater Cape May Chamber of Commerce, PO Box 109, Cape May, NJ 08204, 884-5508.

The Pick of the Past in Massachusetts

Brimfield. The Founding Fathers must have had a premonition when they named the place, because brim it does—on every field as well as sidewalk and front porch and any other place where there is room to set up a booth. Booths cover some 20 fields, each holding about 300 dealers.

Brimfield, Massachusetts, a tiny town near the southern border of the state, is the flea-market capital of the world, the place where thousands of vendors congregate three times a year for a sale that must be seen to be believed. Trinkets, trunks, beer bottles, brass beds, Victorian sofas, vintage postcards—you'll be hard pressed to name any item that won't be for sale somewhere in Brimfield during these weekend gatherings held in May, July, and September each year.

The September date usually brings the best weather for browsing and makes for a perfect end-of-summer weekend, for when you've made the rounds and gathered all the tea caddies and copper pots and other treasures that you can afford, you'll find yourself right next door to the sights of Sturbridge and perfectly positioned for a back-roads meander home through some quaint and undiscovered Connecticut towns.

The gathering of the flea market clans began more than 20 years ago, brainchild of an entrepreneurial dealer named Gordon Reid, who hosted the first affairs at his farm, Antique Acres. Reid's daughters, Jill and Judith, run things now on the same spot, with a flair that must be hereditary, since the show seems to grow both in crowds and dealers yearly. Between them, the Reids corner the cream of the dealers who come to town, but they aren't quite the whole show. There is almost no end in sight to the variety of vendors who show up to take advantage of the crowds. Try to come early, when you can pick and choose with the least amount of elbowing. Whole busloads of shoppers tend to show up as the day goes on.

Sturbridge is only a five-minute drive east of Brimfield on Route 20. The best-known attraction here is Old Sturbridge Village, a 200-acre re-creation of a rural New England village of the early nineteenth century, and one of the outstanding developments of its kind. It's a wonderful place no matter what your age, beautifully landscaped and with more than 40 old buildings moved from their original sites to form a realistic town where costumed "residents" go about the everyday activities of an earlier time.

You'll see the farmer hoe his crops or plow his fields, watch spinners weave wool carded at the water-powered carding mill, find the cobbler's daughter sewing shoe uppers at home, or a woman binding books at the printing office. You just might also be on hand when the farmer appears at the blacksmith shop with a broken hoe to be mended, or find a farm wife picking vegetables to cook over an open hearth for the noon meal, or encounter the members of the Female Charitable Society gathering for their regular meeting.

Every day there are fireplace cooking demonstrations and a dozen different early nineteenth-century crafts in the making. You can hop aboard the horse-drawn wagon or look in on re-created Meetinghouse services on Sunday. Almost every weekend brings a special event. September weekends in recent years have included an Antiquarian Book Fair, an Agricultural Fair, and a Militia Day when historically dressed militiamen practice gunfiring drills and hold a mock battle.

Sturbridge Village can take an hour or a whole day, depending on how much time you have to give it. Snacks and refreshments and whole meals are available on the premises, and there are picnic tables if you want to bring your own fare.

There's a real village of Sturbridge to be explored as well, an authentic New England town with its original green and many historic buildings intact. If you can handle more shopping, here's a town full of shops. Two on Main Street across the driveway from the Public House Inn are of special note—the Green Apple for its excellent stock of antiques, folk art and country furnishings and Sadie Green's Curiosity Shop, whose name does not do justice to the enormous selection of original design jewelry made with luminous antique glass. Many of these pieces are found in New York City shops for far higher prices.

The Seraph has fine reproductions of Early American furniture, and the Shaker Shop features Shaker furniture designs. There's surely a basket for everyone among the hundreds for sale at Basketville, and the

Marketplace, a restored mill, has a little of everything, including a whole top floor of handcrafts. Antiquers will find dozens of lures. Some of the larger selections are available at the Antique Center of Sturbridge, a collective of several dealers, and Sturbridge Antiques to the east on Route 20 with 25 dealers under one roof. To the west on Route 20, watch for Route 148 north and signs for Cheney Orchards for sweet cider and the best of the new apple crop.

If you do Brimfield on Saturday morning, the real Sturbridge in the afternoon, and Sturbridge Village on Sunday, your visit will be more than complete. But if you can tear yourself away with time left for exploring on the drive home, there are some detours in northeast Connecticut that are delightful alternatives to turnpike driving. In fact, this part of the state, which calls itself "the quiet corner," can be an excellent home base, offering some delightful towns and inns.

You'll quickly see why Route 169 gas been declared a "Scenic Highway." One of the prettiest towns on this road is Woodstock, not the famous one but a country cousin, a little town of stone walls and historic houses that date to 1686.

There is no Main Street as such here, just clusters of homes and occasional shops. About midway through the town on the crest of a long ridge is Woodstock Hill, where huge old trees shade handsome country houses spanning a couple of centuries in architecture. One that stands out is Roseland Cottage, a bright pink Gothic-style house built in 1864 for a wealthy gentleman named Bowen, a New York newspaper publisher, who installed the best of everything, right down to a private bowling alley. The house and gardens and barns, owned and operated by the Society for the Preservation of New England Antiquities, are open to visitors. Woodstock Academy is almost directly across the common and about a mile south of Route 169 in Quasset School, a little red-brick schoolhouse (open to the public in the summer months only). The Woodstock Fair each Labor Day weekend is a real old-fashioned country fair, and worth keeping in mind for another visit.

Woodstock offers its own small group of shops near the intersection of routes 169 and 171. In addition to a sampling of local crafts at Scranton's shops, there is the Irish Crystal Company with beautiful imported lead crystal and the Livery Shops with gifts and antiques. Windy Acres has dried and silk flowers as well as fresh blooms, and the Christmas Barn and Shop has 12 rooms of gifts, candles, tree decorations, and fabric. A mile off Route 169 on Woodstock Road in East Woodstock is Brunarhan's, a furniture showroom where hand-crafted pieces in pine and oak are available. Woodstock Orchards (also on Route 169) is the place for the best apples and cider of the season.

The gracious Inn at Woodstock Hill is a recommended stop for lodging or dinner, and the Ebenezer Stoddard House is a pleasant bed-and-breakfast inn. Lord Thompson Manor in nearby Thompson is a 30-room beauty on 40 acres, and the Vernon Stiles Inn in Thompson has been serving meals to travelers since 1814. There are many lovely historic small bed-and-breakfast homes in these unspoiled villages, especially in Pomfret, a pretty town that is home to a prestigious prep school. Several inns host "Learning Weekends" during the year, with workshops in photography, gardening, bird-watching, and a variety of other topics. Write to the Northeast Connecticut Visitors' District for the list.

Keep heading south on Route 169 for Brooklyn, another of those out-of-the-way discoveries off the tourist paths. Brooklyn's New England Center of Contemporary Arts is a charming rustic gallery with changing exhibits of work by recognized living artists. There is usually an artist in residence to talk about his or her work. The Golden Lamb Buttery is a unique dinner stop, offering gourmet fare in a farm setting. Come early for a free hayride through the fields, or to sit on the deck watching the ponies, donkeys, and horses graze.

It's a gentle way back to reality, and if you connect with Route 205 below Brooklyn and then Route 14, you'll soon be back on I-395, the Connecticut Turnpike, and speeding back to the present with all your newfound treasures from the past.

Brimfield Area Code: 413
Sturbridge Area Code: 508
Connecticut Area Code: 203

DRIVING DIRECTIONS New England Thruway or Hutchinson River Parkway and Merritt Parkway to I-91 north; at Hartford cut off to I-86 and continue to Sturbridge, exit 3. Brimfield is about 7 miles west of Sturbridge on Route 20. *Total distance:* about 160 miles.

PUBLIC TRANSPORTATION Amtrak ([800] 872-7245) train service to Worcester, half an hour's drive. Peter Pan Bus Service ([212] 564-8484) to Sturbridge from New York, Hartford, and Boston.

ACCOMMODATIONS *The Publick House,* Main Street (Route 131), Sturbridge, 01566, 347-3313, a charming 1771 inn, $$-$$$ • If you like smaller inns, ask for the *Colonel Ebenezer Crafts Inn,* a restored 1786 home under Publick House management, $$$ • *Country Motor Lodge,* also run by Publick House, $$ • *Old Sturbridge Village Lodges,* Route 20 west, Old Sturbridge Village, 01566, 347-3327 (motel adjacent to the village itself), $$-$$$ • *Oliver Wight House,* 1789 home turned inn, part of Village Lodges, $$-$$$ • *Quality Inn*

Colonial, Route 20, Sturbridge, 01566, motel, tennis, pool, $-$$ • *Sturbridge Host Hotel and Conference Center,* 366 Main Street, Route 20, Sturbridge, 01566, 347-7393, indoor pool, tennis, $$$-$$$$ • *Wildwood Inn,* 121 Church Street, Ware, (413) 967-7798, antique-filled Victorian home, five rooms, serving homemade breads and muffins for breakfast—20 minutes from Sturbridge *and* a bargain, $ CP • *The Inn at Woodstock Hill,* PO Box 98, South Woodstock, CT 06267, (203) 928-0528, English country decor, $$-$$$$ CP • *Ebenezer Stoddard House,* Route 171 and Perrin Road, West Woodstock, CT 06267, (203) 974-2552, ruffles and frills in a bed-and-breakfast home, $$ CP • *Lord Thompson Manor,* Route 200, Thompson, CT 06277, (203) 923-3886, $$-$$$ CP • *Karinn,* Route 169, Pomfret, CT 06250, (203) 928-5492, small restored inn, antiques, fireplaces, $$, CP.

DINING *The Publick House* (see above), $$-$$$, very pleasant tavern for informal meals, $ • *Whistling Swan,* 502 Main Street, Sturbridge, 347-12321, 1800s home and barn, Continental, $$-$$$, Ugly Duckling loft for casual dining, $ • *Salem Cross Inn,* West Brookfield (north of Sturbridge), 867-2345, restored 1705 inn, Yankee fare, open hearth cooking, $$ • *Le Bearn Restaurant Français,* 12 Cedar Street, Sturbridge, 347-5800, French cuisine, quaint atmosphere, $$-$$$ • *Piccadilly Pub,* 362 Main Street, pub fare, popular lounge, $ • *The Harvest at Bald Hill,* Route 169, South Woodstock, 974-2240, setting of plants and flowers, $$-$$$, Sunday brunch, $ • *The Inn at Woodstock Hill* (see above), by reservation only, $$-$$$ • *Vernon Stiles Inn,* Route 200, Thompson, CT, (203) 923-9571, atmospheric 1814 tavern, $$ • *Vanilla Bean Cafe,* 450 Deerfield Road, Pomfret, 928-1562, cafe in a restored barn, excellent for lunch, $ • *Golden Lamb Buttery,* Hillandale Farm, Route 169, Brooklyn, CT, (203) 774-4423, exceptional, open June to December, prix fixe $$$$$.

SIGHTSEEING *Brimfield Flea Market,* Route 20, Brimfield. Outdoor fair dates: mid-May, early July, and mid-September. For current season dates, phone J & J Promotions, (413) 245-3436 or 597-8155 • *Old Sturbridge Village,* Route 20, 347-3362. Hours: daily April to October, 9 A.M. to 5 P.M.; shorter hours off-season. Adults, $15; children 6–15, $7.50 • *Roseland Cottage,* Route 169, Woodstock, CT, (203) 928-4074. Hours: Memorial Day to Labor Day, Wednesday to Sunday noon to 5 P.M.; to mid-October, weekends only. Adults, $4; children, $2 • *New England Center for Contemporary Art,* Route 169, Brooklyn,

CT, (203) 774-8899. Hours: May to November, Wednesday to Sunday 1 to 5 P.M. Free.

FOR FURTHER INFORMATION Contact Sturbridge Information Center, Route 20, Sturbridge, MA 01566, (508) 347-7594, also Northeast Connecticut Visitors' District, PO Box 598, Putnam, CT 06260, (203) 928-1228.

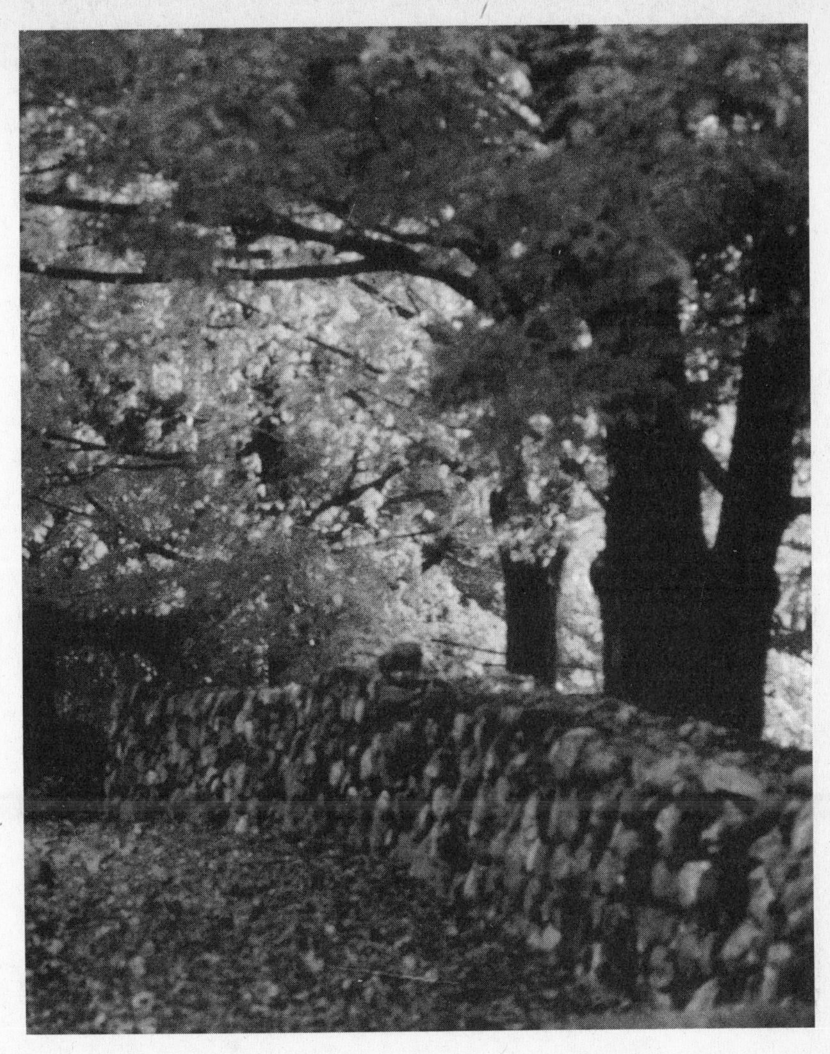

Fall

Autumn in the Litchfield Hills, Connecticut
Photo courtesy of Litchfield Hills Travel Council

Antiquing in Old Connecticut

Any experienced actress knows that a well-staged revival can be big box office. So June Havoc says that although they called her the "Madwoman of the Crossing" when she began in 1978, she had high hopes when she set about to bring Cannon Crossing back to life.

This tiny crossroads village, bounded by the red and white Cannondale railroad station on one side and the Norwalk River on the other, was a serious victim of neglect at the time—paint peeling, roofs sagging, walls on the verge of tumbling down. Today it is as spiffy as a stage set and sometimes close to SRO on busy weekends, when visitors come to browse for antiques, watercolors, candles, fabrics, and other finds housed in the nostalgic nineteenth-century buildings.

A shopping expedition alone doesn't quite justify a whole weekend, of course, not even in such an unusual setting. But by good luck Cannon Crossing is within easy reach of Ridgefield, a beautiful Connecticut town with a long history, a wide Main Street canopied by stately elms, highly regarded restaurants, and some fine country inns. And to cap things on Sunday, you can journey half an hour farther up Route 7 to Kent, another country charmer with lots of shops and a tiny jewel of a museum where tools become works of art.

Route 7, the road that leads to the Crossing north from Norwalk or south from Danbury, used to be known as Antiques Row for its abundance of shops. Shopping centers have taken their toll on the small dealers, but if you drive past some of the more mundane establishments, you'll still find a few choice stores in the Wilton area.

Just about everything is for sale at the Wayside Exchange, a high-quality consignment shop packed full of wooden and upholstered furniture, stacks of dishes and silver, trunks, books, copper pots, and endless miscellany. A stop here might net you a hand-painted child's chest and matching mirror, a tall grandfather's clock, or a silvery dinner bell.

Vallin Gallery is well known for its exquisite Oriental antiques. Chests, tables, lamps, vases, porcelains, and scrolls may be found, all of high quality and priced accordingly.

The names change from time to time but if you keep driving on Route 7, you'll spy other shops with names like Attic Treasures and Country Fair.

Cannon House, featuring antique pine furniture, is on Route 7 at the turnoff to Cannon Crossing. When you spot the sign for the Crossing, turn in and you'll soon have a charming cache of shops to explore, a unpredictable mix of antiques, crafts, baseball memorabilia, teddy bears, and who knows what else. Greenwillow Antiques has a nice selection of country furniture and Penny Ha' Penny offers fine imported foods as well as crafts.

Miss Havoc, incidentally, lives in the restored mill house at the river's edge.

Take a break at the Old Schoolhouse Grill, where the blackboards now bear menus instead of multiplication problems, and then it's on to Ridgefield.

There are more shops to explore on the way to the turnoff on Route 35, as well as on Route 33, an alternative country road connection to Ridgefield that takes you past many lovely Colonial homes. Ask for a complete listing of area antiques shops if you want to do further shopping; it is available in most of the stores. You might take scenic Route 33 anyway, just to see the sights, the next time you return to Route 7.

Either way will bring you onto Ridgefield's broad Main Street, lined with mansions that were once the summer retreats of wealthy residents of New York. The principal bit of history on the street is Keeler Tavern, which was in operation from 1772 to 1907 and has been meticulously restored with authentic furnishings and accessories. Costumed hostesses will show you the sights, including the cannonball that remains embedded in the shingles outside as a memento of a British attack during the Revolutionary War.

Down the street in a 1783 white house, the Aldrich Museum is a surprise in this tradition-oriented town. Its three floors are filled with the latest in modern art, and there is an abstract-sculpture garden in back.

Ridgefield's most highly regarded eating places, both favoring Continental fare, are The Inn and Stonehenge, a 1799 house off Route 7. The scenic surroundings make Stonehenge a favorite for Sunday brunch.

Stonehenge also offers stylishly decorated rooms, 6 in the main building, another 10 in cottages on the grounds. Colonial-style rooms are available at The Elms in town, or you can stay right next door to the Inn at Ridgefield at the West Lane, an elegant Victorian beauty with mahogany paneling, designer fabrics, and working fireplaces in 4 of the 14 rooms. Not far away is Windover Estate, the former summer home of *Life* magazine founder John Ames Michell.

Sleep late, have a hearty breakfast, and then it's Route 7 time again and a half-hour drive north to Kent, another pretty Colonial town loaded with shops and art galleries, plus a special treasure, the Sloane-Stanley Museum. The late artist Eric Sloane's outstanding collection of Early American tools is housed here in a rustic, barnlike building donated to the state by the Stanley Tool Works as a gift marking that company's 125-year anniversary.

Sloane saw handcrafted tools as the nation's first works of art and you'll likely agree when you see his artistic displays of wooden bowls, buckets, and barrels; tiny hinges and huge plows; tools carefully crafted to follow the shape of the grain of the wood from which they are made; and others, such as hoes, rakes, and handles, with shapes by nature that could not be improved upon. Some of the most interesting displays show how the tools were used. Many of the wooden pieces, elegantly carved and highly polished, are unmistakably pieces of art.

One wing holds a reconstruction of Eric Sloane's studio, furnished with his own antiques, books, and fascinating collections, from sand glasses to chessboards and weathervanes.

A pleasant distraction is a visit to Kent Falls State Park, which you will pass on Route 7 on the way to the Sloane-Stanley Museum. If the day calls for a picnic near the falls, the Cobble Cookery on Kent Green can supply the fixings. Otherwise, stop into their cafe for homemade muffins, soups, and sandwiches.

Kent is filled with treasures for shoppers. There are a dozen antiques shops, including the Kent Antiques Center incorporating several dealers, and Pauline's Place has a beautiful selection of fine antique jewelry. Plain Folk will please those in search of country accessories and baskets and the Heron American Craft Gallery has an interesting array of creative handcrafts. Among the art galleries, the Paris–New York–Kent Gallery at Kent Station Square shows top quality work.

Should you like Kent so much you want to stay on or make a return trip, there are some pleasing bed-and-breakfast lodgings in town, as well.

While you are in the area, you might want to sample one of the highly rated restaurants a few miles south in New Milford. Maison LeBlanc has been acclaimed for its country French cooking, and Charles Bistro, a storefront in town, offers lighter French fare and lighter dinner tab as well. In nearby Litchfield, the superb West Street Grill is the place for innovative American fare.

The Silo, a converted stable, silo, and barn in New Milford, is a picturesque stop and a treasure trove of cooking equipment and books. A wide variety of excellent cooking classes and demonstrations are held here on weekends; if cooking is one of your interests, it's well worth checking ahead to see what is happening while you are in the neighborhood.

The Egg and I Farm is a find for those who want to buy hams, ribs, pork, and sausages fresh from the farm. Phone for driving directions.

Finally, when your shopping is done, it's back home to find the right places for all your newly acquired treasures, permanent souvenirs of the weekend.

Connecticut Area Code: 203

DRIVING DIRECTIONS Hutchinson River Parkway to the Merritt Parkway, exit 40, Route 7 north. Cannondale and Cannon Crossing are a right turn clearly marked; routes 33 or 35 lead to Ridgefield. *Total distance:* 60 miles.

PUBLIC TRANSPORTATION Bonanza Bus Lines stops in Kent village, with inns, shops, and restaurants within an easy walk; good getaway for New Yorkers without cars.

ACCOMMODATIONS *West Lane Inn,* 22 West Lane, Ridgefield, 06877, 438-7323, $$$-$$$$ CP • *Stonehenge Inn,* Route 7, Ridgefield, 06877, 438-6511, $$$-$$$$ CP • *The Elms,* 500 Main Street, Ridgefield, 06877, 438-2541, $$$ CP • *Windover Estate B & B,* 194 West Lane, Ridgefield, 06877 (800) 769-WIND, $$$ CP • *Far View Manor,* 803 North Salem Road, Ridgefield, 06877, 438-4753, former school turned B&B $$ CP • *The Country Goose,* Route 7, Kent, 06757, 927-4746, eighteenth-century Colonial, $$-$$$ CP • *Constitution Oak Farm,* Beardsley Road, Kent, 06757, 354-6495, a working farm in the country, like a visit to Grandma's house, $ CP • *Chaucer House,* 88 North Main Street, Route 7, Kent, 06757, 927-4858, small Colonial inn within walking distance of shops and Bonanza bus stop, $$ CP • *Mavis,* 230 Kent Cornwall Road, Route 7, Kent 06757, 1860 Greek Revival home, Victorian roses and ruffles, $$ CP • *Fife 'n Drum,* Route 7, Kent, 06757, 927-3509, rooms in a modern lodge are spacious and well decorated, $$.

DINING *Olde Schoolhouse Grill,* Cannon Crossing, Wilton, 762-8810. lunch and informal dinners, $ • *Stonehenge* (see above), $$$-$$$$, prix fixe dinner, $$$$$ • *Inn at Ridgefield,* 20 West Lane, Ridgefield, 438-8282, $$-$$$, prix fixe dinner, $$$$$ • *Gail's Station House,* 78 Main Street, Ridgefield, 438-9775, great breakfasts, low-key lunch and dinner,$-$$ • *Hay Day Cafe,* 21 Governor Street, Ridgefield, 438-2344, creative American fare adjoining a gourmet market, lunch $, dinner, $$ • *Kismet,* 296 Ethan Allen Highway, Route 102, Ridgefield, 431-1211, suprisingly authentic Indian food and a terrific Sunday buffet brunch, $-$$ • *Fife 'n Drum,* Kent (see above), $$-$$$ • *Maison LeBlanc*, Route 7, New Milford, 354-9931, $$-$$$ • *Charles Bistro,* 51 Bank Street, New Milford, 355-3266, $$ • *Poor Henry's*, 65 Bank Street, New Milford, 355-2274, Bavarian decor, German, Hungarian, and Czech dishes, $$ • *West Street Grill,* 43 West Street, on the green, Litchfield, 567-3885, $$-$$$ • Note: Ridgefield inns require jackets for dinner.

SIGHTSEEING *Cannon Crossing,* Cannondale, off Route 7, Wilton. Hours: most shops open Tuesday through Sunday 11 A.M. to 5 P.M. • *Keeler Tavern,* 132 Main Street, Ridgefield, 438-5485. Hours: February to December, Wednesday, Saturday, and Sunday 1 P.M. to 4 P.M. Adults, $3; children, $1 • *Aldrich Museum of Contemporary Art,* 258 Main Street, Ridgefield, 438-4519 Hours: Tuesday to Sunday 1 to 5 P.M. Adults, $3; students, $2; under 12, free • *Sloane-Stanley Museum,* Route 7, Kent, 566-3005, early May through October, Wednesday to Sunday 10 A.M. to 4:00 P.M. Adults, $3; children, $1.50. Free Thursday and Saturday 11 A.M. to 1 P.M.

FOR FURTHER INFORMATION For Ridgefield, Housatonic Valley Tourism Commission, Box 406, Waterbury, CT 06813, 743-0546 or toll free (800) 841-4488 outside CT. For Kent, Litchfield Hills Travel Council, PO Box 968, Litchfield, CT 06759, 567-4506.

Shakers and Scenery in the Berkshires

The trilevel round stone dairy barn is not only the most striking building at Hancock Shaker Village, but also an apt symbol for the extraordinary people who once lived on this site.

The barn's shape is as ingenious as it is beautiful. Hay wagons could enter at the top, traverse the interior on a sturdy balcony, and dump the hay into the center to a middle level where as many as 54 head of cattle, radiating around the central manger stanchions, could easily be fed by a single farmhand.

The Shakers had a way of finding the most functional way of doing things. The simple classic lines of their chairs and chests made more than a century ago were a precursor of modern design. They were the first to think of packaging garden seeds and herbal remedies, and such handy devices as the circular saw, the flat broom, and the common clothespin were their inventions. They made work easier for themselves as well as for an eager public who bought these products, and thus helped support the community that thrived here for more than 100 years.

The order had all but vanished, done in perhaps by its own rule of celibacy, when the last surviving buildings were acquired in 1960 by a group resolved to create a memorial to the sect by restoring its unique village. It is a fascinating place to visit, conjuring a vivid picture of the life-style of a unique people.

Since the village is also near the heart of the Massachusetts Berkshires, it is an ideal autumn destination, allowing you to enjoy the year-round attractions of the area while the mountains are aflame with autumn color. In early October, you can also attend the Autumn Farm weekend, when old Shaker harvest activities are demonstrated.

Of the original 100 structures on 1,250 acres, 20 have been restored. The visitors' center outside the historical village sells tickets and will provide you with a pamphlet to lead you through the various buildings, where guides are posted to answer questions. Exhibits at the center and throughout the buildings will tell you about the community from its founding in 1790 to the opening of the restoration in 1960. You'll learn that the Shakers were actually an outgrowth of the Quakers, but took a different path, believing that Christ had already returned in the person of their founder, Mother Ann Lee. Mother Ann decreed that religion was to be the dominant force in every area of their lives, requiring separation from the world, communal property, regular confession of sin, and celibacy. Though the sexes were separated, they were considered equal, a very advanced notion in the 1700s. In England they acquired the name Shaking Quakers for the ritual dances that were part of their worship, literally shaking off sin, and were eventually simply dubbed Shakers.

Mother Ann fled from England, where her ways were frowned upon, and came to America to preach her special gospel. Hancock was the third of the 18 communities the sect eventually established throughout the Northeast and Midwest. At the town's zenith in the 1830s there were six "families" in residence, with a total membership of about 300.

At the restoration you'll visit workshops where craftspeople use traditional Shaker materials and methods to produce reproductions of Shaker furniture and crafts, and stroll through gardens planted with some 120 varieties of plants that were part of the Shakers' thriving medicinal herb industry. Vegetable gardens and crop lands utilize heirloom plant varieties, and historic breeds of cattle, sheep, horses, and chickens help re-create the village's agricultural heritage.

One of the most important buildings is the Brick Dwelling, which housed 100 and contained the communal dining room and meeting room used for weekday worship. The basement level contains the 1830 kitchen and the appropriately named Good Room, where homemade baked goodies are sold to visitors. Also in the building are typical sleeping quarters, a pharmacy, a nurse shop, a children's room, and sewing rooms.

In the Brethren's and Sister's shops you'll see some of the industries run by the men, such as the chair and broom making, and weaving rooms that were the women's province. The famous Shaker chairs are made in the Brethren's Shop, and reproductions are sold in the Ministry Shop.

Other sights include the Hired Men's Shop, the Printing Office, the Wash House, and Tan House, where cabinetmaking and blacksmithing are demonstrated, and the Laundry, Machine Shop, and Meeting House, all contributing to a realistic picture of what life was like for this devout band who left the world to build a successful self-sufficient community for themselves.

It takes at least half a day to really appreciate Hancock Shaker Village, and with lunch you'll have just a couple of daylight hours left. Considering the season, you might choose to spend them enjoying the scenery from one of the two prime viewing points, Mount Greylock, the area's highest peak, to the northeast in North Adams, or the next highest point, Mount Everett, to the south in Mount Washington. Mount Washington, a sky-high village with just 100 residents, also gives you a view of Bash Bish Falls, which makes a spectacular 50-foot plunge.

All the inns and restaurants that serve music lovers in the summer are available in fall as well, so you'll have many pleasant choices for dinner and lodgings.

On Sunday you can see some of the sights that are often missed in the busy summer season in Lenox and Stockbridge, which were magnets for both the wealthy and the literary greats of the mid-1800s. Drive around Lenox to see the fine homes in the town that was referred to as the ''inland Newport.'' Longfellow, Melville, Hawthorne, Henry James, and Edith Wharton were among the literati who were attracted by the area's beauty, along with several prominent artists.

Tanglewood's grounds with their magnificent gardens are open for strolling year round, and here you'll see a re-creation of the little house where Hawthorne wrote many of his novels.

If you want to take a break to enjoy the autumn countryside, one way is aboard the Berkshire Scenic Railway, a short ride aboard a 1920 vintage train. Check autumn schedules at the Lenox train station.

The traditional New England main street of Stockbridge was immortalized by one of the area's best known artists, Norman Rockwell. The world's largest collection of his work can be seen in a stunning museum opened in 1993 on a 36-acre former estate just outside Stockbridge. The museum inspires new appreciation for Rockwell's talents at mirroring changing American society. His studio has also been moved to the site. Not the least of the museum's pleasures are the grounds, which offer expansive views of the Housatonic River Valley and the Berkshire countryside.

There are other interesting historic sights in Stockbridge. The oldest house, the 1739 Mission House, was the home of John Sergeant, who was a missionary sent to convert the Indians. It is filled with fine Early American furnishings and has an authentic Colonial herb garden out back. The Merwin House, also known as Tranquility, was built around 1825 and is Victorian in its decor. There are two old churches on the street and the Village Cemetery is the resting place of Indian chiefs as well as early Colonial settlers.

The Children's Chimes, erected in 1878 on the site of the original Mission Church, were built by David Dudley Field as a memorial to his grandchildren; they serenade the town every evening at sunset from apple blossom time until frost.

If you aren't staying there, do stop for a drink or a meal at the Red Lion. It's the most delightful Colonial inn, full of eighteenth-century atmosphere, with charm in every corner. If it is still warm enough, the courtyard is a particularly nice place for refreshments. On Main Street and in other courtyards just off it, you'll also find a interesting shops and galleries for exploring.

Another spectacular home just west of Stockbridge is Chesterwood, where sculptor Daniel Chester French created the working models for his famous "Seated Lincoln" for the Lincoln Memorial in Washington. You can still see the models in the studio along with other bronzes. The home itself, set beside the Housatonic River overlooking Monument Mountain, is certainly a setting that might lead to inspiration. French referred to his estate simply as "heaven." Chesterwood has been beautifully maintained by the National Trust for Historic Preservation.

Other great houses of the Berkshires that can be toured include Edith Wharton's home, "The Mount," and Naumkeag, an 1886 Norman-style home designed by Stanford White with gardens by Fletcher Steele.

Cultural evenings in the Berkshires don't end with the Tanglewood summer season. Evening performances, including adaptations of Edith Wharton novels and stories, continue at The Mount through November, and in Pittsfield, South Mountain Concerts presents chamber music in September and October, the Albany Berkshire Ballet performs at the Koussevitsky Arts Center during the fall, and the Berkshire Public Theater continues year round.

If you still have time to spare, West Stockbridge will hope to provide another kind of inspiration—the spending of cash for the jewelry, folk art, pottery, health foods, dried herbs, and what have you in a little potpourri of shops. Lenox has its own upscale shopping center in the Curtis Shops and on and off Church Street in the village, and a growing number of discount outlets on Route 7 north of town.

If you prefer to concentrate on antiques, drive south on Route 7 to Sheffield, a gracious town with a covered bridge and a main street lined with stately homes—at least a dozen of them transformed into antiques shops. There's no problem finding most of the stores, since they are right on Main Street, but one complex worth seeking out is Twin Fires Antiques on Route 41, consisting of 12 shops in two large barns with lots of special pieces of antique English stripped pine furniture.

By the time you've done the shops, the autumn color should be fading into the twilight, telling you it's time to get back on the highway and home.

Berkshires Area Code: 413

DRIVING DIRECTIONS Saw Mill River Parkway north to the Taconic State Parkway to the New York State Thruway (Berkshire Spur, Route 90), then east to Route 22; north on 22 to Route 295, east on 295 to Route 41, and north on 41. Hancock Shaker Village is at the junction of routes 20 and 41, five miles west of downtown Pittsfield. To get to Lee and Lenox, take exit 2 off Route 90 and proceed north on Route 7. To Pittsfield from Lee or Lenox, continue north on 7, turn west at Route 20. *Total distance:* about 163 miles.

ACCOMMODATIONS AND DINING See "Weekending with the Boston Symphony," pages 98–102.

SIGHTSEEING *Hancock Shaker Village,* Route 20 at 41, Pittsfield, 443-0188. Hours: May 1 to October 31, daily 9:30 A.M. to 5 P.M., April and November daily 10 A.M. to 3 P.M. Adults, $10; children 6–17, $5; family rate, $25 • *Norman Rockwell Museum,* Route 183, Stockbridge, 298-4100. Hours: May to October, daily 10 A.M. to 5 P.M., November to April, weekdays 11 A.M. to 4 P.M., weekends 10 A.M. to 5 P.M. Adults, $8 ($7.50 in winter); children, $2 • *Chesterwood,* Route 183, two miles west of Stockbridge, 298-3579. Hours: May to October, daily 10 A.M. to 5 P.M. Adults, $6; students, $3, children 6–12, $1 • *Mission House,* Main and Sergeant streets, Stockbridge, 298-3239. Hours: late May to mid-October, Tuesday to Sunday 11 A.M. to 4 P.M.; last tour, 3:30 P.M. Adults, $4; children 6–16, $1 • *Merwin House,* 14 Main Street, Stockbridge, 298-4703. Hours: June to mid-October, Tuesday, Thursday, Saturday, and Sunday, noon to 5 P.M. Adults, $4; children 6–12, $2 • *Naumkeag Museum and Gardens,* Prospect Hill, Stockbridge, 298-3239. Hours: Memorial Day to Labor Day, Tuesday to Sunday (and Monday holidays) 10 A.M. to 4:15 P.M. Labor Day to Columbus Day, weekends and holidays only. Adults, $6; children 6–12, $1.50 • *Edith Wharton Restoration, The Mount,* Plunkett Street, Lenox, 637-1899. Hours: Memorial Day through Labor Day, Tuesday to Sunday 10 A.M. to 5 P.M.; September and October, Thursday through Sunday, 10 A.M. to 5 P.M. Adults, $4.50; students, $3 • *Albany*

Berkshire Ballet, 51 North Street, Pittsfield, 442-1307, phone for fall schedule • *South Mountain Concerts,* Route 7, one mile south of Pittsfield, 442-2106, September to mid-October; check current schedules • *Berkshire Public Theater,* 30 Union Street, Pittsfield, 445-4634, phone for current plays • *Berkshire Scenic Railway Museum,* PO Box 2195, Lenox, 637-2210. Trains leave from the Lenox station on Willow Creek Road; phone for seasonal schedules and rates.

FOR FURTHER INFORMATION Berkshires Visitors Bureau, The Common, Pittsfield, MA 01201, 443-9186 or toll free (800) 237-5747 outside MA. Stockbridge Chamber of Commerce, PO Box 224, Stockbridge, MA 01262, 298-5200.

An Autumn Palette in the Catskills

Mention the Catskill Mountains and many people think only of resorts, but the real beauty of the Catskills lies north of the resort belt along the Route 28 corridor.

Here's where the mountains become more rugged and even more scenic, preserved forever wild and beautiful by New York State as the Catskill Forest Preserve, covering a vast 278,000 acres. The hills and woods are a backdrop for a bevy of quaint towns with intriguing shops, and for wilderness areas where you can cast a fishing rod into a rippling river or hike in the woods.

Excellent dining is one of the lures of the corridor, especially along the section that is becoming known as "the French Catskills."

The ski mountains of Belleayre and Hunter also host fall festivals, allowing you to enjoy a bird's-eye foliage panorama from their chair lifts. And two old-fashioned railroads add to the fun with scenic trips into the woodlands, which are favorite outings for families.

A good place to begin exploring is Woodstock, just a few miles north of Route 28. Set smack against a mountain and centered by a village green, this is the prettiest and the best-known town in the area. It was famous early on as an art colony, long before the infamous rock concert held nearby that made the town a symbol of the 1960s.

The Byrdcliffe Crafts Colony was founded here way back in 1902, and the Art Student's League summer school followed just a few years later. In 1910, the Woodstock Artists Association and its gallery came into being and in 1916 the town hosted the nation's first summer chamber music series, the Maverick concerts.

The galleries are still in full swing in the fall, and some concerts carry over, as well. The Artists Association Gallery on the village green is a good place to ask about special events.

Year round, Woodstock is filled with shops as diverse as the crowds that come to browse. Expect to find everything from stained glass and handmade teddy bears to handcrafted jewelry and hand-dyed batiks. Yes . . . tie-dyed clothing and Birkenstock sandals are still on display. Clouds Gallery is the place for high-quality American crafts. You'll have little trouble finding the shops, since they are clustered on Mill Hill Road, which leads into town, and on Tinker, a continuation of Mill Hill beyond the green.

Woodstock is deservedly popular and parking on the street is a problem, so when you arrive it's best to watch the signs and make use of the parking lots thoughtfully provided.

After you've had enough of the shops and filled up at the cafes along Tinker, take a scenic drive north from the green on Rock City Road up to Mead's Mountain for a fantastic view from the fire tower's Overlook Trail. There are more galleries on the way up, if you haven't already overdosed on art.

A detour east on Route 212 for three miles leads to the turnoff for Opus 40, a most unusual outdoor sculpture. It took the late Harvey Fite 37 years to create this monumental environmental display, which is made of hundreds of thousands of tons of fine bluestone and covers more than six acres.

Concerts are often held at Opus 40 in season; check the current schedule.

Ten miles from Woodstock via Route 212 is Saugerties, where you can check out the splashy annual chrysanthemum display in Seamon Park, hunt for treasures in the antique stores, and dine at the Cafe Tamayo, which has gained rave notices from major restaurant critics.

Woodstock lodgings are surprisingly modest for such a special town. The most convenient are Twin Gables, an old-fashioned guest house, and the no-frills Woodstock Inn, a motel. Pinecrest Lodge, on the edge of town, is a rustic complex with rooms in cottages in the woods.

Better inn choices are to the west along Route 212. The first is a charming small bed-and-breakfast, the Ivy Farm Inn, an 1875 farmhouse situated by the side of the road six miles from Woodstock in Lake Hill. Continuing into Mt. Tremper, you'll find the Mt. Tremper Inn, a Victorian haven with lots of charm.

Mt. Tremper is also the beginning of the French influence in the mountains. La Duchesse Ann, a rustic country inn, is one of several area inns where the phone is answered with a delightful French accent. The French connection began many years ago when a waiter at Le Pavillon, one of Manhattan's former French classics, decided to open a restaurant in Shandaken. He called it L'Auberge des Quatre Saisons.

His countrymen came to visit, there was soon a weekend colony, and then more inns with French menus. It is estimated that there are now about 600 French families with permanent or part-time homes in the area.

The scenery takes on a more dramatic look at Phoenicia, as you near the heart of the Catskills. Nearby Esopus Creek, which parallels Route 28 for many scenic miles, has become a favorite for both fly fishing and tubing. For an excellent view of the waterway, board the Catskill Mountain Railroad at the Empire State Railroad Museum in Phoenicia for a scenic round-trip ride along the creek. The museum also has some fine classic rail cars on display.

Phoenicia itself is a funky town that is sprucing up with some interesting new shops. Fishing enthusiasts can get both lessons and equipment at Folkert Brothers, an old-fashioned general store where the wares range from fancy china to hunting gear. Town Tinker is the place to rent tubes for a seat-cooling cruise down the Esopus.

Slide Mountain, the highest Catskill peak at 4,180 feet, is located to the south near Oliverea, where the Mountain Gate Lodge offers another culinary surprise—a dining room with delicious curries and other authentic Indian fare.

Yet another train ride awaits in Arkville, this time aboard the Delaware & Ulster Rail Ride to Halcottsville, a wooded route along the Catskill Scenic Trail.

Make a stop in Margaretville for the antique mall in the old movie theater, local crafts at Catskill Offerings, and the Saturday farmer's market that includes works by area crafts artisans. You might even try out the excellent massages at Body Work. Like all the towns in this area, Margaretville used to be a major summer resort when New Yorkers came to the mountains via the railroad. The fancy hotels are gone, but these towns still have a measure of their old charm and surprising touches of sophistication, though they lack both the crowds and the touristy shops found in Woodstock. Their warm, modest inns serve up real hospitality. Besides reasonable rates year round, all have excellent package rates that include Belleayre skiing in winter.

In fall, this is one of the most beautiful areas in the New York region for hiking. Check your inn or local sports stores for hiking maps.

If you want more activity, check out the ski mountains in the area. At Hunter Mountain, a short, steep scenic drive north of Phoenicia on Route 214, you can take a ride on the ski lift for a 360-degree view from the second highest peak in the Catskill range.

At Belleayre Mountain, a highly recommended family ski area in winter, Columbus Day brings a big, annual fall festival, and a chance to ride the ski lift or get an even loftier view via helicopter.

It's a vista that tells you why people return to the Catskills year after year.

Woodstock Area Code: 914

DRIVING DIRECTIONS New York State Thruway to exit 19 at Kingston, west on Route 28, right on Route 375 north, then left off Route 375 onto Route 212 for Woodstock. *Total distance:* 108 miles to Woodstock.

PUBLIC TRANSPORTATION Adirondack Trailways Bus, (212) 967-2900 or (800) 858-8555. The bus stops in Woodstock, Mt. Tremper, Phoenicia, Shandaken, Pine Hill, Fleischmanns, and Margaretville.

ACCOMMODATIONS *Woodstock Inn,* 38 Tannery Brook Road, Woodstock, 12498, 679-8211, motel, $$ CP • *Pinecrest Lodge,* 77 Country Club Road, Woodstock, 12498, 679-2814, $-$$ • *Twin Gables Guest Home,* 73 Tinker Street, Woodstock, 12498, 679-9479, $ • *Ivy Farm Inn*, Route 212, Lake Hill, 12448, 679-9045, $-$$ CP • *Mt. Tremper Inn,* Route 212 and Wittenberg Road, Mt. Tremper, 12457, 688-5239, $-$$ CP • *Auberge des Quatre Saisons,* Route 42, Shandaken, 12480, 688-2223, rooms in chalet-type motel with private bath, shared bath in lodge, $$$-$$$$ MAP • *Margaretville Mountain Inn,* Margaretville Mountain Road, Margaretville, 12455, (800) 749-5515, homey Victorian, grand views, $-$$ CP • *Susan's Pleasant Pheasant Farm,* #1 Bragg Hollow Road, Halcottsville, 12438, (800) 696-3781, charming rustic restored millhouse, $ CP • *River Run,* Main Street, Fleischmanns, 12430, 254-4884, Victorian in-town inn, $-$$, CP • *Mountain Gate Lodge*, 212 McKinley Hollow Road, Oliverea, 12410, (800) 733-0344, motel-style rooms, great mountain setting, pool in summer, $-$$ CP • *Birchcreek Bed & Breakfast,* PO Box 582 (off Route 28), Pine Hill, 254-5222, $$ CP • *Copper Hood Inn,* Route 28, Shandaken, 12840, 688-9962, mini-resort with indoor pool, tennis, hiking trails, $$$$ MAP • *Hanah Country Inn & Resort,* Route 30, Margaretville, 12455, (800) 752-6494, motel-style rooms, pleasant lodge and scenic golf course, $$$.

DINING *Deming Street Trattoria,* 4 Deming Street (off Mill Hill Road east of town), Woodstock, 679-7858, $-$$ • *Joshua's Cafe,* 51 Tinker Street, Woodstock, 679-5533, excellent Middle Eastern fare, $$-$$$ • *The Little Bear,* Route 212, Bearsville, 679-9497, gourmet Chinese food beside a rippling brook, $-$$ • *La Duchesse Anne,* Wittenberg Road, Mt. Tremper, 688-5260, country French in a rustic setting, $$ • *Auberge des Quatre Saisons* (see above), more fine

French, $$ • *The Bear Cafe,* Route 212, Bearsville, 679-5555, streamside dining, seafood and fresh pasta, $$ • *Emory Brook,* Main Street, Fleischmanns, 254-5945, excellent chef, $$ • *Mountain Gate Indian Restaurant* (see above), $ • *Pine Hill Arms Restaurant,* Main Street, Pine Hill, 254-4012, congenial, reasonable, $$.

SIGHTSEEING *Opus 40 and Quarryman's Museum,* 7480 Fite Road, Saugerties, 246-3400. Hours: Memorial Day through October, Fridays and Sundays noon to 5 P.M., also Saturdays when not reserved for concerts and special events; best to check. Adults, $5; children under 12, free • *Catskill Mountain Railroad Co, Inc.,* Route 28, Mount Pleasant, 688-7400. Hours: late May to mid-September, weekends and holidays ll A.M. to 5 P.M. Adults, $4 one way, $5 round trip; children, any ride, $1 • *Delaware & Ulster Rail Ride,* Route 28, Arkville, (607) 652-2821, phone for this year's schedules and rates • *Chrysanthemum Festival,* Seamon Park, Malden Avenue (go to the end of Main Street and turn left), Saugerties, 9 A.M. to dusk, usually first three weeks in October. Free • The Ulster County Public Information Office free brochure gives a complete list of local wineries and farm markets • For information about summer season events, contact the following: *Maverick Concerts,* PO Box 102, Woodstock, 12498, 679-6482; *Opus 40 Sunset Concerts,* see listing above; *River Arts Repertory Theater,* performances at Byrdcliffe and Bearsville theaters, PO Box 1166, Woodstock, 12498, 679-2100.

FOR FURTHER INFORMATION Woodstock Chamber of Commerce, PO Box 36, Woodstock, NY 12498, 679-6234. Ulster County Public Information Office, PO Box 1800, Kingston, NY 12401, 331-9300.

Foliage Watch on the Connecticut River

A cloud of smoke, a cheerful toot of the whistle, and we were off—chugging our way to a rendezvous with the Connecticut River. Outside the windows of the old steam train, the countryside passed in review, dressed in its best fall colors. Marshes and meadows rolled by, an old freight station here, a tiny lace factory there, until at last we spied the sparkling water and two festive riverboats waiting at the dock to provide the second half of one of the region's most unusual foliage tours.

The Valley Railroad has been operating in Essex, Connecticut, since 1970, offering ten-mile excursions into the past aboard the same kind of steam train that Grandpa might have ridden when he was a boy. More than 140,000 people take the ride each year—a nostalgia trip for some, a new adventure for others. The century-old railroad, abandoned in 1968, is one of scores of steam trains flourishing again across the country by giving samples of what travel was like in the not-too-distant past. But this line is unique for its connection with the Connecticut River.

The stately river completes its 410-mile journey to the sea just a few miles downstream from Essex. For train passengers who board the double-decker riverboats, it offers vistas of untouched woodland, with an occasional diversion—a hilltop mansion, the stone turrets of Gillette Castle, or the gingerbread facade of the Goodspeed Opera House—to whip photographers into action. With the crowning of autumn foliage, it is a spectacular scene.

After the hour-long cruise, the train returns passengers to the depot, where they can have photos taken in costumes that match the train's vintage, dine in a 1915 grill car, visit a minimuseum of the Age of Steam, complete with train whistles to blow and bells to ring, or browse through a shop of memorabilia to warm the hearts of railroad buffs.

During the train ride, conductors oblige railroad fans with a history of the cars in service that day, which may include an open gondola and plush-seated Pullman cars, as well as the standard wicker-seated coaches. In the train yard there are cabooses, work cars, locomotive cranes, and a unique double-ended snowplow. Visitors will be intrigued by the shiny new steam engine powering the trains. It comes from China, the only country where steam engines are still manufactured. The line also recently added elegantly refurbished dining cars, and now offers a dinner run.

When you've had your fill of railroad lore, head for Essex and a second look at the river from one of its most charming landings. The history of Essex, a picture-book town of picket fences and white clapboard Colonial and Federal homes, is inextricably tied to its river. The first wharf at the site of the present Steamboat Dock was in existence in 1656. Essex also thrived as an early shipbuilding center.

The 1878 three-story clapboard Dockhouse with its graceful cupola became a landmark on the river. The Connecticut River Foundation has restored the exterior and a portion of the interior to its warehouse days. It also houses a small but interesting River Museum that tells the story of the waterway with tools, models, and a fascinating model of *The Turtle,* the first submarine, designed in 1776.

You can while away a delightful hour walking around Essex and admiring the fine houses lining the winding lanes in town. Watch for the Pratt House on West Avenue above the Congregational Church. It was restored by the New England Society for Antiquities, and the Essex Garden Club has planted a lovely Colonial herb garden around the home.

There's also shopping galore on Main Street for antiques and all the handicrafts, gifts, and gewgaws you'd expect in a town full of strollers. In keeping with the town, however, everything is tasteful.

By car, River Road offers a scenic drive with glimpses of the water and many fine homes.

There is just one inn in Essex, the famous Griswold, which has been open for business on Main Street since 1776. Spring is not too early to reserve a room for fall foliage season, but it's always worth a call in case of last-minute cancellations. The "Gris" is a must, at least for a meal and a visit. The Tap Room, with its busy antique popcorn machine, was once an early Essex schoolhouse; the Steamboat Room simulates the dining salon of an old riverboat, complete with motion from a gently rocking mural at the end of the room; and the Covered Bridge Dining Room, constructed from an abandoned New Hampshire bridge, contains an important collection of Currier & Ives steamboat prints.

No room at the inn? There are plenty of pleasant alternatives nearby. The Copper Beech in Ivoryton has elegant rooms and a restaurant to match, and the Inn at Chester is a country hotel with an excellent and attractive dining room. The Riverwind Inn in Deep River is a true country charmer, and Bishopsgate in East Haddam is an attractive small inn with a special advantage, because it is within walking distance of one of the area's best attractions, the Goodspeed Opera House.

Musicals of the 1920s and 1930s are served up here in a restored Victorian theater that has been aptly described as a "jewel box." *Annie* and *Man of La Mancha* both debuted at the Goodspeed. The theater is right on the banks of the river, and the bar where refreshments are served between acts offers a beautiful view. Reserve weekend tickets far in advance; the Goodspeed is deservedly popular.

New musicals are now performed at a branch of the Goodspeed in Chester. The National Theater for the Deaf is also headquartered here and sometimes performs locally. Check at your inn for schedules.

Come Sunday one of the most pleasant afternoon diversions along the river is a picnic at Gillette Castle State Park, where you'll munch your sandwiches with a spectacular clifftop view. A tour of the castle is a unique experience. It was built by actor William Gillette, a somewhat eccentric gentleman who gained fame and fortune for his portrayal of Sherlock Holmes on stage. The structure cost over a million dollars, quite a pretty penny when it was built in the early

1900s, and was meant to emulate the Rhine Valley castles Gillette had admired in Europe—with turrets, balconies, and the rest.

The interior of the castle is a curiosity. Each of the 24 rooms bears witness to Gillette's eccentricity. No two of the 47 doors are alike, and all are fitted with wooden locks operated by hidden springs. A system of mirrors enabled Gillette to observe visitors without being seen, and a secret panel in the study permitted him to escape if he didn't like what he saw.

Gillette also apparently had an aversion to metal. He insisted that no nails or other metal objects be exposed, and even his light switches are made of wood. The interior walls are also made of hand-hewn and carved oak. There is so much wood that Gillette had fire hoses and a sprinkler system installed, safety features that were many years ahead of their time.

After the castle, there are plenty of diversions in either direction. A short drive north in Higganum is the Sundial Herb Gardens, with formal gardens for touring and a delightful shop selling herbs and tasteful gifts. Teas and tours are offered on many Sunday afternoons.

Downriver a bit, pretty little Chester is a perfect town for browsing. The shops include the Connecticut River Artisans Cooperative, with fine crafts by local artists, and Chester Gallery, another showcase for local work, including contemporary baskets.

If you want to dine on the river, Camelot Cruises in Haddam offers lunch, dinner, or Sunday brunch cruises.

Continuing east, the Great American Trading Company in Deep River is a treasure of toy nostalgia, filled with old-time favorites like wooden pick-up sticks, marbles, and Chinese checkers. Heading toward Old Saybrook, the Essex-Saybrook Antiques Village has a little bit of everything, with 80 dealers under one roof.

In Old Saybrook, where the Connecticut River meets Long Island Sound, there's another opportunity for cruising, as well as the chance to wind up the weekend with a fine seafood dinner. Take your pick of the handsome dining room at the Saybrook Point Inn, the nautical ambience and water views at Dock and Dine, or the informal Saybrook Fish House, which often gets the vote from *Connecticut Magazine* readers for serving the best seafood in the state.

Essex Area Code: 203

DRIVING DIRECTIONS New England Thruway (I-95) to exit 69; Route 9 north three miles to Essex (exit 3). *Total distance:* about 100 miles.

PUBLIC TRANSPORTATION Amtrak rail service to Old Saybrook, toll free (800) USA-RAIL with a connection to Essex.

ACCOMMODATIONS *Griswold Inn,* 36 Main Street, Essex, 06426, 767-1812, $$-$$$$$ CP • *Copper Beech Inn,* Main Street, Ivoryton, 06442, 767-0330, $$$-$$$$$ CP • *Bishopsgate Inn,* Goodspeed Landing, East Haddam, 06423, 873-1677, $$-$$$ CP • *The Inn at Chester,* 318 West Main Street, Route 148, Chester, 06412, 526-9541, $$-$$$, CP • *Riverwind Inn,* Main Street, Deep River, 06147, 526-2014, wonderful country decor, $$-$$$$ CP • *Chester Village Bed & Breakfast,* 123 Main Street, Chester, 06412, 526-9770, a budget choice, walking distance to town, $-$$, CP.

DINING *Griswold Inn* (see above), dinner entrées $$-$$$; Sunday hunt breakfast $$ • *Copper Beech Inn* (see above), dinner entrées $$$-$$$$ • *Oliver's Taverne,* Route 152, Essex, 767-2633, informal, popular, $-$$ • *The Post and Beam,* The Inn at Chester (see above), $$$ • *Restaurant du Village,* 59 Main Street, Chester, 526-5301, country French bistro, $$$-$$$$ • *Fiddler's Seafood Restaurant,* 4 Water Street, Chester, 526-3210, country decor, good food, $$ • *Fine Bouche,* Main Street, Centerbrook, 767-1277, fine French food, $$-$$$ • *The Dock & Dine,* 145 College Street, Saybrook Point, Old Saybrook, 388-4665, $-$$$ • *Saybrook Fish House,* 99 Essex Road, Old Saybrook, 388-4836, $-$$ • *Saybrook Point Inn,* 2 Bridge Street, Old Saybrook, 388-0212, $$-$$$.

SIGHTSEEING *Valley Railroad,* exit 3 off Route 9, Essex, 767-0103. Call for current schedule and rates • *Connecticut River Museum,* foot of Main Street, Essex, 767-8269. Hours: Tuesday to Sunday 10 A.M. to 5 P.M. Adults, $3; children under 12, free • *Goodspeed Opera House,* East Haddam, 873-8668, April to November. Phone for current offerings • *Gillette Castle,* Gillette Castle State Park, Hadlyme, 526-2336. Hours: mid-May to mid-October, daily 10 A.M. to 5 P.M.; October to mid-December, weekends only 10 A.M. to 4 P.M. Adults, $4; children 6–12, $2. No fee for visiting park • *Camelot Cruises,* 1 Marine Park, Haddam, 345-8591, phone for current schedules and rates for lunch and dinner cruises • *Deep River Navigation Company,* River Street, Deep River, 526-4954. Phone for information about cruises out of Old Saybrook.

FOR FURTHER INFORMATION Connecticut River and Shoreline Visitors Council, 393 Main Street, Middletown, CT 06457, 347-0028 or toll-free (800) 486-3346.

Serene Scenes in New Jersey

Frenchtown and Milford are small river towns with much in common. Each has charm, unpretentious airs, and a generous share of history. In the 1700s, each town was a ferry landing, later a flourishing mill town with industries powered by the river. The main street of each was named Bridge Street in the 1800s because it ended in a bridge across the Delaware.

When industry moved elsewhere, the area languished. The period small-town look remained because the towns were too poor to "modernize."

Frenchtown, circa 1741, was the site of grist and sawmills that helped supply the Continental Army. It was considered so vital during the Revolutionary War that its ferry operator and his employees were exempted from military duty. The mills continued to grind into the early 1900s, supplying corn for rural Hunterdon County's poultry farmers.

But fires and floods brought hard times to Frenchtown later in this century. Concerned citizens got together a few years back and applied for a state grant for upgrading. Now the little town has regained its quaint original charm, complete with stone-paved sidewalks and old-fashioned street lamps.

Frenchtown's two-story, gingerbread-trimmed nineteenth-century buildings now have some very interesting tenants. Among them are some choice spots for antiques and fine crafts, and two gourmet havens. Frenchtown Inn serves up four-star French fare by candlelight amidst brick walls and beams, while the Race Street Cafe is known for innovative cuisine in an informal setting that doubles as an art gallery. All the paintings on the walls are for sale.

On the funkier side, Blue Fish, in a restored mill on the edge of town, is known nationally for hand-block tinted and hand-dyed clothing.

The local lodging is Old Hunterdon House, an elegant three-story 1865 Italianate mansion with Victorian furnishings, carved plaster ceilings, working fireplaces, and a cupola. The National Hotel, circa 1851, also offers simple rooms and is definitely worth a stop for a drink at its century-old wooden bar. One of the best spots in town on a sunny day is the Bridge Cafe, a takeout deli with soups, quiches, sandwiches, and treats that can be enjoyed at patio tables by the riverside. The homemade yogurt is delicious.

Milford, population 1,350, is a town that satisfies a city dweller's fantasy of a true country getaway. The main street, with its old-fashioned church and library, is a reminder of a more peaceful era. The town bulletin board advertises Tupperware parties and church suppers.

When some 1940s vintage cars drove through town one weekend on their way to an auto rally, they looked as though they belonged there.

A sign on the bulletin board invites visitors to "Slow down, relax, and enjoy our slower, more gentle pace." That's an easy order to follow when you're rocking on the front porch of Chestnut Hill, a small, cozy Victorian inn facing the Delaware.

While Milford is wonderfully free of T-shirt emporiums or touristy shops, there is a bit of browsing to be done. Especially pleasing are the country gifts and culinary wares at the Little Shop in the old train station. The Little Shop also sells terrific takeout lunches for a pleasant pastime in the area, walking part of the scenic 15-mile riverside path that runs from Frenchtown to Stockton.

Almost everyone in Milford stops by The Baker, where Greg Adams, a former pastry chef at Le Cirque, arrived in 1984 to build a thriving business baking a dozen kinds of organic whole-grain breads and rolls for big city stores. They sell here for a fraction of city prices. There are also warm-from-the-oven muffins and croissants for sale. The smells are heavenly.

Along Bridge Street are two eating spots that are happy surprises in a small village. Olde Mill Ford Oyster House has absolutely fresh seafood, as proven by the displays in the adjoining fish market. The old town tavern is now the Ship Inn, a place to enjoy English, Irish, Scottish, and Welsh beers on draught, served in an authentic pub atmosphere. The menu offers fare such as steak and kidney pie and roast beef and Yorkshire pudding.

To discover more small-town charm, just follow Route 78 east to Clinton, one of New Jersey's unsung gems. Just at the point where the south branch of the Raritan River joins Spruce Run Creek, Clinton's main street begins with a waterfall almost 200 feet wide, anchored at either end by an old mill, set against limestone cliffs and a ten-acre park. It's a picture-book setting little changed since the 1700s.

The red mill with the waterwheel is the Clinton Historical Museum. The turning waterwheel recalls bygone days when grain, flaxseed, limestone, graphite, and talc were processed here. The four floors of exhibits in the mill represent daily rural life in northwestern New Jersey over the past 300 years, and include objects from farm tools and spinning wheels to clothing, china, silver, and glass. The articles are arranged in tableaux depicting the lives of the people who used them. Other buildings house a blacksmith shop, a turn-of-the-century general store and post office, an 1860 schoolhouse, and a log cabin. There are also an herb garden and machinery sheds on the grounds, and in summer, the base of the 150-foot limestone cliff forms a natural amphitheater for concerts. A Harvest Jubilee is held each year in early October. The park itself makes for a delightful stroll beneath the willows and along the stream, where you can watch ducks and geese paddle by.

The mill across the way, an old stone building with a gambrel roof, was still a working gristmill into the 1950s. Now it's the Hunterdon Art Center, an active community center with changing exhibitions of art and crafts as well as classes, films, and concerts. Many interesting original crafts can be found here in the Sales Gallery.

Clinton's Main Street couldn't be a more charming representation of a nineteenth-century town. Visitors tend to browse in a small shopping complex across the street from the mill, where there is an outdoor cafe on the river that is the perfect spot for light refreshments.

Leigh Way is a modest bed-and-breakfast home within walking distance of Main Street should you want to stay in town.

If you want to get out in the autumn air, Spruce Run State Park is just three miles north of Clinton.

A final picturesque stop off Route 78 is the town of Oldwick, a little village that was once known as New Germantown for the Germans who settled it in the 1740s. The entire center of town is a historic district filled with tilty 200-year-old clapboard homes, many of them now antique shops. If you don't find your heart's desire in town, ask at the shops for the Central New Jersey Antique Trail Guide, which lists some four dozen shops in the general vicinity.

Make a stop at the Magic Shop to feel like a kid again, by taking a slide down the rabbit hole past fairy-tale scenes. The shop is a fund-raising venture for a local school for boys and offers toys and music boxes along with its magical slide.

Oldwick makes a perfect lunch break, whether you choose to sample the rightfully famous onion rings at the quaint Tewksbury Inn or the homemade soups and sandwiches at the General Store. The inn also has a more elegant dining room upstairs for dinner. The prize dinner spot, however, is to the south a few miles in Whitehouse, where the Ryland Inn wins raves for its chef, formerly of Manhattan's five-star Bouley.

Oldwick is surrounded by the hills of Hunterdon County and the Cold Brook Preserve, which encompasses the town and a surrounding area of 298 acres, keeping the rural heritage of Hunterdon safe for future generations. The area includes large numbers of apple and peach orchards and two cider mills, where you can pick up some of the season's favorite beverage.

Just beyond the inn on King Street is one of those orchards, Town Farm, where you can detour for cider and apples. One of the most scenic drives around continues on King Street, winding up, down, and around as the scenery turns to woodlands, with handsome homes nestled in the trees. Continue on King as the name changes to Potterstown Road, and when you cross a bridge, make a left to Rockaway Road, driving past a picture-book horse farm and beside a rippling brook to Mountainville, a quaint dot on the map that will surely charm you with its old houses. The Kitchen Caboodle here offers kitchen wares and country furniture, as well as excellent homemade lunches. One of the handful of antique shops is in the former Old Mountainville Hotel.

Turn right at the junction with Mountainville onto Sawmill Road, then right again just past the schoolhouse to Old Turnpike Road, Route 517, which will take you back into Oldwick.

The villages and rolling hills of upper Hunterdon Country are at their very best in their fall colors. Remember to bring along a camera—or a canvas.

North Jersey Area Code: 908

DRIVING DIRECTIONS New Jersey Turnpike to exit 14, then take Route 78 west and continue to Route 31 south. From 31, take Route 12 west into Frenchtown. For Milford, take exit 11, Route 614 south (toward Pattenburg), turn left on Route 519, then right onto Bridge Street into town. *Total distance:* about 85 miles.

PUBLIC TRANSPORTATION Regular bus service to Frenchtown and Milford; trip from Manhattan is under two hours. Get information from the Port Authority Bus Terminal, (212) 564-8484.

ACCOMMODATIONS *Old Hunterdon House,* 12 Bridge Street, Frenchtown, 08825, 996-3632 $$$-$$$$ CP • *National Hotel,* 29 Race Street, Frenchtown, 08825, 996-4871, $-$$ CP • *Chestnut Hill,* 65 Church Street, Milford, 08848, 995-9761, $$-$$$ CP • If these are full, just across the river in upper Bucks County, PA, are: *Bridgeton House,* PO Box 167, River Road, Upper Black Eddy, PA 18972, (215) 982-5856, $$-$$$$ CP; or the elegant *Evermay,* River Road, Erwinna, PA 18920, (215) 294-9100, $$-$$$$ CP • Other alternatives: *Leigh Way,* 55 Leigh Street, Clinton, 08809, 735-4311, $-$$ CP; *Holly Thorn House,* 141 Readington Road, Whitehouse Station (south of Oldwick), 08889, $$ CP.

DINING *Frenchtown Inn,* 7 Bridge Street, Frenchtown, 996-3300, $$$-$$$$ • *Race Street Café,* 2 Race Street, Frenchtown, 996-3179, $$$ • *Ryland Inn,* Old Route 22, Whitehouse, 534-4011, superb chef, worth the expensive tab, $$$ • *Old Milford Oyster House,* Bridge Street, Milford, 995-9411, $$ • *Sergeantsville Inn,* Route 523, Sergeantsville, (609) 397-3700, romantic, worth a drive, $$$ • *Tewksbury Inn,* Main Street, Oldwick, 439-2641, downstairs dining room, $-$$, country French dinner in handsome upstairs dining room, full dinners $$-$$$ • *General Store,* Main Street, Oldwick, 439-2642, lunches and takeout only, $.

SIGHTSEEING *Clinton Historical Museum,* 56 Main Street, Clinton, 735-4101. Hours: April to October, Tuesday to Sunday 10 A.M. to 4 P.M. Adults, $5; children 6–12, $1.50 • *Hunterdon Art Center,* 7 Center Street (off Main), Clinton, 735-8415. Hours: Thurday and Friday 12:30 P.M. to 4:30 P.M., Saturday and Sunday 1 to 5 P.M. Adults, $3, children, $1. Combination ticket with Clinton Historical Museum, $5.50.

FOR FURTHER INFORMATION Hunterdon County Chamber of Commerce, 2200 Route 31, Box 15, Lebanon, NJ 08833, 735-5955.

Tailgating and Other Diversions in New Haven

Though some may dispute their claim, it's a matter of pride in New Haven, Connecticut, that football was born here. The first Yale intramural game was played on the village green some 200 years ago, and football has been a welcome fall tradition ever since.

The origins of tailgate picnics are more obscure, but a visit to the Yale Bowl parking lot on a football weekend clearly demonstrates that this diversion, too, has become a local tradition—and one that is observed with style. Hibachis and outdoor grills send out tempting aromas, cocktail shakers clink merrily, folding tables are set with cloths and cutlery, and even the informal picnickers seem to have particularly attractive hampers.

It's a happy custom on a fine fall day—the picnic, the game, the Yale marching band clad in blue blazers putting a bit of wit into its casual halftime show—and if you want to join the fun, you'll find yourself in a town that has a lot to offer both before and after the game.

New Haven has a long history, the largest collection of British art to be found outside Britain, Yale's magnificent Gothic campus for strolling, top museums, some of the best regional theater in the country, and last—but certainly not least—pizza that is unsurpassed. It will take some juggling to fit it all in. One plan might be to do the campus Saturday morning, take in a bit of New Haven history after the game, and reserve Sunday for museums and some autumn leaves in the city's scenic parks.

Begin by visiting the Information Center at One Long Wharf, off I-95, exit 46, where you can pick up a walking tour map, then head for the green. One of the nine squares laid out in 1638 in America's first planned city, the green offers three particularly fine churches, one Gothic, one Federal, and one Georgian in design. The Center Congregational (1813) is considered a masterpiece of American Georgian architecture.

The main entrance to Yale is just off the green through the William Lyon Phelps Gate on College Street. Free one-hour tours of the campus are offered from the Information Center inside the gate at 10:30 A.M. and 2 P.M. weekdays and 1:30 P.M. weekends, but you can spend an equally pleasant if less informed hour just roaming through the ivied courtyards and past the Gothic facades of the college. Though Yale is now a university of 11,000 students that spreads over many blocks, the heart of the school still remains the old campus bounded by Chapel, High, Elm, and College streets. Nathan Hale, Noah Webster, and William Howard Taft all studied in Connecticut Hall, the oldest intact building on campus.

The green and Yale recall New Haven's Colonial and cultural history, but the city also has an important industrial history. Among its famous products are New Haven clocks, Winchester rifles, and Gilbert toys, which include that all-time favorite, the erector set. Eli Whitney manufactured his cotton gin here and in 1812 led the way to mass production by turning out rifles with interchangeable parts. New Havenite Charles Goodyear invented vulcanized rubber in this town.

After the game, visit the New Haven Colony Historical Society, where you can see samples of some of these early products, Whitney's cotton gin among them, as well as displays of decorative arts, tableware of New Haven from 1640 to 1840, and antique dolls and toys. Nearby at High and Grove streets, an impressive Egyptian gateway leads to the Grove Street Cemetery, a parklike retreat where Whitney and Goodyear are buried, along with Samuel F. B. Morse and Noah Webster.

If your favorite kind of history is found in antique stores, head for the 800 block of Whalley Avenue, where eight stores are clustered. Another dozen are in neighboring Milford, many of them located on Broad Street.

Audubon Street is a revitalized neighborhood that is developing into an arts district, with a number of galleries, bookstores, and shops and changing exhibits at the Creative Arts Workshop at 80 Audubon.

New Haven has many excellent restaurants patronized by the many visitors to Yale and by theatergoers in town, but at dinner hour many make a beeline straight for Wooster Street, the heart of the Italian district. Some of the restaurants here are highly regarded, too, but it is the pizza that makes Wooster Street legendary. It is authentic Italian tomato pie—you have to order mozzarella on top if you want it—and it is *delicious*. There is a long-standing war between devotees of Pepe's (medium-thick crust) and Sally's (superthin), but there are enough fans to do justice to both. Come very early, or be prepared for long *lines*.

Early dinner isn't a bad idea anyway, since you will probably want to get to the theater in the evening. Those who follow theater will need no introduction to Long Wharf, the regional company named for its home in a former food terminal near the water. Long Wharf is a pleasant theatergoing experience, a small and intimate theater-in-the-round with invariably creative staging.

Yale Repertory Theater is another place where you will usually find well-performed experimental theater in New Haven. And recently the old Shubert, home of countless pre-Broadway tryouts in the past, has been renovated and brings in touring companies and concerts, while the new Palace has its own roster of musicals and top-name performers, making for a bounty of evening entertainment in New Haven. You can check for current offerings at all by calling (203) 498-5050, ext. 1310.

Another kind of evening entertainment is next door in Milford, where jai alai is played daily June through December. The game is fast and the betting furious. If you've never seen it played, here's your chance.

Since museums don't open until the afternoon on Sunday, you might sleep late, enjoy brunch, or take a drive to one of New Haven's parks. The city's flat terrain is interrupted by two towering, red rock cliffs that are centerpoints for two lovely parks, each with a view of the harbor and Long Island Sound. East Rock Park is also the site of the city's arboretum, Pardee Rose Gardens, a bird sanctuary, and hiking trails at their peak of autumn color. West Rock Park contains a 40-acre zoo.

Your first museum stop should be one of Yale's finest attractions, the Yale Center for British Art. This modern structure holds the extensive Paul Mellon collection covering British life and culture from Elizabethan times to the present, with numerous paintings by Turner, Constable, and other noted British artists. There are often concerts and lectures scheduled here on weekends; check the desk for the current offerings.

Across Chapel Street, the Yale University Art Gallery, the nation's oldest college art museum, has a varied collection of American and European art of all periods, American decorative art spanning three centuries, African sculpture, pre-Columbian, and Near and Far Eastern art. There is also a sculpture garden.

Another unique attraction is the Yale Collection of Musical Instruments, 850 antique and historical instruments dating from the sixteenth to the nineteenth centuries. The Peabody Museum of Natural History is also an excellent one of its kind, and the Beinecke Library has many rare displays, including a Gutenberg Bible, original Audubon bird prints, and medieval manuscripts.

There is a lot to see—you'll have to pick and choose. And then you'll have the pleasant prospect of picking one of those many fine restaurants in the city to finish off the day.

New Haven Area Code: 203

DRIVING DIRECTIONS Take I-95 or the Hutchinson, Merritt, and Wilbur Cross parkways to downtown New Haven exits. *Total distance:* 75 miles.

PUBLIC TRANSPORTATION Metro-North services New Haven ([212] 532-4900) as does Amtrak ([800] 523-8720). Some bus transportation is available in town.

ACCOMMODATIONS *The Inn at Chapel West,* 1201 Chapel Street, 06510, 777-1201, New Haven's only inn, and a beauty, lavish Victorian decor, $$$$ CP • *New Haven Medical Hotel,* 229 George Street, 06510, 498-3100, near the medical center, pleasant quarters for recovering patients and for all, indoor pool, $$$ • *Residence Inn by Marriott,* 3 Long Wharf Drive, 06511, 776-5337, pool, $$$ CP • *Park Plaza Hotel,* 155 Temple Street, 06510, 772-1700, $$-$$$ • *Colony Inn,* 1157 Chapel Street, 06511, 776-1234, $$-$$$ • *Holiday Inn at Yale,* 30 Whalley Avenue, 06511, 777-6221, $$-$$$ • *Howard Johnson's Long Wharf,* 400 Sargent Drive, 06511, 562-1111, $-$$ • *Quality Inn,* 100 Pond Lily Avenue, 06525, 387-6651, indoor pool, $$.

DINING *Bruxelles,* 220 College Street, 777-7752, upbeat ambience, upscale pizza and rotisserie specialties, $$ • *Bagdon's,* 9 Elm Street, 777-1962, Continental, stylish decor, $$ • *Leon's,* 321 Washington Avenue, 777-5366, Italian old-timer, $$-$$$ • *Azteca's,* 14 Mechanic Street, 624-2454, upscale Southwestern, $$ • *Gennaro's Ristorante D'Amalfi,* 937 State Street, 777-5490, excellent Italian, $$ • *Sally's Apizza,* 237 Wooster Street, 624-5271, $ • *Pepe's,* 157 Wooster Street, 865-5762, $ • Caffe Adulis, 228 College Street, 777-5081, Ethiopian, definitely a change of pace, $ • *New Haven Brewing Company,* 458 Grand Avenue, 772-2739, come for a brew or a tour, $.

SIGHTSEEING *Yale Football,* contact Yale Department of Athletics, PO Box 402A, Yale Station, New Haven, CT 06520, 436-0100, for current schedule and ticket prices • *New Haven Colony Historical Society,* 114 Whitney Avenue, 562-4183. Hours: Tuesday to Friday 10 A.M. to 5 P.M., Saturday and Sunday 2 P.M. to 5 P.M. Adults, $2; children, $1 • *Yale University,* guided one-hour walking tours from Phelps

Gateway off College Street at New Haven green. Call 432-2300 to check current schedule. Free • *Yale Center for British Art,* 1080 Chapel Street, 432-2800. Hours: Tuesday to Saturday 10 A.M. to 5 P.M., Sunday noon to 5 P.M. Free • *Yale University Art Gallery,* 1111 Chapel Street, 432-0600. Hours: Tuesday to Saturday 10 A.M. to 5 P.M., Sunday 2 to 5 P.M. Free • *Peabody Museum of Natural History,* 170 Whitney Avenue, 432-5050. Hours: Monday to Saturday 10 A.M. to 5 P.M., Sunday noon to 5 P.M. Adults, $3.50; children, $2 • *East Rock Park,* East Rock Road. Hours: daily during daylight. Free • *West Rock Park,* Wintergreen Avenue. Hours: zoo (West Rock Nature Center), 787-8016, open Monday to Saturday 10 A.M. to 4 P.M., Sunday noon to 4 P.M. Free • *Long Wharf Theater,* 222 Sargent Drive, 787-4282 • *Yale Repertory Theater,* Chapel and York streets, 432-1234 • *The Palace,* 1000 Chapel Street, 624-TIXS • *Shubert Theater,* 247 College Street, 562-5666 • *Milford Jai Alai,* 311 Old Gate Lane (I-95, exit 40), (800) 243-9660 in CT, (800) 972-9650 out of state; 877-4242 locally. Hours: June to November, Monday, Wednesday through Saturday 7 p.m, matinees Monday, Wednesday, Saturday, Sunday at noon. General admission, $2; reserved seats, $2.25–$6.

FOR FURTHER INFORMATION Contact New Haven Convention and Visitors' Bureau, Inc., One Long Wharf Drive, New Haven, CT 06511, 777-8550 or toll-free (800) 322-STAY. Open Monday to Friday 8:30 A.M. to 4:30 P.M.

A Vision of the Past in Deerfield

Many consider The Street in Old Deerfield, Massachusetts, the loveliest in all New England—and you'll find it at its very best in autumn.

More than 60 fine Colonial and Federal homes line this mile-long avenue, each one carefully restored to its original condition. In the 14 houses open to the public, visitors can see more than 100 rooms filled with china, glassware, silver, pewter, fabrics, and furniture that are a testament to the good taste of our early settlers.

The difference between Deerfield and other restorations is that this town remains alive and well today. People still live in its historic homes. Even the museum-houses have apartments in the rear for the faculty of Deerfield Academy, the noted prep school that has stood on

The Street since 1797. From the moment you arrive, you will sense the town's continuity with the past.

Seeing this peaceful, elm-shaded village today, it is hard to believe it was once a frontier outpost whose fate was uncertain from day to day. Twice Deerfield was almost destroyed by Indian attacks, in the Bloody Brook Massacre of 1675 and the Deerfield Massacre of 1704. Fifty settlers died in the latter battle, and another 111 were taken prisoner and marched off on a brutal midwinter trek to Canada.

But instead of fleeing, the survivors set out to rebuild their town and rework their farms. The town revived and thrived as a center of the wheat industry and an important cattle market. Its more primitive houses were replaced by gracious clapboard homes in the Connecticut Valley tradition. Though rustic compared to homes of this period in Boston or Philadelphia, their very simplicity makes them seem all the more beautiful today.

Deerfield's hard-bitten farmers used the new wealth to bring in the finest furnishings they could buy, particularly the work of the excellent craftsmen and cabinetmakers of their own valley.

By a combination of luck, vision, energy—and money—this era of good taste has been preserved. When the center of farming moved away from New England in the mid-nineteenth century, Deerfield, by then the home of three schools, survived as a center of education. In the next 100 years many local residents began efforts at restoration, but the town's real renaissance was fostered by Mr. and Mrs. Henry Flynt, who came to Deerfield in the 1930s because their son was enrolled at the Academy. The Flynts' first move was to buy and restore the white-columned 1884 Deerfield Inn in the center of town. They next acquired one of the old houses for themselves, and from there one house led to another. In 1952 Mr. and Mrs. Flynt founded Historic Deerfield, Inc.

Though Deerfield is only a village, you can't rush through it in an hour or two. Allow at least a full day—or better yet, a weekend.

A visit to Historic Deerfield includes a walking tour of the village, but you might prefer to start on your own by strolling The Street, with time to savor the town's setting among wooded hills and observing the exteriors of the saltbox houses, with their steep-pitched gambrel roofs, weathered clapboard siding, and distinctively carved doorways. Note the Academy buildings, the old Brick Church, and the delightful post office, a replica of a 1696 meetinghouse.

You may want to take a detour onto the Channing Blake Meadow Walk, a half-mile footpath leading from the village into the nearly 1,000 acres of beautiful meadows that surround the western and northern edges of the community. It gives a close-up view of the fields that have been farmed continuously for more than three centuries and brings into focus the critical roles of agriculture in past and present-day rural New England.

Then head for the Hall Tavern Information Center, where color photos will help you make the difficult choice of which houses to visit during a limited stay. Each house tour takes 30 minutes.

You can begin with Hall Tavern itself, once a hostelry for travelers. One of its seven rooms is an unusual ballroom with gaily stenciled walls.

A must on any tour is Ashley House (circa 1730), the home of Deerfield's Tory minister during the American Revolution. Many may have quarreled with the Reverend Jonathan Ashley's politics, but no one could fault his taste. The north parlor, with blue walls setting off red shell-crowned cupboards, a gold satin settee, and rich Oriental rugs, has been called one of the most beautiful rooms in America.

Each of the other houses has its own special attractions and a knowledgeable guide to point them out. Many of the guides are longtime local residents who have family stories to add to the town's history.

The Sheldon-Hawks House (1743), home of the town's historian, contains fine paneling, a display of sewing equipment, and a memorable bedroom with brilliant flame-stitch bed hangings and red moreen curtains and chairs. Behind the austere, Colonial facade of the Wells-Thorn House (1717/1751) are a series of rooms furnished to depict changing periods in Deerfield's history. The Dwight House (1725) has an elegant parlor and a doctor's office behind its weathered exterior.

The Asa Stebbins House (1799), the town's first brick edifice, was built by the wealthiest landowner and decorated with French wallpapers and freehand wall drawings. Like many of Deerfield's homes, this one has an excellent collection of early export china.

Mr. Stebbins also built the town's other brick house for his son, Asa, Junior, in 1824. Now called Wright House, it is distinguished for its exquisite collection of Federal furniture.

Frary House (1720/1768), a home with a double history, is another highly recommended stop. Its location on the town common made it a refuge for the Frary family in pioneer days and a profitable tavern for the Barnards later on. The house contains a ballroom, many examples of country furniture, and a variety of cooking, spinning, and weaving equipment. There is also a "touch it" room where children and adults may handle some of the tools that are off-limits elsewhere.

The newest home on the tour is the Ebenezer Hinsdale and Anna Williams House, opened to the public in 1993 after 12 years of painstaking restoration and research to interpret the life and times of nineteenth-century Deerfield residents. The furnishings are based on the personal inventory of household property owned by Hinsdale Williams at his death on June 1, 1838.

For a change of pace, step into some of the specialized buildings such as the Henry Needham Flynt Silver and Metalware Collection, a farmhouse containing a smith's workshop, a pewter collection, and an outstanding display of American and English silver. The house dates from around 1810. Inside a Victorian barn is the Helen Geier Flynt Textile Collection, a remarkable assemblage of American, English, and European needlework, textiles, quilts, bed hangings, and costumes.

Historic Deerfield sponsors many special events, including antiques forums, open hearth cooking demonstrations and craft fairs. Ask for a listing of programs in advance and you may be able to plan your visit to coincide.

Last stop, and a delightful place to stay, is the Deerfield Inn, where you can end the day with tea before a roaring fire or stronger refreshments in the tavern room. The inn serves excellent meals in an elegant, candlelit dining room. From May to November, evening carriage rides can be combined with dinner at the inn.

With luck you'll be able to get a room at the inn. If not, there are other good inns in the college towns nearby, and wherever you stay, you're in good position on Sunday for a tour of the Pioneer Valley, home of the well-known Five Colleges, haven for craftsmen, and a bucolic area with more than its share of autumn scenery.

A college tour is a good plan for seeing the sights, and you'll be getting a good cross section of college architecture while you're at it—Amherst with its halls of ivy and picture-book green; the modern University of Massachusetts, a virtual city that actually has a building tall enough for a top-floor restaurant with a view; rustic Hampshire College; and the mix of old and new along the quadrangles of Smith in Northampton and Mount Holyoke in South Hadley. Smith has an outstanding plant house and botanical garden, as well as an excellent and varied art museum with French impressionists, Renaissance sculpture, eighteenth-century English paintings, and much more. Amherst's Mead Art Gallery is smaller but has a large collection of American art from the eighteenth to twentieth centuries, as well as a curiosity, the Rotherwas Room, dating from 1611 and given to the college by an alumnus who had it brought to America from a British castle. Walnut carved paneling, an ornate mantel, and stained-glass windows give the room an authentic baronial flavor.

There's interesting shopping in this region, particularly for lovers of fine handcrafts. The Pioneer Valley has developed into a major center for artisans, with some 1,500 living in the area. Their work can be seen in many galleries in Northampton, the arts and dining center of the area. Don Muller at 11 Bridge Street and the Ferrin Gallery and Pinch Pottery on Main Street are of special note. Ferrin's annual October Tea Party features wonderful teapots from craftspeople all over the country. Thorne's Marketplace on Main is also an interesting spot, a one-time department store turned into a complex with galleries, shops, and eating places.

Northampton's Center for the Arts has exhibits throughout the year, as does The Hart Gallery, on the lower level of the Guild Art Center. Antiquers will find more than half a dozen shops, including the three-level, multidealer Antique Center of Northampton, all within a few yards of each other on Market Street.

Among Northampton's creative residents are the folks who invented the Ninja Turtles. They opened a local museum of sequential art, the Words and Pictures Museum, where you can sample the latest comic books and graphic novels, or step over the frame of a comic to become part of the action.

For foliage vistas, try Mount Tom on U.S. 5 in Holyoke, where an observation tower is open daily until 8 P.M. On Mount Sugarloaf, off Route 116 in Sunderland near Amherst, another state park with an observation tower offers a sweeping view of the river valley and the flaming hillsides on either side.

Heading home, you may want to make a detour into Springfield, where four museums for art, fine arts, and natural history are clustered together in a quadrangle downtown.

Of more interest to any sports fans along may be the Naismith Memorial Basketball Hall of Fame, a wonderful showcase of the sport in the town where it was born in 1891. This is a museum full of color and life. Among its many pleasures are uniforms tracing the sport's changes, life-size action blow-ups of Hall of Famers, and a movie that puts you smack into the middle of center court during a game. On the way out, you can try your shooting arm on a moving walkway with a ready supply of balls to be aimed at baskets at a range of distances. Some of the targets are so close that almost everyone can leave feeling like a champ.

Deerfield Area Code: 413

DRIVING DIRECTIONS Take I-95 or Hutchinson River Parkway and Merritt Parkway to I-91; follow I-91 north to exit 24 and follow Route 5 six miles into Deerfield center. *Total distance:* 187 miles.

PUBLIC TRANSPORTATION Amtrak trains to Springfield, phone toll free (800) USA-RAIL. Peter Pan Bus Lines connect Springfield, Amherst, and Northampton to New York and Boston, phone toll free (800) 237-8747 in Massachusetts, (212) 564-8484 in New York.

ACCOMMODATIONS *Deerfield Inn,* Main Street, Deerfield, 01342, 774-5547, $$$ • *Lord Jeffery Inn,* 30 Boltwood Avenue, Amherst, 01002, 253-2576, $$-$$$ • *Hotel Northampton,* 36 King Street, Northampton, 01060, 584-3100, nicely refurbished town landmark, $$-$$$ • *Autumn Inn,* 259 Elm Street (Route 9), Northampton, 01060, 584-2576, pleasant motel near Smith campus, $$ • *Quality Hotel,* 1 Atwood Drive, U.S. 5 and I-91, Northampton, 01060, 586-1211, motel, indoor pool, tennis, $$-$$$.

DINING *Deerfield Inn* (see above) $$ • *Lord Jeffery Inn* (see above), $$ • *Eastside Grill,* 19 Strong Avenue, Northampton, 586-3347, Cajun specialties, $-$$ • *Wiggins Tavern,* Hotel Northampton (see above), 200-year-old tavern, New England specialties, $$ • *The Depot,* 125A Pleasant Street, Northampton, 586-5366, stylishly renovated train station, varied menu. $-$$ • *Spaghetti Freddy's,* next to The Depot, Northampton, 586-5366, good pasta at good prices, $-$$ • *Fitzwilly's,* 23 Main Street, Northampton, 584-8666, local gathering spot, $-$$ • *India House,* 45 State Street, Northampton, 586-6344, tandoori specialties, $ • *Paul and Elizabeth's,* 150 Main Street in Thorne's Market, Northampton, 584-4832, local vegetarian favorite, $-$$ • *La Cazuela,* 7 Old South Street, Northampton, 586-0400, Mexican and Southwestern dishes, $-$$ • *Green Street Cafe,* 64 Green Street, Northampton, 586-5650, European flavor, lunch and dinner, $-$$ • *The Northampton Brewery,* 11 Brewster Court, Northampton, 584-4176, brew-pub, very popular, $-$$ • *Yankee Pedlar Inn,* 1866 Northampton Street, Holyoke, 532-9494, Colonial ambience, longtime favorite in the area, $$ • *The Log Cabin,* Route 141, Easthampton Road, Holyoke, 536-7700, rustic setting and fine views, $$ • *Student Prince and Fort,* 8 Fort Street, Springfield, 734-7475, German food, great collection of beer steins, $-$$$ • *Tavern Inn Restaurant,* 91 West Gardner Street, Springfield, 781-2882, near the Basketball Hall of Fame, sports decor, $ • *Peking Duck House,* 1535 Main Street, Springfield, 734-5604, relative of New York's Chinatown standby, $-$$ • For a light lunch, try *The Black Sheep Deli,* 79 Main Street, Amherst, or *Coolidge Park Cafe* in the Hotel Northampton, Northampton.

SIGHTSEEING *Historic Deerfield,* PO Box 321, Deerfield, MA 10342, 774-5581. Hours: daily 9:30 A.M. to 4:30 P.M. Adults, $10; children, $5 • *Mead Art Gallery,* Amherst College, 542-2335. Hours: weekends 1 to 5 P.M., weekdays 10 A.M. to 4:30 P.M. Free • *Smith College Museum of Art,* Elm Street, Northampton, 585-2760. Hours: Tuesday to Saturday noon to 5 P.M., Sunday 2 to 5 P.M. Free • *Words and Pictures Museum,* 244 Main Street, Northampton, 586-8545. Hours: Tuesday to Sunday, noon to 5 P.M. Donation • *Naismith Memorial National Basketball Hall of Fame,* 1150 West Columbus Avenue (off I-91, Downtown Springfield exit), Springfield, 781-6500.

Hours: September to June, daily 9 A.M. to 5 P.M., July to Labor Day, to 6 P.M. Adults, $7; children 7–15, $4.

FOR FURTHER INFORMATION Franklin County Chamber of Commerce, 395 Main Street, Greenfield, MA 01301, 773-5463; Greater Springfield Convention and Visitors' Bureau, 34 Boland Way, Springfield Civic Center, Springfield, MA 01103, 787-1548; Northampton Chamber of Commerce, 62 State Street, Northampton, MA 01060, 584-1900.

A Capital Trip to Albany

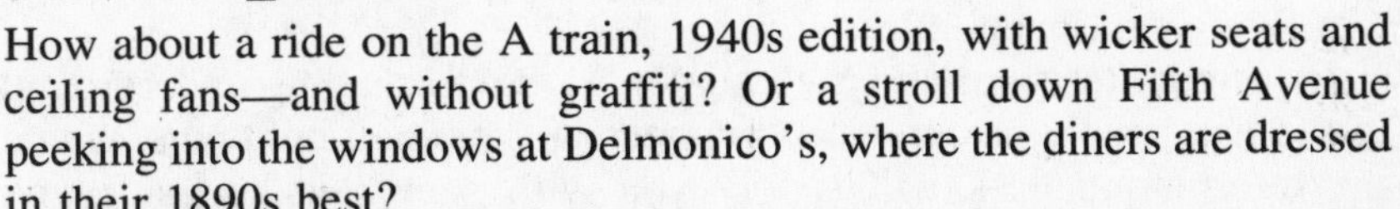

How about a ride on the A train, 1940s edition, with wicker seats and ceiling fans—and without graffiti? Or a stroll down Fifth Avenue peeking into the windows at Delmonico's, where the diners are dressed in their 1890s best?

These and much, much more—replicas of a tenement sweatshop, the old port of New York, an old Chinatown store, an antique trading post from the Stock Exchange, the "Sesame Street" TV set, and a 1925 city bus—are among the features of the "The New York Metropolis," the most comprehensive exhibit on the city ever assembled.

But if you want to see it, there's a catch. You'll have to travel 150 miles from Manhattan to the New York State Museum, part of the Empire State Plaza in Albany.

New York's state capital is rarely thought of as a weekend destination, but there's more than enough here to pack a pleasureful weekend of sightseeing, plus some beautiful surrounding countryside to explore when you're done in town. The scenery is at its best in fall, when apple picking, hiking, a cruise on the Hudson, and a look at the fascinating history of the Shaker sect are all possibilities for the weekend scenario.

The prime attraction in Albany is the Empire State Plaza, the legacy of late Governor Nelson Rockefeller. Not everyone agreed with Rockefeller's colossal plan to clear 98 acres of downtown land and dislocate 3,000 people in order to build glass and marble monuments costing a billion dollars of taxpayers' money. Not everyone approved of the architecture, either. Though they were built in the 1970s, some of the buildings still seem futuristic in design, as does the equally unorthodox Knickerbocker Arena nearby, which houses sports, concerts, and conventions.

Still, there's no denying that Albany has gained not only a striking government complex but a first-rate cultural center. The stupendous plaza art collection assembled by Mr. Rockefeller adds to the pleasure of a visit. It is the nation's largest publicly owned collection of modern art.

Your first stop definitely should be the plaza, perhaps for a bird's-eye view from the forty-second-floor observation deck of its tallest building, known simply as the Tower. Across the mall four smaller Agency Towers house many state departments. At one end of the mall are the lower-scale structures of the Legislative Office Building and the Justice Building; and at the other end is the handsome Cultural Education Center, which contains the State Museum. The many-tiered steps to the center form a seating area that can accommodate 2,500 people for the free music and entertainment that frequently take place on the mall.

Next to the Tower is a restaurant, and next to that the most unusual of all the edifices, the Performing Arts Center, universally known as The Egg. The name's origin will be obvious when you see the shape of this flying saucer on stilts.

Having gotten your perspective, you'11 be descending underground to the half-mile concourse that connects all the mall buildings, where the information desk will supply you with pamphlets to guide you through the extraordinary art collection, some 92 works created in the 1950s and 1960s. Many of the artists were members of the New York School. These include Jackson Pollock, Franz Kline, and Mark Rothko. The art is found inside the state agency buildings, all along the concourse and outdoors on the plaza. Among the important sculptures are Alexander Calder's Triangles and Arches, in the south end of the reflecting pool on the plaza, and five works by David Smith, located in the Corning Tower. Smith lived in Bolton Landing, north of Albany.

Other well-known artists represented include Frankenthaler, Motherwell, Oldenburg, Kelly, Gottlieb, Nevelson, and many others.

You'll probably want to linger in the State Museum. It is the nation's largest state museum and has amazing resources for an institution in a city the size of Albany. In addition to the many unique features of the New York metropolis exhibit, there are some interesting special effects in the section called ''Adirondack Wilderness,'' particularly a small dark room where you can hear the awesome sound of a giant tree falling in the forest. Another exhibit portrays the Native Peoples of New York, tracing the state from the Ice Age to the first settlements of Native Americans.

Another spot for lingering is the New York State Vietnam Memorial in the courtyard south of the Justice Building. It was designed as a place for reflection and serenity, with trees, shurbs, benches, a fountain, and a pool. A bronze honor roll lists the names of the over 4,000 New Yorkers who were killed or listed as missing in Vietnam. On the first floor of the Justice Building are two other parts of the memorial, a resource center with books and films on the war, and a gallery with changing exhibits of artwork and photographs by Vietnam veterans. The indoor sections are open on weekdays only.

When you've had your fill of the plaza, you might take a walk to the west (behind the agency buildings) to Hamilton Street and Robinson Square, a series of galleries, shops, and restaurants in restored nineteenth-century brownstones. The entire area behind the plaza known as Center Square, once a slum, is being restored house by house into a totally charming neighborhood; it is well worth the time for a stroll to appreciate the fine Victorian architecture. The area is bounded by Washington and Madison avenues, Lark and South Swan streets.

After lunch on Hamilton or in one of the plaza restaurants, it's time for a second free tour, this time a look at the ornate state capitol building with its "million-dollar staircase," adorned with carvings, and the beautifully restored Senate and Assembly chambers. Free guided tours leave from the tour desk on the main floor.

The Albany Urban Cultural Park Visitors' Center is the place to see exhibits and an audio-visual program exploring the rest of Albany's history, including charming re-creations of the city during its early Dutch days. The center is stocked with brochures of all area attractions and a free walking-tour brochure to guide further explorations.

One important stop is the Albany Institute of History and Art, depicting four centuries of regional history. This is one of the oldest museums in the nation, founded in 1791, and its Dutch limner portraits are some of the earliest examples of portraiture in America. Offerings in the galleries run the gamut: exquisite Albany-made silver; nineteenth-century furniture, pewter, and ceramics made in the state; a collection of cast-iron stoves manufactured in Albany and Troy; and paintings by the Hudson River School of artists.

There are several prize historic homes and churches to visit. Choice among the houses are Cherry Hill, whose furnishings reflect the changing life-styles of five generations of the Van Rensselaer family, who lived here from 1787 to 1963, and the Schuyler Mansion, home of the prominent early family and a center of activities during the Revolutionary War. George Washington, Benjamin Franklin, and Alexander Hamilton visited this house; Hamilton, in fact, married Elizabeth Schuyler at the mansion.

Among the most notable churches are First Church, whose pulpit, carved in Holland in 1656, is the oldest in America; St. Peter's, a Gothic Revival structure containing a silver communion service donated by Queen Anne; the first Episcopal cathedral in America, with stalls built by monks in 1623 and some of the finest European wood carving in America; and Congregation Beth Emeth, one of the first four reform Jewish congregations in America, with a great folded roof reminiscent of the tent Moses prepared as a desert tabernacle.

Or you may decide to forget sightseeing altogether, and get a different perspective on the Capital District aboard a cruise on the Hudson River or the Erie Canal.

As the state capital, Albany is accustomed to visitors, and there are numerous places to stay and dine in the area, including one small bed-and-breakfast, the Mansion Hill Inn, with TV and other motel conveniences. If you want to make this a country weekend, choose the the Appel Inn, a delightful historic home on six acres just 12 miles from the city. Another good choice a bit further away is the Greenville Arms, a comfortable Victorian homestead with attractive grounds, about 28 miles southwest in a peaceful tiny town on the edge of the Catskills.

As for evening entertainment, if you are in the city you should find something of interest going on in one of the two arenas of The Egg, which has an ongoing schedule of drama, dance, and music, or at the Knickerbocker Arena. The Capitol Repertory Company also presents a program of plays in their downtown theater from October through June.

Come Sunday, if you want to see some of the lovely countryside, you'll have to pick and choose your destinations. One strong recommendation is to bring along your hiking shoes and make your first stop the John Boyd Thatcher State Park, about 18 miles west of the city on Route 157. The clifftop view here is one of the best around; on a clear day you can see the peaks of the Adirondacks, the Massachusetts Taconics, and Vermont's Green Mountains, plus the Hudson-Mohawk Valley and the profusion of trees covering the slopes—oaks, elms, red maples, birches, lindens, and white pines—producing a rich palette of fall color.

The hiking shoes are for the half-mile Indian Ladder trail paralleling the Helderberg Escarpment, a cliff of limestone and shale that geologists have declared to be one of the richest fossil-bearing formations in the world. The trail takes about 45 minutes.

If you continue from the park to Route 156, you can pick your own peck of apples at Indian Ladder Farms in Voorheesville. Depending on the season, you may find raspberries or blueberries ripe for picking as well, and there's always fresh-pressed cider for sale as well as fresh-grown vegetables.

From here you can choose your direction. One possibility is to take in a game at Heritage Park, where the AA Albany-Colonie Yankees play, and where you might just see a future Mantle or DiMaggio in the making. The intimacy and informality of a minor league park is a refreshing experience.

If you continue west on Route 20 for perhaps 20 miles you'll come to a natural wonder, Howe Caverns. An 80-minute tour here of the underground caves and subterranean waterways includes an underground boat ride. If you are going to the caverns, bring a jacket; temperatures in the caves are in the chilly fifties.

Nearby is the new Iroquois Indian Museum, tracing the lives of the tribe that inhabited this part of New York. The Museum offers a special section for children, where they can experience some of the activities of the young Iroquois.

Another alternative if you have children along is to drive south to the Catskill Game Farm on Route 32. Otherwise on to Route 23A, the spectacular road to Hunter Mountain, with cliffs and waterfalls along the way and more magnificent foliage vistas. If you take this route, make a detour to Elka Park for Sunday dinner at the Redcoat's Return, a rustic farmhouse whose book-lined dining room is highly recommended in the area.

Or you might choose to make your way back about 20 miles southeast of Albany for a visit to the Shaker Museum on Route 66 in Old Chatham. This complex of eight buildings in a calm and beautiful farm setting shows the enterprise and ingenious simple designs of this industrious sect, who invented such practical aids as the circular saw, the flat broom, and the clothespin. You will see a cabinetmaker's shop; a small chair factory; a smith's shop; galleries of textiles and the looms that produced them; craft shops used by tinsmiths, cobblers, and broom makers; the Shaker seed and medicine industries; an herb house adjacent to the herb garden; and nine period rooms and a Shaker schoolroom. Each room is incredibly neat, spare, and functional, with the clean-lined furniture that has inspired so many latter-day craftsmen. If the Shakers interest you, make a note that the third Saturday in September is the annual Crafts Day at the museum, when special demonstrations are scheduled. Also note that the museum store sells reproductions of Shaker furniture and of their handsome oval storage boxes.

If time remains, take a drive through the appealing old towns and the pastoral countryside of the various Chathams and New Lebanon. If you drive home via Route 22, there are some splendid choices for dinner. Two in Hillsdale are the L'Hostellerie Bressane, highly acclaimed for French food, and the Swiss Hutte. The third, farther down in Patterson, though not noted for its fine dining, is a real curiosity. It's an offbeat Mexican restaurant called the Texas Taco, where you'll share eating quarters with the most amazing collection of odd memorabilia and animals, including parrots and a monkey. Some people find it so appealing they make a special point of driving home via this route just to stop in again.

Albany Area Code: 518

DRIVING DIRECTIONS New York State Thruway (Route 87) to exit 23. Follow signs to I-787 into Albany, watching for signs to the

Empire State Plaza. Elevated traffic loop leads into and under the Empire State Plaza. Parking is available in underground garages and is free after 5 P.M. and on weekends. *Total distance:* 150 miles.

PUBLIC TRANSPORTATION Amtrak ([800] 523-8700) to Albany is the most scenic route you can take, paralleling the Hudson River almost all the way.

ACCOMMODATIONS Most Albany-area lodgings have lower rates for weekend packages; be sure to ask. • *Omni Albany,* Ten Eyck Plaza, 12207, 462-6611, convenient downtown location, $$$-$$$$ • *Econo Lodge Downtown,* 300 Broadway, 12207, 434-4111, budget choice downtown, $ CP • *Mansion Hill Inn,* 115 Philip Street at Park Avenue, 12202, $$-$$$ CP • Two pleasant choices near the airport: *Albany Marriott,* 189 Wolf Road, Colonie, 12205, 458-8444, $$$-$$$$ • *The Desmond,* 660 Albany Shaker Road, Colonie, 12211, 869-8100, $$$-$$$$ • Bed-and-breakfast inns outside the city: *Greenville Arms,* Greenville, 12038, 966-5219, $$-$$$ CP • *Appel Inn,* PO Box 18, RD 3, Altamont, 861-6557, $-$$ CP.

DINING *Ogden's Restaurant,* Howard Street at Lodge Street, 463-6605, interesting menu, in restored office building, $$-$$$ • *Nicole's Bistro at L'Auberge,* 351 Broadway, 465-1111, French fare in restored steamship ticket office, $$-$$$ • *Jack's Oyster House,* 42 State Street, 465-8854, noisy, old favorite downtown eatery with famous cheesecake, $-$$ • *La Serre,* 14 Green Street, 463-6056, French and fine, in a restored factory, $$$-$$$$ • *Café Capriccio,* 49 Grand Street, 465-0439, regional Italian, $$-$$$ • *Yono's,* 289 Hamilton Street, 436-7747, Indonesian, $$ • *Michael's Restaurant,* 851 Madison, 489-4062, deli with takeout counter if you want a picnic lunch, $ • *Stone Ends,* 9 Frontage Road, Route 9W, Glenmont, 465-3178, art deco decor, New American menu, excellent reports, $$-$$$$ • *Redcoat's Return,* Dale Lane, Elka Park, 589-6379, $$-$$$ • *L'Hostellerie Bressane,* off Route 22, Hillsdale, 325-3412, $$-$$$ • *Swiss Hutte,* Route 22, Hillsdale, 325-3333, $$-$$$ • *Texas Taco,* Route 22, Patterson, 878-9665, $.

SIGHTSEEING Empire State Plaza, visitors' assistance and information, north end of the underground concourse, 474-2418. Hours: Monday to Friday 9 A.M. to 4 P.M. Observation deck, daily 9 A.M. to 5 P.M. Free • *New York State Museum,* Empire State Plaza, 474-5877. Hours: daily 10 A.M. to 5 P.M. Free • *State Capitol Building,* Empire

State Plaza, 474-2418. Tours: on the hour, daily 9 A.M. to 4 P.M. Free • *Cherry Hill,* 523½ Pearl Street, 434-4791. Hours: February to December, Tuesday to Saturday 10 A.M. to 3 P.M., Sunday 1 to 3 P.M. Adults, $3.50; children 6–16, $1 • *Schuyler Mansion,* 32 Catherine Street, 434-0834. Hours: Wednesday to Sunday 10 A.M. to 5 P.M. Donation • *Albany Institute of History and Art,* 125 Washington Avenue, 463-4478. Hours: Tuesday to Friday 10 A.M. to 5 P.M., Saturday and Sunday noon to 5 P.M. Donation • Churches, usually open daytime hours, but phone to check; all free: *First Church in Albany,* North Pearl near Clinton, 463-4449; *St. Peter's Church,* State and Lodge streets, 434-3502; *Cathedral of All Saints,* 62 South Swan Street, 465-1342; *Congregation Beth Emeth,* 100 Academy Road, 436-9761 • *Albany Urban Cultural Park/Visitors' Center,* 25 Quackenbush Square, 434-6311. Hours: Monday to Friday 10 A.M. to 4 P.M. year-round, weekends spring through fall • *Dutch Apple Cruises, Inc.,* 1668 Julianne Drive, Castleton, NY, 463-0220. Hours: daily May 1 to October 31. Hudson River and canal cruises from downtown Albany at Broadway and Quay streets, phone for current schedules and rates • *Albany-Colonie Yankees,* Heritage Park, Watervliet-Shaker Road, 869-9236. Phone for current schedule and prices • *John Boyd Thatcher State Park,* Route 157 off Route 85. Hours: 9 A.M. to 10 P.M. through Labor Day; closes earlier after Labor Day. Free • *Indian Ladder Farms,* Route 156 (two miles west of Voorheesville), 765-2956. Hours: Monday to Saturday 9 A.M. to 6 P.M.; Sunday 10 A.M. to 6 P.M. • *The Shaker Museum,* Route 66, Old Chatham, 794-9100. Hours: May 1 to October, daily 10 A.M. to 5 P.M. Adults, $6; children 8–17, $3; family rate, $14 • *Howe Caverns,* Route 7, Howes Cave. Hours: daily 9 A.M. to 6 P.M. Adults, $10.50; children 7–12, $6; children under 7 free • *Iroquois Indian Museum,* Caverns Road, Howes Cave, 296-8949. Hours: daily 10 A.M. to 5 P.M. Adults, $5; children, $2.50 • *Catskill Game Farm,* Route 32, Cairo, 678-9595. Hours: April 15 to October 31, daily 9 A.M. to 6 P.M. Adults, $11.75; children 4–11, $7.50.

FOR FURTHER INFORMATION Albany County Convention and Visitors' Bureau, Inc., 52 South Pearl Street, Albany, NY 12207, 434-1217.

Hounds and Houses in Chester County

For more than 50 years, it has been a ritual. Promptly at 9 A.M. on the first Saturday in October, the huntsman's horn sounds in Chester County, Pennsylvania. It is the signal for the running of horses and hounds for one of the frequent fox hunts in this fabled horse country—and it is the traditional start of the once-a-year celebration known as Chester County Day.

For the rest of the year much of this lush hilly region, roughly midway between Philadelphia and Pennsylvania Dutch country, is somewhat private about its charms, except for the three major sights on the fringe of the county: Longwood Gardens, the Brandywine River Museum, and Valley Forge. But for this one day only, the entire county blows its own horn for the benefit of the local hospital, showing off dozens of its finest residences as well as the covered bridges, old mills, Quaker meetinghouses, gardens, and other historic sites that are all the more appealing just because they aren't widely touted. The day is so special that ticket sales are limited to 5,000—and many more must be turned away.

The crowds don't get overwhelming because so many houses are open, everything from Federal-era row houses and columned mansions on the brick-paved streets of West Chester, the county seat, to stone manors and restored barns and carriage houses in the country. With so many homeowners taking part in the day, a choice of daylong itineraries is offered in different areas. Some of the owners also help to make the day more memorable with touches like the aroma of fresh-baked bread from the kitchen and spectacular arrangements of flowers and fruit in the rooms.

One of the particular pleasures of the tour is occasionally meeting some of the hosts whose families have lived in this area for generations. Chester County has been strongly influenced by its Quaker origins. People here don't show off. Their homes and possessions were made to last, and many live quietly every day with family furniture, antiques, and china that would do credit to a museum.

When the owners aren't present, helpful guides will point out some of the treasures.

Because the county covers such a large area, tours alternate locale and emphasis, taking on a different quarter of the territory each year.

Slide-show previews of the homes included are offered on Friday night at Longwood Gardens and the West Chester courthouse to help visitors make the difficult choice of which houses they want to see most. The slide shows are included in the price of the tour. For those who prefer not to drive, bus tours are available from the hospital in West Chester on Saturday morning.

A good plan is to write well in advance for a copy of the *County Day* newspaper, which is usually published in August and outlines the year's current tours. The itineraries may influence where you decide to stay for the weekend, but two safe bets any year are West Chester and the Longwood area, since both have plenty of accommodations.

The tour will keep you so busy on Saturday you probably won't want to take time for a long lunch. However, a stop at the Marketplace Deli in West Chester center will equip you with a fine portable meal to be enjoyed along the way. Come dinnertime, you can choose from a whole roster of charming country inns.

If you can spare a few minutes, do have a look at the exceptional Chester County Historical Society Museum in West Chester. It is filled with exquisite clocks, furniture, inlaid chests, embroidery, Tucker porcelain, and majolica pottery, the kinds of pieces often featured on the covers of antiques magazines. There are six fine period room settings. The Museum hoped to break ground in 1994 for a major expansion that will add the neighboring YMCA building to its complex, greatly expanding the exhibit space, library, and facilities and creating a regional history center.

Sunday offers other delightful possibilities. You might want to head for Marshalton to see the annual Triathalon Race, with festivities beginning at 9 A.M., sponsored by the Marshalton Inn. It's a unique and wacky event, with competitors from 6 to 69 racing via canoe, bicycle, and Olympic walk-step. Though it is a fun race that anyone can enter, for many it is a serious competition, which makes it all the more fun to watch. Normally this is a quaint quiet village, but on this day the place is jumping all afternoon and into the evening, with lively music and food stands set up outdoors.

If you didn't really see much of the town on Saturday, a walking tour of West Chester is a quieter and quite interesting occupation. The town is a parade of architectural variety—green serpentine stone, brick town houses, gingerbread porches, porticoed doorways, iron-lace fences, Greek columns. The courthouse, a bank, and a church are massive-columned Greek Revival structures designed by the architect of the nation's capitol, which once caused the little town to be dubbed the Athens of Pennsylvania. The firehouse and public library are Gothic buildings adorned with Tiffany windows. The residential life of the 1800s can be seen in restored houses on Portico Row, Pottery Row, Stone Row, and Wayne Square.

Another special pleasure in the area is the little Dilworthtown Country Store, located south of West Chester on Brinton Bridge Road just off Route 202. It has been at the same stand since 1758, and the original stone walls and low beams add atmosphere to a tantalizing stock of penny candy, country antiques, bolts of calico, hand-fired tools, hand-dipped candles, folk toys, baskets, quilts, and all manner of one-of-a-kind creations from neighborhood craftspeople. The Dilworthtown Inn right next door is one of the best in the area, a good bet for Saturday or Sunday dinner.

Take a drive up Birmingham Road, just past the inn, to see the magnificent gentlemen's farms, a Quaker meetinghouse, an octagonal schoolhouse, and a historic old cemetery.

If the day is fine and you want to enjoy the outdoors, take a stroll around the Brandywine Battlefield State Park near Chadds Ford, where you can visit restorations of Washington's and Lafayette's headquarters. Or a half hour's drive will take you to the 2,200-acre national park at Valley Forge, resplendent in autumn colors. Longwood Gardens and the Brandywine River Museum with its Wyeths are other perennial attractions, different with each change of season.

Between Longwood and the museum, Route 1 is lined with antiques shops, and a busy flea market is in action every weekend. While you are in Kennett Square, you can also make a stop at the Mushroom Museum and Shop at Phillips Place. The giant mushrooms for sale here in the town that calls itself the world's mushroom capital will make the ones in your local supermarket look like miniatures.

The back roads of Chester County don't get a lot of attention compared to those in nearby Bucks or Lancaster counties, yet they are full of unexpected discoveries—historic, scenic, and just plain fun. You'll find that whatever direction you choose to explore, it's almost impossible to make a wrong turn.

Chester County Area Code: 610

DRIVING DIRECTIONS Take the New Jersey Turnpike south to exit 6, Pennsylvania Turnpike, then west to exit 24, Schuylkill Expressway (Route 76), then south to Route 202 to West Chester. Continue on 202 to Route 1 south to Longwood Gardens. *Total distance:* 120 miles.

ACCOMMODATIONS Bed-and-breakfast inns in the scenic nearby countryside include: *Meadow Spring Farm*, 201 East Street Road (Route 926), Kennett Square, 19348, 444-3903, folksy, warm, a working farm, $-$$$ CP • *Sweetwater Farm,* Sweetwater Road, PO Box 86, Glen Mills, 19342, 459-4711, elegant, $$$-$$$$ CP • *Highland Farm Bed and Breakfast,* 314 Highland Farm Road, West Chester, 19382, 431-7026, gracious 1850 hilltop stone mansion, beautifully furnished, $$$-$$$$ CP • *Hamanassett*, PO Box 129, Lima, 19037, 459-3000, 28-room stone 1870 mansion in secluded wooded setting, $$ CP • *The Log House,* Fairville Road, Chadds Ford 19317, 388-7087, two private suites, in an eighteenth-century log home on five acres or a nearby historic stone house, $$ CP • *Lenape Springs Farm,* PO Box 176, Pocopson, 19366, 793-2266, modest modern rooms in 1850 stone farmhouse, peaceful 32-acre setting, hot tub and billiards table, $-$$ CP • Two good choices in West Chester: *Franklin House*, 339 North Franklin Street, West Chester, 19380, modernized 150-year home, quilts and four-posters, sunny and welcoming, $$ CP; and *Faunbrook*, 699 West Rosedale Avenue, West Chester, 19382, 436-5788, art-filled Victorian showplace tucked away on the edge of town, $$ CP • Hotel choices with inn ambience: *Fairville Inn,* Route 52, Fairville, 19357, 388-5900, restored 1820s home, lovely decor, new carriage house with private decks, $$$-$$$$ CP and afternoon tea • *Brandywine River Hotel,* Routes 1 and 100, Chadds Ford, 19317, 388-1200, intimate 40-room hotel, $$$ CP • *Duling-Kurtz House,* South Whitford Road, Exton, 19341, 524-1830, charmingly furnished, $$-$$$ CP. There are many motels in the area; write to Brandywine Valley address below for full list.

DINING All of the following are attractive old country inns; pick one that is convenient and phone for exact driving directions • *Chadds Ford Inn,* Route 1, Chadds Ford, close to Wyeth Museum, 388-7361, $$-$$$ • *Mendenhall Inn,* Route 52, Mendenhall, 388-1181, convenient to Longwood Gardens, $$-$$$ • *Coventry Forge Inn,* Route 23, Coventryville, 469-6222, worth a drive for classic French food in a pre-Revolutionary house, $$-$$$$, prix fixe Saturdays, $$$$ • *Historic Dilworthtown Inn,* 1390 Old Wilmington Pike and Brinton Bridge Road, Dilworthtown (south of West Chester), 399-1390, $$-$$$ • *Historic General Warren Inne,* Old Lancaster Avenue, Malvern, 296-3637, $$–$$$$ • *Marshalton Inn,* 1300 West Strasburg Road (Route 162), Marshalton, 692-4367, $$-$$$ • Other choices: *La Cocotte,* 124 West Gay Street, West Chester, 436-6722, French local favorite, $$-$$$ • *Pace One,* Thornton-Concord Road, Thornton, 459-9784, restored barn, good Sunday brunch, $; dinner, $$-$$$ • *Vickers,* Welch Pool Road and Gordon Drive, Lionville, 363-7998, gourmet dining in a former underground railroad station, $$-$$$$ • *Duling-Kurtz House,* Exton (see above), $$-$$$ • *Lenape Inn,* Routes 52 and 100, West Chester, 793-2005, on the Brandywine River, $$-$$$ • *Crier in the Country,* Route 1, Glen Mills, 358-2411, varied menu, $$-$$$.

SIGHTSEEING *Chester County Day,* tickets, $25 (no children under 12); bus tours from Chester County Hospital beginning at 9 A.M.

$35; tickets include slide-show previews. For information, tickets, or a copy of *Chester County Day* advance newspaper, write *Chester County Day,* PO Box 1, West Chester, PA 19381 • *Longwood Gardens,* US 1, Kennett Square, 388-6741. Hours: April to October, daily 9 A.M. to 6 P.M.; rest of year, to 5 P.M.; conservatories 10 A.M. to 5 P.M. Adults, $10; children 6–14, $2 • *Brandywine River Museum,* US 1, Chadds Ford, 388-7601. Hours: daily 9:30 A.M. to 4:30 P.M. Adults, $5; children 6–12, $2.50 • *Brandywine Battlefield Park,* US 1, Chadds Ford, 459-3342. Hours: Tuesday to Saturday 9 A.M. to 5 P.M.; Sunday noon to 5 P.M. Battlefield free. Building tours, Adults, $3.50; children, $1 • *Phillips Mushroom Museum,* US 1, Kennett Square, 388-6082. Hours: daily 10 A.M. to 6 P.M. Adults $1.25; children, $.50 • *Valley Forge National Historical Park,* near Pennsylvania Turnpike, exit 24, 783-1077. Hours: daily 8:30 A.M. to 5 P.M. Park is free, fee for guided bus tours • *Chester County Historical Society,* 225 North High Street, West Chester 692-4800. Hours: Tuesday, Thursday, Friday, and Saturday, 10 A.M. to 4 P.M.; Wednesday 1 to 8 P.M.; Sunday noon to 4 P.M. Adults, $2.50; under 18, $1.50.

FOR FURTHER INFORMATION *Brandywine Valley Tourist Information Center* at Longwood Gardens, Route 1, Kennett Square, PA 19348, 388-2900, or toll free (800) 228-9933. Ask about Brandywine Valley Sampler Packages.

Fairs, Festivals, and Big Apples in the Nutmeg State

There was music coming from a carousel on the midway, an oxen draw scheduled at one, a corn-husking contest at two, and a Wild West show about to begin.

But for one towheaded four-year-old named Billy, it was all an anticlimax. The highlight of his day had been a new acquaintance named Elsie. She was the first cow he had ever seen outside a storybook.

From July to October country fairs are in high gear all over the state of Connecticut, a harvest ritual that gives farmers a showcase for their crops and livestock, homemakers a place to exhibit their prize baking and canning, and everyone the opportunity for some old-fashioned fun.

For many a suburban or city parent, however, the best show of all is watching youngsters like Billy wide-eyed at their first sight of real, live farm animals. A self-addressed stamped envelope will get you a full listing of current dates and times of fairs in the Nutmeg State from the Association of Connecticut Fairs.

Often the last fairs of the season offer a bonus since they are strategically located in scenic central and northwestern parts of the state that offer fine foliage as well as other special fall pleasures—hayrides, harvest festivals, apple picking, and a dazzling display of thousands of chrysanthemums in bloom.

Fairs are usually scheduled in late September and early October for the towns of Durham, Berlin, Harwinton, and Riverton. Each one offers its own attractions. Durham, an institution for over 70 years, may present racing pigs and magic shows along with crafts and top-name country music acts. There may be nail-driving and corn-husking contests, a frog jump, and a turtle race in Berlin. Harwinton has featured an Early American display with demonstrations of old-time crafts and a country store, while Riverton, the smallest of the fairs, offers competitions in sawing and chopping as well as a pie-eating contest. Exact events may change, but the general pattern does not.

Whichever fair you choose you'll see fine specimens of sheep, goats, poultry, rabbits, pigs, and other livestock competing for blue ribbons, plus prize crops, cooking, and baking and such down-home competitions as horse, oxen, and tractor pulls. All the fairs offer entertainment as well.

No matter which fair you attend, you'll be within a short drive of Bristol, where there's an attraction with special appeal for families. The New England Carousel Museum is a real treat, a chance to marvel at the master carvers who created an important form of American folk art, the colorful and whimsical steeds of the old-fashioned carousel. Some 300 ornately carved horses, elephants, giraffes, cats, and other legendary beasties are displayed in a turn-of-the-century factory building, a replica of the kind of place where these craftsmen would have worked. Upstairs, visitors are invited to watch woodcarvers and painters at work restoring carousel creatures and repairing the machinery that sets them in motion.

While you are in Bristol, have a look at the American Clock and Watch Museum, one of the few of its kind in the country. There are more than 3,000 timepieces of every size and shape, most made in Connecticut. It's fun to be here at noon, when the chiming clocks are set to strike simultaneously.

Bristol also stages an annual Mum Festival in late September, honoring the brilliant flowering of the chrysanthemums. Activities include a parade, carnival, and craft fair.

Not far away in Terryville, which stages its own fair in mid-September, you can sample another kind of fall country tradition: a hayride. Just climb aboard with Ken Wood of Wood Acres, and you'll go lumbering off for an hour's drive through the woods, ensconced in a wagon piled high with sweet-smelling hay and pulled by a picture-book pair of giant dapple-gray Percheron horses.

If the Riverton Fair is your destination, be sure to stop at the Hitchcock Museum to see examples of the famous nineteenth-century chairs. The present Hitchcock factory here maintains many of the old handmade procedures and has a showroom and gift shop open to the public. There's also a Seth Thomas clock outlet store here, and other pleasant shops.

Fair or not, foliage watchers will want to head to Riverton for a drive through the People's State Forest nearby, a ride that parallels the Farmington River and is made even more beautiful by the reflected colors in the sparkling reservoir running beside the road. There are several scenic stop-offs on the forest road, many of them with picnic areas.

Finally, if you travel during the first two weeks of October, you'll find the annual Apple Harvest Festival in full swing around the village green in Southington, an easy stop-off on your way home.

An old-time parade, and all kinds of races are the order of the day, including the wild and woolly "bed race," in which cribs, four-posters, and brass bedsteads come careening downhill to the delight of cheering spectators.

On the second weekend of the festival, an arts and crafts fair is held, and food stands offer pies, fritters, caramel apples, cider, and just about everything having to do with fall's favorite crop. There's another way to get a lofty perspective of the festival and the fall foliage in Southington—via New England Hot Air Balloons. They'll take you up early morning or late afternoon any day when the wind is right. Phone ahead if you are interested.

If all the festivities inspire you to want to do some apple picking on your own, there are orchards in the area where you are invited to do just that.

As for the apple festival, it's all authentic small-town Americana, unsophisticated fun for everyone, and as traditional as—you guessed it—apple pie.

Connecticut Area Code: 203

DRIVING DIRECTIONS Take I-95, New England Thruway. For Durham, get off at exit 48, take the I-91 connection at New Haven, then follow I-91 to exit 15, Route 68 east. For Berlin, from I-91 take Routes 5 and 15, Berlin Turnpike, at Meriden. For Harwinton and Riverton, get off I-95 at Route 8 (exit 27), just past Bridgeport.

Harwinton is east of Route 8 on Route 118; Riverton is farther north and also east on Route 20. *Total distance:* about 110 miles.

ACCOMMODATIONS *Radisson Inn,* 42 Century Drive (off Route 229), Bristol, 06010, 589-7766, $$ • *Comfort Inn,* 120 Laning Street, Southington, 06489, $-$$ • *Susse Chalet,* 462 Queen Street, Southington, 06489, 621-0181, $ CP • *Hawthorne Motor Inn,* 2387 Wilbur Cross Highway (Route 15), Berlin, 06037, 828-4181, near miniature golf and a nature center, $ • *Old Riverton Inn,* Route 20, Riverton, 06065, 379-8678, $-$$ CP • *Yankee Pedlar Inn,* 93 Main Street, Torrington (off Route 8), 06790, 489-9226, convenient for Harwinton, $-$$ • *Chimney Crest Manor*, 5 Founders Drive, Bristol, 06010, 582-4219, a bed-and-breakfast that is truly a baronial manor, $$-$$$ CP • *Cobble Hill Farm Inn,* Steele Road, New Hartford, 06057, 379-0057, a real charmer on 22 acres with a pond, $$-$$$ CP (with a big farm breakfast) • *Captain Josiah Cowles Place Bed & Breakfast,* 184 Marion Avenue, Southington, 276-0227, 1740 Colonial, $ CP.

DINING *Yankee Pedlar Inn* (see above), $-$$ • *Old Riverton Inn* (see above), $-$$ • *Hawthorne Motor Inn* (see above), $$ • *The Tributary,* 19 Rowley Street, Winsted, 379-7679, pleasant and unpretentious, $$ • *Jessie's Restaurant,* Route 44, Winsted, 379-0109, Italian, outdoor dining in season, $-$$ • *Brannigan's,* 176 Laning Street, Southington, 621-9311, ribs are the specialty, good family choice, children's menu, $-$$.

SIGHTSEEING *Country Fairs.* For free listing of fair dates, send a self-addressed, legal-size envelope with $.75 postage to Association of Connecticut Fairs, Box 753, Somers, CT 06071 • *Southington Apple Harvest Festival.* Contact Greater Southington Chamber of Commerce, 7 North Main Street, Southington, CT 06489, 628-8036, for current festival information and dates • *Bristol Mum Festival,* last week in September, phone 584-4718 for information • *New England Hot Air Balloons,* PO Box 706, Southington, 621-6061 • *New England Carousel Museum, 95* Riverside Avenue (Route 72), Bristol, 585-5411. Hours: April to October, Monday to Saturday 10 A.M. to 5 P.M., Sunday noon to 5 P.M.; rest of year, closed Monday and Tuesday. Adults, $4; children, $2.50 • *American Clock and Watch Museum,* 100 Maple Street, off Route 6, Bristol, 583-6070. Hours: March to November, daily 10 A.M. to 5 P.M. Adults, $3.50; children 8–15, $1.50; under 8, free • *Hitchcock Museum,* Route 20, Riverton, 738-4950. Hours: April to December, Thursday to Sunday noon to 4 P.M.

Donation • Hayrides: *Ken Wood,* Wood Acres, Terryville, 583-8670. Phone in advance for rates, reservations, and driving directions • Apple Orchards: Phone to confirm hours before you go: *Rogers Orchards–Home Farm,* Long Bottom Road, Southington, 229-4240; *Rogers Orchards–Sunnymount Farm,* Meriden-Waterbury Road, Route 322, Southington, 879-1206; *Lewis Farms*, 391 Belleview Avenue, Southington, 628-9736; *Minor's Farm,* 409 Hill Street, Bristol, 589-0861; *Hickory Hill Orchard,* 351 West Meriden Road, Cheshire, 272-3824; *Bishop Farms,* 500 South Meriden Road, Cheshire, 272-8243; *Lyman Orchards,* junction of Routes 147 and 157, Middlefield, 349-3673.

Family Parade to West Point, Storm King, and Museum Village

The thing that takes many first-time visitors to West Point by surprise is the sheer beauty of the place. The same point high above the Hudson that once allowed Colonial troops to watch out for British ships up and down the river now serves as a peaceful outlook over river and plains, with a remarkable perspective on the glorious fall foliage of the Hudson Valley.

For many who don't consider themselves pro-military, there is a second surprise in the impressiveness of the stone buildings and the contagious pride you sense in the young cadets who are continuing the "long gray line" of patriots who marched here before them.

As a result, lots of parents who come to the U.S. Military Academy primarily for the kids wind up loving the place themselves, particularly if they are able to make it on a football weekend, when the cadets are out for a full-dress parade.

Football or not, a day at West Point combined with an art excursion to Storm King and a Sunday visit to the old-time craftspeople at Orange County's excellent Museum Village at Monroe is an ideal itinerary for fall family foliage watching—maximum scenery for the front seat, with minimum driving to inspire complaints from the back.

A phone call to the Visitor Information Center of the Public Affairs office will give you an up-to-date schedule of games and news of any other special events around the time you plan to visit. Even if you are able to get tickets to a game, you may have trouble finding a motel room nearby. But since the drive is short and scenic, it is easy enough to start from home Saturday morning and move out of the area for the night. You can see the cadet parade whether you see the game or not, and if you bring along a picnic lunch, the day at West Point won't cost you a cent. All the sites are free to visitors.

First stop at the academy is the Visitor Information Office outside the new granite-towered Thayer Gate, which was donated to the academy in 1988 as a forty-fifth-reunion gift from the class of 1943. A movie on West Point is shown here, and there are some interesting exhibits that take you through a cadet's typical day, including a model of a spartan dormitory room, displaying the order and neatness that is part of military training. Nothing is overlooked, from hospital-corner sheets to shined shoes and neatly rolled socks.

A good plan is to see the academy, then visit the splendid West Point Museum near the Information Center. If you are a good walker, you can pick up a guide and see the sights on your own. But on a first visit, a highly recommended introduction is aboard one of the bus tours that goes out from the visitors' center. Many of the well-informed guides are wives or officers or enlisted men who live at West Point, and have interesting, firsthand stories of life here today as well as a store of military history to relate.

The tour takes you uphill past Michie (pronounced my-key) Stadium to the magnificent Gothic Cadet Chapel, which has outstanding stained-glass windows and the largest church organ in the world (18,000 pipes), and farther on past the gracious nineteenth-century homes of the superintendent and the commandant, facing the parade grounds known as The Plain.

Among the roster of cadets who have marched here are presidents Ulysses S. Grant and Dwight D. Eisenhower, Jefferson Davis, General George Armstrong Custer, and Edward White, the first astronaut to walk in space. Major General George W. Goethals, who designed the Panama Canal, was another West Point alumnus, as was Abner Doubleday, a Union commander in the Civil War who is far better known as the inventor of baseball.

A tip: If you plan to see a parade, arrive at The Plain early for good viewing.

Trophy Point is a favorite spot for most young children, who love clambering over the cannons. Among the many relics on display at the point overlooking the river are links from the giant chain that was once stretched across the Hudson from West Point to Constitution Island to block the progress of the British fleet. The links weigh 300 pounds apiece.

A statue of the Polish soldier who masterminded this blockade strategy, Thaddeus Kosciuszko, is elsewhere on the grounds. The battle monument at Trophy Point is dedicated to the men of the Union army who were killed in the Civil War.

The old Cadet Chapel, dating from 1836, is Colonial in decor and has its own simple beauty. The walls are lined with battle flags and marble shields commemorating the American generals of the Revolutionary War. One shield bears only a date and no name; it belonged to Benedict Arnold, who tried to betray the fort to the British when he was in command of his post in 1780. Some other remaining sights are the Chapel of the Most Holy Trinity, a Catholic church in Norman Gothic style patterned after an abbey church in England, and Fort Clinton, a Revolutionary War station.

An uphill trek will take you to Fort Putnam, which gives you an idea of a soldier's living conditions during the time of the American Revolution, as well as a splendid view of West Point and the river. A couple of tour boat lines offer cruises on the Hudson, a fine way to get a river's-eye view of the foliage when your touring is done.

Save energy to appreciate the West Point Museum, one of the largest collections of military history in the Western hemisphere. There are six galleries tracing the history of the academy, the U.S. Army, American wars, and world warfare from ancient times to the nuclear age. Among the high points are uniforms through the years and miniature re-creations of some of the world's most famous battles. Two galleries sure to provoke interest display small and large weapons, including the beloved "jeep" of the Second World War, as well as tanks and cannons, including the one that fired the first shot of the First World War.

Unless you have brought along a picnic to enjoy at designated sites on the grounds, the choice spot for lunch or dinner is the Hotel Thayer, which is used by many visiting families of cadets. It's a fine place to stay if you can get in, as well as a reasonable choice for a family dinner. If you want fast-food establishments or an ice cream parlor, you'll find them in Highland Falls outside the gate, and there are also places here that will prepare a picnic for you if you haven't brought one from home.

If you can't get a room at the Thayer or in Highland Falls, the pleasant rustic Bear Mountain Inn is just a few miles away, Cromwell Manor Inn offers beautifully furnished luxury quarters in an old estate nearby. And there are a few winning small inns in Cold Spring, an antiquers' mecca just across the Hudson. Otherwise your best bet is Newburgh, where there are motel accommodations as well as a couple of bed-and-breakfast inns. Newburgh itself is a historic town with many Revolutionary War sites. Two of the principal ones are the Jonathan Hasbrouck house on Liberty Street, Washington's final headquarters during the war, and the New Windsor Cantonment off Route 32, a reconstruction of the last American encampment, which also has the only surviving log structure actually built by the troops.

One very good reason to head toward Newburgh is the drive along the Old Storm King Highway from West Point to Cornwall, a magnificent scenic route. An even better reason is that the turn off Route 32 south of Newburgh leads to the Storm King Art Center. This remarkable sculpture park must be seen to be believed: 100 acres of lawns, fields, and woodlands artfully landscaped to form green "galleries" for more than 130 works by masters of modern sculpture. This is one art showcase that even young children can enjoy, since one of the prize exhibits, Isamu Noguchi's 40-ton granite *Momo Taro,* is a sculpture that was created to be touched and climbed.

The hilltop is a green gallery offering views of the large works in the distance as well as the chance to inspect some of Storm King's most important works close up. These include Henry Moore's sleek *Reclining Collected Forms* and Louise Nevelson's *City on the High Mountain.* Admirers of the whimsical work of David Smith make pilgrimages to Storm King, where eight of his pieces are displayed on one lawn. Spread across an expansive meadow below are five stabiles by Alexander Calder, whose monumental 56-foot work *The Arch* welcomes visitors at the entrance gate.

The woodlands and fields provide opposite experiences. The former invites visitors to travel winding gravel paths and discover sculptures in its wooded enclaves. The fields below offer a broad, almost endless canvas for huge modernistic sculptures, some as high as a four-story building. As a backdrop for this unparalleled display of art are mountain vistas that are at their most breathtaking in the fall.

When you've done justice to Storm King, you may want to drop in on Woodbury Common, to the south at the junction of Route 17 and the New York State Thruway, where well over 100 prominent fashion names offer discount outlets. The famous labels include Anne Klein, Calvin Klein, Burberry, Brooks Brothers, Donna Karan, Ellen Tracy, and dozens more.

A very different kind of experience awaits if you drive farther south on Route 87 and turn west on Route 17 to exit 129 at the Museum Village in Orange County. This is New York's largest "living history" museum, with more than 30 buildings telling the story of the making of crafts in nineteenth-century America, from handwork to the beginnings of modern technology. It offers an interesting and entertaining bit of history with demonstrations of pottery and broom making, weaving, blacksmithing, printing, and other trades and crafts. Among the buildings you can tour are a one-room school, a general store, a blacksmith's shop, an apothecary, and a log cabin. In addition to special events throughout the season, on October weekends you'll see special demonstrations of "putting by for winter," autumn chores such as grinding and drying corn, preserving, cidering, and other typical activities on a farm in the fall season 150 years ago. There is a cafe on the museum grounds and, once again, picnic facilities.

From here it's a short drive to Route 12 and Sugar Loaf, a village full of crafts shops where you can watch latter-day artisans at work and possibly pick up an original souvenir of your trip. If you can stay a while, there's also a new state-of-the-art theater in town, the Lycian Centre, presenting a wide variety of entertainment.

Sugar Loaf makes for a pleasant transition back to the present and you may still have enough light to get in some last foliage watching as you connect back to Route 17 and an easy drive home.

West Point Area Code: 914

DRIVING DIRECTIONS George Washington Bridge to Palisades Interstate Parkway to Bear Mountain Circle (end of parkway), then Route 9W north, following signs to Highland Falls and West Point. *Total distance:* 50 miles.

PUBLIC TRANSPORTATION Shortline Bus service to West Point, Newburgh, Vails Gate (near Storm King), and to Museum Village, toll free (800) 631-8405.

ACCOMMODATIONS *Hotel Thayer,* U.S. Military Academy grounds, West Point, 10986, 446-4731, $-$$ • *Palisades Motel,* Route 218 off 9W, Highland Falls, 10928, 446-9400, $$ • *West Point Motel,* 361 Main Street, Highland Falls, 10928, 446-4180 $ • *Howard Johnson's Motor Lodge,* 95 Route 17K at Thruway exit 17, Newburgh, 12550, 564-4000, $$ • *Holiday Inn,* 90 Route 17K at Thruway, Newburgh, 12550, 564-9020, $$ CP • *Bear Mountain Inn,* Bear Mountain State Park, 10911, 786-2731, $$ • *Cromwell Manor Inn,* Angola Road, Cornwall, 12518, 534-7136, $$$-$$$$ CP • *Stockbridge-Ramsdell Bed & Breakfast,* 158 Montgomery Street, Newburgh, 12550, 561-3462, restored Victorian, Hudson views, $-$$ CP • *Hudson House,* 2 Main Street, Cold Spring, 10516, $$-$$$, 265-9355, country inn near the river, $$-$$$$ • *Pig Hill Bed & Breakfast,* 73 Main Street, Cold Spring, 10516, 265-9247, charming B&B/antiques shop—if you like your furniture, you can buy it! $$$$ CP • *Plumbush,* Route 9D, Cold Spring, 10516, 265-3904, Victorian estate, $$-$$$ CP.

DINING *Hotel Thayer* (see above), $-$$ • *Bear Mountain Inn* (see above), food court lunch, $; Wildflower dining room, $$; Sunday buffet, $$ • *Banta's Steak & Stein,* Union Avenue, New Windsor, 564-7678, steaks, salad bar, children's plates, $-$$ • *North Plank Road Tavern,* 18 North Plank Road, Newburgh, 565-6885, nineteenth-century roadhouse, Victorian decor, Continental menu, $$ • *Brewster*

House, 1762 Temple Hill Road, New Windsor, 561-1762, \$-\$\$\$ • *Il Cenacola,* 152 Route 52, Newburgh, 564-4494, a find for Northern Italian food, \$\$ • *Painter's Tavern,* Route 218 on the village square, Cornwall-on-Hudson, 534-2109, eclectic menu, recommended \$\$ • *Gasho of Japan,* Route 32, Central Valley (near Monroe), 928-2277, cooking at your table, kids love it, \$\$ • *Barnsider Tavern,* King's Highway, Sugar Loaf, 469-9810, warm, rustic, \$ • For dining in Cold Spring, see page 220.

SIGHTSEEING U.S. *Military Academy:* Visitor Information Center outside Thayer Gate, 938-2638, Hours: daily 9 A.M. to 4:45 P.M. Phone for parade schedules, Army Band concert dates, and other information. Football information from Athletic Office, 446-4996. *West Point Museum,* daily 10:30 A.M. to 4:15 P.M.; *Chapel,* daily 8:30 A.M. to 4:15 P.M. except Sunday from 1 P.M.; *Fort Putnam,* late May to early November, Thursday to Monday 11 A.M. to 3 P.M. All free • *West Point Guided Tours,* from Visitor Information Center, 446-4724. Hours: April to November, Monday to Saturday approximately every 20 minutes from 10 A.M.; Sunday tours beginning at 11:30 A.M.; December to March Monday to Saturday tours at 11 A.M. and 1 P.M., Sunday tour 2:30 P.M. Adults, \$4; children under 12, \$2 • *Storm King Art Center,* Old Pleasant Hill Road, Mountainsville, 534-3115 (watch for signs off Route 32, 5 miles south of Newburgh). Hours: April to November, daily 11 A.M. to 5:30 P.M. Adults, \$5; students, \$3; under 5, free • *Museum Village in Orange County,* Museum Village Road (New York Route 17, exit 129), Monroe, 782-8247. Hours: May to early December, Saturday and Sunday noon to 5 P.M., Wednesday to Friday 10 A.M. to 2 P.M., open weekdays to 5 P.M. in July and August. Adults, \$8; ages 6–15, \$5 • *Washington's Headquarters State Historic Site,* 84 Liberty Street, Newburgh, 562-1195. Hours: mid-April to late October, Wednesday to Saturday 10 A.M. to 5 P.M., Sunday from 1 P.M. Free • *New Windsor Cantonment State Historic Site,* Temple Hill Road, Route 300, New Windsor, 561-1765. Hours: April to October, Wednesday to Saturday 10 A.M. to 5 P.M., Sunday from 1 P.M. Free • Hudson River Cruise information: *Hudson Highlands Cruises,* PO Box 265, Highland Falls, 10928, 446-7171.

INFORMATION Orange County Tourism, 30 Matthews Street, Suite 111, Goshen, NY 10924, 294-5151 or toll free (800) 7 OC-TOUR.

Color-Full History in Connecticut

The oldest house in the oldest town in Connecticut has a colorful gallery of ghosts in its past—and a guide who delights in telling about them.

"Here's the happy couple," she began, pointing to dour-faced portraits of Lieutenant and Mrs. Fyler, the home's original owners. "And here's the cupboard where they hid the booze when the parson came to call."

The woman's lively commentary proved an appropriate introduction to Windsor, and a part of Connecticut that seems to relish its history. The small towns circling Hartford have the look of old New England and more than their share of sightseeing variety. Within their peaceful environs, you can tour prize historic homes, prowl the passages of a notorious underground prison, have a look at aviation history, or follow the hoopla of America's elections from George Washington to George Bush.

Meanwhile, there's every opportunity to enjoy the autumn outdoors at its finest, with a bonus ending—a drive through the scenic woodlands of the state-maintained People's State Forest.

A good place to begin your tour is Windsor, a town that was already 140 years old when the Declaration of Independence was signed in 1776. Windsor's historic district still boasts its village green, a 1630 white-steepled church, the original town burying ground, and about three dozen houses built before the Revolutionary War. Six of the houses date to the 1600s. Almost all are still occupied.

The Lt. Walter Fyler House, the oldest of the houses, has been meticulously cared for and filled with furnishings that reflect its rich history as a home, a shop, and the town post office. Adjacent Wilson Museum displays more mementos of the town's past. If you're lucky you'll get the guide who'll fill you in on the juicier details. The Dr. Hezekiah Chaffee House, a 1765 residence just behind the Fyler home, is included in the tour. Also open to visitors is the Oliver Ellsworth Homestead, home of one of the five men who drafted the U.S. Constitution and the third Chief Justice of the United States.

This is also the heart of the tobacco-farming area that once gave the area the name of "Tobacco Valley." Connecticut Shade Grown Tobacco was known through the world as the finest wrapper available for quality cigars. Many of the farms are disappearing as the land gives way to developers, but you may still spy the tobacco growing under netting on some of the back roads.

Head north on Palisado Avenue, Windsor's main street, and you'll get yourself right back to U.S. 91. Head north and take the exit for

Route 20 to East Granby, where you'll come upon one of the most unusual of our national historic landmarks, the Old New-Gate Prison and Copper Mine. First chartered as a mine in 1707, it was converted into a prison in 1773, designated as a place of confinement for burglars, horse thieves, robbers, and counterfeiters. During the Revolution it was used for Tories and prisoners of war. During its 42-year history as a prison, more than 800 prisoners were committed to New Gate's underground cells.

Today you can go down into the mine for a well-lit, self-guided tour of the winding passages where the prisoners lived in total darkness. Bring a sweater—mine temperatures can be in the mid-forties even on sunny days.

Plane buffs will want to detour here on Route 75 near Bradley Airport in Windsor Locks, where the New England Air Museum displays some 75 historic aircraft, including a 1911 Bleriot, a World War II 'Warbird,'' and the actual plane used in Clark Gable's 1938 movie *Test Pilot. You* can also try out an authentic training cockpit simulator and see the prizewinning film *To Fly.*

Continue from here south on Route 202 to Simsbury, in the Farmington River Valley, where some of the earliest coins minted in the original Granby mines are on display at Massacoh Plantation. This 22-acre site traces three centuries of Simsbury history. On the grounds are a Victorian carriage house, manufacturing exhibits, a sleigh shed, a one-room schoolhouse, an icehouse, and a seventeenth-century meetinghouse. One of the favorite exhibits is a Yankee peddler's wagon, loaded with gewgaws and knickknacks.

Massacoh's Phelps House is one of the finest remaining examples of an old Connecticut tavern. Be sure to note the narrow, lighted cupboard over the mantel. It is a rarity that is believed to have been built by a retired shipwright since it is reminiscent of a sailing ship's forecastle. Look carefully and you'll see that the paneling in the tavern room includes witches' crosses meant to keep evil spirits away while the men enjoyed their liquid spirits.

Simsbury, with its wide, tree-shaded main street, is one of the valley's most charming villages, and has the area's best lodgings. It's also an ideal place for browsing. Simsburytown Shops is a complex of boutiques featuring everything from cookery to Indian jewelry to homemade pâté. The Ellsworth Art Gallery at Massacoh Plantation has contemporary art of high quality.

The Gallery on the Green in nearby Canton, operated by the local Artists' Guild, is another good place to see changing art exhibits in two galleries. Canton offers a cache of antiques shops as well.

A few miles south in Avon on Route 44 is another pleasant browsing spot, the Farmington Valley Arts Center—a collection of artists' studios and a gallery housed in a historic stone building that was once an explosives plant.

Many of the local artists are inspired by their beautiful rural surroundings in the Farmington Valley, and if it is a fine fall day, you may want to spend some of your weekend enjoying the outdoors. There are many ways to do that. Roaring Brook Nature Center in Canton has woodland walking trails and many naturalist-led walks. You'll spot lots of canoers out on the Farmington River when the water is right, and if you want to join them, the local visitors' bureau has a list of canoe rental outfitters. The most popular outdoor pastime in the fall is climbing to the top of Heublein Tower in Talcott Mountain State Park, off Route 185 in Simsbury. It's a not-so-tough trek to a 1½-mile ridge trail with a fantastic five-state view.

The Connecticut Hang Gliding Association has its headquarters at Talcott Mountain on weekends when the wind is right, providing added entertainment for spectators. Should you get the urge to join the birdmen, Tek Flight Products offers certified one- and two-day courses. Or you can soar even higher by signing up for one of the half-dozen hot- air balloon rides available in the valley.

One attraction that should not be missed is the drive into West Hartford to experience a one-of-a-kind place, the Museum of American Political Life. Featured is a special kind of American folk art—the colorful trappings of our political campaigns.

The displays begin with a life-size torchlight parade and continue through a time line of the nation's history, marked by buttons, banners, bandannas, posters, and all the other paraphernalia of our national elections. There are some 60,000 items in the collection, most once belonging to one avid collector, J. Doyle DeWitt, a former president of the Travelers Insurance Company who willed the priceless treasures to the university in his company's town. A recent donation of three-quarter-scale perfect replicas of inaugural gowns worn by First Ladies adds another dimension to the display.

All of this merits close inspection, but the most mesmerizing section for most visitors moves into the present, showing the changes television brought to presidential campaigning. It's hard to pull away from the screens showing clips from the commercials and debates such as the Kennedy-Nixon encounters that have changed the course of our history.

One other interesting bit of the past in West Hartford is the eighteenth-century saltbox home where Noah Webster was born. It offers a look at the most widely used textbook in America, the *Blueback Speller,* authored by Webster in 1783, and America's first dictionary, compiled in 1828.

Of course, if the fall color is beckoning, you may decide to save museums for a return visit and concentrate on foliage watching instead. For a prime route, take Route 44 going west out of Avon, turn right at Route 318 past New Hartford, and watch for the road that takes you through the People's State Forest and eventually to Riverton. It's a drive made even more beautiful by the reflections in the sparkling reservoir that runs beside the road, and there are several scenic stopoffs along the way to let you enjoy the view, many with picnic areas.

To end the day with a last look at the colorful Connecticut hills, take Route 20 west out of Riverton and connect with Route 8 south. You'll enjoy panoramic vistas almost all the way back to the junction of the Merritt Parkway before Bridgeport.

Connecticut Area Code: 203

DRIVING DIRECTIONS Hutchinson River Parkway to the Merritt Parkway to I-91. Take exit 37, Route 305, to Windsor. Bear left onto Route 159 across the Farmington River into the historic district. *Total distance:* About 123 miles.

ACCOMMODATIONS There are many weekend packages in this area; be sure to ask about them when you reserve. *Simsbury Inn,* 397 Hopmeadow Street, Simsbury, 06089, 651-5700, elegant small hotel with antique reproduction furnishings, an indoor pool and health club, $$-$$$$ • *Simsbury 1820 House,* 731 Hopmeadow Street, Simsbury, 06070, 658-7658, beautifully restored historic home, $$ CP • *Avon Old Farms Hotel,* Routes 44 and 10, Avon, 06001, 677-1651. The handsome new wing of this 164-room hotel is the choicest, but the older rooms are good value. Original art by local artists throughout. $$-$$$$ CP • *Residence Inn by Marriott,* 100 Dunfey Lane, Windsor, 06095, 688-7474 or (800) 331-3131, 06095, $$ CP • *Courtyard by Marriott,* 1 Day Hill Road, Windsor, 06095, 683-0022, $$ • *Stephine Potwine House,* 84 Scantic Road, East Windsor, 06088, 623-8722, 1831 country farmhouse overlooking a pond, $-$$ CP • *The Old Mill,* 63 Maple Street, Somersville (10 minutes northeast of Windsor), 06072, 763-1473, $$ CP.

DINING *Evergreens,* Simsbury Inn (see above), elegant dining, $$-$$$ • *Simsbury 1820 House* (see above), fine Continental fare, $$-$$$ • *Hop Brook,* 77 West Street, Simsbury, 651-1118, gristmill overlooking pond, $$-$$$ • *Chart House,* 4 Hartford Road, Simsbury, 658-1118, former 1780 tavern, now part of better-than-average chain with steak and seafood menu, $$-$$$$ • *Avon Old Farms Inn,* 1757 inn across from hotel (see above), Colonial decor and menu, $$-$$$$ • *Seasons Cafe,* Avon Old Farms Hotel (see above), contemporary, reasonable menu in pretty dining room surrounded by woods, $$ • *One-Way Fare,* 4 Railroad Street, Simsbury, 658-4477, burgers, chile, etc., served up in the old 1874 railroad station, $ • *Max-A-Mia,*

Fairway Shops, 70 East Main Street, Avon, 677-6299, lively informal local favorite for Italian, worth the wait, say residents, $$ • *Madeleine's,* 1530 Palisado Avenue, Windsor, 688-0150, Continental, elegant, $$-$$$.

SIGHTSEEING *New England Air Museum,* Route 75 at Bradley International Airport, Windsor Locks, 623-3305. Hours: daily 10 A.M. to 5 P.M. Adults, $6.50; children 6–11, $3 • *Lt. Walter Fyler House and Wilson Museum,* 96 Palisado Avenue, Windsor, 688-3813. Hours: April to November, Tuesday to Saturday 10 A.M. to noon and 1 to 4 P.M. Adults, $2; children under 12 with adult, free; tours include the Dr. Hezekiah Chaffee House • *Old New Gate Prison,* Newgate Road, East Granby, 566-3005. Hours: mid-May to October, Wednesday to Sunday 10 A.M. to 4:30 P.M. Adults, $3; children 6–17, $1.50 • *Massacoh Plantation,* 800 Hopmeadow Street, Simsbury, 658-2500. Hours: May to October, Sunday to Friday daily 1 to 4 P.M., Saturday by appointment only. Adults, $5; children 5–18, $2.50 • *Talcott Mountain State Park,* off Route 185 at Blooomfield-Simsbury town line. Hours: Tower open Memorial Day to Labor Day daily, September and October, weekends only. Grounds open year round. Free • *Museum of American Political Life,* University of Hartford, 200 Bloomfield Avenue, West Hartford, 243-4090. Hours: Tuesday to Friday, 11 A.M. to 4 P.M., Saturday and Sunday, noon to 4 P.M. Donation • *Farmington Valley Arts Center,* Avon Park North, off Route 44, Avon, 678-1867; *Fisher Gallery,* Hours: Wednesday to Saturday 11 A.M. to 4 P.M. Free. Artists may be found working almost any time, but Saturday is usually the best day. • Hang gliding instruction: Phone *Tek Flight Products,* 379-1668 • Ballooning: Check with *Farmington Valley Visitors' Association* at address below.

FOR FURTHER INFORMATION Greater Hartford Tourism District, 1 Civic Center Plaza, Hartford, CT 06103, 520-4180 or toll free (800) 793–4480, or Connecticut's North Central Tourism Bureau, 111 Hazard Avenue, Enfield, CT 06082, 763-7578 or (800) 248-8283.

Year-round Color in Pennsylvania Dutch Country

It may be at its scenic best against a backdrop of autumn foliage, but there's plenty of color left even after the leaves fall in Pennsylvania Dutch Country.

Picture-book farms, bright hex signs, windmills, and covered bridges dot the landscape. You'll still find yourself sharing the roads with black-frocked men and bonneted women driving shiny horse-and-buggy rigs into town. And the auctions, farmers' markets, and colorful shops await anytime you visit this unique corner of America.

The host of things to see and do here draws as many as four million visitors a year, which is not necessarily good news, since the numbers mean touristy shops and attractions.

So start by picking an unspoiled home base. One way to do that is to stay on a farm, a special treat for families. Both the Mennonite Information Center and the Pennsylvania Dutch Visitors' Bureau publish lists of working farms that welcome guests.

If an inn is more your style, choose one of the towns that has retained its old-fashioned charm. One very pleasant stop is Lititz (accent on the first syllable), seven miles north of Lancaster, one of the most carefully preserved towns in Lancaster County and one with the special flavor of its Moravian origins. A walk down Main Street in Lititz takes you past more than a dozen homes dating to the mid-1700s, and the brick and stucco buildings of the Moravian Church Square, which include the church itself and the old Brethren's and Sisters' houses.

At 221 Main Street you can visit the Pretzel House, where owner Julius Sturgis made the first commercial pretzels in the United States in an adjoining bakery. (You'll have a chance to try your own hand at fancy twisting.) The Museum-House of Johannes Mueller at 137 Main is virtually unchanged since Mr. Mueller lived there in 1792.

The delicious aroma that hangs over Lititz is from Wilbur's Chocolate Factory, where you are invited in to see displays of historical candymaking equipment.

The town is known for two of its special observances, on the Fourth of July and at Christmas.

Lititz lodgings include the General Sutter Inn, a pleasant little hotel; the Alden House, a restored and atmospheric 1850s residence on Main Street; and a delightful surprise on a hilltop outside of town, the Swiss Woods Inn, which offers views and the decor and charm of an Alpine hideaway.

Strasburg is another special stop. The town center, dating to the

1730s, retains many of its original homes and is a National Historic District. There are two vintage lodgings on Main Street, the Strasburg Village Inn, originally a tavern, circa 1787, and the authentically restored Limestone Inn, a 1786 Colonial home.

This is a railroading mecca. At the Strasburg Rail Road's Victorian railroad station, you can board a steam train for the scenic ride to Paradise. Paradise turns out to be just a whistle stop, but the ride runs right through the heart of Amish farm country, a fascinating close-up view of families at work in the fields.

Strasburg is also the home of the fine Railroad Museum of Pennsylvania, with one of the country's best collections of vintage trains, as well as the Museum of the Toy Train Association of America, a gold mine of nostalgia. You can even choose to spend the night at the Red Caboose, a motel whose lodgings are authentic, comfortably rigged out cabooses with modern conveniences, including a TV lodged in the potbelly stove. You can have lunch or dinner in a Victorian dining car, or go one better by dining while you are riding aboard the Strasburg Rail Road Dinner Train. Lunch is also available in the dining car on every run.

Farther to the east, Churchtown is another unspoiled spot set on the crest of a ridge overlooking Amish farm country. The church that inspired the name is the Bangor Episcopal, which was established in the 1700s by Welsh immigrants. The stone walls are a new world version of old Welsh building styles. There's little commercialism here, but there are some excellent artisans such as Lena Clark, known for her quilts, and Steve Witmer, the resident potter who specializes in traditional saltware. Among the old gray stone houses lining the main street are two recommended lodgings, the Inn at Twin Linden and the Churchtown Inn.

One other alternative is to stay in a bed-and-breakfast home in Lancaster, the attractive small city that is a central hub convenient to all area towns and attractions. It is also the home of some of the very best dining. The King's Cottage, a bed-and-breakfast home conveniently located at the edge of town, has attractive furnishings and a big homemade breakfast that will keep you going most of the day. For country charm, the winner is the Gardens of Eden, an antique-filled early Victorian home surrounded by gracious grounds and gardens and decorated with the dried floral arrangements that are the specialty of Marilyn Ebel, the lady of the house.

Pennsylvania's capital during the Revolutionary War and America's largest inland Colonial town, Lancaster can easily fill up a day on its own. A good way to get the lay of the land is on one of the Historic Lancaster Walking Tours, offering a 90-minute stroll through the town's past. Then the first stop is the Central Market, right in the center of town. It is the biggest and most historic of the region's famous farmers' markets, and an institution since the 1700s. Awaiting you are potpourris of fresh fruits and vegetables; savory homemade bologna, sausage, and scrapple; and home-baked pies, cakes, and cookies, as delicious to the eye and nose as to the tummy. You'll find many Amish selling and buying here.

Another downtown attraction is the Heritage Center Museum at Lancaster County in the Old City Hall, which houses a fine collection of Lancaster-made antiques, including furniture, clocks, silver, pewter, needlework, and weaving. Several shops around this area are worth a browse, particularly the arts and crafts in Chestnut House on Market Alley.

Then there are two historic homes that merit a call. Wheatland, the beautifully preserved home of President James Buchanan, is furnished as it was when Buchanan lived there from 1848 to 1868. Rock Ford Plantation is the 1792 Georgian brick home of George Washington's adjutant, General George Hand. The barn on the grounds is a mini-museum of folk artifacts.

Wherever you decide to spend your day, be sure to save time for drives along the beautiful country roads and farmlands that are the real heart of Pennsylvania Dutch Country. The flat, fertile fields and pristine white farms flanked by silvery silos are a serene picture that will linger long in your memory.

Start at the Visitors' Bureau off Route 30 just east of Lancaster, where you can arm yourself with maps and information and see a film to prepare you for the sights ahead. You'll learn that the people of the region are not Dutch but German *(Deutsch* became *Dutch* to the American ear) and that the Amish are only one of many sects among the "Plain People" who live in this area.

It is a firm belief among the "Old Order" of the Amish that duty to God means living simply and tilling the soil. Cars, phones, and electricity are forbidden, not because they are considered evil in themselves but because they are temptations to a more worldly life. A more liberal sect, called "Church Amish" because they hold services in church rather than at home, does allow the use of electricity and cars—but only plain black sedans. Some Mennonites are similar to the Old Order; their buggies can be spotted because they are flat-roofed and black, while the Amish vehicles have rounded roofs and are painted gray.

You can see the beautiful farmlands on any of the side roads between Routes 30 and 340 or off Route 741. You'll recognize the Amish homesteads by their windmills and the absence of electric wires; note also the distinctive additions on some of the farms. Known as "Gross Dawdis," they are an Amish solution to the generation gap. When a farmer reaches retirement age, an annex to the main house is built, allowing him to enjoy the fruits of his labor and to be part of the family without getting in the way of the younger generation. Sometimes you'll see double additions, marking a three-generation home.

If you want a guided back-roads tour, the Mennonite Information Center provides guides who will come out with you in your own car for a reasonable hourly rate.

There are attractions along the way, such as the Amish Farm and House, that show you a re-creation of the interior of a typical Amish or Mennonite home. Or you can see the real thing by having a meal with the Meyer family, members of the River Brethren sect who invite guests in for traditional family-style dinners, followed by a hymn sing. Their six children make charming waiters and waitresses.

A bit more austere is dinner with the Emanuel Fishers, a chance to visit an Old Order Amish family. If you call to make a reservation, let the phone ring for a while; it is located outside of the house.

Another way to visit is by stopping at one of the many frame houses along the road that have a sign outside advertising Quilts. This is a fascinating experience. Some women have only their own work for sale, but an entrepreneur like Emma Witmer on Route 23 in New Holland stocks more than 100 quilts in her upstairs bedrooms, all hand-stitched at home by Amish and Mennonite women. The quality varies with the intricacy of the stitching and the fineness of the colors—and so does the price.

Antique Amish quilts in bold, dark colors have become serious collectors' items, and go for many thousands of dollars. Some fine examples are displayed at the Quilt Museum in Intercourse. It is part of a complex of shops clustered around the People's Place, a center for Amish and Mennonite arts and crafts. There are films here on the Amish (for a fee), a courtyard gallery with free art exhibits, and a well-stocked book and craft shop. The associated shops across the road include the Old Country Store, with crafts and quilts, and Village Pottery, both featuring work by Mennonite artisans. Old Road Specialties next door offers fine reproductions of the antique designs of a noted Amish furniture maker, Henry Lapp.

There are many talented artisans still working in the area. Marilyn Stoltzfus-White at the Clay Distelfink in Smoketown creates bright hand-painted pottery, including personalized plates to mark a birthday or anniversary. Ned Foltz is well known for his high-quality Pennsylvania redware pottery. His home studio can be found by taking Route 897 west to Peartown Road and making a right turn. The pottery is up the road on the left in a grove of trees.

The Weathervane Shop at the Landis Valley Museum just outside Lancaster is another place to see fine crafts. The museum itself is excellent, comprising more than 30 buildings filled with 250,000 items showing rural life and the role of farming in Pennsylvania history. There are four period homes from 150 years ago. Other structures are shops, a school, and a tavern. The annual Harvest Days celebration held here the second weekend of October is a chance to see old-fashioned crafts and activities of the season such as apple drying, apple-butter making, and corn drying and grinding.

A more contemporary, year-round pastime these days is shopping for bargains at the giant outlet center that has grown up at the intersections of Routes 30 and 896. There are dozens of brand-name manufacturers from Lenox to L'eggs. When it comes to dining in Pennsylvania Dutch Country, there are two ways to go: plain and fancy. ''Fancy'' means Continental and creative American fare. The best is found in Lancaster at Market Fare or the posh Windows on Steinman Park, or at the Log Cabin in Leola. ''Plain'' means a no-frills setting and hearty servings of traditional local dishes and garnishes that often include ''seven sweets and seven sours,'' such as pickled beets, pepper cabbage, olives, pickles, piccalilli, applesauce, or dried apricots. For dessert, there's that gooey molasses-flavored delicacy known as shoo-fly pie. There are lots of places to sample this kind of meal, most of them labeled ''family restaurant.''

Both plain and fancy is the fare at Groff's Farm. It is well worth a drive into the country to taste the area's very best traditional dishes, cooked with contemporary flair and served in a charming farmhouse. Be sure to make reservations. Mount Joy has another interesting restaurant, Catacombs, housed in a historic brewery.

Come Sunday, make your way back north on Route 222 to Mennonite country and one of its most interesting settlements, Ephrata. You might well decide to play another trip to this quieter region, as Ephrata offers some prime inn choices, particularly Smithton, a sunny and welcoming place with canopy beds, Pennsylvania Dutch quilts, and working fireplaces in every room. One of the finest small collections of quilts in the area is for sale here.

The prize attraction here is Ephrata Cloister, the restored community of a monastic sect founded in 1730. You'll have to duck your head to enter the low doorways (a reminder of humility) and go single file down the narrow halls (symbols of the straight and narrow path) to see where these dedicated people lived and the narrow wooden ledges where they slept—with eight-inch wooden blocks for pillows. There are eight surviving buildings, a fascinating look at the austere way of life once practiced here. Ephrata offers some fascinating browsing, as well.

Doneckers, proprietors of a classy store and restaurant and four village homes converted to inns, have recently taken on a new project, the Artworks, a former factory now home to studios and shops for more than 50 quality artisans, many of whom can be seen at work. Photography, pottery, quilts, leather game boards, handmade kaleidoscopes, photography, paintings, and whimsical folk carvings are just a few of the offerings. There's also a big farmers market in the complex Thursday through Saturday.

Some other interesting places in town include Martin's Chair Shop on East Farmersville Road, for handcrafted furniture, and the Self-Help Crafts Center on Route 272, which is run by the Mennonite Central Committee to help people in developing nations earn a living through the sale of their traditional crafts. Both the Artworks and the Self-Help Center have pleasant little cafes for lunch.

If you can get to Ephrata on Friday, you can visit one of the region's most colorful sights, the Green Dragon, the largest farmers' market in Pennsylvania. The grounds are overflowing with good food and just about everything else imaginable, including cows, goats, chickens, and rabbits, which are auctioned off in the morning. You may even spot an emu farmer selling his exotic birds.

From Ephrata, drive north toward Reading, where you might want to detour for more dozens of outlet stores and for the famed wild-mushroom cookery at Joe's restaurant. Beyond Reading, you're into Gay Dutch country, famous for its enormous banked barns decorated with giant versions of those brightly painted geometrical designs known as hex signs. Contrary to the name, the signs have nothing to do with warding off evil and are there only for their color and beauty, or as the Pennsylvania Dutch say, "chust for nice."

Old Route 22, which parallels Route 78, is known as Hex Highway for the large number of barns. Continue west on Route 78 to Lenhartsville, turn south on Route 143, and watch for the covered bridge on the left, then make a right to a side road that boasts nine prize barns. If you drive north on Route 143, you'll come to a bird-and-nature-lover's retreat, Hawk Mountain, the only designated sanctuary for birds of prey. This is the place to spot eagles and hawks on their migratory patterns in the fall, as well as to get spectacular views of the entire area spread below.

Then connect with Route 78 and a direct drive back to New York—which may suddenly seem much farther than a three-hour drive from the spirit of Pennsylvania Dutch Country.

Lancaster Area Code: 717
Reading and Churchtown Area Code: 215

DRIVING DIRECTIONS New Jersey Turnpike to Pennsylvania Turnpike to Route 222, then south to Route 30 into Lancaster. Turn south on Route 896 about 5 miles east of Lancaster and proceed 3 miles for Strasburg; go north on Route 501 to Lititz, 7 miles. *Total distance*: 159 miles to Lancaster.

PUBLIC TRANSPORTATION Amtrak (800) 523-8720 has quick and easy direct service from New York to Lancaster; National Car Rental is within walking distance of the station.

ACCOMMODATIONS *General Sutter Inn,* 14 East Main Street, Lititz, 17543, 636-2115, $$ • *Alden House Bed and Breakfast,* 62 East

Main Street, Lititz, 17543, 627-3363, $$-$$$ CP • *Swiss Woods,* Blantz Road, Lititz, 17543, 594-8018, $$-$$$ CP • *Strasburg Village Inn,* 1 West Main Street, Strasburg, 17579, 687-0900, $$ CP • *Limestone Inn,* 33 East Main Street, Strasburg, 17579, 687-8392, $$ CP • *Red Caboose Motel,* Route 741, Paradise Lane, Strasburg, 17579, 687-6646, $-$$ • *Gardens of Eden,* 1894 Eden Road, Lancaster, 17601, 393-5179, $$ CP • *The King's Cottage,* 1049 East King Street, Lancaster, 17602, 397-1017, $-$$ CP • *Cameron Estate Inn,* RD 1, Donegal Springs Road, Mount Joy, 653-1773, out of the way, but this restored estate is one of the area's most elegant lodgings, $$-$$$$ CP • *The Inns at Doneckers,* 318-324 North State Street, Ephrata, 733-9502, $$-$$$$ CP • *Smithton Inn,* 900 West Main Street, Ephrata, 17522, 738-9502, $$-$$$ CP • *The Inn at Twin Linden,* Route 23, Churchtown, 17555, (215) 445-7619, $$-$$$ CP • *Churchtown Inn,* Route 23, Churchtown, 17555, (215) 445-7794, $$-$$$ CP. Two area resorts with indoor pools, tennis, and golf: *Lancaster Host Resort,* 2300 Lincoln Highway East, Lancaster, 299-5500, $$-$$$$; and *Willow Valley Resort,* 2416 Willow Street Pike, Lancaster, 464-2711, $$-$$$.

DINING *Groff's Farm,* Pinkerton Road, Mount Joy, 653-2048, delicious Pennsylvania Dutch specialties in a farmhouse, $$-$$$ • *Catacombs,* 102 North Market Street, Mount Joy, 653-2056, another Mount Joy winner, Continental menu; in the cellar are aging vaults of a former brewery, $$$ • *Log Cabin,* 11 Lehoy Forest Drive, Leola, 626-1181, wooded setting through a covered bridge—call for driving directions, $$-$$$$ • *Market Fare,* 25 West King Street, across from Central Market, Lancaster, 299-7090, paintings, classical music, a tasty and reasonable menu, $$. Also informal upstairs cafe for lunch, $ • *Windows on Steinman Park,* 16-18 West King Street, Lancaster, 295-1316, fine and fancy French, $$-$$$$ • *Hunt Club,* The Inn at Twin Linden (see above), weekends by reservation only, excellent reputation, book well in advance, $$-$$$ • *Red Caboose* (see above), 687-5001, dinner in the dining car, $-$$ • *The Restaurant at Donecker's,* 333 North State Street, 738-2421, lunch, $, dinner, $$$ • *Strasburg Rail Road Dinner Train,* 687-6486, reserve ahead for prix fixe dinner, $$$$ including train fare • *Joe's,* 450 South Seventh Street, Reading, 373-6794, worth a detour for the wild-mushroom cookery, $$$-$$$$ • To sample Pennsylvania Dutch specialties, commercial settings but bountiful servings, try *Leola Family Restaurant,* 2491 New Holland Pike, Leola, 656-2311, $-$$ or *Good and Plenty,* Route 896, Smoketown, 394-7111, $$. For information on a family-style dinner in a traditional "Plain People's" home, contact Jack and Dee Dee Myers, 664-4888, or Emanuel Fisher, 768-3691.

SIGHTSEEING *Central Market,* Penn Square, Lancaster, 291-4740. Hours: Tuesday and Friday 6 A.M. to 4:30 P.M., Saturday 6 A.M. to 2 P.M. • *Historic Lancaster Walking Tours,* 100 South Queen Street, Lancaster, 392-1776. Hours: usually April to October, Monday to Saturday 10 A.M. and 1:30 P.M., Sunday 1:30 P.M. by advance reservation. Schedules may change with the season, best to phone for current schedules and rates • *Heritage Center Museum of Lancaster County,* Penn Square, Lancaster, 299-6440. Hours. May to mid-November, Tuesday to Saturday 10 A.M. to 4 P.M. Free • *People's Place Quilt Museum,* Main Street, Intercourse, 768-7171. Hours: Monday to Saturday 9 A.M. to 5 P.M. Adults, $3; children, $1.50 • *Strasburg Rail Road,* Route 741, Strasburg, 687-7522. Hours: late March to December, hours vary with seasons. Best to check. Adults, $7; children 3–11, $4 • *Railroad Museum of Pennsylvania,* Route 741, Strasburg, 687-8628. Hours: May to October, Monday to Saturday 9 A.M. to 5 P.M., Sunday noon to 5 P.M.; closed Mondays November to April. Adults, $6; ages 6–17, $4 • *Toy Train Museum,* Paradise Lane (off Route 741), Strasburg, 687-8976. Hours: daily May to October 10 A.M. to 5 P.M., weekends only November and December. Adults, $3; children 7–12, $1.50 • *Landis Valley Museum,* 2451 Kissel Road (Route 272 North), Lancaster, 569-0401. Hours: Tuesday to Saturday 9 A.M. to 5 P.M., Sunday noon to 5 P.M. Adults, $7; ages 6–17, $5 • *Amish Farm and House,* Route 30 east of Lancaster, 394-6185. Hours: daily summer 8:30 A.M. to 6 P.M., spring and fall to 5 P.M., winter to 4 P.M. Adults, $4.75, children 6–11, $3 • *Rock Ford Plantation,* 881 Rock Ford Road, Lancaster, 392-7223. Hours: April to November, Tuesday to Saturday 10 A.M. to 4 P.M., Sunday noon to 4 P.M. Adults, $3.50; ages 6–18, $1.50 • *Wheatland,* 1120 Marietta Avenue, Lancaster, 392-8721. Hours: daily April to November 10 A.M. to 4:15 P.M. Adults, $5; students, $3; children 6–12, $1.75 • *Sturgis Pretzel House,* 219 East Main Street, Lititz, 626-4354. Hours: Monday to Saturday 9 A.M. to 5 P.M. Free • *The Artworks at Doneckers,* 100 North State Street, Ephrata, 738-9503. Hours: Monday, Tuesday and Thursday 11 :45 A.M. to 5 P.M., Friday 11:45 A.M. to 7 P.M.; Saturday 10 A.M. to 5 P.M.; Sunday noon to 4 P.M. Free • *Green Dragon Farmers' Market,* 995 North State Street (off Route 272), Ephrata, 738-1117. Hours: Friday 9 A.M. to 10 P.M. year-round.

FOR FURTHER INFORMATION For extensive lodgings list, including motels, farms, and bed-and-breakfast homes, plus more on area attractions, contact the Pennsylvania Dutch Convention and Visitors' Bureau, 501 Greenfield Road, Lancaster, PA 17601, 299-8901 or toll free (800) 735-2629. For a list of Mennonite farms accepting guests and information on private guides, contact the Mennonite Information Center, 2209 Millstream Road, Lancaster, PA 17602, 299-0954.

Winter

Ballooning in Connecticut's Farmington Valley
Photo courtesy of Eleanor Berman

Uncovering the Past Near Hartford

At the turn of the century, when upper-middle-class women were expected to stick close to their elegant hearths and homes, Theodate Pope Riddle of Farmington, Connecticut, would have none of it.

The daughter of a multimillionaire industrialist and wife of an ambassador to Russia and Argentina, Ms. Riddle was a trailblazer, studying to become one of the first licensed women architects in the country. She designed several Connecticut schools, but her most notable achievement came at the precocious age of 16 when she helped Stanford White design a home for her parents, a mansion unique because it was deliberately planned to show off the collection of Impressionist art that astute Alfred Atmore Pope acquired before the rest of the world had recognized such talents as Manet, Degas, and Monet.

Twenty major works of art were all that Mr. Pope had room for amid the Empire sofas and four-poster beds, the porcelains, bronzes, and etchings that filled his home; and he made his choices wisely, including two of Monet's haystack paintings, Degas's famous *Dancers and Jockeys,* and portraits by James Whistler and Mary Cassatt.

Hill-Stead, as the Mount Vernon–like hilltop mansion was called, is now a public museum, one of the few places where museum-quality art can be seen in a gracious residential setting. This little-heralded art treasure in a Hartford suburb is one of many surprises awaiting visitors to Connecticut's state capital. The nation's oldest statehouse, one of its earliest and finest art museums, the flamboyant Victorian home of Mark Twain, and the priceless firearms collection of Sam Colt are among many unexpected finds in and around Hartford, hidden from passersby on the whizzing turnpike by the glass-sided mini-skyscrapers that mark America's insurance center.

Whether to stay in the city or in a neighboring town is the first decision to be made. Hartford's hotels offer convenience to the city's attractions and dining; Farmington and Wethersfield have more old New England ambience.

Wherever you settle, you'll quickly find out that Hartford is more than insurance companies. The Old State House, a 1796 Federal-style masterpiece by Charles Bullfinch, sits smack in the middle of those new office towers. It was scheduled for demolition to make way for a parking lot when Hartford's aroused citizens raised millions to save this memento of the city's historic past.

Now the courtroom and original Senate and House chambers are restored to their former splendor, and visitors to Hartford can tour the architectural landmark where seven former U.S. presidents from Adams to Grant also once paid their respects. The painting of George Washington hanging in the Senate chambers is the only Gilbert Stuart portrait of Washington still hanging in its original commissioned space.

After further refurbishing of the building, all of this is expected to be open to the public once again in the fall of 1994. Plans include the installation of a Connecticut Hall of Fame, and returning the green in front of the building to its original use as a town meeting place.

At the visitors' center in the Old State House, you can pick up maps and booklets on the city as well as a printed, self-guided walking tour that offers a quick and easy overview.

The most important of Hartford's sights is the Wadsworth Atheneum on Main Street, America's first free public art museum, established in 1842. It now occupies five buildings and a sculpture court. First-time visitors may be amazed at the size and breadth of the museum collections. The generosity of Hartford native J. P. Morgan accounts for many of the treasures. The private collections he donated include some 3,000 pieces of priceless porcelain and many valuable paintings. Morgan also purchased and donated the Wallace Nutting collection, the nation's finest assemblage of very Early American furniture from the Pilgrim era.

Another focus of the museum is its comprehensive selection of American paintings spanning 200 years. Important nineteenth-century works were given by another local collector, Mrs. Samuel Colt. Other special strengths are paintings by the Hudson River School and by Hartford-born artist Frederick Church, who advised Mrs. Colt in her collecting. Outside the museum, Alexander Calder's soaring stabile *Stegosaurus* straddles Burr Mall.

A more controversial outdoor sculpture is the Stone Field on Gold Street, 36 glacial boulders ranging in weight from 1,000 pounds to 11 tons. Sculptor Carl Andre received $87,000 for this rock collection, which may or may not be a work of art, depending on whom you ask.

With walking tour in hand, you're now prepared to explore the curious mix of old and new that marks downtown Hartford. You'll see, for example, the white steeple of Center Church, circa 1807, reflected in the gold-mirrored walls of the Bushnell Tower, designed by I. M. Pei in 1969; view one of the earliest successful urban renewal efforts at Constitution Plaza, as well as one of the city's oldest homes at 396 Main Street. The 1782 Butler-McCook Homestead is well worth a stop.

Some interesting stops for shoppers (and diners) are the Richardson Mall, an 1875 department store converted to shops and a food court, and the Pavilion shopping mall near the Old State House.

Open only on weekdays is another worthwhile sight, the Museum of Connecticut History, housing the Colt collection of guns, which is recognized as one of the finest collections of firearms anywhere. The

1,000 guns tell the long history of the company that Sam Colt founded in 1836 and moved to his native Hartford in 1847. By 1855 he had the world's largest private armory, and Colt revolvers were known the world over. The guns on display range from Wyatt Earp's six-shooter, to Colt's then-revolutionary Gatling machine guns, to M2 and M3 aircraft guns. In a curious way the guns are markers of the nation's history. The museum also has a fine collection of timepieces by early Connecticut clockmakers, and many historical documents, including the charter once hidden in the state's fabled Charter Oak.

Across the street, on a knoll dominating the city's 41-acre Bushnell Park, is the gold-domed state capitol building. Its Moorish interior is also open to the public only on weekdays in winter, but the exterior deserves more than a passing glance. The complex architectural style offers everything from Gothic spires to classical arcades, and many fine statues decorate the facade, depicting allegorical figures as well as some of the state's early heroes.

Bushnell Park's other pride is its meticulously restored 1914 carousel, a favorite of Hartford youngsters in the summertime.

To see some of Hartford's historic surroundings, drive just a few miles south to Old Wethersfield, a gem of a town, dating to 1634 and with more than 150 remaining homes built before 1850. The Buttolph-Williams House is one of the oldest. It dates to the turn of the eighteenth century and is furnished in the style of the early Pilgrims. The three main attractions in town, the eighteenth-century Webb-Deane-Stevens homes, are part of one excellent historic tour. A town museum and cultural center offer exhibits, as well.

Another interesting stop here is the Comstock Ferre seed company, the nation's first, which sells over 800 varieties of garden seeds. The Standish House is a properly historic inn on Main Street, a nice stop for lunch or dinner, and the Chester Bulkley House offers bed-and-breakfast lodgings in an 1830 home.

Come Saturday night, you may want to visit the Hartford Stage Company, a first-rate regional theater, see the Hartford Whalers, the city's National Hockey League entry, or take in the action at jai alai. You could also check the newspaper for concerts or special events at Bushnell Auditorium or on the campus of Trinity College.

Sleep late on Sunday, fortify yourself with a hearty brunch, and head for Hartford's major literary landmark, Nook Farm. This Victorian enclave, settled during the second half of the nineteenth century, was a colony populated by prominent actors, editors, and celebrities of the day. Among them were Harriet Beecher Stowe and Samuel Clemens, better known as Mark Twain. Their restored homes and two former carriage houses preserve an important portion of this unusual neighborhood. The Stowe House is a simple cottage furnished with many of its original pieces and decorated with the delicate watercolors the author produced between books.

The Clemens household, however, is quite a different affair. Built in 1874 for the then-princely sum of $130,000, it is a showplace, with its carved mantels, goldleaf wallpapers, inlaid mahogany furniture, and decorative work by the likes of Louis Comfort Tiffany. The Twain humor is evident, however, in touches like the optical illusion fireplace and the cigar, pipe, and billiard cue ceiling decor of the third-floor study. The story goes that Clemens gave up his second-floor study because his children were too noisy to suit him and retired upstairs, where he wrote his masterpieces with a billiard table at his side.

The billiard room leads to two balconies, one of which Clemens called the Texas Deck because it reminded him of the uppermost deck of a riverboat steamer. Clemens himself once described his home as part steamboat, part medieval stronghold, and park cuckoo clock.

From Nook Farm, continue west down Farmington Avenue and you'll soon arrive at Farmington. This town contains more than 100 houses built prior to 1835, and most of the original village is a state historic district. You may want to make your first stop a look at the Stanley Whitman House, a gracious seventeenth-century New England home full of furnishings and other artifacts of earlier days. Then you'll have saved the best for last—a visit to Ms. Riddle's regal Hill-Stead. The last tour begins at 4 P.M.

Hartford Area Code: 203

DRIVING DIRECTIONS The quickest way is to follow the New England Thruway (I-95) into Connecticut to New Haven, then connect with I-91 straight to Hartford. The more scenic route follows the Hutchinson River Parkway into the Merritt Parkway, making the I-91 connection just before Wallingford. In daylight, the Merritt is well worth an extra few minutes. Take the Hartford exit marked CAPITAL DISTRICT. *Total distance:* 113 miles.

PUBLIC TRANSPORTATION Amtrak (800) 523-8720 serves Hartford from New York's Penn Station. Most of the city sights are walkable from downtown hotels in decent weather. Take a cab to reach Nook Farm.

ACCOMMODATIONS Center-city hotels all have weekend packages: *Goodwin Hotel,* 1 Haynes Street, Hartford, 06103, 246-7500, Hartford's only small luxury hotel, in a historic building, $$$$ • *Ramada Inn–Capitol Hill,* 440 Asylum Street, 06103, 246-6591, $$ • *Holiday Inn–Downtown Civic Center,* 50 Morgan Street, 06120, 549-2400, $$-$$$ • *Sheraton-Hartford,* 315 Trumbull Street at Civic

Center Plaza (connected to Civic Center), 06103, 728-5151, $$$ • *Susse Chalet Motel,* 185 Brainard Road (I-91 exit 27), 06114, 525-9306, $ • *Centennial Inn of Farmington,* 5 Spring Lane, Farmington, 06032, 677-4647, all-suite hotel, $$-$$$$ CP • *Barney House,* 11 Mountain Spring Road, Farmington, 06032, 677-9735, handsome old home, $$ CP • *Farmington Motor Inn,* 827 Farmington Avenue, Farmington, 06032, 677-2821, $$$ CP • *Chester Bulkley House,* 184 Main Street, Wethersfield, 06109, 563-4236, B&B home, $$ CP.

DINING *Carbone's Restaurant,* 588 Franklin Avenue, 249-9646, Italian restaurant popular with politicos, $$ • *Gaetano's,* Hartford Civic Center, second level, 249-1629, excellent French and Italian, $$ • *Max on Main,* 205 Main Street, 522-6500, sophisticated bistro, very popular, $$-$$$ • *Hot Tomato's,* 1 Union Place, 249-5100, popular Italian, lotsa pasta, $-$$ • *Congress Rotisserie,* 7 Maple Avenue, 560-1965, grill specialities, $-$$ • *Amarillo Grill,* 309 Asylum Street, 247-7427, Texas barbecue ribs, good for families, $-$$ • *Peppercorns Grill,* 357 Main Street, 547-1714, excellent Italian dishes and more, $$ • *Pierpont's,* Goodwin Hotel (see above), attractive formal setting for fine dining, $$$ • *Capitol Fish House* 391 Main Street, 724-3370, in a restored nineteenth-century hotel, $$-$$$ • *Truc Orient Express,* 735 Wethersfield Avenue, 296-2618, first-rate Vietnamese food, $ • *Apricots,* 1593 Farmington Avenue, Farmington, 673-5405, French, longtime favorite, $$-$$$$ • *The Whitman,* 1125 Farmington Avenue, Farmington, 678-9217, attractive, interesting menu, music on weekends, $-$$$ • *Standish House,* 222 Main Street, Wethersfield, 721-1113, lovely 1790 home, varied menu, $$-$$$.

SIGHTSEEING *Wadsworth Atheneum,* 600 Main Street, 278-2670. Hours: Tuesday to Sunday 11 A.M. to 5 P.M. Adults, $5; students, $2; under 13 free. Free to all on Thursday and Saturday 11 A.M. to 1 P.M. • *Old State House,* 800 Main Street, 522-6766. Hours: Best to check hours after reopening. Free • *Capitol Building,* 210 Capitol Avenue, 240-0222. Hours: Monday to Friday 9 A.M. to 3 P.M.; free tours 9:15 A.M. to 1:15 P.M. Saturday tours April through October, 10:15 A.M. to 2:15 P.M. Free • *Museum of Connecticut History,* 231 Capitol Avenue, 566-3056. Hours: Monday to Friday 9 A.M. to 4:15 P.M., Free • *Butler-McCook Homestead,* 396 Main Street, 522-1806. Hours: May 15 to October 15, Tuesday, Thursday, and Sunday noon to 4 P.M. Special Christmas displays in December. Adults, $3; children, $1 • *Mark Twain Memorial,* 351 Farmington Avenue at Forest Street (I-84 exit 46), 525-9317. Tours: Tuesday to Saturday 9:30 A.M. to 5 P.M., Sunday noon to 5 P.M. Open Mondays also June 1 to Columbus Day and in December. Adults, $6.50; children under 16, $2.75 • *Hill-Stead Museum,* 35 Mountain Road, 677-4787. Hours: April to October, Tuesday to Sunday 10 A.M. to 5 P.M.; November to March, Tuesday to Sunday 11 A.M. to 5 P.M. Adults, $6; children 6-12, $3 • *Stanley Whitman House,* 37 High Street off Route 4, 677-9222. Hours: March, April, November, and December, Sunday noon to 4 P.M.; May to October, Wednesday to Sunday noon to 4 P.M.; closed January and February. Adults, $3; children 6-14, $2 • *Webb-Deane-Stevens Museum,* 211 Main Street, Wethersfield, 529-0612. Hours: May to October, Wednesday to Monday 10 A.M. to 4 P.M., rest of year, Saturday and Sunday only; last tour begins 3 P.M. Adults, $6; students, $4; children, $1.

FOR FURTHER INFORMATION Contact the Greater Hartford Convention and Visitors' Bureau, 1 Civic Center Plaza, Hartford, CT 06103, 728-6789 or toll free (800) 793-4480.

Christmas Cheer at Bear Mountain

One of the younger natives was getting restless.

She had oohed at the 40-foot Christmas tree, listened happily to the first of the carols. But now, with frosty puffs punctuating her words in the wintry night air, she could be heard plaintively asking her dad, "When's he coming?"

Almost as if on cue, the choral group broke into "Here Comes Santa Claus," and there was the great man himself, making a grand entrance in a flurry of "Ho, ho, ho's," singing a few carols in a belly-deep baritone, and inviting everyone to come to call the next day when he was settled in his quarters downstairs in the Bear Mountain Inn. And pretty soon, the sky was lit up with fireworks.

The youngster's grin was ear to ear once again.

Santa's arrival on the first Friday in December annually marks the start of the season for the kids as well as the opening of the traditional Bear Mountain Christmas Festival, a regular event since 1968 under the sponsorship of the Palisades Interstate Park Commission and the Bear Mountain Inn. Right through until the start of the New Year, this is family time at the inn, with warm hospitality, Santa in residence, lots to do, and a setting that would do credit to a Christmas card.

The Bear Mountain Festival is neither huge nor slick, but it has a pleasant down-home flavor. The community is invited to get involved, by lending crafts and creations such as gingerbread villages and candy cottages. The displays change from year to year. Recently they have ranged from Early American quilts and antique toys to Hummel figurines and decorated Ukrainian eggs. Working toy-train layouts are perennial favorites, as are the Christmas trees decorated in original motifs. During the week, church choirs and school choruses drop by to add music to the festivities.

Santa welcomes children to his workshop (which is off in a wing by itself), where they find him surrounded by a retinue of bigger-than-life animated friends, including a toy soldier, a Raggedy Ann doll, a panda bear, a snowman, and a group of mechanical carolers. The kids love it.

Bear Mountain Inn is a rustic fieldstone and timber affair with big beams and a giant fireplace that stretches from floor to ceiling. You can choose from rooms in the inn building or lodges on the grounds. Out the windows of the lodge, brightly garbed families can be seen ice skating against a backdrop of mountains and evergreens. At night, when the rink is lit and a dozen trees around the perimeter also light up along with the giant tree and a 40-foot star on the mountaintop, it's fairyland time.

When the weather cooperates, the days fly by, filled with skating, sledding, and playful snowball fights. Should you seek further diversion, West Point is just north on Route 9W, or you can cross the bridge and head a few miles north on Route 9 to Cold Spring. Pick up a walking tour brochure in one of the shops and see the historic sights of the picturesque village; then if the kids will cooperate, you can visit some of the 50-plus antiques shops that crowd each other in a three-block stretch of Main Street, which runs down to a bandstand on a little spit out into the Hudson. The view is outstanding.

Another shopping option is a ten-minute drive west on Route 6 to Route 32 in Central Valley and the Woodbury Common, a shopping outlet where over 100 factory outlets from Corning to Anne Klein offer all kinds of gifts and clothing at savings.

Late in the day, head back south on Route 9 to Garrison, where you can enjoy another area holiday tradition, a candlelight tour at Boscobel. This beautiful nineteenth-century mansion with its columns and porticoes is an outstanding example of New York Federal architecture, and its period furnishings take on a special elegance in the candle glow. Musicians are on hand to enhance the mood, and the house smells invitingly of the warm cinnamon-flavored cider refreshments waiting at the end of the tour.

Like Cold Spring, incidentally, Garrison has an overlook with a splendid Hudson view. There are two places to treat yourself to a special dinner in Garrison. Xaviar's is the place for flawless New American cuisine in a classy setting, or you can settle in front of the fireplace in the low-ceilinged, atmospheric dining room of the Bird and Bottle Inn, a restored eighteenth-century tavern. In Cold Spring, Plumbush offers a lovely Victorian setting, while Northgate provides river views and Hudson House, simple country charm.

To wind up the weekend on a traditional note, head home via Route 9 and stop in at the Sleepy Hollow Restorations. Each of the three buildings has a different offering: Van Cortlandt Manor in Croton-on-Hudson presents the traditional decorations of St. Nicholas Day; Sunnyside in Tarrytown displays the ways that Washington Irving entertained his family and friends at Christmas; and Philipsburg Manor in North Tarrytown is filled with the traditional trimmings for Twelfth Night or Old Christmas. Each building also offers candlelight tours; check the schedules to see if they coincide with your own.

Bear Mountain Area Code: 914

DRIVING DIRECTIONS Across George Washington Bridge to Palisades Interstate Parkway to Bear Mountain Park. *Total distance:* about 50 miles.

PUBLIC TRANSPORTATION Shortline Bus service to Bear Mountain, (212) 736-4700.

ACCOMMODATIONS *Bear Mountain Inn,* Bear Mountain, NY 10911, 786-2731, $-$$ • See also Cold Spring and West Point.

DINING *Bear Mountain Inn* (see above), $-$$ • *Hotel Thayer, U.S.* Military Academy grounds, West Point, 446-4731, $-$$ • *Xaviar,* Highland Country Club, Route 9D, Garrison, 424-4228, prix fixe $$$$$ • *Bird and Bottle Inn,* off Route 9, Garrison, 424-3000, $$-$$$; Saturday prix fixe dinner, $$$$$ • *Northgate,* 1 North Street, Cold Spring, 265-5555, $$ • *Plumbush,* Route 9D, Cold Spring, 265-3904, $$$ or prix fixe, $$$$$ • *Hudson House,* 2 Main Street, Cold Spring, 265-9355, $$-$$$.

SIGHTSEEING *Bear Mountain Christmas Festival,* Bear Mountain Inn, 786-2731. Hours: early December to January 1, daily 10 A.M. to 6 P.M.; Santa's arrival (with tree lighting, caroling, and fireworks), first Friday in December, usually beginning at 7 P.M. Santa's house to December 24; exterior light displays to January 1. Call for current hours and events • *Boscobel,* Route 9D, Garrison, 265-3638. Hours: April to October, 9:30 A.M. to 5 P.M.; March, November, and December, 9:30 A.M. to 4 P.M. Adults, $5; children, $2.50; candlelight tours, adults, $6; children, $3 • *Sleepy Hollow Restorations,* 150 White Plains Road, Tarrytown, NY 10591, 631-8200. Phone or write for holiday exhibits, tour dates, hours, and holidays fees. General fees, each house, adults, $6; children, $3.

FOR FURTHER INFORMATION Contact Palisades Interstate Park Commission, Bear Mountain, NY 10911, 786-2701.

Catching the Brandywine Spirit

The ghost of Christmas past is alive and well in the Brandywine Valley.

Teddy bears and toys that delighted children a century ago, trees festooned with nature's own ornaments, a New England winter scene populated by antique dolls, the foods and feasts of Early America, Victorian garlands and wreaths, candlelight, carols, and cascades of red poinsettias—these are a sampling of some of the things that light up this rural area where Delaware and Pennsylvania meet. There's a contagious, noncommercial spirit that even old Ebenezer Scrooge would have found hard to resist. If you're feeling a bit cynical about the season, there's no better antidote than a dose of Brandywine cheer.

All the hotels in Wilmington are decked out for the season and offer special weekend package rates that make them ideal holiday headquarters. Planning an itinerary is more of a challenge, since the list of annual events runs into the dozens. One practical approach is to work around the major attractions, starting with the ones closest to Wilmington.

The Delaware Art Museum delights visitors young and old with its old-fashioned displays. One special, recent favorite was the antique toys of Pennsylvania collector Richard Wright. Called "Remembrances of Holidays Past: Dolls, Toys, and Teddy Bears," the exhibit included European and American dolls in porcelain, wood, wax, cloth, china, and bisque, early Disney characters and Steiff bears, miniature furniture, and a choice dollhouse.

The museum's Christmas crèche is another area favorite, an elaborate eighteenth-century Nativity scene with more than 40 hand-carved and amazingly lifelike figures.

Children love the downstairs White Whale gallery, where participatory exhibits allow them to express their own creativity. Parents, meanwhile, will be free to visit the museum shop, with its array of unusual gifts, and the gallery, where contemporary art is for sale.

The works of Howard Pyle, the Wyeths, and other noted American artists remain on display during the Christmas season.

Follow Route 52 out of town to Winterthur, and you'll find that the museum that holds one of the nation's greatest collections of early American furnishings filled with displays re-creating traditions of early American holiday entertaining. For the annual "Yuletide at Winterthur" celebration, the antique-filled rooms are set up for festivities of an earlier time such as dessert parties, musicales, punch parties, holiday feasts, after dinner games and entertainment, and a hunt breakfast. Evening tours are magical, with the displays shown off in the soft illumination of candlelight. The Conservatory is especially lovely, with banks of poinsettias highlighted by an 18-foot Christmas tree decorated as it was when the museum was the home of Henry Francis du Pont.

Foods, ranging from suckling pigs to pheasant, syllabub to oysters, and homemade cakes and cookies, are all so lifelike you'll want to dig right in. A recent, festive eighteenth-century Southern dinner had the table laden with turkey, steaks, oysters, vegetables, pies, cakes, tarts, and sweets galore, all set up before the beautiful fireplace of the great Marlboro Room.

All the foods are based on documented evidence of early Yuletide customs.

If it all leaves you feeling starved, the Country Mouse Cafe is a convenient lunch stop nearby on Route 52 in Greenville Crossing.

Hagley Museum, situated right on the Brandywine River, was created to show how the river's water power built early manufacturing that helped industrialize the nation, including du Pont's black powder mills. The exhibits tracing industry from the 1600s into this century are interesting, as are the restored mills and shops. All of the property is festively decorated during the holiday season, including the nineteenth century machine shop where visitors can see demonstrations of steam toys.

But the standout is Eleutherian Mills, the 1803 Georgian home of E. I. du Pont. It is decorated upstairs and down with original creations using fruit, greenery, and other natural materials. The apple and pineapple door fans, pine ropes, ivy wreaths, cranberry trees, and Victorian natural tree ornaments may well give you lots of new ideas for your own home holiday decor.

A popular recent exhibit in Hagley's Henry Clay Mill Gallery featured "The Magic of Miniature," with operating toy trains and model steam engines from the machine age. A holiday shop also includes train items, along with children's gifts, Nativity scenes, old-fashioned ornaments, and cast-iron reproductions of toys from the 1800s.

Hagley offers evening candlelight tours of the du Pont home the week before Christmas and the day after the holiday, an event made more festive by the melodious voices of the Hagley Carolers.

If you've chosen the second weekend of December for your visit, you'll want to get back in time to attend the annual candlelight house tour in Colonial New Castle, six miles south of Wilmington on Route 9. Time seems to have stood still in Delaware's onetime capital, leaving the red-brick Georgian and Federal homes of the town looking much as they did in the 1700s. They are a real delight decked out for the holidays. Candles flicker in every window and along the paths outside, and carolers add to the Yuletide atmosphere with their songs of the season.

Other evening Christmas festivities usually can be found at the Grand Opera House on Wilmington's Market Street Mall, where Christmas concerts and all kinds of seasonal entertainment are among the attractions scheduled each December.

On Sunday, head across the Pennsylvania border for two of the valley's prime attractions. It's hard to imagine a cheerier scene than the Brandywine River Museum, where tiny fingers can be seen pointing in all directions as children urge parents to "Look, look" at the wondrous sights. The December features have become a local tradition, repeated year after year, and are always eagerly anticipated.

Every other year, in one section of this museum which displays so many works by the Wyeth family, Ann Wyeth McCoy offers a gift to the children of the community, an exhibit featuring her magnificent collection of antique porcelain dolls. A doll's Christmas tree is one of the scenes put together by Mrs. McCoy and her artist husband, John, and each year there is a special scene such as a winter landscape of dolls congregating in front of a New England church, each quite literally "dolled up" in Victorian finery. It's so realistic that there's even a crying youngster who has slipped trying to cut across the frozen river.

Another gallery here whizzes and hums with five toy trains winding their way along thousands of feet of track, through mountains and valleys, past houses and factories, on their way to a huge railroad yard. Grown-ups love it just as much as the small fry. The model O-gauge railroad is a serious year-round interest of the museum, which employs a special full-time "engineer" to restore and maintain the antiques and other toy trains and the extensive scenery.

Other museum galleries, as always, feature the artistic efforts of Brandywine artists, including the Wyeths and Howard Pyle, but they take second place in December to the giant trees in the hallway, festooned with munchkins, mice, beguiling angels, and other totally wonderful whimsical "critters" made by museum volunteers each year from natural materials found in abundance in the woods outside. Critters are for sale in the museum gift shop, or you can buy a little booklet to show you how to make these tiny treasures for your own tree. There are other unique gift ideas in the shop, as well as Wyeth prints.

Things become even merrier in the museum when choral groups appear during the day to put the festivities to music. On weekends, outside the rustic, converted mill there are vendors in the courtyard offering roasted chestnuts and handmade gifts—dolls, quilts, and tree ornaments among them.

It's hard to leave the good cheer at the Brandywine, but you'll find ample compensation when you proceed on Route 1 to Kennett Square and Longwood Gardens. Santa's figure in an antique sleigh pulled by sparkling reindeer greets you from the main terrace, and inside, the conservatory is resplendent with more than 2,000 poinsettias, graceful cyclamens, colorful tulips, and fragrant narcissi—a breathtaking red and white holiday display.

Prizewinning trees decorated by local garden clubs are just a prelude to Longwood's traditional 18-foot beauty, and to further enhance the holiday mood, organ recitals and choral concerts are offered in the adjacent ballroom daily through most of December. In the Visitor Center, the popular 12-foot Victoria and Albert Tree glows with hundreds of old-fashioned hand-blown glass ornaments.

The theme and decor of the celebration changes each year, and there are new special features, as well. Recently the East Conservatory was home to an animated three-quarter-life-size village with mechanized residents in eighteenth-century garb and a special display featuring old-fashioned sleds. No telling what each year will bring, but you can be sure it will be delightful.

If you stay until the sun goes down, 35,000 lights will twinkle outside, bedecking dozens of trees near the parking area and the walkways. Weather permitting, the fountains of the Open Air Theatre dance to music every half-hour during the day and continuously from 5 to 9 P.M.

And these are just the major sights in the valley. Every weekend there are open houses in historic homes, Victorian displays at Wilmington's Rockwood Museum, traditional Swedish and Colonial celebrations, tree displays, fairs featuring homemade gifts and fresh baked goodies, more candlelight tours, caroling, tree-trimming parties, and many other classic holiday delights. And as a bonus along the way, the winter landscape of the valley is a typical Andrew Wyeth scene come to life.

It's an extraordinary Christmas celebration here in the Brandywine Valley—one you may well decide to make a tradition of your own.

Delaware Area Code: 302

DRIVING DIRECTIONS Take the New Jersey Turnpike to its end and cross the Delaware Memorial Bridge, then pick up Route 295 to I-95 north into Wilmington. *Total distance:* 121 miles.

ACCOMMODATIONS See page 39. Ask about special holiday packages.

DINING See page 39.

SIGHTSEEING *Winterthur Museum,* Winterthur, (800) 448-3883. Tuesday to Saturday 9 A.M. to 5 P.M.; Sunday noon to 5 P.M. General admission: adults, $8, students 12–18, $5; under 12, $3. General admission includes a tour of the Galleries, a self-guided garden walk, and year-round tram. Yuletide at Winterthur tours, late November through December, by reservation only, adults, $6; children, $3 • *Delaware Art Museum,* 2301 Kentmere Parkway, Wilmington, 571-9590. Hours: Tuesday to Saturday 10 A.M. to 5 P.M., Sunday noon to 5 P.M. Adults, $4; children, $2.50 • *Hagley Museum,* Route 141, Greenville, 658-2400. Hours: April to December daily 9:30 A.M. to 4:30 P.M.; January to March, Monday to Friday, one tour at 1:30 P.M.; Saturday and Sunday 9:30 A.M. to 4:30 P.M. Adults, $9.75; children 6–14, $3.50 • *Brandywine River Museum,* Route 1, Chadds Ford, Pennsylvania, (610) 388-7601. Hours: daily 9:30 A.M. to 4:30 P.M. Adults, $5; children, $2.50 • *Longwood Gardens,* Route 1, Kennett Square, Pennsylvania, (610) 388-6741. Christmas hours: Conservatories, daily 10 A.M. to 9 P.M.; Visitor Center, daily 9 A.M. to 9 P.M.; outdoor displays, daily 5 P.M. to 9 P.M. Adults, $10 ($6 on Tuesdays); children, $2; under 6, free • *Historic New Castle Candlelight Tour.* For current dates and fees, phone 322-8411.

FOR FURTHER INFORMATION Contact Brandywine Valley Tourist Information Center at Longwood Gardens, Route 1, Kennett Square, PA 19348, (610) 388-2900 or toll free (800) 228-9933, for a complete listing of Brandywine Valley Christmas activities. Greater Wilmington Convention and Visitors' Bureau, 1300 Market Street, Suite 504, Wilmington, DE 19801, toll free (800) 422-1181, or 652-4088.

All Aboard for a Connecticut Christmas

The conductor looks familiar. There's something about the pudgy build, the bright red suit. And why is he handing out goodies instead of punching tickets?

The reason, of course, is that Santa Claus himself presides aboard Connecticut's North Pole Express, a huffing, puffing steam train that rides the rails every season between the towns of Essex and Chester.

The Express is one of the many happy traditions that make Christmas special for children in Connecticut. Take a weekend off with the family, and you can share that ride with Santa, visit with his reindeer and toymakers, mail your cards from a picture-postcard village called Bethlehem, go caroling or sleigh riding, see a magnificent eighteenth-century Italian crèche, load down the trunk with one-of-a-kind gifts, and maybe even head home with a tree you've chosen and chopped down yourself.

This is a rambling trip, but it isn't difficult since no two points in this compact state are more than two hours apart. And there are so many interesting stops along the way, it's doubtful that you'll hear many complaints coming from the back seat.

For your first stop, drive north past New Milford, past gracious white clapboard homes and kids skating on ponds, to a unique shop where the children may actually let you get some shopping done because they'll be so intrigued with the giant tree that is a holiday tradition at The Silo. This converted stable, silo, and barn, normally filled with finds for cooks, are chock-full of gifts made by local craftspeople during the holidays—everything from baskets and batiks to quilts and statues. Even the ornaments on the eye-boggling 18-foot tree are handmade. The gingerbread, dough, blown-glass, and stained-glass creations can be purchased right off the tree.

From New Milford, drive east on Route 109 through the handsome Colonial village of Washington, continuing on to Route 61, then south to Bethlehem, where the post office on intersecting Route 132 will not only postmark your cards but will offer an assortment of 24 rubber stamps dating back over the years to personalize your envelopes. It's a good idea to bring extra paper for the kids, most of whom seem determined to try out every stamp design at least twice.

As you might expect in a little town of Bethlehem, there is a super Christmas shop—the state's largest—located at 18 East Street and full of imported ornaments and toys.

Bethlehem also holds an annual Christmas Festival, usually the second weekend in December, with dozens of artisans and craftspersons on hand with a bounty of original gifts, food stalls on the green, strolling carolers, hayrides, and Santa himself to say hello to the crowd. He does get around this time of year.

About a mile south of Bethlehem village green, in a weathered barn on the grounds of the Regina Laudis priory, is an eighteenth-century Neapolitan crèche of museum quality. It is, in fact, the gift of a wealthy collector of religious art whose other endowments now rest with New York's Metropolitan Museum.

The crèche is 16 feet long by 4 feet high by 5 feet deep. The setting is a blend of a scene from an eighteenth-century Italian hillside village and a classical Nativity, and the detail in the 60 carved figures is fascinating. All the clothes are of silks, satins, and brocades in rich muted shades; each figure is a lifelike re-creation of the townsperson going about his or her daily tasks. It is a rare work of art in a remarkable rural setting.

The Abbey also offers handmade crafts, Christmas trees, and wreaths for sale during the holiday season.

Continuing north to Torrington, you'll find another kind of creation, the town's annual Christmas Village. Santa Claus has been in residence here the week before Christmas for more than 30 years, receiving young guests in a comfortable, oak-beamed living room with logs crackling in the fireplace. After a chat and a small gift from Santa, the children can go across the corridor to the toy shop, where local "elves" are busily working on toys for youngsters in the town hospital.

On the grounds near the rear of the building is a Nativity scene with almost life-size figures. And nearby is Santa's sleigh, a favorite spot for photographers with pint-size models along. Eight reindeer are waiting in a pen close at hand, as is Rudolph, a red-nosed reindeer with his own gingerbread house. There's also Snowflake, a baby deer who's a favorite with the youngest visitors. There is no admission charge to the village and nothing is for sale here. It's a Christmas gift from Torrington residents for the enjoyment of children.

If you want to add an old-fashioned sleigh ride to your agenda, make advance arrangements with Ken Wood in Terryville, located about midway between Bethlehem and Torrington.

You can stay the night in Torrington if you've had enough driving for one day, but it's worth considering the less-than-an-hour's trip to Hartford via Routes 202 and 44 eastbound for the annual Festival of Lights in that city's Constitution Plaza. In the midst of the 250,000-bulb spectacular are sculptured angels with brass trumpets, reindeer, a Nativity scene, a 75-foot Christmas tree decked with hundreds of tiny lights and a 6-foot starburst, and the South Plaza Fountain, a cascade of shimmering light.

Check the papers to see if the Hartford Ballet is doing its holiday run of *The Nutcracker,* just in case you couldn't get tickets at Lincoln Center.

Sunday morning you'll set out on I-91 to Route 9 for Essex, but if the dates are right, you may want to make a shopping stop along the way at Wesleyan Potters in Middletown. The work of more than 200 fine craftspeople is for sale here from late November through mid-December—pottery, jewelry, weaving, wood, leather, glass, and pewter—all one of a kind and all high quality.

The North Pole Express leaves the Essex depot afternoons and evenings on Friday, Saturday, and Sunday in December. The cars are lit with toy-shaped Christmas lights, the caroling begins as soon as the train whistle blows, and the Connecticut countryside outside the window is bedecked with special Christmas lights and decorations supplied by friendly residents along the train's route. The ride has a special charm at night when the decorations are aglow.

Since the first train rides of the day aren't until noon, you'll have time to take a stroll through Essex, a lovely old seaport town whose beautifully preserved homes are a delight any time of year, but are especially wonderful with Christmas decorations decking the doors and windows. After a snowfall, Essex is a Christmas card come to life.

Have your lunch—or the big late Sunday hunt breakfast—or at least a look inside the Griswold Inn on Main Street. A village landmark since 1776, the inn is a must, not only for its Colonial ambience but also for the many collections that make it almost a mini-museum of nautical lore.

After you ride the train, you can head east on I-95 to Mystic Seaport, which is transformed every December into a nineteenth-century celebration of Christmas. Evergreens sprout atop the masts of historic ships, doorways are festooned, and homes are decorated for the holiday. Costumed guides lead groups to selected exhibits of Christmas past, and Lantern-Light Tours are held in the evening. Advance reservations are needed for tours.

You may want to stay for the romantic lantern-light strolls or the wassail and plum pudding that are available at the Seaman's Inne. Or you may want to get an earlier start back onto I-95, where any of several easy detours will bring you to farms where you can pick out your Christmas tree and chop it down yourself. Just don't forget to come prepared with enough rope to anchor the tree to the car roof.

Properly laden with memories and your tree, you should be set to keep up the holiday spirit after you get home.

Connecticut Area Code: 203

DRIVING DIRECTIONS Take the Hutchinson Parkway to I-684 to I-84 east. Take exit 4, Route 202 to Brookfield and New Milford; then Route 202 north, Route 109 east, Route 61 south to Bethlehem. Then Route 61 north to Litchfield, Route 202 north to Torrington,

Route 202 and Route 44 west into Hartford. Middletown and Essex are on Route 9 east of Hartford. Mystic is east on Route 95. *Total distance:* to Torrington, 109 miles; to Hartford, 113 miles; to Essex 100 miles.

ACCOMMODATIONS *Yankee Pedlar Inn,* 93 Main Street, Torrington, 06790, 489-9226, $-$$ • *Griswold Inn,* Main Street, Essex, 06426, 767-1812, $$-$$$ CP • For Washington accommodations, see page 74; for numerous hotel-motels in Hartford, see pages 216–217; for more on Essex, see page 160; for Mystic Seaport, see page 34.

DINING *Yankee Pedlar Inn* (see above), $-$$ • *Griswold Inn* (see above), $$, Sunday hunt breakfast, $-$$.

SIGHTSEEING *Valley Railroad,* Essex, 767-0103; usually late November to December 23, Thursday through Sunday and daily the week before Christmas; best to phone for current schedule and rates • *Bethlehem Post Office,* 266-7910. Hours: December 1 to 23, weekdays 8 A.M. to 5 P.M., Saturday to 12:30 P.M. Free • *Bethlehem Christmastown Festival,* usually first or second weekend in December. Phone 266-5702 for dates and events • *Abbey of Regina Laudis,* Flanders Road off Route 61, Bethlehem, 266-7637. Hours: throughout the holiday season and to mid-January, weather permitting, daily 10:30 A.M. to 4:30 P.M. Free • *Christmas Village,* Alvord Memorial Playground, Church Street, Torrington, 489-2274. Hours: mid-December to Christmas Eve, best to check for current hours. Free • *Sleigh Rides,* Ken Wood, Wood Acres, Griffen Road, Terryville, 583-8670 • *Mystic Seaport,* 50 Greenmanville Avenue, Mystic, 572-0711. Hours: November to March, 9 A.M. to 4 P.M. Lantern-light tours daily 5 to 9 P.M. in December. Phone for this year's times and rates. Daytime admission: adults, $15; children, $7.50 • Cut Your Own Christmas Tree Farms: For a list of the farms, contact the Connecticut Department of Agriculture, Marketing Division, State Office Building, 165 Capitol Avenue, Hartford, CT 06106, 566-4845.

FOR FURTHER INFORMATION For a complete schedule of Christmas events in Connecticut, contact the Tourism Division, Department of Economic Development, 865 Brook Street, Rocky Hill, CT 06067, toll free (800) CTBOUND.

Winter Pleasures Around Williamstown

He's a die-hard skier, one of the first on the slopes no matter what the weather.

She's ambivalent. If the sun isn't bright, the snow isn't powdery, and the temperature isn't above 20 degrees, she'd just as soon be inside a good museum.

Can they find happiness together on a winter weekend?

If there is any area equipped to handle both athletes and aesthetes, it is the northern Berkshires of Massachusetts. For skiers there is a choice of Brodie Mountain, Jiminy Peak, or Bousquet, which are challenging enough for all but the most expert, and Vermont areas like Haystack and Bromley are within an hour's drive for the really determined.

This is also good territory for cross-country skiers. The center at Brodie has 5 miles of packed trails and 50 acres of rolling fields, plus a network of 25 miles of unplowed roads adjacent to the magnificent 11,000 acres of Mount Greylock State Reservation.

But for those who want no part of wintry winds, here's an area with more sophisticated pleasures than most destinations farther north, beginning with one of the most inviting and impressive small museums to be found anywhere, Williamstown's Sterling and Francine Clark Art Institute.

Sterling Clark had the good fortune to be heir to the fortune his grandfather amassed as a partner to Isaac Singer, the sewing machine king. Clark began using his inheritance to collect fine art around 1912, beginning with works of the Old Masters. But with the encouragement of his French-born wife, he shifted emphasis in the 1920s and 1930s to concentrate on nineteenth-century French painting, especially the Impressionists, with some attention also to American artists like Sargent, Remington, and Winslow Homer, who is represented by seven choice oils.

Clark's grandfather attended Williams, and he was also friendly with Karl Weston, a Williams art history professor who helped to garner important alumni collections for the Wiliams Museum of Art. So in the 1950s, when the Clarks decided to build a structure to house their collection, they chose Williamstown for the beauty of its pastoral setting and had a building designed to make the most of it. Tall windows in the corridors look out on natural scenes that are works of art in themselves and that add to the pleasure of visiting the museum.

The fact that the galleries are done to drawing-room scale and furnished in many cases with fine antiques also makes a visit to the museum more rewarding.

You'll see excellent examples of some of the world's greatest painters here, dating from the Renaissance and later, including Van Ruisdael, Hals, Gainsborough, Tiepolo, Goya, Turner, and Mary Cassatt. There is also a remarkable silver collection, five centuries of the most exquisite pieces of the silversmith's art.

The French works include Géricault, Courbet, Daumier, Corot, and Millet, but the real heart of the museum, the paintings that may remain in your mind's eye long after you've left the galleries, are the exceptional works by Rubens, Monet, Degas, and Renoir. There are more than 30 Renoirs in the collection. Among the most memorable pieces are Monet's *Tulip Fields at Sassenheim* and one from his Rouen Cathedral series, and Renoir's *At the Concert* and *Sleeping Girl with Cat.*

There are grander and more famous museums than the Clark Art Institute, but few that offer a more satisfying visual experience.

All of Williamstown, in fact, is a visual delight. It is a beautiful old New England town with a college dating to 1793 at its center. Williams is so much a part of its hometown that it is hard to distinguish where the campus begins and ends. College buildings occupy much of Main Street, and most of the landmarks on the town's printed historical walking tour belong to the school. The architecture runs the gamut from Georgian to Greek revival to mansard-roofed Victorian Gothic. There are many buildings worth a visit.

The Hopkins Observatory, built between 1836 and 1838, is the oldest astronomical observatory in the United States. It is open to the public. The Chapin Library on the second floor of Stetson Hall has an extensive collection of rare books—some 17,000 of them—and changing exhibits on English and American literature.

The Williams College Museum of Art is exceptional, with a notable collection of sculpture and painting dating from ancient Assyrian stone reliefs to the last self-portrait by Andy Warhol. There are prints by Dürer and Rembrandt, oils and watercolors by Homer, Inness, Rivers, and Hopper, and contemporary sculptures by George Segal and Anthony Caro. Highlights include a whole room devoted to Spanish art, a section of Early American paintings and furnishings and the Bloedel Collection of Twentieth-Century American Art.

The addition to the museum built in 1983 is a work of art in itself. The architecture repeats the octagonal design of the original 1846 neoclassical rotunda in soaring new skylit galleries.

If you've absorbed your artistic limit for the day, walk over to Water Street (Route 43) and poke through the half-dozen shops that include custom leather goods, gold and silver jewelry, two gift shops with a mix of wares, and The Potter's Wheel, a gallery of high-quality stoneware, glass, metal sculpture, and jewelry. The view of the frozen brook behind the gallery is one of its prize exhibits.

The most elaborate lodging in Williamstown is The Orchards, which is not Colonial from the outside, but most definitely is within, done in handsome period decor. The Williams Inn is actually a hotel, but manages to maintain the feeling of New England warmth, and has the bonus of an indoor pool. Other alternatives are bed-and-breakfast homes, the attractive accommodations at Jiminy Peak, the Berkshire Hilton in Pittsfield, the many inns in Lenox 20 miles to the south, or the very cozy alpine-style Mill House Inn, just across the New York state line, about 12 miles from Williamstown.

If the weather remains willful on Sunday, some driving is required to see the remaining sights in the area. About 20 minutes to the north is Bennington, Vermont. Old Bennington with its green, monument, Colonial homes, and church is worth quite a few snapshots. The Bennington Museum has among its many treasures a whole room of original oils by Grandma Moses. Another recommended stop is Bennington Potters to see (and buy) some of the well-known stoneware produced here. Hawkins House in nearby Shaftsbury is another crafts gallery of working studios and shops set in a landmark Colonial home and barns on the property. Quilts, carvings, glass, pottery, sculpture, wrought-iron pieces, jewelry in gold and silver, candles, and drawings are some of the works you'll find being turned out in the studios.

Back in Massachusetts, Pittsfield has the Berkshire Museum, which has been handsomely renovated. The collections are quite diverse. History exhibits range from tools to dolls to a Woodland Indian collection. Six galleries of natural science feature extensive displays of rocks, minerals, and shells; miniature dioramas of dinosaurs; and an aquarium with over 100 live animals and fish. The heart of the art collection is nineteenth century work by masters such as Inness, Church, Bierstadt, Copley, and Peale. The twentieth century is also well represented, with many paintings by artists with ties to the Berkshires.

And if you are a lover of Herman Melville and *Moby Dick,* phone ahead for an appointment to visit Arrowhead, where Melville lived while he wrote his epic. The home is now headquarters of the Berkshire County Historical Society.

If there is still time to spare while one partner is up on the slopes, both Lenox and West Stockbridge offer more shops and galleries to explore. Or you'll find the lodge at Brodie a very congenial place to pass the time—Irish decor, good company, and good Irish coffee.

By now you should be back together again and ready to enjoy dinner in one of the many good Berkshire inns farther south on your way home, a happy ending to an exhilarating winter weekend.

Williamstown Area Code: 413

DRIVING DIRECTIONS Saw Mill River Parkway north to the Taconic Parkway to the New York State Thruway, Berkshire spur

(Route 90); east to exit 2, then follow Route 102 to U.S. 20 past Lenox and Pittsfield into Route 7 and Williamstown. *Total distance:* 175 miles.

ACCOMMODATIONS *The Orchards,* 222 Adams Road, Williamstown, 01267, 458-9611, spacious, gracious, $$$$ (ask about weekend packages) • *Williams Inn,* on the green, Williamstown, 01267, 458-9371, $$$-$$$$ • *River Bend Farm,* 643 Simonds Road, Williamstown, 01267, 458-3121, charming authentically restored 1770 Georgian Colonial on the National Register, $$ CP • *Field Farm Guest House,* 554 Sloan Road, Williamstown, 01267, 458-3135, art-filled modern home on 254 scenic acres, $$ CP • *The House on Main Street,* 1120 Main Street, Williamstown 01267, 458-3031, pleasant home, walking distance to town, $$ • *Goldberry's,* 39 Cold Spring Road (Route 7), Williamstown, 01267, 458-3935, attractive 1830 home, also within a walk of town, $$ CP • *Jiminy Peak Mountain Resort,* Corey Road, Hancock, 01237, 738-5500, inn building $$$$, condos with kitchens $$$$$; less on weekdays and off-season • *Berkshire Hilton Inn,* Berkshire Common at West Street on Route 7, Pittsfield, 01201, 499-2000, $$$-$$$$ • *Mill House Inn,* Route 43, Stephentown, New York 01268, (518) 733-5606, $$-$$$ CP • *1896 Motel,* Route 7, Williamstown, 01267, 458-8125, pleasant motel on lovely grounds, $-$$ CP. For Lenox accommodations and dining, see pages 101–102.

DINING *Le Jardin Inn,* Route 7 and Cold Spring Road, Williamstown, 458-8032, converted estate, French menu, $$-$$$ • *Savories,* 123 Water Street (Route 43), Williamstown, 458-2175, New American, $-$$ • *Williams Inn* (see above), $$-$$$ • *The Orchards* (see above), $$-$$$$ • *Hobson's Choice,* Water Street, Williamstown, 458-9101, cozy, informal, $$ • *Truffles and Such,* Allendale Center, Pittsfield, 442-0151, creative chef, excellent reviews, $$-$$$. For lunch and light fare almost any time, a best bet is the *Erasmus Café at the College Bookstore,* 76 Spring Street, Williamstown, open Monday to Saturday 9 A.M. to 10 P.M.

SKIING *Jiminy Peak,* Corey Road, Hancock, 738-5500, daily and night skiing. Phone for current rates • *Brodie,* Route 7, New Ashford, 443-4752, daily and night skiing • *Bousquet Ski Area,* Tamarack Road, Pittsfield, 442-8316, daily and night skiing • For winter brochure with details on vertical drops, number of trails, lift ticket prices, and special ski packages available at local lodgings, write to Berkshire Visitors' Bureau (see address, p. 234).

SIGHTSEEING *Sterling and Francine Clark Art Institute,* 225 South Street, Williamstown, 458-9545. Hours: daily except Monday 10 A.M. to 5 P.M. Free • *Williams College Museum of Art,* Lawrence Hall, 597-2429. Hours: Tuesday to Saturday 10 A.M. to 5 P.M. Sunday 1 to 5 P.M. Free • *Chapin Library,* Stetson Hall, 597-2462. Hours: Monday to Friday 10 A.M. to noon, and 1 P.M. to 5 P.M., closed on weekends. Free • *Berkshire Museum,* 39 South Street (Route 7), Pittsfield, 443-7171. Hours: Monday to Saturday 10 A.M. to 5 P.M., Sunday 1 to 5 P.M.; open Monday July and August. Adults, $3; children, $2. Free admission Wednesday and Saturday morning • *Arrowhead,* 780 Holmes Road, Pittsfield, 442-1793. Phone for appointment in winter. Summer hours: Memorial Day to October 31, daily 10 A.M. to 4:30 P.M. Adults, $4; children 6–16, $2.50.

FOR FURTHER INFORMATION Contact the Berkshire Visitors' Bureau, Berkshire Common, Pittsfield, MA 01201, toll free (800) 237-5747 or 443-9186.

Philadelphia for All Seasons

Name an East Coast city with more than 100 museums, a world-renowned orchestra, the most Rodin sculptures to be found outside of Paris, an opera house that is compared to La Scala, 75 dance troupes, and the company *Time* magazine called "The foremost presenters of new and unusual music theater works in the country."

No, it isn't New York, but you're close. Philadelphia, just 100 miles to the south, is coming into its own as a star attraction.

Staid William Penn still presides atop the block-square City Hall at Broad and Market streets, but he has been joined by Claes Oldenburg's giant *Clothespin* across the way, one of the visible symbols of the new contemporary beat throughout the city, along with the skyscrapers that now look down on Mr. Penn.

It all began in the late 1960s when the National Park Service rescued beautiful Independence Hall and the rest of the city's pre-Revolutionary buildings, razing the warehouses and urban blight that had all but hidden them, and transforming the area into a handsome historic urban park.

While the park was taking form, neighboring Society Hill also began to revive, with restorations of its cobbled streets and charming red-brick Colonial town houses. Now the waterfront itself has been refurbished, and renamed Penn's Landing. Old piers and ramshackle buildings have given way to a park and sculpture garden, a maritime museum, and a floating nautical museum of permanently moored historic ships at the pier. This is also the departure point for ferries to the excellent new New Jersey Aquarium just 10 minutes across the river in Camden.

The waterfront now also swings by night, with some of the piers along the Delaware transformed into night clubs that are the favorite haunts of young Philadelphians.

And good things just kept happening. A restaurant renaissance turned the city into a culinary capital. Gleaming new hotels and elegant shopping centers added more lures for visitors. And now there is an explosion of arts, especially theater and dance.

With all of the new, plus the best of the old—the museums, the fine Philadelphia Orchestra, the bustling Italian market and historic Germantown, the cheese-steak shops and pretzel vendors, the world's largest city park—a weekend is hardly enough time to take it all in. But a winter weekend, when many of the better hotels offer tempting bargain packages, is a perfect time to begin to get acquainted.

The logical place to start is where our nation started—in Independence National Historical Park. Make a first stop at the city's excellent midtown visitors' center at 16th Street and JFK Boulevard for free walking tours and maps, then either a pleasant 15-minute walk or the Number 76 bus will take you to the oldest part of the city.

There are few places that can re-create so vividly the charged atmosphere of a new colony daring to challenge the powerful English crown. A film at the park visitors' center sets the stage, and the enthusiastic park guides help to make the past events come alive with colorful stories about the eventful days that saw the nation declare its independence. In Independence Hall you'll stand in the room where it all happened, just a few strides from the chair where Benjamin Franklin sat and the rostrum where John Hancock presided over the signing of the Declaration of Independence. This room is also where the Constitutional Convention met. The square just outside is where the Declaration was first read to the citizens of Philadelphia—and to the world.

The many visitors who take the 25-minute tour of Independence Hall and only glance at the other buildings making up the park are missing out on interesting sights. Flanking Independence Hall are Congress Hall, where the first American Congress met, and the Old City Hall, which housed the first Supreme Court. In Congress Hall you'll learn that the Senate became known as the upper house quite literally because it was quartered on the second floor.

Carpenters' Hall has been restored to the way it was when the First Continental Congress met there, the Second National Bank has become a portrait gallery of the nation's founders, and down the block is the house where Dolley Payne lived when she met her future husband, James Madison, a delegate to the Constitutional Convention.

Don't overlook Franklin Court, tucked away in an alleyway between 3rd and 4th streets off Market. Only a steel frame remains as a symbol of Franklin's home, but the museum underground would almost certainly have pleased the ingenious Mr. Franklin. The entry is history, disco-style—a mirrored hall with flashing signs citing Franklin's many roles as statesman, inventor, wit, and much more. There is a bank of telephones and a listing of numbers to dial to talk to people like John Adams, George Washington, and John F. Kennedy about Franklin's importance to the country. A dial-it computer produces Franklin witticisms on almost any subject, his many inventions (including library steps hidden in a chair and the first pair of bifocals) are on display, and a changing marionette gallery depicts his adventures as ambassador for his country. It's an altogether delightful way to learn about a remarkable man.

And then, of course, there is the Liberty Bell, housed in a glass pavilion, accessible to the throngs who want to gaze at the famous crack and touch the bell for luck. The bell, you'll learn, was actually ordered in 1751, the fiftieth anniversary of the democratic constitution granted by William Penn to his colony, but its motto, Proclaim Liberty, became prophetic for a new nation. It had been recast before, but the final crack that put it out of service came in 1835 as the bell tolled the death of Chief Justice John Marshall, according to local lore.

If you do it justice, Independence Park will take the entire morning, finishing just in time for a historic lunch in the 1773 City Tavern, once called "the most genteel tavern in America" by John Adams. The menu still includes old English favorites, and your waitress will be dressed as she might have been in Adams's day.

After lunch there are many nearby sights for exploring. Society Hill, south of the park, roughly between Lombard and Walnut and 2nd and 7th streets, has become a prototype for urban restoration with its many blocks of Colonial town houses lovingly restored within the past few decades. A walk through the area also takes you past several historic churches, all clearly labeled with informative signs, and past some intriguing shopping areas to get you out of the cold, including Head House Square, a red-brick restored marketplace, and South Street, a mix of funky shops, restaurants, and nightlife.

North of Chestnut Street is the Old City, the old commercial district, which is still a bit rundown. Do walk over, however, to see Elfreth's Alley, the perfectly charming cobbled avenue lined with 37 houses built between 1713 and 1811, the oldest continually occupied street in America. Not far away is historic Christ Church, where Washington and many members of the Continental Congress worshiped, and the tiny Betsy Ross House, where the nation's first flag was made.

If the weather is conducive and there is time, you may also want to tour the ships and the submarine at Penn's Landing. There are interesting indoor exhibits nearby at the Maritime Museum.

Or, if you are feeling flush this weekend, you might return to the center of the city to explore the shops at the Bellevue, which include names like Ralph Lauren, Gucci, and Tiffany. The shops are part of the renovation of a 1902 landmark, the old Bellevue-Stratford Hotel, now known as the Hotel Atop the Bellevue. If you can't afford the tab, come for afternoon tea in the nineteenth-floor Barrymore Room, one of the many rooms that have been restored to their original turn-of-the-century elegance.

This is one of a trio of luxury hotels that have opened in the city center in recent years. The other two are the Rittenhouse and the very elegant Ritz-Carlton, which has its own adjoining exclusive shopping complex, Liberty Place.

Philadelpia has more shopping diversions for every taste and pocketbook. The Gallery Mall, at Ninth and Market, is one of the largest urban malls in the nation, with 110 shops and restaurants. The chic designer shops are clustered on Walnut Street, and antiquers won't want to miss the cluster of interesting shops on Pine Street, east of Broad Street. If bargains are more your beat, take a short drive to Franklin Mills just north of the city, where there are outlets by the score, including clearance centers for Saks Fifth Avenue, Macy's, J C Penney, and Sears. Take I-95 north to the Woodhaven Road exit to Franklin Mills Boulevard.

When it comes to luxury dining, the city's best-known spot is the five-star Le Bec Fin, but it has plenty of competition in the gourmet sweepstakes. An excellent time to visit Philadelphia is during the annual "Book and the Cook" weekend in mid-March, when dozens of star cookbook authors, including some of the nation's most famous chefs, oversee the kitchen of the restaurant that comes closest to their specialties. You not only get a delicious meal, but a chance to meet the chef. The choices range from fancy French to down-home Southern.

The city's other March extravaganza is its lavish flower show, widely regarded as the country's best. If you decide to come, get there as soon as the doors open—the crowds can be overwhelming.

A few more culinary tips: The best brunch in town is the lavish spread at the Four Seasons. If you want to sample the haute cuisine of junk food, a Philadelphia cheese-steak sandwich, Jim's Steaks at Fourth and South streets is one of the local favorites.

After dinner, you can sample Philadelphia's rich arts scene. This is the place to preview talent before it gets to New York. Over 100 productions have had their world or American premieres here in the last few years. The American Music Theater Festival, a national center for contemporary musical theater, has gained increasing critical acclaim since it opened in 1984, and the Philadelphia Festival Theater for New Plays at the Annenberg Center at the University of Pennsylvania is the only theater in the country offering a year-round schedule devoted to new plays.

Or you can hear the renowned Philadelphia Orchestra at the Academy of Museum, a National Historic Landmark building whose ornate horseshoe-shaped auditorium was loosely patterned after Milan's La Scala.

If you want livelier action, head for the riverfront where clubs like Egypt, Katmandu, and Dave and Busters will surely be swinging. The club names may change, but the scene will be the same under any name.

Sunday is the day to board the Olde Town trolley that leaves the tourist center for tours through Fairmount Park. It will take you past lush meadowland and rustic trails, restored mansions, outdoor theaters, the zoo, and even a Japanese teahouse. In spring and summer, regattas rowing out from the boathouses on the river adjoining the park are a regular sight. Not all of the attractions stay open in winter, but there's enough to keep you happily occupied.

Philadelphia's best-known museums, located at the entry to Fairmount Park on broad Benjamin Franklin Parkway, know no seasons. The Philadelphia Museum of Art takes you anywhere from an Amish farmhouse to a Peking palace. The art collections are large, the American wing is outstanding, and the Oriental section is a knockout, with a Buddhist temple, a palace reception room, a Chinese scholar's study, and many magnificent pieces of rosewood furniture from the Ming dynasty. If you climb the banks of steps outside it that *Rocky* made famous, you'll be rewarded with a striking vista of the city.

Across the parkway in the Rodin Museum is the largest collection of the sculptor's works to be found outside France, including such masterpieces as *The Thinker, The Burghers of Calais,* and *Gates of Hell,* all a gift to his fellow citizens from a little-known Philadelphian named Jules E. Mastbaum.

The Franklin Institute Science Museum on the other side of the boulevard is a change of pace and one of the most innovative institutions of its kind, with participatory exhibits that let you steer a ship, ride a 350-ton locomotive, and walk through a giant human heart.

The latest addition to this fabulous museum is the nation's only Futures Center, a whirring, blinking, hands-on world that shows what we can expect in the years ahead, from medicine to transportation to fashion.

One of the most popular exhibits in the Futures Center is the Musser Choices Forum, where each person in the audience votes electronically on the best techniques to solve future problems such as global warming or preserving the rain forest, then gets to compare answers with the rest of the group. Often the vote is on regulations under consideration by Congress, and the consensus is sent to Washington to help guide legislators.

Other attractions include sky shows at the Fels Planetarium and the Omniverse Theater, where a giant screen puts you in the midst of the action.

With the park and the museums, the day will be done before you know it, and you still won't have been to Germantown or the Italian Market or the Mummers Museum, or seen the excellent American art collection at the Museum of American Art of the Pennsylvania Academy of the Fine Arts or the famous Mummy Room at the University Museum, which has shared many archaeological expeditions with the British Museum. And then there are the U.S. Mint and the ''Please Touch'' Museum and the gardens . . . and later in the year the outdoor activity at Fairmount Park and the non-stop festivals at Penn's Landing . . . and when the Barnes Foundation reopens in 1995, you'll surely want to travel to suburban Merion, just outside Philadelphia, to see America's greatest private collection of Impressionist art.

If you're like most first-time visitors to Philadelphia, you'll leave town calculating how soon you can come back.

Philadelphia Area Code: 215

DRIVING DIRECTIONS Take the New Jersey Turnpike to exit 4, then Route 73 north to Route 38. Follow Route 38 west to U.S. 30 and continue west over the Benjamin Franklin Bridge into the city. *Total distance:* 98 miles.

PUBLIC TRANSPORTATION Amtrak (800) 523-8720 has frequent service to Philadelphia, and the city's sights are easily accessible on foot or via public transportation. Best buy is the SEPTA Day-pass—$5 for a day of unlimited rides on city buses, streetcars, elevated lines and subway. Passes are sold at the Visitor Center.

ACCOMMODATIONS Many Philadelphia hotels, including the most elegant, offer excellent weekend package deals. The Convention and Visitors' Bureau has a complete current list of packages. Luxury hotels: *Four Seasons,* 1 Logan Square, 19103, 963-1500 or (800) 268-6282, indoor pool, $$$$$ • *Hotel Atop the Bellevue,* Broad and Walnut streets, 19102, 893-1776 or (800) 222-0939, $$$$$ • *Ritz-Carlton,* 17th and Chestnut at Liberty Place, 19103, 563-1600, $$$$$ • *The Rittenhouse,* 210 West Rittenhouse Square, 19103, 546-9000, $$$$ • *Embassy Suites Hotel,* 1776 Benjamin Franklin Parkway, 19103, 561-1776, spacious quarters, good location, $$$-$$$$ (with free breakfast and cocktail hour) • *Omni at Independence Park,* 4th and Chestnut streets, 19106, 925-0000, indoor pool, $$$$$ •

Sheraton Society Hill, 2nd and Walnut streets, 19106, 238-6000 or (800) 325-2525, $$$-$$$$ • *Latham Hotel,* 17th and Walnut streets, 19103, 563-7474, $$$$ • More moderate-price choices: *Barclay,* 237 South 18th Street, 19103, 545-0300, $$-$$$$ • *Holiday Inn City Centre,* 1800 Market Street, 19103, 561-2556, $$$-$$$$ • *Warwick Hotel,* 17th at Locust Street, 19103, 735-6000, $$$-$$$$ • *Wyndham Franklin Plaza Hotel,* 17th and Vine streets, 2 Franklin Plaza, 19103, 448-2000, indoor pool, health club, $$-$$$$ • *Best Western Independence Park Inn,* 235 Chestnut Street, 19106, 922-4442, small, quite attractive, $$$-$$$$ • *Ramada Inn Center City,* 501 North 22nd Street, 19130, 568-8300, $$-$$$ • *Comfort Inn–Penn's Landing,* Delaware Avenue and Race Street, 19106, 627-7900, $$-$$$ • *Quality Inn Historic Downtown Suites,* 1010 Race Street, (Chinatown), 19107, $$-$$$ • Bed-and-breakfasts in the city: *Thomas Bond House,* 129 South 2nd Street, 19106, 923-8523, $$-$$$ CP • *Shippen Way Inn,* 416-18 Bainbridge Street, 19147, 627-7266, $$-$$$ CP • *La Reserve,* 1804 Pine Street, 19103, 735-1137, center-city townhouse, $$ CP.

BED-AND-BREAKFAST *Bed and Breakfast Connections,* PO Box 21, Devon, PA 19333, 687-3565 or toll free (800) 448-3619 • *Bed and Breakfast, Center City,* 1804 Pine Street, Philadelphia, PA 19103, 735-1137.

DINING Literally hundreds of possibilities. A few suggestions: *Le Bec Fin,* 1523 Walnut Street, 567-1000, splurge at the city's five-star best, $$$$$ • *Deux Cheminees,* 1221 Locust Street, 790-0200, more fine French, $$$$$ prix fixe • *The Fountain,* Four Seasons Hotel (see above), Continental, excellent, $$$$; notable Sunday brunch, $$-$$$ • *La Truffe,* 10 South Front Street, 925-5062, French, both traditional and nouvelle, $$-$$$$ • *Ciboulette,* Hotel Atop the Bellevue (see above), 790-1210, a top choice for contemporary French dishes, $$$-$$$$ • *Alouette,* 334 Bainbridge Street, 629-1126, mix of French and Thai influences, $$-$$$ • *Susanna Foo,* 1512 Walnut Street, 545-2666, Chinese with a French accent, $$-$$$ • *Cutter's Grand Cafe,* 2005 Market Street, 851-6262, seafood specialties, glitzy, lively, $$ • *Marabella's,* 1420 Locust Street, 545-1845, and 1700 Ben Franklin Parkway, 981-5555, trendy spots for burgers, pasta, $-$$ • *DiLullo's Centro,* 1407 Locust Street, 546-2000, elegant decor, fine Italian food, $$-$$$ • *Mike Schmidt's at the Main Event,* 8th and Walnut streets, 413-2200, sports star owner, popular, $$-$$$ • *DiNardo's Famous Crabs,* 312 Race Street, 925-5115, the name says it, $-$$ • *White Dog Cafe,* 3420 Sansom Street, 386-9224, university area, informal, interesting menu, $$ • *La Veranda,* Penn's Landing, Pier 3 between Delaware Avenue and Arch Street, 351-1898, riverside Italian with fine views, very popular, $$-$$$ • *City Tavern,* 2nd and Walnut, 923-6059, Revolutionary history, good choice for lunch, $; dinners, $$-$$$ • *Dickens Inn,* 421 South 2nd Street, 928-9307, pub atmosphere, roast beef, Yorkshire pudding, $-$$$ • *Philadelphia Fish & Co.,* 207 Chestnut Street, 625-8605, fresh fish, fair prices, $$ • *Pasta Blitz,* 2nd and Walnut streets, 299-0499, reasonable pasta, $$ • *Dock Street Brew House,* 2 Logan Square, 496-0413, eclectic menu, home brew, singles favorite, $-$$ • South Street area: *Cafe Nola,* 328 South Street, 627-2590, favorite for Cajun and Creole, $$-$$$$ • *Saloon,* 750 South Seventh Street, 627-1811, a favorite for Italian, $$-$$$ • *Tiramisu,* 528 North Third Street, 925-3335, hearty Italian, $$-$$$$ • *Monte Carlo Living Room,* Second and South streets, 925-2220, elegant Northern Italian, $-$$$$ • *San Carlo,* 214 South Street, 592-9777, Italian with terrific antipasto, $$-$$$ • Two old-timers near the Italian market, no decor, big portions, small tabs: *Dante's & Luigi's,* 762 10th Street, 922-9501, $-$$ • *Strolli's,* 1528 Dickinson Street, 336-3390, $ • For a feast of sights, sounds, and food selections at lunchtime, visit the stalls at Reading Terminal Market, the nineteenth-century marketplace still thriving at 12th and Arch streets.

SIGHTSEEING *Independence National Historical Park Visitor Center*, 3rd and Chestnut streets, 597-8974. Hours: daily 9 A.M. to 5 P.M. Free • *Christ Church,* 2nd Street above Market Street, 922-1695. Hours: Monday to Saturday 9 A.M. to 5 P.M., from 11 A.M. in winter; Sunday 1 to 5 P.M. Free • *Betsy Ross House,* 239 Arch Street, 627-5343. Hours: Tuesday to Sunday 10 A.M. to 5 P.M. Donation • *Philadelphia Museum of Art,* 26th Street and Benjamin Franklin Parkway, 763-8100. Hours: Tuesday to Sunday 10 A.M. to 5 P.M. Adults, $6; under age 18, $3; free on Sunday until 1 P.M. • *Rodin Museum,* 22nd Street and Benjamin Franklin Parkway, 763-8100. Hours: Tuesday to Sunday 10 A.M. to 5 P.M. Donation • *University Museum of Archaeology and Anthropology,* 33rd and Spruce streets, 898-4000, Tuesday to Saturday 10 A.M. to 4:30 P.M., Sunday 1 to 5 P.M. Adults, $5; students, $2.50; children, free • *Mummers Museum,* 2nd Street and Washington Avenue, 336-3050. Hours: Tuesday to Saturday 9:30 A.M. to 5 P.M., Sunday noon to 5 P.M. Adults, $2.50; children, $2 • *Norman Rockwell Museum,* 6th and Sansom streets, 922-4345. Hours: daily 10 A.M. to 4 P.M. Adults, $2; children under 12, free; no charge to see mosaic in building lobby • *U.S. Mint,* 5th and Arch streets, 597-7350. Hours: January to April and September to December, Monday to Friday 9 A.M. to 4:30 P.M.; May and June, also open Saturday; July and

August, open Saturday and Sunday. Free • *Barnes Foundation,* 300 Latches Lane, Merion, 667-0290; due to reopen in 1995 after renovations, phone for new hours and fees. For additional Philadelphia sightseeing, see pages 48–49.

FOR FURTHER INFORMATION For current dates of Philadelphia Flower Show, "The Book and the Cook" weekend, schedules of theater, music and dance, a listing of hotel weekend packages, and a complete city guide, contact Philadelphia Convention and Visitors' Bureau, 16th Street and JFK Boulevard, Philadelphia, PA 19102, 636-1666. Visitor Center at that address is open daily 9 A.M. to 5 P.M. For information packet only, call toll free (800) 537-7676.

Snow and Snuggling in the Litchfield Hills

It's just as the song pictures it. Outside, there's a sleigh waiting to jingle you through the snow. Unless, of course, you'd rather skate on the pond, or practice your cross-country strides, or head for a ski area where snowaking guarantees that 95 percent of the slopes are always ready for action.

If it's too cold or too warm for all that, how about antiquing or sightseeing, or snapping photos of white-steepled churches and picture-book village greens? Or you could always just join that contented tabby cuddled in front of the inn fireplace.

Weekends are all but weatherproof in the Litchfield Hills of Connecticut, where winter sports share billing with New England villages, interesting shops, and old-fashioned inns where hospitality is warm, whatever the weather.

For skiers, the major attraction here is Mohawk Mountain, Connecticut's largest, yet a small, friendly area with many of the amenities of a bigger complex. Mohawk is unusually attractive, set in the middle of a state forest, reached via an arching bridge over a surrounding brook, with lakes that are sometimes used for ice skating. The chalet-style cedar lodge has a wall-size picture window and a large deck for enjoying the view. And this is one of the few lodges that worries about creating inviting indoor atmosphere, with potted trees and green plants, rafters hung with sleighs, wagon wheels, and old wooden skis, and even a wall of books next to the fireplace for those who aren't skiing for the day.

Mohawk is an ideal place to learn to ski. There are special day rates for novices and even a separate, slower chairlift for beginners. Cross-country lessons and rentals are also available, and there are miles of beautiful trails in the adjacent Mohawk State Forest. If Mohawk's 24 downhill trails are not as steep as those farther north in Vermont, there's the compensation of lift lines that seldom call for more than five to ten minutes' wait.

At day's end welcoming fires and refreshments await in a number of inns in the area. A few are particularly noteworthy, making for a pleasant winter weekend with or without skiing.

For a small, secluded spot away from it all, head for the Under Mountain Inn, north of Mohawk in the charming village of Salisbury. Each of the seven rooms is decorated differently, many with reproductions of Early American wallpapers. The British owner-chef prepares tasty fare like fish and chips, Scottish salmon, or steak and kidney pie as well as Continental specialties to be enjoyed in the fireplace-warmed dining room, and you can be sure of a proper pot of English tea, kept warm in its own cozy. From this inn, you can ski cross-country on quiet country lanes right down the road.

Another Salisbury landmark is the venerable White Hart on the village green, the very model of classic New England inn, and with an excellent dining room, as well.

Salisbury is a haven for tea lovers. Chaiwalla, a delightful tea room, offers delicious lunches as well as rare teas. If you want to buy more fine teas, walk directly across the street to the real estate office, and in the front room you'll find a surprise: a selection of teas from Harney & Sons, Ltd., who supply some of the finest restaurants in the country. The teas are brewed right in the back room.

Just below Salisbury in Lakeville, the home of the prestigious Hotchkiss School, Interlaken Inn is an attractive modern complex, with a big health and fitness center indoors offering exercise equipment, aerobics classes, racquetball, and a sauna. There is ice skating on neighboring ponds, and plenty of cross-country skiing territory nearby. A couple of period homes on the property have been redecorated for those who prefer inn atmosphere.

Set away from town, high on a hill in Lakeville, is the Wake Robin Inn, a handsome columned former private school that has been renovated into an inn. Though all are nicely decorated, the rooms vary greatly—some are very nice, some are very small. Ask questions when you reserve and check your options before you settle in. The dining room here gets good reviews.

Three appealing inns beckon to the east in Norfolk. Mountain View is a homey Victorian, while Manor House is an elegant turn-of-the-century showplace with carved stairs and Tiffany windows. They'll pamper you here with breakfast in bed, and the big front bedroom has a warming fireplace of its own. Greenwoods Gate is a 1797 Colonial bed-and-breakfast home whose stylishly decorated bedrooms could easily wind up on a magazine page.

Norfolk has cross-country skiing nearby at Haystack Mountain State Park, and downhill skiing at the small, family-friendly Sundown ski area in New Hartford.

About 20 minutes below Mohawk Mountain, near New Preston, two inns around Lake Waramaug are also tempting choices. The Inn at Lake Waramaug, housed in a 1791 Colonial, offers an indoor pool and sauna, Ping-Pong, and a pool table for the kids, and plenty of room to ice skate or cross-country ski over the snow-covered lake. Twenty modern units on the property are motel style, but do come with canopy beds and fireplaces.

The Boulders is a more gracious inn in a rustic 1800s stone building with an antique-filled living room that offers an unbeatable view of lake and hills from its big picture window. You can choose from handsome period rooms upstairs or cottage rooms on the grounds with working fireplaces.

Lake Waramaug is in New Preston, a tiny river village where a cache of interesting shops have occupied picturesque old buildings along the one main street in town. A onetime garage, for example, now houses J. Seitz and Co., which has an exceptional stock of Southwestern furniture, clothing, and jewelry; Black Swan Antiques with its rare treasures from Europe; and the New Preston Antiques Center, a collective with a variety of wares. The Grey Squirrel holds treasures for folk art enthusiasts, and there are several other antiques and accessory shops with a little bit of everything.

The Cafe is an excellent stop for light meals or dessert, and if you head toward the lake, you'll find the Hopkins Vineyard, where you are welcome to taste the local wines.

From Lake Waramaug, it's just a few miles to Litchfield, one of the area's most historic and photogenic towns, and a fine place for browsing through shops and galleries (see page 74). From town, drive to Bantam Lake off Route 209 and you can watch ice boaters in action on winter afternoons. The White Memorial Foundation park bordering the lake offers 35 miles of cross-country ski trails, and you can rent cross country skis at the Wilderness Shop on Route 202 in Litchfield.

For sleigh rides, the man to call is Ken Wood at Wood Acres. Drive over to his farm in Terryville and you'll go dashing through the snow on a sled pulled by a team of Percheron draft horses. When there is no snow, they hitch up the wagon for a hayride. Afterwards, you can warm up in a cozy barn next to the wood stove.

Unless, of course, you decide to forget it all, and stick to the most traditional winter activity in northwest Connecticut—sitting by the fire alongside that contented cat.

Litchfield Hills Area Code: 203

DRIVING DIRECTIONS For New Preston, take I-684 north to exit 9E, I-84 east to exit 7, U.S. 202 north. From New Preston follow signs and lakeside road to Inn at Lake Waramaug. For Salisbury use above route but continue on I-684 north to the end (it becomes N.Y. 22), then take U.S. 44 east. Continue east on Route 44 for Norfolk, or head north via the Hutchinson River Parkway to the Merritt Parkway and take Route 8 north, then 44 west to Norfolk. For Lakeville, follow 41 south from Salisbury. For Mohawk Mountain, follow Route 7 north to Route 4 east at Cornwall Bridge and follow signs.

Total distance: to New Preston, 83 miles; Salisbury, 115; Lakeville, 113; Norfolk, 130.

ACCOMMODATIONS Ask about weekend and ski packages. *Under Mountain Inn,* Undermountain Road (Route 41), Salisbury, 06068, 435-0242, $$$$ MAP • *The White Hart,* Village Green, Salisbury, 06068, 435-0030, $$-$$$$ • *Yesterday's Yankee,* Route 44, Salisbury, 06068, 435-9539, Cape Cod cottage B&B, $$-$$$ CP • *Interlaken Inn,* Route 122, Lakeville, 06039, 435-9878, $$-$$$$ • *Wake Robin Inn,* Route 41, Lakeville, 06039, 435-2515, $$$$ CP, motel unit, $$ CP • *Mountain View Inn,* Route 272, Norfolk, 06058, 542-5595, $-$$$ CP • *Manor House,* PO Box 701, Maple Avenue, Norfolk, 06058, 542-5690, $$-$$$$ CP • *Greenwoods Gate,* Greenwoods Road East, Norfolk, 06058, 542-5439, $$$-$$$$ CP • *Inn at Lake Waramaug,* Lake Waramaug Road, New Preston, 06777, 868-0563, $$$$-$$$$$ MAP • *Boulders Inn,* Route 45, New Preston, 06777, 868-0541, $$$$$ MAP.

DINING *Under Mountain Inn* (see above), $$-$$$ • *The White Hart* (see above), $$$, Tap Room, informal meals, $$ • *Savarin,* Wake Robin Inn (see above), $$$ • *The Pub and Restaurant,* Station Place, Norfolk, 542-5716, $-$$ • *Woodlands,* Route 41, Lakeville, 435-0578, $-$$ • *Cannery Cafe,* Route 44, Canaan, 824-7333, $-$$ • *Boulders Inn* (see above), • *The Cafe,* Route 45, New Preston, 868-1787, $$-$$$ • *Le Bon Coin,* Route 202, New Preston, 868-7763, French in a country house, $$$.

SLEIGH RIDES *Wood Acres,* Griffen Road, Terryville, 567-0785. Reservations required. Phone for current information and driving directions.

SKIING *Mohawk Mountain Ski Area,* Cornwall, 672-6464. *Ski Sundown,* New Hartford, 379-9851. Call for current information.

FOR FURTHER INFORMATION Litchfield Hills Travel Council, PO Box 968, Litchfield, CT 06759, 582-5176.

Yankee Winter Weekends in Sturbridge

Open fires and roasting chestnuts set the scene. Your welcoming drink is a steaming eighteenth-century concoction known as syllabub. The hostesses are in Yankee costumes, and you never know when a strolling minstrel may wander in singing Colonial songs. Another Yankee winter weekend is under way.

The weekends, held throughout January, February, and March, were initiated by the Publick House Inn, no doubt as a way to drum up winter business, but they've proven so popular that they are now a tradition past its fortieth year, anticipated and carried out in grand style each year in cooperation with Old Sturbridge Village. The notion is to revive Early American winter pleasures to make our twentieth-century winters a little more bearable, concentrating on the many facilities at Sturbridge Village and a luscious menu that was obviously devised in less calorie-conscious times. Recently guest chefs have been invited—a new one each week—to add their own unique winter menus to the Saturday night feast.

Saturday, for example, begins with a big breakfast—anything you want from the menu. To work it off, bundle up and take a stroll around old Sturbridge Village, the 40-building reconstruction of a typical Colonial town. Even if you've been here before, the village takes on a new dimension in the winter as it concentrates on cold weather activities of its time. The usual crafts demonstrations—weaving, printing, tinsmithing, and the like—are in order in the winter, and the artisans have more time to chat and answer questions. The school teacher will give you a colorful introduction to education as it was in the 1830s, guaranteed to fascinate all ages. And you finally may have time to take a look at some of the indoor exhibits that usually are forgotten in the summer. There are seven galleries to be seen, filled with firearms, lighting devices, folk art, textiles, blown and molded glass, mirrors, scientific instruments, hand-sewn and knitted garments, weaving and quilts, and much more. The Clock Gallery adjoining the Visitor Center is a standout.

Hot mulled cider and the Great Room Buffet luncheon await at Bullard Tavern, and after lunch you'll get to see how they used to make maple sugar candy by hardening the syrup in the snow, and be treated to a rollicking sleigh ride around the common.

Country pâté, roast leg of venison, mincemeat pie, and pheasant are the kinds of things you can expect on the dinner menu; afterward it is back to Old Sturbridge Village, where an evening of nineteenth-century magic tricks keeps everyone amazed and amused.

The Publick House is a delightful setting for this kind of festivity. It is a onetime coaching tavern opened in 1771, and the atmosphere probably hasn't changed a lot since then. Period furniture, low ceilings, and tilty floors and doorframes remain, though the carpeting and TV sets upstairs are strictly twentieth century.

One very equally appealing alternative is the Ebenezer Crafts Inn, under the same management, a restored 1786 Colonial home with airy bedrooms furnished in Colonial style and sweeping views of the snow-covered hills from the windows. Other accommodations are at the Inn's Motor Lodge or the Chamberlain House, a nearby residence.

Incidentally, you can stay at the inn and enjoy visits to Old Sturbridge Village without participating in the Yankee Winter Weekend program.

Those who do take part are back to the inn on Sunday for yet another glorious breakfast—a hearty, all-you-can-eat buffet, complete with apple cobbler. Figuring that half the guests can't move anyway, the rest of the day is unplanned. You can return to Sturbridge or visit some of the many area shops on Main Street and Route 20, any of which can supply excellent souvenirs of the weekend. Yankee Winter Weekend guests get a discount at many area shops.

One other possibility is to take the less-than-half-an-hour's drive farther east on I-84 to I-90 and discover a surprising New England town. Worcester, Massachusetts, is mainly (and accurately) thought of as a factory town, but it is much more. New England's second largest city, it has a Colonial heritage that dates to 1673, an attractive hilly terrain, and lovely residential areas. It is the home of twelve colleges and some fine museums.

The New England Science Center is a creative way to learn with hands-on science exhibits, as well as to find out about animal behavior, seashells, and any number of other fascinating topics that fit loosely under the heading of natural science. The 60-acre complex includes a planetarium, a primate center, re-created African communities, and a zoo. Winter favorites are a polar bear family that really enjoys the great outdoors when it's cold outside. A special window also lets you watch them swimming underwater.

Of interest to kids as well as their parents is the Higgins Armory Museum. The Great Hall takes you back to the days of knights, with displays of armor and weapons from ancient Greece to feudal Japan. The Quest Gallery lets you actually try on armor and castle clothes, and offers storytelling and crafts.

The Worcester Art Museum may surprise you. The traditional stone building contains some fine exhibits, including a thirteenth-century French chapel rebuilt here stone by stone. The brochure describes the collection as "the development of man as seen through 50 centuries of his art," and they've shown just that through displays from Greek and Roman vases to Persian and Indian miniatures to Rembrandts, Goyas,

Matisses, and Picassos. The painting galleries are separated by schools, including Dutch, French, Spanish, and Italian.

Worcester's museums are easy to find, as signs are posted pointing the way no matter how you enter the city. The contrasting exhibits make for a rewarding afternoon, and when you're done you'll discover that some of those dull factories associated with the city are now converted into very lively places for food and drink. One good choice right around the corner from the art museum is Northworks on Grove Street—casual, congenial, and inexpensive with a menu of burgers, fried zucchini, and other light foods that may be welcome after all the Colonial feasting in Sturbridge.

If you have a more elegant dinner in mind there's Maxwell Silverman's Tool House. And Worcester now has a Legal Sea Foods and other new spots in a transformed police station–firehouse complex.

Reliving the past and discovering a promising small city of the present—it's a winning combination for a winter weekend.

Worcester and Sturbridge Area Code: 508

DRIVING DIRECTIONS Hutchinson River and Merritt parkways or I-95 north to I-91 to Hartford; from Hartford take I-84 toward Boston. Sturbridge is exit 3. The Publick House Inn is on Route 131 in the center of Sturbridge, south of Route 20. *Total distance:* 160 miles.

ACCOMMODATIONS *Sturbridge Yankee Winter Weekends.* Lodging, two dinners, two breakfasts, Saturday luncheon, and all admissions, starting from $199 per person, double occupancy • Weekends run January through mid-March. Choice of accommodations: Publick House Inn, Chamberlain House, Ebenezer Crafts Inn, or Publick House Country Motor Lodge. For information, contact Publick House Inn, Sturbridge, MA 01566, 347-3313. For additional Sturbridge lodging, see pages 138–139.

DINING *Northworks,* 106 Grove Street, Worcester, 755-9657, $-$$ • *Maxwell Silverman's Tool House,* 25 Union Street, Worcester, 755-1200, $$-$$$ • *Legal Sea Foods,* Exchange Place, Exchange and Walden streets, Worcester, 792-1600, $$-$$$$ • For more area dining, see page 139.

SIGHTSEEING *Worcester Art Museum,* 55 Salisbury Street, 799-4406. Hours: Tuesday to Friday 11 A.M. to 4 P.M., Saturday 10 A.M. to 5 P.M., Sunday 1 to 5 P.M. Adults: $5; students, $3; under 13, free; free to all Saturday 10 A.M. to noon • *New England Science Center,* 222

Harrington Way, 791-9211. Hours: Monday to Saturday 10 A.M. to 5 P.M., Sunday noon to 5 P.M. Adults, $6; children 3–16, $4 • *Higgins Armory Museum,* 100 Barber Avenue, Worcester, 853-6015. Hours: Tuesday to Saturday 10 A.M. to 4 P.M., Sunday noon to 4 P.M. Adults, $4.75; children, $3.75 • *Old Sturbridge Village,* Route 20, 347-3362. Hours: daily April to October 9 A.M. to 5 P.M.; shorter hours off-season. Adults, $15; children 6–15, $7.50; valid for two consecutive days.

FOR FURTHER INFORMATION Sturbridge Area Tourist Association, PO Box 66, Route 20, Sturbridge, MA 01566, or call toll free (800) 628-8379. Worcester County Convention and Visitors' Bureau, 33 Waldo Street, Worcester, MA 01608, 753-2920.

Snowtime in the Poconos

Invigorating days outdoors and a cozy inn at day's end. For many people that's the perfect formula for a winter weekend, but in the past it was a hard order to fill in Pennsylvania's Pocono Mountains. Though there is plenty of scenery and an abundance of outdoor activity in this area so convenient to reach from the city, the Poconos have been associated mostly with large resorts or honeymoon havens.

But not anymore. Now there is a choice of inviting country inns in the Poconos. And once you've found them you've found the best of both worlds. You can be snug and secluded when you want, but when you don't feel like sitting home by the fire, not only are there major ski areas at your disposal, but also the facilities at many of those big resort hotels as well. Many of them are ideal if you are a cross-country skier or even just beginning at downhill.

First then, pick an inn. The number-one choice is the Inn at Meadowbrook, a lovely retreat in the countryside outside East Stroudsburg. The house is light and airy, with big windows to take in views of the lovely grounds, and rooms are tasteful and furnished with English florals, brass beds or four posters, ruffles and wicker. Cross-country skiing or ice skating is available right on the property, the stable next door offers trail rides and riding lessons in an indoor arena—and there's a welcoming fire when you come inside. Come back in the summer, and you can enjoy tennis and a pool—all at very moderate rates.

Three more winning contenders are in the town of Canadensis. The Overlook Inn is welcoming, done in soft shades of blue, with lots of plants and pillows, comfortable seating in front of the fire, and a game room–library that invites guests to mingle; Brookview Manor is a pleasant, spacious country home; and Pine Knob is cozy, warmed with personal touches like the owner's collections of quilts and cookie jars.

Two possibilities await north of Canadensis in South Sterling. The Sterling Inn is a mini-resort with the old-fashioned feel of a country inn. Activities include cross-country skiing, ice skating, sledding, and swimming in an indoor pool. French Manor, a turreted fieldstone mansion, was built in the 1930s by famed art collector Albert Hirschorn, and has nonstop views from its very private perch atop Hackleberry Mountain. Rooms are lavishly furnished, and a multi-course dinner is served by candlelight in the great room, which has a cathedral ceiling and giant fireplaces at either end.

Now, having made your choice of inns, enjoyed your breakfast, and resisted the lure of the fire, you have the pleasant prospect of planning an outdoors day in the Poconos. Skiing is gentle here, but there are compensations since even Camelback, the closest and largest of the ski areas, is able to offer snow-making over the entire mountain. There is also night skiing, if you are so inclined. Between Camelback and other areas such as Big Boulder, Jack Frost, or Shawnee, there should be enough to suit all but the really expert skier. Write ahead to the Pocono Mountains Vacation Bureau, and they'll send you a free guide to all the areas so you can choose your slope in advance.

If you are a beginner, you may want to consider heading for Pocono Manor. The gentle trails and baby slopes are served by a J-bar and a T-bar. The Manor also maintains a Nordic Ski Touring Center, with rentals and lessons and miles of groomed trails for all abilities.

The Manor is one of the grand old mountaintop hotels that were once the pride of the Poconos. It is refurbishing to adjust to a new resort era, and if the hotel isn't what it used to be, the views and 3,000-acre grounds are as spectacular as ever.

One of the most beautiful Poconos resorts is Sky Top Lodge, standing on a mountaintop overlooking 5,500 unspoiled acres. Recently renovated, it is a gracious reminder of another era, a place where gentlemen wear coats for dinner and service is impeccable. You can come for dinner, but you must stay here to use the many facilities. The prices are not exorbitant considering the services and activities included, plus three meals daily and afternoon tea. Take a look and put it down for a possible return stay.

At Mount Airy, a flashier kind of resort, you'll find not only downhill, cross-country, and snowmobile trails available to you, but guaranteed snow for all three. They actually make snow for the cross-country and snowmobile trails, taking no chances on disappointing their guests. If the weather is hopeless, you can also use Mount Airy's Indoor Sports Palace for a fee, complete with tennis, ice skating, a health club, heated pool, and basketball and handball courts.

The Poconos area is not one for quaint villages, but if shopping is your favorite sport, there is enough to keep you occupied for a pleasant couple of hours. A good place to start is route 390 in Mountainhome. Among the interesting shops are Jabara, with discount prices on fine Portuguese linens, ceramics, and sweaters, and Viva, with a stock of unusual clothing and home accessories. Come upstairs, over the Theo. B. Price hardware store, to the Country Store for the area's best selection of folk art and country gifts, and to Christmas Memories for holiday spirit, music boxes, and interesting ornaments year-round.

An unusual stop is the Pocono Mineral and Gem Company in Colony Village, south of Canadensis, where there is a mini-museum of natural gems plus a fine selection of gem jewelry at reasonable prices. Antiquers should head for The Other Woman in Mountainhome, as well as Kelly's in Swiftwater. Don't overlook the Sunday market at Collectors Cove off Route 33 south of Stroudsburg, where over 100 dealers participate. The Village at Fox Hill in East Stroudsburg offers an upscale collection of shops, or you can hunt for bargains at the many outlets in Stroudsburg.

While you are out driving, take the scenic drive up through Big Pocono State Park to the top of Camelback Mountain for mountain vistas. There are tables here for a picnic with a view or you can have lunch at the Cameltop restaurant atop the mountain.

Some Pocono food stops give you a show with your shopping. Callie's Candy Kitchen in Mountainhome, for example, has chocolate-covered everything from strawberries to potato chips, plus laugh-a-minute candy-making demonstration from the colorful Mister Callie. Dozens of kinds of pretzels can be sampled at Callie's Pretzel Factory, where you can watch the pretzel bender in action, and try bending one of your own.

One last kind of recreation widely available in the Poconos is horseback riding. A number of stables offer horses and/or guided trail rides, and on the right day there's really nothing like the beauty of moving past untouched snow through the winter stillness. Many stables offer hayrides, as well.

''Pocono People Love Winter'' is the slogan from the local vacation bureau, and considering the many ways they have to enjoy the season, it's no wonder.

Poconos Area Code: 717

DRIVING DIRECTIONS Take the George Washington Bridge to I-80 west to exit 52 in Pennsylvania. Follow Route 447 north to Canadensis. Ask your inn for more specific directions to its door. *Total distance:* 109 miles.

ACCOMMODATIONS *The Inn at Meadowbrook,* Cherry Lane Road, RD 7, Box 7651, East Stroudsburg, 18301, 629-0296, $-$$ CP

• *The Overlook Inn,* Dutch Hill Road, Canadensis, 18325, 595-7519, $$$$ MAP • *The Pine Knob Inn,* Route 447, Canadensis, 18325, 595-2532, $$$$ MAP • *Brookview Manor,* Route 447, Canadensis, 18325, 595-2451, $$-$$$$ CP • *The French Manor,* PO Box 39, Huckleberry Road, South Sterling, 18460, 676-3244, $$$$$ MAP, $$$$ CP • *Sterling Inn,* South Sterling 18460, 676-3311 or toll free (800) 523-8200, $$$$-$$$$ MAP.

DINING *Pump House Inn,* Skytop Road, Route 390, Canadensis, 595-7501, $$-$$$ • *Overlook Inn* (see above), $$-$$$ • *French Manor* (see above), $$$-$$$$ • *Pine Knob Inn* (see above), $$-$$$ • *Homestead Inn,* Sandspring Drive, Cresco, 595-3171, $$-$$$ • *Hampton Court Inn,* Route 940 East, Mt. Pocono, 839-2119, $$-$$$ • Golden Goose, Route 191, Cresco, 595-3145, $$ • *The Inn at Meadowbrook* (see above), $$ • *Sky Top Lodge,* Sky Top, toll free (800) 345-7SKY, in PA (800) 422-7SKY, prix fixe $$$$$ • *Hazard's Raintree Restaurant,* Route 191, South Sterling, 676-5090, $$-$$$, nice country setting, excellent American menu, $-$$.

FOR FURTHER INFORMATION *Pocono Mountains Vacation Bureau,* 1004 Main Street, Stroudsburg, PA 18360, 421-5791.

Winter Warm-ups in Connecticut

So the days are cold and dreary and you long to get away for the weekend. But you don't ski—in fact, you hate being out in the cold. Where can an indoors lover find fun in the winter?

Fortunately, you don't have to travel far for a cozy retreat with plenty to do besides battling the weather. Lower Litchfield County has a number of happy alternatives for those who prefer indoor sports.

Take Woodbury, for example. Known as "the antiques capital of Connecticut," this is a classic New England town of white-steepled churches and lovely homes along Main Street—and many of those homes are antique shops. In all, there are more than two dozen places where you can browse among beautiful things in warm comfort.

Even more picturesque is neighboring Washington, with a picture-perfect green, dominated by the tall-spired Congregational Church and surrounded by magnificent white clapboard homes set off with dark shutters. This is a very private town—old wealth, old homes, two prestigious prep schools—but it still offers pleasures for visitors, from shops and galleries to a quite exceptional small Indian museum.

Of course, a warm winter getaway should include a wonderful inn, and there are a range of choices in this neighborhood. In Southbury, the Heritage Inn is actually a small resort hotel, where you'll be welcomed by a blazing fire in the big stone fireplace, and find a host of indoor activities, including a billiards room, a fitness center, an indoor pool, a sauna, and whirlpools. There's also a timbered dining room with a lavish Sunday brunch and, adjoining the inn, a multilevel shopping complex where you can while away the hours without ever having to go outdoors.

If Colonial is more your style, drive north on U.S. 6 to Woodbury, and the Merryvale Bed and Breakfast, an antique-filled 1789 home still boasting its original wide oak floorboards and fireplaces. Also in Woodbury is the Curtis House, the oldest hostelry in the state and a best bet for budget-watchers. It's a modest place, where you can sleep in a canopy bed and dine in Early American surroundings.

Should you feel you deserve a splurge to cheer you up during this dreary season, consider the Mayflower Inn in Washington, one of poshest (and priciest) lodgings in Connecticut. Opened in 1992 after a restoration reputed to have cost $15 million, this is the very model of a country hotel, done with exquisite taste. The traditional gray shingle architecture of the original inn and several added buildings is called "American Shingle." It reflects New England, but the furnishings inside would be quite at home in the English countryside. The main sitting room looks like a page from "House Beautiful," with its velveteen upholstery and cozy clutter. The panelled library, whose bay window is all that is left of the original inn, has a fireplace and cozy cashmere throws over the back of the chairs, tempting guests to take one of the books off the shelves and settle in for the afternoon.

None of the 25 guest rooms are alike. They are decorated in fine prints with coordinated stripes and solids and with lovely antiques. There are canopy beds, sleigh beds, and country iron headboards; some rooms have fireplaces, others, bay windows. Room color schemes are soft blue, to deep red, green, or peach. Number 18 in the main building, the smallest of the rooms, is also one of the coziest, with puff drapes, a canopy bed, and a bay window with a view that makes you feel you are in a tree house. All the rooms have a small library and exquisite accessories such as alarm clocks of English leather, Spode plates on the night stand, a miniature Staffordshire china bouquets and hand-painted soap dishes in the lavish mahogany-trimmed bathrooms.

If you can't stay here, come for dinner. The food is excellent and the inn is worth seeing.

Washington offers many pleasant ways to pass the day. The Gunn Museum is small but packed with interesting mementos of the past.

Silver, pewter and china, furniture, tools and kitchenware, dolls and dollhouses, clothing, and paintings of Washington people and by Washington artists are among its collection.

Washington Depot, just a couple of miles away on Route 47, offers some very special shops. English and French antiques, as well home accessories and a kitchen shop, can be found at Washington House, and a big and tasteful selection of furniture accessories at The Tulip Tree. The Hickory Stick Bookstore also is exceptional, and makes for fine browsing. The Pantry in Washington Depot is a highly recommended stop for lunch. Many of the good things made here can be bought to take home.

Washington's most unusual offering is the Institute for American Indian Studies, dedicated to showing the life of the earliest inhabitants of the Northeastern woodlands. The recently enlarged museum, one of the few devoted to Indian life in this part of the country, aims to become a major center where the histories and cultures of New England's Native-American populations can be shared. It is expanding and improving by the year. "As We Tell Our Stories," features tapes of actual Algonkian people interpreting their own history, including the memories of tribal elders. Other exhibits tell about some of the important elements in the lives of early natives—deer that furnished clothing, corn for nourishment, clay to make pots, baskets and wampum that were used for trade. One gallery is devoted to rotating exhibits, which include contemporary Indian art.

Outdoors is a reconstructed Algonkian village, a typical Indian encampment of the 1600s, with both reed- and bark-covered wigwams and a longhouse where a chief might have lived.

Films and other programs are scheduled for Saturday and Sunday afternoons throughout the winter, and there is an excellent gift shop. Parents may want to note that the institute holds many interesting workshops for children in summer.

Antiquers, however, may have difficulty getting anywhere beyond the shops of Woodbury. This town of 7,500 attracted dealers initially with zoning laws that allowed them to run businesses from their homes. Since so many houses were—and still are—filled with antiques, the transition seemed a natural one. Many of the houses still double as homes for the owners, so everything is kept low key to maintain the New England look of the town. Signs can be no larger than two feet by two feet, and open banners and sandwich boards are prohibited.

No one town has a greater assortment of furniture, especially on the upscale end. You'll need no guidebook to find the shops—the long Main Street, Route 6, is lined with them. They range from museum quality at David Dunton to rustic Canadian pieces at Monique Shay to country French at Country Loft. British Country antiques offers lots of pine and oak, painted armoires and other English specialties; Gerald Murphy has a nice mix of American and English, country and formal;

and Grass Root offers a variety of dealers and moods. The names may change as shops change hands, but the variety and quality of the shops is constant.

One of most beautiful shops in Woodbury is the Mill House, located a few miles outside town on Route 6. The main shop, a seventeenth-century gristmill, and several out-buildings along the Nonewaug River hold a vast variety of eighteenth-century English and French furniture and accessories.

If you want to read up before you buy, stop at Books About Antiques, a shop with volumes on almost any collectible you can name.

Should you should come back in warm weather, make a stop at Woodbury's Glebe House, a home dating from the late 1600s that is credited as the birthplace of the American Episcopal Church. The house boasts the only garden in the United States by noted English designer Gertrude Jekyll.

In case you have more time (and money) to spend, Litchfield's galleries and crafts artisans and the shops of New Preston are just a few minutes drive away, more of the pleasures that make this corner of the state a winner for a winter weekend.

Connecticut Area Code: 203

DRIVING DIRECTIONS Hutchinson River Parkway to I-684 north to exit 9E, I-84 east to exit 15, U.S. 6 north to Southbury. Follow Route 6 north to Woodbury, then 47 northwest to Washington. *Total distance:* about 100 miles.

ACCOMMODATIONS Ask about weekend and winter packages • *Heritage Inn,* Village Green, Heritage Village, Southbury, 06488, 264-8200, $$-$$$ • *Curtis House,* Main Street, Woodbury, 06798, 263-2101, $-$$ CP • *Merryvale Bed & Breakfast,* 1204 Main Street South, Woodbury, 06798, 266-0800, $$ CP • *Mayflower Inn,* Route 47, Washington, 06793, 868-9466, $$$$$.

DINING *Carole Peck's Good News Cafe,* 694 Main Street South, Route 6, Woodbury, 266-4663, admired local chef, modern American food, art gallery, music on weekends, $$-$$$ • *Curtis House* (see above), $$-$$$ • *Fritz's*, 10 Sherman Hill Road, Route 6, Woodbury, 263-3036, German specialties, $$ • *The Olive Tree Restaurant,* Routes 6 and 64, Woodbury, 263-4555, Continental with a Greek flair, $$ • *Mayflower Inn* (see above), $$-$$$ • *Bacci's*, 900 Main Street South, Southbury, 262-1250, Northern Italian, attractive, $$ • *Heritage Inn* (see above), good bet for Sunday brunch, $$-$$$ • *The*

Pantry, 5 Titus Road, Route 47, Washington Depot, 868-0258, gourmet shop and unbeatable stop for breakfast, lunch, or tea, $ • See also Litchfield and Lake Waramaug, page 74.

SIGHTSEEING *Institute for American Indian Studies,* 38 Curtis Road, off Route 199, Washington, 868-0518. Hours: January to March, Wednesday to Saturday 10 A.M. to 5 P.M., Sunday noon to 5 P.M., rest of year open daily. Adults, $4; children, $3 • *Gunn Museum,* on the green at Wykeham Road (Route 47), Washington, 868-7756. Hours: Thursday to Saturday, noon to 4 P.M. Free • *Glebe House,* Hollow Road, off Route 6, Woodbury, 263-2855. Hours: April to November, Wednesday to Sunday, 1 to 5 P.M. Admission $3.

FOR FURTHER INFORMATION Litchfield Hills Travel Council, Box 968, Litchfield, CT 06759, 567-4506.

Newport: Snug Harbor in the Off-season

The winter waves were whipping against the cliff. A couple, knitted hats pulled down against the wind, arms wound around each other's ski parkas, were standing on the Cliff Walk, mesmerized by the sight.

Newport, Rhode Island, summer haven for the socialite, the sailor, and the sightseer, has a fascination of its own in the winter's chill. The Ocean Drive looking out to sea is even more spectacular, the Cliff Walk along the bluffs more dramatic, and the harbor takes on a special serenity in its unaccustomed stillness.

With the fabled mansions still receiving visitors, the sights still worth seeing, and dozens of shops and restaurants still open for business, Newport remains a snug harbor for a weekend by the sea.

There's more reason to come out of season every year, in fact, because Newport is changing. You can see it as soon as you enter town to be greeted by the big Gateway Transportation and Visitors' Center, with a 16-screen multimedia presentation and space to handle the thousands who jam the picturesque streets in summer. There's enough room in back for a fleet of tour buses. Bigger hotels like the Marriott next door and a new conference center mean that uncrowded winter is really the best time to appreciate the wonderful old charm that attracted so many in the first place. It's also a chance to enjoy fine dining without waiting on long lines to get in. To make things even nicer, lodging rates go way down, and the town has instituted a February Winter Festival filled with food, festivities, and fun.

The town is now chockablock with lodging choices, many right on the harbor, but the coziest accommodations by far are the inns. Top pick for a romantic outlook is the Inn at Castle Hill on Ocean Drive. The rambling Victorian mansion has spacious rooms, an unmatched view of rocky coast, and a crackling fire downstairs to ward off winter chills.

There are many appealing smaller guest houses in the historic district. Among the best are the three "Admirals." My favorite is the modest Admiral Farragut on Clarke Street, a quiet block that is just a stroll from all the action in town. The inn is filled with handmade Shaker-style furniture, painted chests, hand-glazed walls, and whimsical original folk art murals. The Admiral Benbow, now an old-timer in rapidly changing Newport, still has loyal fans for its spacious rooms. The newer Admiral Fitzroy is another with lots of hand-painted touches, this time in a Victorian mood.

The Francis Malbone House, a neighbor of the Fitzroy on Thames Street, is one of the most elegant lodgings, a 1760 mansion beautifully furnished in Federal style and with a lovely garden out back, a rarity in crowded Newport. The John Banister House, a less formal 1751 Colonial, is also filled with antiques and has a fireplace in every room. A delightful choice closer to the beach is Elm Tree Cottage, done in elegant country style by the artistic young innkeepers.

In The Point, oldest section of town near the waterfront, the Sanford-Covell Villa Marina is a grand 1870s Victorian right on the water and with dazzling views. The Stella Maris Inn, a fine residence circa 1853, and the more intimate 1871 Sarah Kendall House are across the street, but have their own views from the front bedrooms.

To get a sense of the city, begin by taking the well-marked 10-mile Ocean Drive past all the mansions and along the bluffs looking out to sea. If the weather is kind, turn off along Bellevue Avenue and follow some of the 3½-mile Cliff Walk, a path along the bluffs giving you views of lawns and mansions on one side and an eagle's-eye ocean view on the other.

To warm up, you can take a tour of the mansions. If you think we had no royalty in this country, you may well change your mind when you see the massive scale, the marble floors, chandeliers, ballrooms, and priceless brocades of these summer "cottages" of America's nineteenth-century industrial magnates, some with as many as 70 rooms. Two of the museum homes under the aegis of the Preservation Society of Newport County are open weekends during the winter: Marble House, designed by Richard Morris Hunt for William K. Vanderbilt and so named because of the many kinds of colors of marble used in its construction and decoration, and Chateau-sur-Mer, one of the most lavish examples of Victorian architecture in America and the site of Newport's first French ballroom.

There are other mansions to be toured, as well. Belcourt Castle, an 1891 Hunt estate designed in the style of Versailles, is another look at the lavish world of yesterday. The Astor's Beechwood also takes you back to 1891, when Caroline Astor ruled as queen of American society, bringing the gilded era alive with theatrical performances.

Back in town everything centers around the harbor. Sailboats and yachts have replaced the clipper ships that once dropped anchor here with treasures from around the world. The first American navy was established in Newport in 1775 to protect against the British HMS *Rose.* As a result the town was burned by the British not only during the Revolutionary War but again during the War of 1812.

Newport kept her navy ties and was home to a large fleet of ships up until 1973. It was after the navy destroyers moved out that the yachts and America's Cuppers moved in, and shops began to spring up along the restored wharf areas. The two principal centers are Bowen's and Bannister's wharves right on the waterfront and the Brick Market Place across the way.

Along the wharves, in old restored warehouses and new structures with Colonial-modern lines, you'll find shops with wares from around the world, original gold and silver jewelry designs, handcrafted leather goods, children's clothing and toys, and a candy store noted for its homemade fudge. The Brick Market Place is a cobbled maze of condominiums and 30 shops with a wide variety of goods—crafts and art, Irish fabrics and hand-knits, and Scandinavian imports, to name a few.

If antiquing is your goal, you'll find shops on Thames Street, on parallel Spring Street, and on Franklin Street, tucked in between. Note that Newport shop hours can be irregular in the off season, but most are open sometime over the weekend. If you miss one or two, there are plenty to take their place.

On Sunday, you can sample some of the city's other numerous and varied attractions. Drive or walk the narrow streets near the town center, where scores of seventeenth-century Colonial homes have been lovingly restored, painted rainbow hues, and occupied by proud residents. Stop at the lovely Colonial-style Touro Synagogue, the nation's oldest, and the Trinity Church designed by Christopher Wren. The Tennis Hall of Fame on Bellevue Avenue offers aficionados a look at early racquets and quaint costumes. Come back in summer and you can play on its grass courts by the hour or have a round of croquet on the lawn.

There are changing exhibits at the Newport Art Museum, housed in a fine 1862 building designed by Richard Morris Hunt. Hammersmith Farm, the girlhood home of Jacqueline Kennedy Onassis, is a fascinating house filled with Kennedy memories. It is open weekends only in March and November; fit it in if you can.

The Winter Festival grows larger by the year. Horse-drawn hayrides, snow sculptures, an ice-carving competition, and a scavenger hunt through town are among over 100 events. Magicians, clowns, and fireworks are all part of the fun. When the weather is right, a favorite feature is the Cliffwalk Society Winter Stroll, a guided walk along Newport's scenic path above the sea.

One of the tastiest sides of this festival is food. A festival ticket entitles you to visit restaurants all around town who cooperate for samplings of their specialties. Recent menus included Southwestern ribs, New England clam chowder, fiery ''festival shrimp,'' pastas, nachos, hors d'oeuvres, cider, tea and beer tastings, and bruschetta bread. Restaurants also feature dinner specials during festival week, including progressive dinners.

Come evening, jazz concerts and candlelight tours of historic homes are on the agenda.

There are more than enough reasons for a warming visit to Newport in winter. But who could blame you if you were to decide to forget them all and just return to the Cliff Walk to memorize that mesmerizing vista of the sea?

Newport Area Code: 401

DRIVING DIRECTIONS Take I-95 east to exit 3 in Rhode Island, then Route 138 east to Newport. *Total distance:* about 185 miles.

PUBLIC TRANSPORTATION Amtrak (800) 523-8720 to Providence or Boston; bus and shuttle service from Providence, from T. F. Green Airport, and from Boston's Logan Airport. Much of the town is walkable.

ACCOMMODATIONS Rates listed are for high season; all are considerably lower in winter, some as much as 50 percent. Ask about special rates, and send for the hotel package brochure printed by Convention and Visitors' Bureau. All zip codes are 02840. Inns and guest houses (check to make sure inns provide parking space): *Inn at Castle Hill,* 590 Ocean Drive, 849-3800, $$-$$$$$ CP • *The Admirals:* reservations for all at 846-4256, or toll free (800) 343-2863 outside Rhode Island; *Admiral Farragut Inn,* 31 Clarke Street, $$-$$$$ CP; *Admiral Fitzroy,* 398 Thames Street, $$$-$$$$$ CP; *Admiral Benbow,* 93 Pelham Street, $$-$$$$ CP • *Francis Malbone House,* 392 Thames Street, 846-0392, $$$$-$$$$$ CP • *Elm Tree Cottage,* 336 Gibbs Avenue, 849-1610, $$$-$$$$$ CP • *Sanford-Covell Villa Marina,* 72 Washington Avenue, 847-0206, $$-$$$$$ CP • *Sarah Kendall House,* 47 Washington Street, 846-7976, $$$-$$$$ CP •

Stella Maris Inn, 91 Washington Street, 849-2862, $$-$$$$ CP • *The Jailhouse Inn,* 13 Marlborough Street, 847-4638, offbeat choice, the renovated 1772 Newport jail, $$-$$$ CP • *The Inntowne,* 6 Mary Street, 846-9200, hotel comforts in an inn setting, $$$-$$$$ • *John Banister House,* Pelham and Spring streets, 846-0050, $$$-$$$$ CP • Some other appealing small guest houses: *The Inn at Old Beach,* 19 Old Beach Road, 849-3479, elegant Victorian, $$-$$$ CP • *The Victorian Ladies,* 63 Memorial Boulevard, 849-9960, nicely decorated, $$-$$$$ CP • *Melville House,* 39 Clarke Street, small and cozy, 847-0640, $$-$$$ CP (closed January and February); *Brinley Victorian,* 23 Brinley Street, modest, cheerful, $$-$$$$ CP • *Wayside,* Bellevue Avenue, 847-0302, imposing home on mansion row, $$-$$$ CP • *Cliffside Inn,* 2 Seaview Avenue, 847-1811, breezy Victorian near the beach and the Cliff Walk, $$$-$$$$ CP. If you come back in season, consider *The Willows,* 8 Willow Street, The Point, 846-5486, open April to October, where the hostess specializes in romance, serves breakfast in bed, $$-$$$ CP • Resorts and larger hotels: *Doubletree Islander Resort,* Goat Island, 849-2600, on a private island, $$$$-$$$$$ • *Newport Harbor Hotel and Marina,* America's Cup Avenue, 847-9000, on the harbor, $$$-$$$$$ • *Newport Marriott,* 25 America's Cup Avenue, 849-1000, also on the harbor, $$$$-$$$$$ • *Inn on the Harbor,* 359 Thames Street, 849-6789 or (800) 225-3522, modern 58-suite hotel with mini-kitchens, $$$-$$$$$.

DINING Top of the line: *La Petite Auberge,* 19 Charles Street, 849-6669, renowned French chef, $$$ • *Le Bistro,* 250 Thames Street, 849-7778, French cafe, one flight up, $$-$$$ • *Clark Cooke House,* Bannister's Wharf, 849-2900, elegant eighteenth-century dining room, $$-$$$ • *Black Pearl,* Bannister's Wharf, 846-5264, converted wharf warehouse, $-$$$ • *White Horse Tavern,* Marlborough and Farewell streets, 849-3600, nation's oldest continuously operating tavern, $$-$$$$ • *Canfield House,* 5 Memorial Boulevard, 847-0416, gracious 1841 home, $$-$$$ • *Rhumbline,* 62 Bridge Street, 849-6950, snug Colonial home, $$ • Other good choices: *La Forge Casino,* 186 Bellevue Avenue, 847-0418, French and American, overlooking tennis courts, $$-$$$ • *Yesterday's,* 28 Washington Square, 847-0116, informal, $, or The Place, wine bar and grill $$ • *Pronto,* 464 Thames Street, 847-5251, Italian, $-$$ • *Elizabeth's,* Brown and Howard Wharf, Lower Thames Street, 846-6862, attractive decor, varied menu includes Welsh and English specialties, $$-$$$ • *Sardella's,* 30 Memorial Boulevard, 849-6312, traditional Italian, popular, $$-$$$ • *Puerini's,* 24 Memorial Boulevard, tiny, reasonable, always crowded Italian, b.y.o.b., $-$$ • *The Pier,* West Howard Wharf off Lower Thames Street, 847-3645, overlooking the harbor, entertainment on weekends, busy, $-$$$$ • *Sea Fare's American Cafe*, 151 Swinburne Row, Brick Marketplace at Thames, 849-9188, pizza to full meals, regional American, $$ • For seafood: *Scales and Shells,* 527 Thames Street, 846-3474, $-$$ • *Shore Dinner Hall,* Waites Wharf (off Lower Thames Street), 848-5058, totally informal, counter service, $-$$ • For light and reasonable fare, both the *Black Pearl* and *Clark Cooke Honse* (see both above) have cafe adjuncts; also try *Brick Alley Pub,* 140 Thames; *Sala's*, 345 Thames Street, or *Cobblestone Restaurant,* 206 Thames. For brunch with a smashing view, *The Inn at Castle Hill* (see above) can't be beat.

SIGHTSEEING *Newport Mansions,* Preservation Society of Newport County, 118 Mill Street, 847-1000. Hours: Marble House and Chateau-sur-Mer: November to March, Saturday, Sunday (and Monday holidays) 10 A.M. to 4 P.M., except December; open daily early December until Christmas week and December 26–30. Other mansions open weekends in April, daily May to October, 10 A.M. to 5 P.M.; later hours in summer. $6 to $7.50 at each house. Two houses: adults, $12; children, $5; three houses, adults $17.50; children, $6 • *International Tennis Hall of Fame and Tennis Museum,* Newport Casino, Bellevue Avenue, 849-3990. Hours: November to April, daily 11 A.M. to 4 P.M.; rest of year, daily 10 A.M. to 5 P.M. Adults, $6; children, $3 • *Touro Synagogue,* 72 Touro Street, 847-4794. Hours: Sunday only through spring, 1 to 3 P.M. Rest of the year daily except Saturday, 10 A.M. to 5 P.M. Free • *Trinity Church,* Church and Spring streets, 846-0660. By appointment except in summer, daily 10 A.M. to 4 P.M. Free • *Newport Art Museum,* 76 Bellevue Avenue, 848-8200. Hours: Labor Day to Memorial Day, Tuesday to Saturday 10 A.M. to 4 P.M., Sunday 1 P.M.to 4 P.M. summer daily 10 A.M. to 5 P.M. Adults, $4; under 18, free • *Belcourt Castle,* 657 Bellevue Avenue, 846-0669. Hours: February to Memorial Day and mid-October to November, daily 10 A.M. to 4 P.M. Memorial Day to mid-October to 5 P.M., December to early January, Monday to Saturday 10 A.M. to 3 P.M. Closed January. Adults, $6.50; students, $4; children 6–12, $2 • Astor's *Beechwood,* 580 Bellevue Avenue, 846-3772. Hours: mid-May to October, daily 10 A.M. to 5 P.M. November to mid-December, 10 A.M. to 4 P.M. Weekends only February to mid-May, closed mid-December through January. Adults, $7.75; children, $6 • *Hammersmith Farm,* Ocean Drive, 846-0420. Hours: daily April to mid-November, weekends March and November, 10 A.M. to 5 P.M., to 7 P.M. in summer. Adults, $6.50; children 6–12, $3.

FOR FURTHER INFORMATION Contact the Newport Convention and Visitors' Bureau, 23 America's Cup Avenue, Newport, RI 02840, 849-8098 or toll free (800) 326-6030.

Tapping the Maples in Stamford

The calendar says winter, but the crackling fires and the boiling syrup kettles tell you not for long. Maple sugaring is the first sure sign we've made it through another winter, and it's a perfect reason for an early March Connecticut weekend not too far from home.

Though maple sugaring is largely associated with the farms of Vermont, New Hampshire, and upstate New York, a pleasant sampling is available just 40 miles away at the Stamford Museum and Nature Center. The museum puts up its sugar shed as soon as the sap starts to rise and taps the sugar maple trees that dot its 100-acre grounds.

You'll spy the collection buckets on the trees as soon as you arrive, but you may be surprised to see that the sap running is as thin and clear as water. The filled buckets are taken to the shed, where the sap is emptied into an evaporator to simmer slowly over a wood fire until it thickens into golden, gooey, delicious syrup. Staff members tending the fire are generous with free tastes and will allow you to chop a log or two for the fire if the outdoor spirit moves you.

Maple sugaring is a time-honored occupation, and you'll also see demonstrations of how the Indians did it—in a hollowed tree trunk using heat from stones that had been baked in the fire—as well as the way the Colonists used to boil down their syrup in giant black kettles.

Maple sugaring usually takes place one of the first two or three weekends in March, but the museum warns visitors to call ahead to be sure the sap is running and the weather cooperating before you plan to come. Since you are only an hour or so from New York, if the stars are shining Friday night you can also take advantage of the weekly open house at the Stamford Museum Observatory from 8 to 10 P.M. It's exciting to look through a professional telescope and discover that the stars are really round and that you can clearly see the rings around Saturn.

Stamford's emergence as a corporate headquarters center has created a boon for weekenders. The many new hotels that have gone up to serve visitors to more than 50 top corporations in the area are looking for customers when the business week is over, and all offer good-value weekend packages, some as much as half off regular rates.

The hotels are quite cosmopolitan for a small city. My favorite is the Sheraton, with a lobby as light and airy as a greenhouse.

The Hyatt Regency on the Greenwich-Stamford border is also attractive, with a four-story atrium and an indoor garden. The Marriott, the city's biggest, has a lively disco and revolving rooftop restaurant, and like its near-neighbor, the Holiday Inn Crowne Plaza, is within walking distance of Stamford's Town Center, the ultimate in shopping centers. You will find not only Macy's, Saks Fifth Avenue, and JC Penney stores here, but a wealth of upscale boutiques, from Williams Sonoma to Ralph Lauren, Brooks Brothers to Brookstone, all under one convenient roof.

If you prefer inn ambience, your best bet is the Homestead Inn in Greenwich, an elegantly refurbished Colonial home with an excellent dining room.

Come Saturday your first stop should be United Housewrecking Company, off exit 9 on the Connecticut Turnpike. It's hard to imagine anyone who wouldn't have fun at this one-of-a-kind emporium. As the name suggests, the company began by selling off the contents of homes and buildings that had been torn down. It was a place where the locals came to browse outdoors among surplus phone booths, gasoline pumps, soda fountains, and church pews, or to search for bargains in secondhand storm windows, doors, fireplace tools, or furniture.

When it was discovered by decorators and out-of-town shoppers, the variety of wares grew even wackier to meet the new demands, and the company moved to new quarters, now mostly indoors. Today you might find a canopied wicker beach chair on wheels for $350 or an old New York City subway sign for $10. The surprises are part of the fun.

One of United Housewrecking's prime attractions is the possibility of finding old things to convert into nostalgic new ones. Some possibilities are ship's wheels, portholes, and hatch covers for tabletops, old-fashioned sewing machine heads for lamps, and wooden type cases whose many small compartments are ideal for showing off knickknacks and collections. Since the tourists started coming, many new versions of these old favorites are available and there are dozens of sizes and shapes of new wrought-iron pieces.

The scene changes dramatically when you drive into downtown Stamford, where you'll note all manner of futuristic architecture in the apartments, office buildings, corporate headquarters, and department stores that have transformed the city in recent years. The sloped sides of Landmark Square, the round glass buildings of St. Johns Towers, and the inverted pyramid of the GTE headquarters are some of the many unusual designs. Note that there is an outpost of the Whitney Museum in the Champion International Paper headquarters.

One of the city's longtime architectural attractions is the First Presbyterian Church, a few blocks north of downtown on Bedford Street. Known as the Fish Church for its shingled contemporary shape, the building has extraordinary windows made of more than 20,000 pieces of inch-thick colored glass imported from Chartres, France. The glass is set in an abstract depiction of the Crucifixion and the

Resurrection, and the panes are a glorious sight as the jewel-hued light varies with changes in the sun and clouds outside.

Continue north straight up Bedford Street until it becomes High Ridge Road and you are on your way to the Stamford Museum. In addition to watching the maple sugaring, you'll be able to see a reconstruction on the museum grounds of an old-fashioned Connecticut farm.

One of the last remaining eighteenth-century barns in the state was rescued, brought down from Cheshire, Connecticut, plank by weathered plank, and painstakingly reassembled here as the centerpiece of a model farm. Half a dozen kinds of seventeenth- and eighteenth-century fencing have been re-created by hand to enclose the fields, and an exhibit in a second barn shows how the early farmer accomplished so much with so little in the way of tools. The entire crop cycle is depicted, from plowing, harrowing, and sowing to cultivating, harvesting, and preserving, with displays of the authentic pre-machine-age implements that were used for each task.

Maple sugaring is just one of the many seasonal demonstrations of farm activities here, such as apple cidering, ice harvesting, and sheep shearing. All year round you'll see a barnyard full of the tamest and most appealing farm animals to be found anywhere outside of Mother Goose. They are longtime residents of the museum's Hecksher Farm for Children, which has been incorporated into the new display.

There is also a small zoo of native Connecticut wildlife, a pond inhabited by dozens of varieties of ducks and geese, miles of nature trails, and an imposing Tudor mansion up the hill, once the home of retail magnate Henri Bendel and now housing nature and art exhibits. The museum also holds many folk music concerts, including the High Ridge Folk Festival in July.

In the evening, you may find opera, ballet, concerts, or theater at the Stamford Center for the Arts on Atlantic Street.

Greenwich provides a variety of Sunday diversions for visitors. On pleasant days its Audubon Center offers 485 acres of beautiful woodland with many walking trails. The Bruce Museum, recently refurbished and doubled in size, has fine and decorative arts, as well as natural science and history exhibits and a saltwater aquarium.

Bush-Holley House in Cos Cob, home of the Greenwich Historical Society, traces another kind of history. It is a seventeenth-century saltbox home has been restored and authentically furnished, with impressive Jacobean fireplaces, as well as fine paneling and many rare early furniture pieces.

Greenwich, incidentally, is one of those towns like Southampton and Newport where you can pass a pleasant hour just driving and gazing wistfully at the mansions. Northbound roads such as Lake Avenue, North Street, and Round Hill Road and their environs offer ample opportunities for scenery- and estate-watching.

Connecticut Area Code: 203

DRIVING DIRECTIONS Take I-95, the New England Thruway, which becomes the Connecticut Turnpike. Greenwich exits are 3 to 5. Stamford exits are 6 to 9, just beyond. If you are going directly to the Stamford Museum, take the Hutchinson River Parkway to the Merritt Parkway, turn left at exit 35 (High Ridge Road), and proceed 1¼ miles. The museum is on the left. *Total distance:* 40 miles.

ACCOMMODATIONS Rates listed are for weekdays; weekends are much less—but because packages change—are difficult to list. Ask for current packages at all. • *Sheraton Stamford,* First Stamford Place, Stamford, 06902, 967-2222, $$$ • *Hyatt Regency,* 1800 East Putnam Avenue (Route 1), Old Greenwich (on the Stamford–Old Greenwich line), 06870, 323-6900, $$$$ • *Radisson Tara Stamford,* 2701 Summer Street, Stamford, 06905, 359-1300 (located between downtown and the museum), $$$ • *Stamford Marriott Hotel,* 2 Stamford Forum (off exit 8), Stamford, 06901, 357-9555, indoor pool and game and exercise room, $$$$, weekend packages often available • *Holiday Inn Crowne Plaza,* 700 Main Street, Stamford, 06901, 358-8400, $$$ • *Homestead Inn,* 420 Field Point Road (off I-95, exit 3), Greenwich, 06830, 869-7500, $$$-$$$$ CP.

DINING *Amadeus,* 201 Summer Street, Stamford, 348-7775, Mozart on the piano, Viennese specialties, convenient for the Center for the Arts, $$ • *La Bretagne,* 2010 North Main Street, Stamford, 324-9539, formal French, $$$-$$$$ • *Il Forno,* 45 Atlantic Street, Stamford, 357-8882, handsome decor, lively ambience, good Italian food, $$ • *Columbus Park Cafe,* 205 Main Street, Stamford, 967-9191, Italian and Continental, tiny and popular so make reservations, $$ • *Kathleen's,* Bank Street, Stamford, 323-7785, artful decor, inventive American cuisine, $$ • *Crab Shell,* 46 Southfield Avenue, Stamford, 967-7229, seafood on the water, casual, $-$$$ • *Pellici's,* 98 Stillwater Avenue, Stamford, 323-2542, no atmosphere but reasonable and good basic southern Italian home cooking, $-$$ • *La Grange,* Homestead Inn (see above), $$$$ • *Bertrand,* 253 Greenwich Avenue, Greenwich, 661-4618, rave reviews for the chef-owner, formerly of Lutèce, $$$-$$$$$ • *Jean Louis,* 61 Lewis Street, Greenwich, 622-8450, haute French, haute prices, $$$-$$$$ • *C'est Si Bon,* 151 Greenwich Avenue, 869-1901, small French cafe, $$ • *La Strada,* 48 West Putnam Avenue, Greenwich, 629-8484, stylish Northern Italian, $$ • *Le Figaro,* 372 Greenwich Avenue, Greenwich, 622-0018, French bistro, $$-$$$ • *Terra Ristorante Italiano,* 156 Greenwich Avenue, Greenwich, 629-5111, superb Italian food, $$$ • *Bec Fin Fish Market and Cafe,* 199 Sound Beach Avenue, Old Greenwich, 637-4447, lunch only, terrific seafood, $$.

SIGHTSEEING *Stamford Museum and Nature Center,* 39 Scofieldtown Road, 322-1646. Hours: Monday to Saturday 9 A.M. to 5 P.M., Sunday and holidays 1 to 5 P.M. Admission for nonresidents: adults, $4; under age 14, $3; Planetarium shows, adults, $2; children, $1; Observatory night, Friday 8 to 10 P.M., adults, $3; children, $2 • *United Housewrecking Company,* 535 Hope Street, Stamford (Connecticut Turnpike exit 9), 348-5371. Hours: Monday to Saturday 9:30 A.M. to 5:30 P.M., Sunday noon to 5 P.M. • *First Presbyterian Church,* 1101 Bedford Street, 324-9522. Hours: Monday to Friday 9 A.M. to 5 P.M. Donation • *Whitney Museum of American Art,* 1 Champion Plaza, 358-7652. Hours: Tuesday to Saturday 11 A.M. to 5 P.M. Free • *Audubon Center of Greenwich,* 613 Riversville Road, 869-5272. Hours: Tuesday to Sunday 9 A.M. to 5 P.M. Adults, $3; children, $1.50 • *Bush Holley House,* Strickland Road, Cos Cob, 869-6899. Hours: Tuesday to Friday noon to 4 P.M., Sunday 1 P.M. to 4 P.M. Adults, $3; children, $.50 • *Bruce Museum,* One Museum Drive, Greenwich, 869-0376. Hours: Tuesday to Saturday 10 A.M. to 5 P.M., Sunday 2 P.M. to 5 P.M. Adults, $3.50; children, $2.50.

INFORMATION Greater Fairfield Tourism District, 297 West Avenue, Norwalk, CT 06850, 854-7825 or toll free (800) 866-7925.

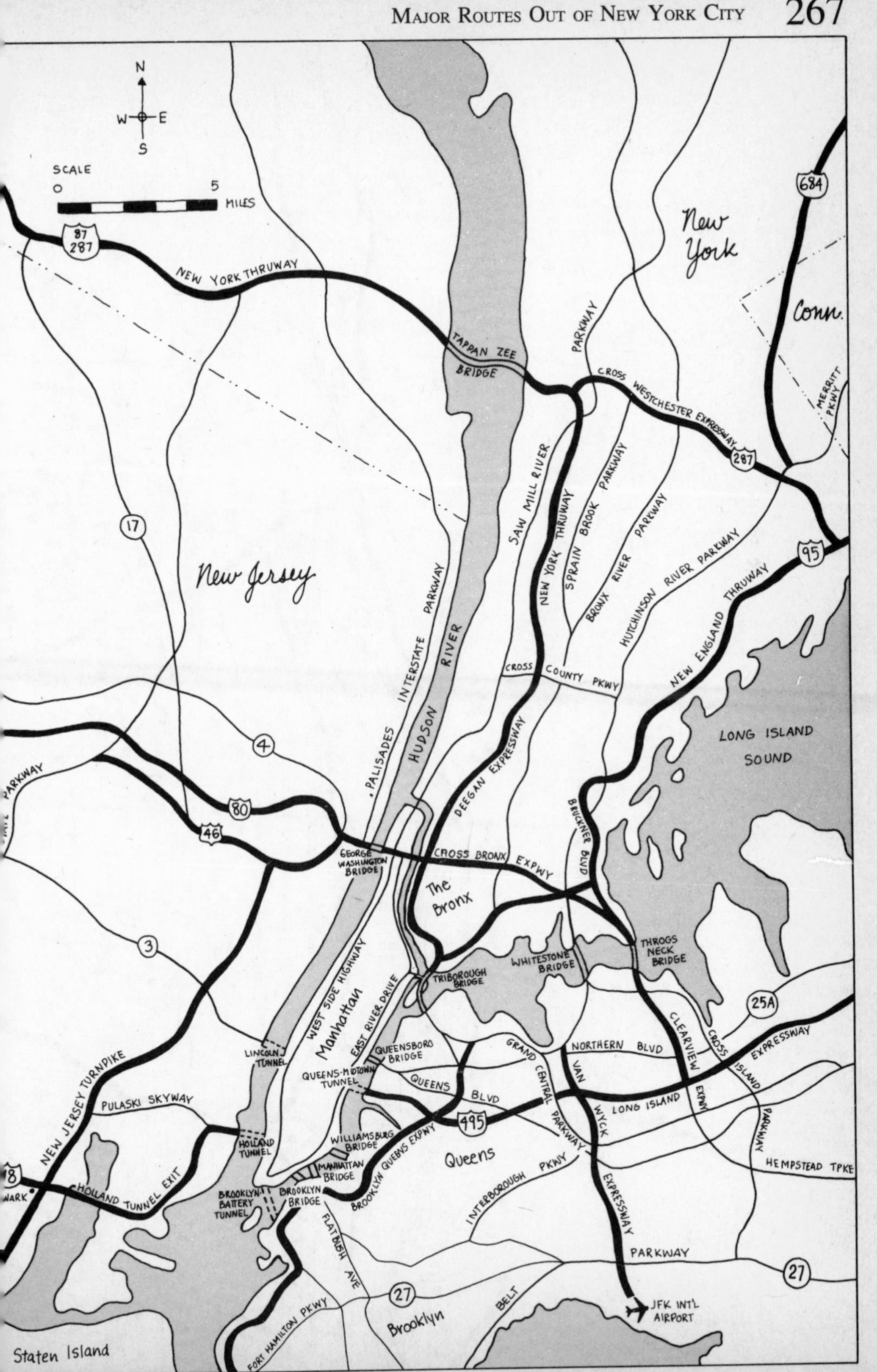
N
W
E
S
SCALE
0
5
MILES
New York
Conn.
New Jersey
684
87
287
NEW YORK THRUWAY
TAPPAN ZEE BRIDGE
PARKWAY
CROSS WESTCHESTER EXPRESSWAY
MERRITT PKWY
287
SAW MILL RIVER
NEW YORK THRUWAY
SPRAIN BROOK PARKWAY
BRONX RIVER PARKWAY
HUTCHINSON RIVER PARKWAY
NEW ENGLAND THRUWAY
95
17
PALISADES INTERSTATE PARKWAY
HUDSON RIVER
CROSS COUNTY PKWY
DEEGAN EXPRESSWAY
LONG ISLAND SOUND
4
80
46
PARKWAY
BRUCKNER BLVD
GEORGE WASHINGTON BRIDGE
CROSS BRONX EXPWY
The Bronx
3
WHITESTONE BRIDGE
THROGS NECK BRIDGE
TRIBOROUGH BRIDGE
WEST SIDE HIGHWAY
Manhattan
EAST RIVER DRIVE
25A
CLEARVIEW EXPWY
CROSS ISLAND PARKWAY
EXPRESSWAY
LINCOLN TUNNEL
QUEENSBORO BRIDGE
GRAND CENTRAL PARKWAY
NORTHERN BLVD
VAN WYCK EXPRESSWAY
QUEENS-MIDTOWN TUNNEL
QUEENS BLVD
LONG ISLAND
NEW JERSEY TURNPIKE
PULASKI SKYWAY
495
WILLIAMSBURG BRIDGE
HOLLAND TUNNEL
Queens
HEMPSTEAD TPKE
MANHATTAN BRIDGE
BROOKLYN QUEENS EXPWY
INTERBOROUGH PKWY
HOLLAND TUNNEL EXIT
BROOKLYN-BATTERY TUNNEL
BROOKLYN BRIDGE
FLATBUSH AVE
PARKWAY
27
27
BELT
JFK INT'L AIRPORT
FORT HAMILTON PKWY
Brooklyn
Staten Island

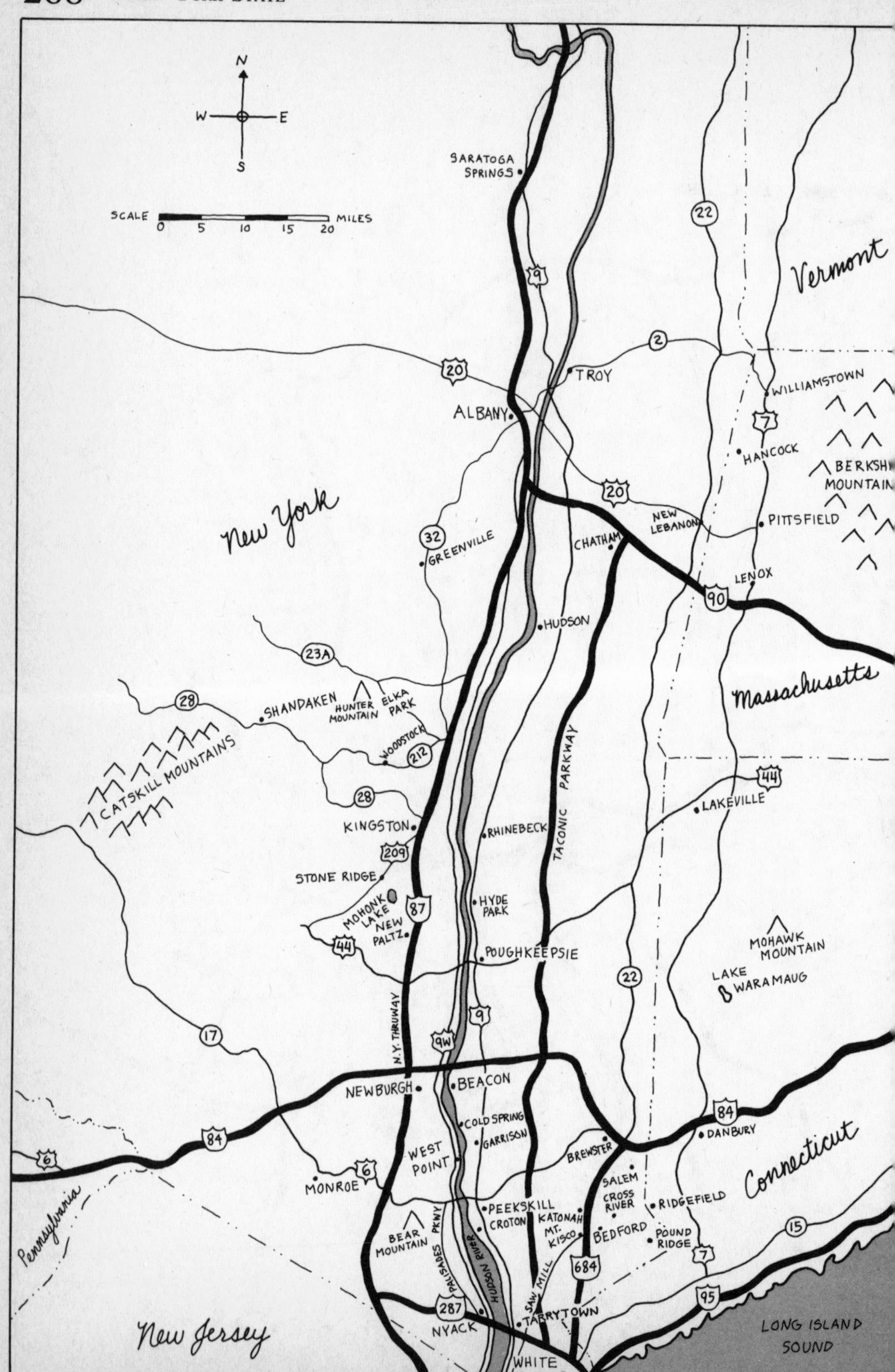
N
W
E
S
SCALE
0 5 10 15 20
MILES
SARATOGA SPRINGS
Vermont
TROY
WILLIAMSTOWN
ALBANY
HANCOCK
BERKSHI
MOUNTAIN
New York
NEW LEBANON
PITTSFIELD
CHATHAM
GREENVILLE
LENOX
HUDSON
Massachusetts
SHANDAKEN
HUNTER MOUNTAIN
ELKA PARK
WOODSTOCK
CATSKILL MOUNTAINS
TACONIC PARKWAY
LAKEVILLE
KINGSTON
RHINEBECK
STONE RIDGE
HYDE PARK
MOHONK LAKE
NEW PALTZ
POUGHKEEPSIE
MOHAWK MOUNTAIN
LAKE WARAMAUG
N.Y. THRUWAY
NEWBURGH
BEACON
COLD SPRING
GARRISON
WEST POINT
BREWSTER
DANBURY
Connecticut
MONROE
SALEM
CROSS RIVER
RIDGEFIELD
PEEKSKILL
CROTON
KATONAH
MT. KISCO
BEDFORD
POUND RIDGE
BEAR MOUNTAIN
PALISADES PKWY
HUDSON RIVER
SAW MILL
Pennsylvania
TARRYTOWN
NYACK
New Jersey
WHITE PLAINS
LONG ISLAND SOUND
22
9
2
20
7
20
32
90
23A
28
212
28
44
209
87
44
22
9
17
9W
84
6
84
6
15
7
684
95
287

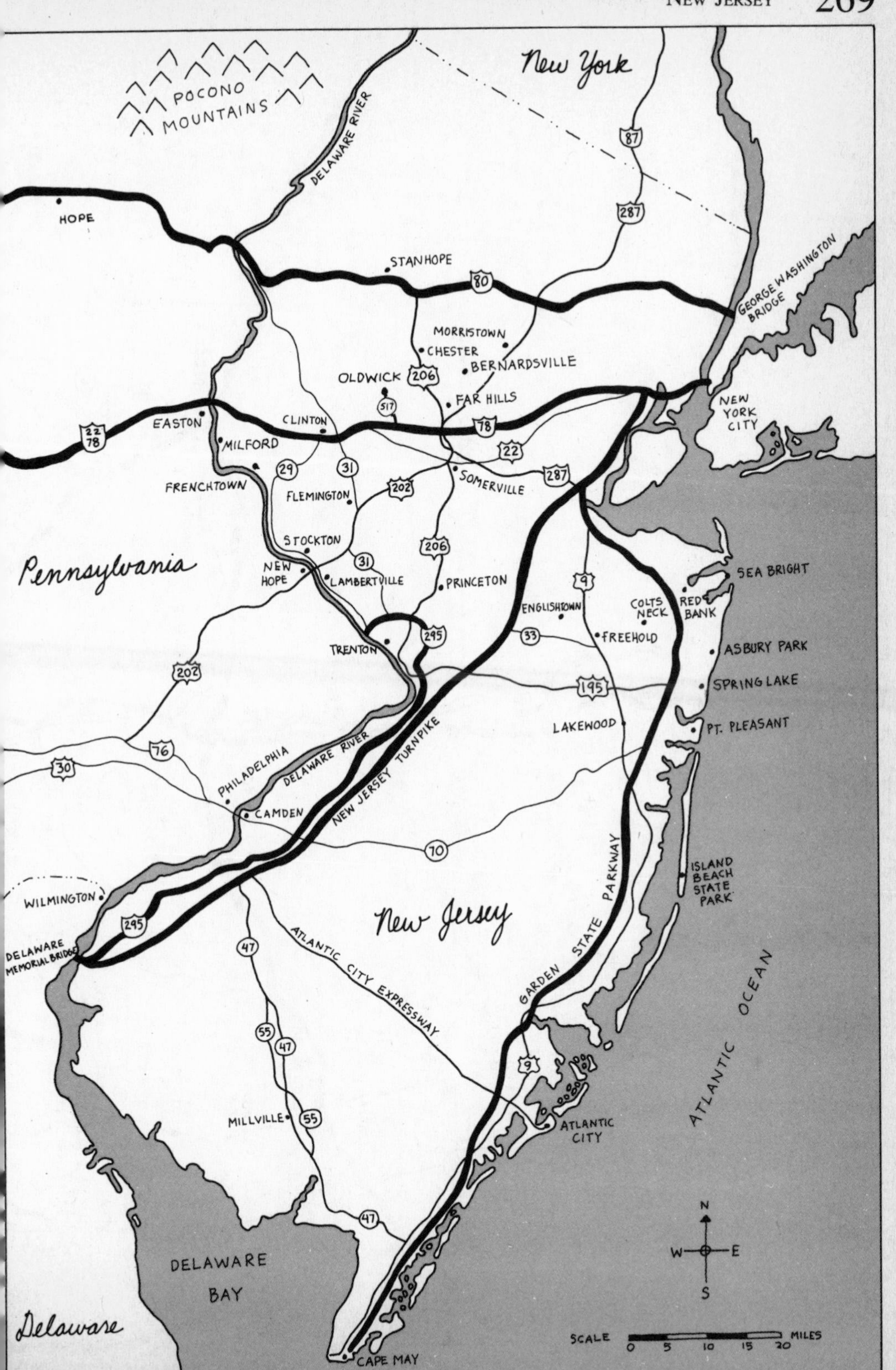
New York
Pocono Mountains
Delaware River
87
287
Hope
Stanhope
80
George Washington Bridge
Morristown
Chester
Bernardsville
Oldwick
206
Far Hills
517
78
New York City
22
78
Easton
Clinton
Milford
22
29
31
287
Frenchtown
202
Somerville
Flemington
Stockton
206
Pennsylvania
New Hope
31
Lambertville
Princeton
Sea Bright
9
Englishtown
Colts Neck
Red Bank
295
33
Freehold
Trenton
Asbury Park
202
195
Spring Lake
Lakewood
Pt. Pleasant
76
30
Philadelphia
Delaware River
New Jersey Turnpike
Camden
70
Island Beach State Park
Wilmington
295
New Jersey
Garden State Parkway
47
Atlantic City Expressway
Delaware Memorial Bridge
Atlantic Ocean
55
47
9
Millville
55
Atlantic City
47
N
W
E
S
Delaware Bay
Delaware
Scale
0 5 10 15 20
Miles
Cape May

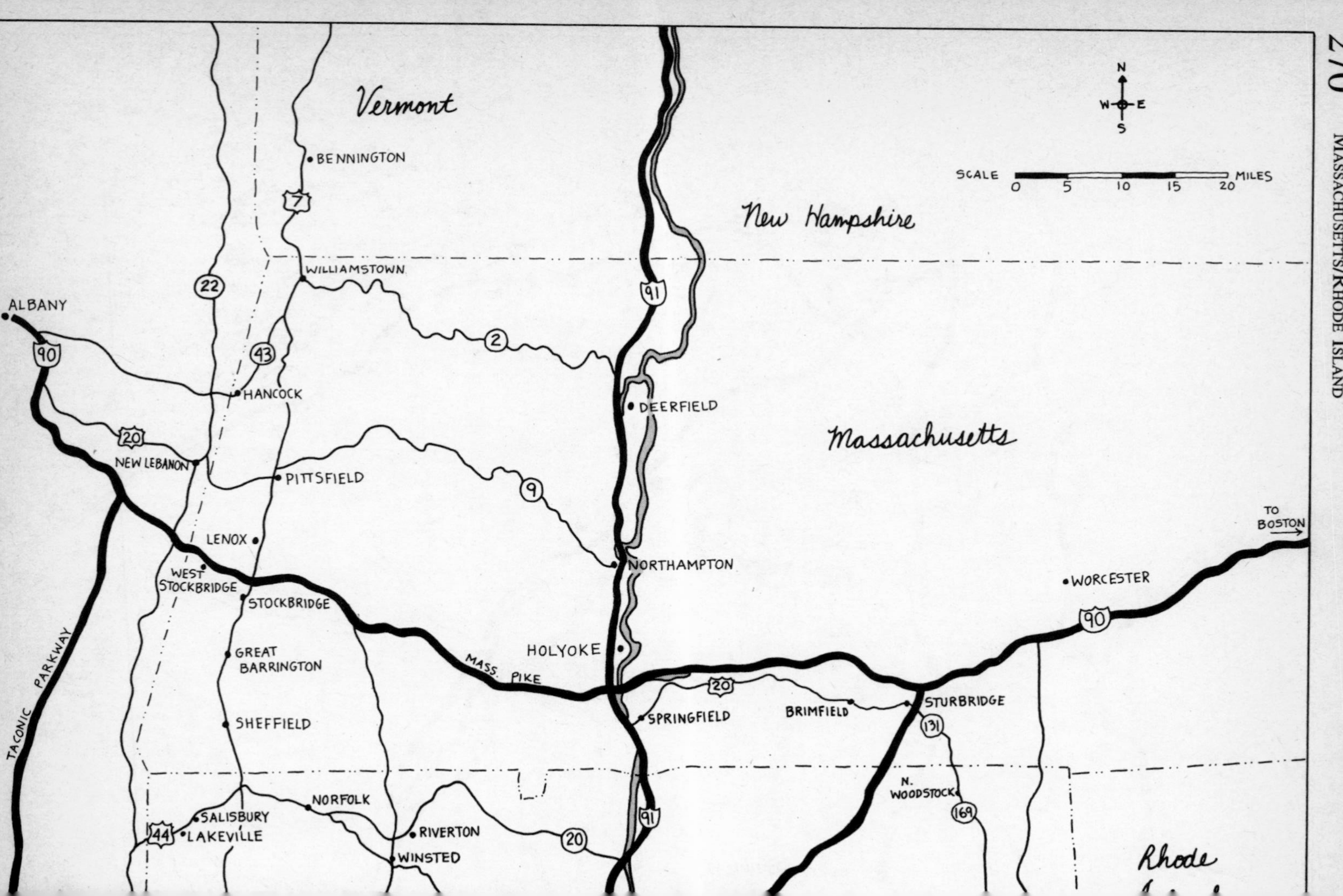

Vermont
N
W
E
S
BENNINGTON
7
SCALE
0
5
10
15
20
MILES
New Hampshire
WILLIAMSTOWN
22
91
ALBANY
90
2
43
HANCOCK
DEERFIELD
Massachusetts
20
NEW LEBANON
PITTSFIELD
9
TO BOSTON
LENOX
NORTHAMPTON
WEST STOCKBRIDGE
STOCKBRIDGE
WORCESTER
90
HOLYOKE
GREAT BARRINGTON
MASS. PIKE
TACONIC PARKWAY
20
SPRINGFIELD
BRIMFIELD
STURBRIDGE
131
SHEFFIELD
N. WOODSTOCK
NORFOLK
169
91
SALISBURY
44
LAKEVILLE
RIVERTON
20
WINSTED
Rhode

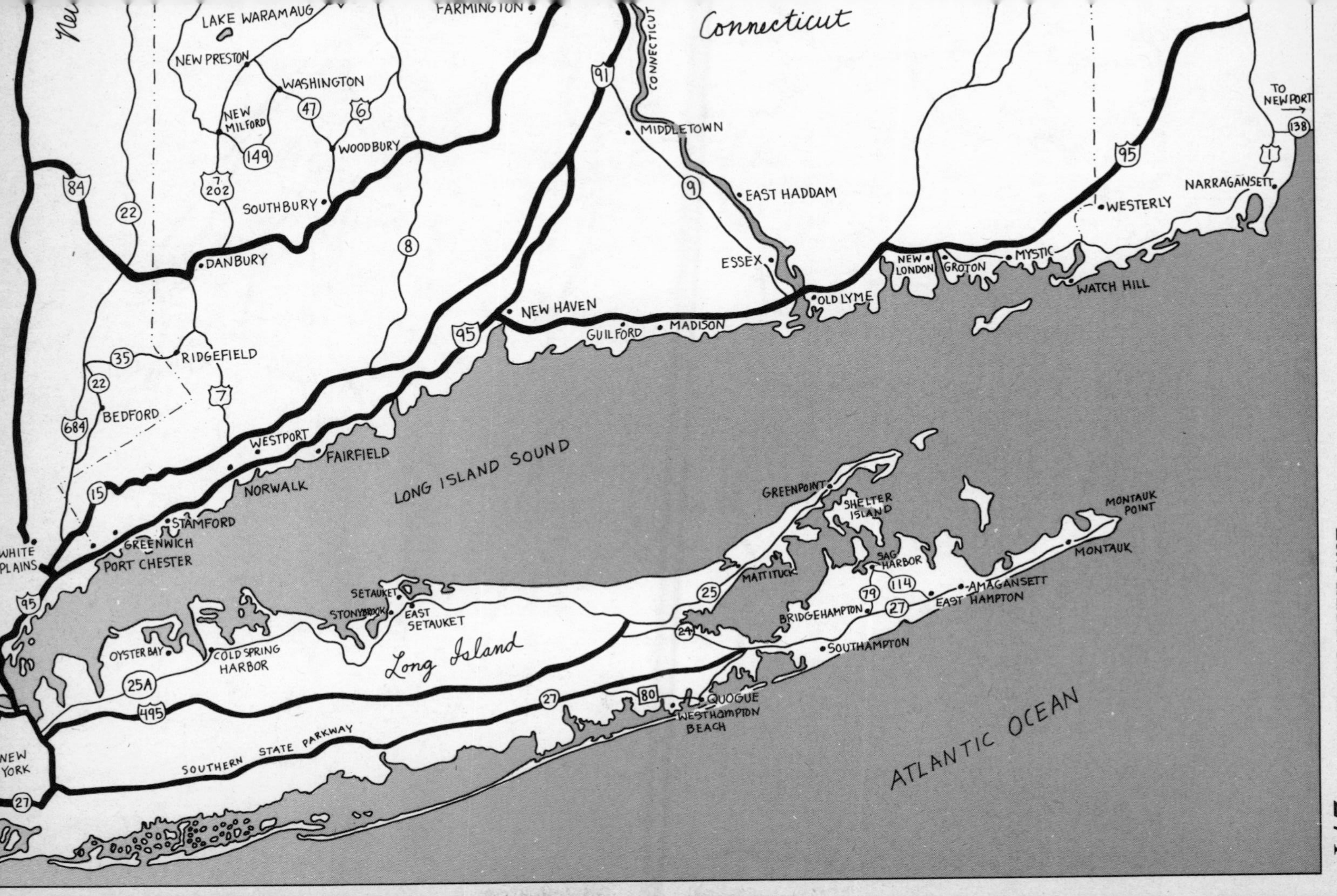
Connecticut
LAKE WARAMAUG
FARMINGTON
NEW PRESTON
WASHINGTON
NEW MILFORD
WOODBURY
SOUTHBURY
DANBURY
RIDGEFIELD
BEDFORD
CONNECTICUT
MIDDLETOWN
EAST HADDAM
ESSEX
OLD LYME
NEW LONDON
GROTON
MYSTIC
WATCH HILL
WESTERLY
NARRAGANSETT
TO NEWPORT
NEW HAVEN
GUILFORD
MADISON
WESTPORT
FAIRFIELD
NORWALK
STAMFORD
GREENWICH
PORT CHESTER
WHITE PLAINS
LONG ISLAND SOUND
GREENPOINT
SHELTER ISLAND
MONTAUK POINT
MONTAUK
SAG HARBOR
MATTITUCK
AMAGANSETT
EAST HAMPTON
BRIDGEHAMPTON
SOUTHAMPTON
SETAUKET
STONYBROOK
EAST SETAUKET
OYSTER BAY
COLD SPRING HARBOR
Long Island
QUOGUE
WESTHAMPTON BEACH
ATLANTIC OCEAN
SOUTHERN STATE PARKWAY
NEW YORK
84
22
7
202
149
47
6
91
9
95
138
1
8
35
684
15
25
24
79
114
27
25A
495
80

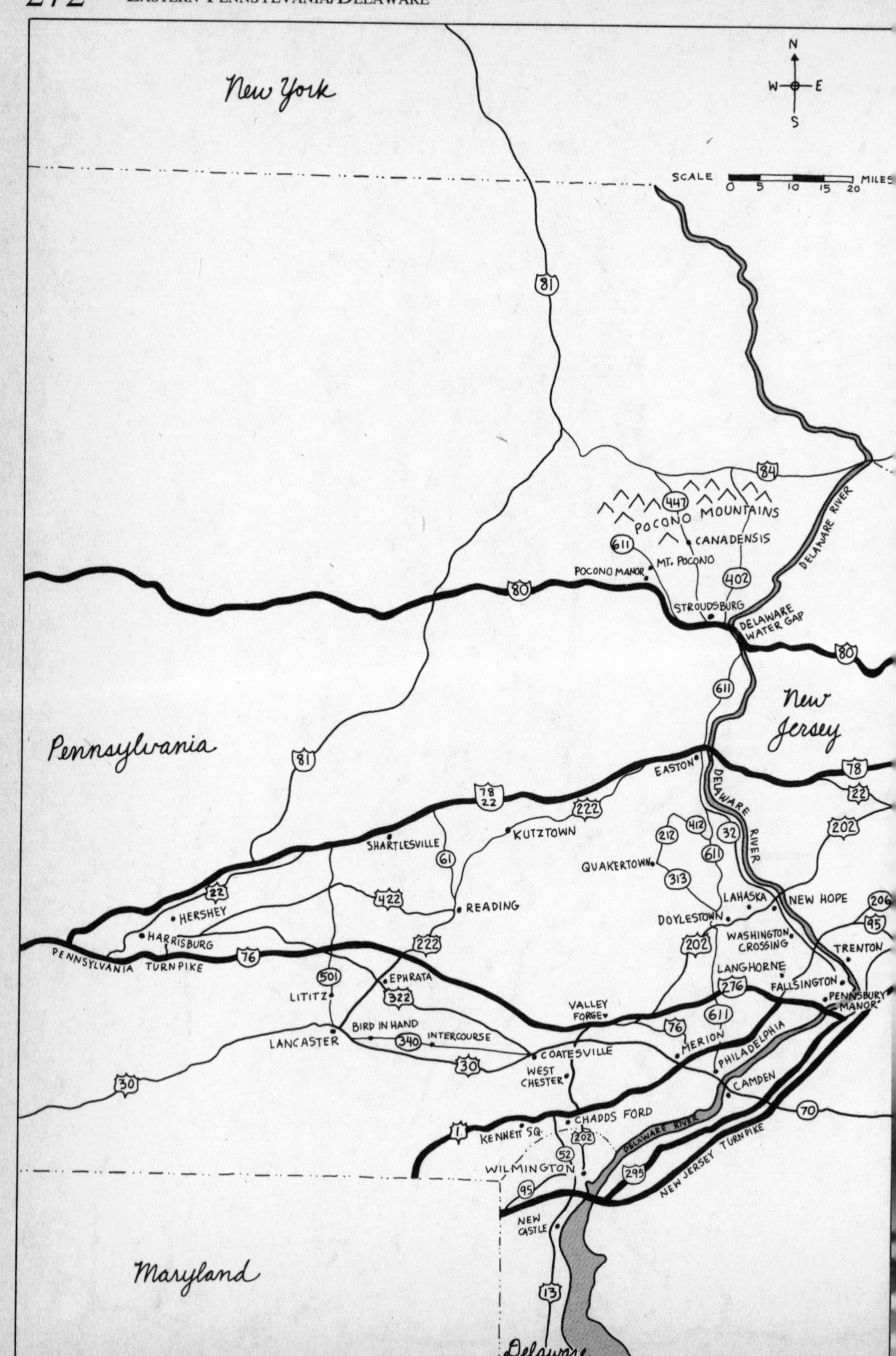
New York
N
W
E
S
SCALE
0 5 10 15 20 MILES
POCONO MOUNTAINS
CANADENSIS
MT. POCONO
POCONO MANOR
STROUDSBURG
DELAWARE WATER GAP
DELAWARE RIVER
New Jersey
Pennsylvania
EASTON
KUTZTOWN
SHARTLESVILLE
QUAKERTOWN
READING
HERSHEY
HARRISBURG
PENNSYLVANIA TURNPIKE
LAHASKA
NEW HOPE
DOYLESTOWN
WASHINGTON CROSSING
TRENTON
LANGHORNE
FALLSINGTON
PENNSBURY MANOR
EPHRATA
LITITZ
VALLEY FORGE
BIRD IN HAND
INTERCOURSE
LANCASTER
MERION
PHILADELPHIA
COATESVILLE
WEST CHESTER
CAMDEN
CHADDS FORD
KENNETT SQ.
DELAWARE RIVER
NEW JERSEY TURNPIKE
WILMINGTON
NEW CASTLE
Maryland
Delaware
81
84
447
611
402
80
78
22
222
212
412
32
313
202
206
95
61
422
76
501
322
276
340
30
70
1
52
295
13

General Index

Category Index

Music and Dance

Nature

Parks and Beaches

Shopping